THE *CORSAIR* AFFAIR

KIERKEGAARD'S WRITINGS, XIII

KIERKEGAARD

THE *CORSAIR* AFFAIR
AND ARTICLES RELATED TO THE WRITINGS

Edited and Translated
with Introduction and Notes by

Howard V. Hong and
Edna H. Hong

PRINCETON UNIVERSITY PRESS
PRINCETON, NEW JERSEY

Copyright © 1982 by Howard V. Hong
Published by Princeton University Press,
41 William Street, Princeton, New Jersey 08540
In the United Kingdom: Princeton University Press, 6 Oxford Street,
Woodstock, Oxfordshire OX20 1TW

All Rights Reserved

Third printing, and first paperback printing, 2009
Paperback ISBN: 978-0-691-14075-9

The Library of Congress has cataloged the cloth edition of this book as follows

Kierkegaard, Søren Aabye, 1813–1855.
The Corsair affair.
(Kierkegaard's writings ; 13)
Bibliography: p.
Includes index.
1. Kierkegaard, Søren Aabye, 1813–1855—Addresses,
essays, lectures. 2. Corsaren—Addresses, essays,
lectures. 3. Goldschmidt, Meïr Aron, 1819–1887—
Addresses, essays, lectures. 4. Møller, Peder Ludvig,
1814–1865—Addresses, essays, lectures. I. Hong,
Howard Vincent, 1912– . II. Hong, Edna Hatlestad,
1913– . III. Title. IV. Series: Kierkegaard, Søren
Aabye, 1813–1855. Works. English. 1978 ; 13.
B4376.K48 1981   198'.9   80-7538
ISBN 0-691-07246-9

British Library Cataloging-in-Publication Data is available

Printed on acid-free paper. ∞

Designed by Frank Mahood

press.princeton.edu

Printed in the United States of America

3 5 7 9 10 8 6 4

CONTENTS

HISTORICAL INTRODUCTION vii
CHRONOLOGY xxxix

I. Articles, 1842-1851
1

PUBLIC CONFESSION
3

WHO IS THE AUTHOR OF EITHER/OR
13

A WORD OF THANKS TO PROFESSOR HEIBERG
17

A LITTLE EXPLANATION
22

AN EXPLANATION AND A LITTLE MORE
24

A CURSORY OBSERVATION CONCERNING A DETAIL IN DON GIOVANNI
28

THE ACTIVITY OF A TRAVELING ESTHETICIAN AND HOW HE STILL HAPPENED TO PAY FOR THE DINNER
38

THE DIALECTICAL RESULT OF A LITERARY POLICE ACTION
47

AN OPEN LETTER
51

II. Addenda
61

vi   *Contents*

A LETTER
63

ANOTHER LETTER
66

[A LETTER]
69

LITERARY QUICKSILVER
73

SUPPLEMENT   87
  Key to References   88
  P. L. Møller, M. Goldschmidt, *The Corsair*, and Related
  Publications, 1841-1848   91
    From *The Corsair*, 1841-1845   91
    "A Visit in Sorø," by P. L. Møller   96
    "To Mr. Frater Taciturnus," by P. L. Møller   104
    From *The Corsair*, 1846-1848   105
    From Meïr Goldschmidt's Autobiography   138
  Selected Entries from Kierkegaard's Journals and Papers
  Pertaining to   153
    Articles   153
    The *Corsair* Affair   157
      Drafts of Writings for Possible Publication   157
      Journal Entries   208
    "An Open Letter"   241

EDITORIAL APPENDIX   265
  Acknowledgments   267
  Collation of Articles in the Danish Editions of
  Kierkegaard's Collected Works   269

NOTES   271

BIBLIOGRAPHICAL NOTE   309

INDEX   311

HISTORICAL INTRODUCTION

THE *CORSAIR* AFFAIR

"I hope that someone will soon write a fully documented history of the *Corsair* affair," declared W. H. Auden a decade ago.[1] In an elemental way, the present volume is intended to be a fulfillment of that hope. Instead of being a documented history, it is in large part a collection of the most pertinent documents by the main figures: Søren Kierkegaard (1813-1855), Peder Ludvig Møller (1814-1865), and Meïr Goldschmidt (1819-1887).[2]

The *Corsair* affair has been called the "most renowned controversy in Danish literary history."[3] The immediate occasion was literary—P. L. Møller's review of Kierkegaard's *Stages on Life's Way* (see Supplement, pp. 96-104)—and those involved were writers, but the issues were more ethical, social, and philosophical than literary. Similarly, the consequences of the controversy for the participants were ethical, philosophical, and religious, with appropriate effects upon their writing.

The relation between Goldschmidt, the editor of *The Corsair* (1840-1846) and the pseudonymous author of the novel *En Jøde* (A Jew; 1845), and Kierkegaard was one of mutual admiration: on the one hand, a young writer who sought the esteem and advice of a more acknowledged writer, who, on the other hand, discerned the talent and possibilities of the younger man. They first met at a party in 1838, and Goldschmidt recounts that Kierkegaard's eyes were "sagacious, lively, and masterful, with a mixture of good humor

---

[1] W. H. Auden, "A Knight of Doleful Countenance," *New Yorker*, May 25, 1968, p. 41.

[2] Kierkegaard and Møller had been students at the University of Copenhagen in the 1830s; Goldschmidt, a young journalist in Næstved, came to Copenhagen in 1840 and started *The Corsair* that year.

[3] Paul Rubow, *Goldschmidt og Nemesis* (Copenhagen: Munksgaard, 1968), p. 118 (ed. tr.).

and malice" and that in conversation he "constantly remained much superior to me."[4]

Their second meeting[5] occurred after the appearance in *The Corsair* of an inadequate review (October 22, 1841),[6] which Goldschmidt had amended in a postscript, of Kierkegaard's dissertation, *The Concept of Irony*. As they conversed, Kierkegaard advised Goldschmidt to apply himself "to comic writing, that was my task. I took his words as good advice kindly meant, which they also undoubtedly were. . . . But what was the task assigned to me: comic writing? I could not very well ask him about that, and I did not know what it was."[7] During other meetings on the street, Goldschmidt recounts, "the question was always on the tip of my tongue: What is the task you have assigned me? What is comic writing? But neither did I have the right talents for raising the question, nor did his personality make such an approach easier."[8]

When *Either/Or*, edited by Victor Eremita, appeared in 1843, Møller and Goldschmidt were "more or less agreed that Victor Eremita was the most brilliant Greek to emerge again on the scene. There was a wealth of thought, wit, irony, mastery, especially the last. He was masterly in everything and could himself be Either/Or, Both/And, if not personally, then in his thought." Goldschmidt even sent Victor Eremita and Møller an invitation to a celebration (with a "flask of rare Italian wine"), although, of course, the guest of honor could be present only invisibly.[9] In *The Corsair*,[10] the book was praised, albeit in a typically offhanded way.

In 1845, *The Corsair* lauded the editor of *Stages on Life's Way* by suggesting that it would be more enjoyable "to eat dry bread and drink water with Hilarius Bookbinder than to

[4] See Supplement, p. 138. [5] See Supplement, p. 139.
[6] See Supplement, pp. 92-93.
[7] See Supplement, p. 139.
[8] See Supplement, p. 141. Later, in a letter (January 8, 1879) to Otto Borchsenius, Goldschmidt confirms that Kierkegaard "called me to esthetics and comic writing." *Breve fra og til Meïr Goldschmidt*, I–II, ed. Morten Borup (Copenhagen: 1963), Letter 411, I, p. 225 (ed. tr.).
[9] See Supplement, pp. 141-42. [10] See Supplement, pp. 93-95.

drink champagne with Mr. Böotius."[11] The climax of *The Corsair*'s always gentle and often laudatory treatment of the pseudonymous Kierkegaard came in the fateful phrase in the issue of November 14, 1845: "Lehman will die and be forgotten, but Victor Eremita will never die."[12]

Goldschmidt's esteem for Kierkegaard and the pseudonymous works was genuine, as were Kierkegaard's admiration of and expectations for Goldschmidt. As reputed editor of *The Corsair*, Goldschmidt had made himself something of an outsider in a way consistent with the paper's flamboyant motto: "His hand shall be against all, and the hands of all against him." Whatever Kierkegaard thought about the paper, he thought well of the young writer, and Goldschmidt appreciated the older writer's interest and his willingness to converse with him publicly. According to Rikard Magnussen, at that time "the position of Jews in Denmark was still such that the oppression of the race could force upon the gifted Jew a constrictive inner insecurity and a passionate need for recognition, a need that in reality still contained a certain contempt for the society whose recognition it sought . . .."[13]

Goldschmidt edited the satirical, oppositionist weekly paper for six years, from 1840 to 1846, a time called "*The Corsair*'s reign of terror." Magnussen writes of "the tyranny the scandal sheet *The Corsair* exercised over the citizenry at the time."[14] Georg Brandes declares, "At that time *The Corsair* seemed to have at least as much power as the dominant so-called serious press in our day."[15] With the largest circulation in the city and in the country, with talented anonymous writers and cartoonists of wit and malice, with a series of straw men as "responsible editor," with disdain for public position and personal privacy, *The Corsair* gathered and cleverly exploited fact, rumor, and gossip—"and with good reason all feared being treated in that paper, and it could be fateful for a

---

[11] See Supplement, p. 96. [12] Ibid.
[13] Rikard Magnussen, *Det særlige Kors* (Copenhagen: 1942), p. 161 (ed. tr.).
[14] Ibid., pp. 164-65 (ed. tr.).
[15] Georg Brandes, *Søren Kierkegaard, Samlede Skrifter*, I-XVIII (Copenhagen: 1899-1910), II, p. 378 (ed. tr.).

man's reputation and his future."[16] The second line of *The Corsair*'s masthead motto, "Ça ira, Ça ira," from the so-called "*Carillon national*" of the French Revolution, reads: "les aristocrates à la lanterne" (hang the aristocrats). Thousands in Denmark delighted in seeing others being hanged in the satire, ridicule, malice, and caricature that overshadowed the political and esthetic lead pieces in the paper, and everyone—almost everyone—was apprehensive of being the next to receive the *Corsair* treatment. In 1880, J. Davidsen, in referring to the *Smuds- eller Skandalepresse*[17] (gutter or scandal press), says that what Kierkegaard later wrote about *The Corsair* "is hard, but it is not untrue."[18]

"Then P. L. Møller loomed up."[19] This short sentence is central in Volume I of Goldschmidt's autobiography, and the very verb *(tonede frem,* the basis of Goldschmidt's own coinage, *Fremtoning)*[20] gives a special accent to its significance. Chapter VIII, on P. L. Møller, is the "main section of the book."[21] In the autumn of 1842, the relation between Møller and Goldschmidt commenced and developed. Goldschmidt knew Møller's reputation as something of a genius who had won a gold medal for his writing and also as "an extremely dangerous, not only satirical but malicious person; but this could not frighten me, who had the same thing on hand and was not afraid."[22] For some time, Møller became the chief influence on Goldschmidt. Paul V. Rubow declares that Møller's relation to Goldschmidt was comparable to that of Henrich Steffens and Adam Oehlenschläger.[23] When Goldschmidt

[16] Magnussen, p. 165 (ed. tr.).
[17] *Fra det gamle Kongens Kjøbenhavn*, I-II (Copenhagen: 1880-81), I, p. 206.
[18] Ibid., p. 207 (ed. tr.).
[19] Meïr Goldschmidt, *Livs Erindringer og Resultater*, I-II (Copenhagen: 1877), I, p. 297 (ed. tr.).
[20] See *JP* VI, note 2967.
[21] Rubow, p. 117 (ed. tr.).
[22] Goldschmidt, *Erindringer*, I, p. 301.
[23] Rubow, p. 117. Steffens's lectures on German romantic philosophy and literature in Copenhagen (1802-1804) were overwhelmingly impressive to many of the Danish intelligentsia. The most famous relationship developed between Steffens and the poet Oehlenschläger, who spent many hours in

was sentenced to "six times four days" for violation of the press laws, Møller became his chief defender through an article in his own publication, *Arena*.[24] During Goldschmidt's absence at student meetings in Sweden in June 1843 and his journey to Paris in the autumn of 1843, Møller was in charge of *The Corsair*.[25] "Both on this occasion and in his entire *Corsair* activity, Goldschmidt's relation to P. L. Møller must be taken into consideration, for even though historically Goldschmidt was definitely the primary and proprietary leader of the paper... he himself was under the direction or in any case under the decisive influence of P. L. Møller...."[26]

Møller had entered the University of Copenhagen in 1832, Kierkegaard in 1830. Møller won the gold medal in 1841 for his essay on French poetry; Kierkegaard submitted and successfully defended his dissertation on irony in the same year. Møller moved from medicine to theology to esthetics; Kierkegaard began in theology, became occupied with esthetics and literature, and wrote a philosophical dissertation. During this prolonged student decade, they must have known each other, although there are no references to Møller in Kierkegaard's extant journals and papers from that time. Frithiof Brandt, however, convincingly makes a case for the thesis that P. L. Møller, the Byronic esthete, a modern Don Juan type, was the model for Johannes the Seducer in Volume I of *Either/Or* (1843).[27] Three years later, Kierkegaard, in affirming his interest in "a psychological familiarity with actual people," stated, "Such an actual person is Mr. P. L. Møller."[28]

After winning the gold medal for his essay, Møller nourished the hope that he might become Adam Oehlen-

---

conversation with Steffens about romantic nature philosophy. Oehlenschläger's poem "*Guldhornene*" was the immediate and prophetic result.

[24] "*Corsaren og Goldschmidt,*" *Arena, et polemisk-æsthetisk Blad*, ed. P. L. Møller, no. 3-4, June 1843, pp. 49-83.

[25] *Meïr Goldschmidts Breve til hans Familie*, I-II, ed. Morten Borup (Copenhagen: 1964), I, p. 18.

[26] Magnussen, p. 163 (ed. tr.).

[27] Frithiof Brandt, "*P. L. Møller. Modellen til Johannes Forføreren?*" in *Den unge Søren Kierkegaard* (Copenhagen: 1929), pp. 160-304. Cf. *The Point of View, KW* XXII (*SV* XIII 277-78 fn.).

[28] P. 45.

schläger's successor as professor of esthetics at the University of Copenhagen. As a contribution to that end, he began a series of three esthetic yearbooks entitled *Gæa*, which provided a means of publishing his own criticisms and poetry and of developing associations with influential critics and writers, including the poet Carsten Hauch and Oehlenschläger himself. Victor Eremita (Kierkegaard), too, had been asked to contribute to *Gæa* but had declined.[29] *Gæa . . . 1846* (actually published in December 1845) included Møller's "A Visit in Sorø,"[30] the main part of which was a clever and in some ways discerning, but generally uncomprehending, review of Kierkegaard's *Stages on Life's Way*, cast in the form of a discussion among the author and various persons at Sorø Academy.

Carsten Hauch, in whose house the discussion presented in "A Visit in Sorø" supposedly took place, was involved in Møller's writing of the piece, although Kierkegaard did not know or suspect it. In a letter to Møller, Hauch wrote: "The observations I have expressed regarding Kierkegaard I gladly turn over to you for your use, since I am assured that you will use them with discretion; meanwhile, you will thereby bring upon yourself a heavy battle with Denmark's most subtle dialectician."[31]

Georg Brandes later characterized Møller's piece in *Gæa* as "a frivolous and dishonorable article: frivolous, because its

---

[29] *Kierkegaard: Letters and Documents*, *KW* XXV, Letter 121, to P. L. Møller:

Christmas Day [1845]
Dear Sir:
Through Mr. Giødwad I received your highly esteemed and confidential note today. My reply to you and to anyone who makes or has made a proposal of this sort: I never have anything completed, and I never bind myself with promises.

Yours respectfully,
Victor Eremita.

[30] See Supplement, pp. 96-104.
[31] In Archives, Royal Library, Copenhagen, NkS 3217, 4°, quoted by Helge Toldberg, "*Goldschmidt og Kierkegaard*," in *Festskrift til Paul Rubow* (Copenhagen: 1956), p. 235 (ed. tr.).

author had made no attempt whatsoever to put himself into what he wrote about, and dishonorable, because it (under the guise of evaluating Kierkegaard's authorship), as is customary in this kind of article, dealt with street gossip about his private life, accused the hero in the diary of 'placing his betrothed on the experimental rack, of dissecting her alive, of torturing her soul out of her drop by drop,' all of which accusations were made as if directed against Kierkegaard himself."[32]

Goldschmidt, thinking of Møller's desire to establish himself as critic and esthetician, saw the piece as giving "the impression of being a manifesto originating at or supported by Sorø Academy.... It was a kind of cunning that perhaps only poets have; they are so simple-minded that in their craftiness they become both ludicrous and pathetic as a result.... Møller created the impression that such gentlemen seemed to lend their authority, and in many respects the whole work was splendid, perhaps the most lively and energetic he had written. But he had caught a Tartar."[33]

The Tartar responded directly with an article in the newspaper *Fædrelandet* (December 27, 1845)—"The Activity of a Traveling Esthetician and How He Still Happened to Pay for the Dinner,"[34] an attack on Møller and also *The Corsair*, but not on Goldschmidt. The sting came at the end: "*Ubi* P. L. Møller, *ibi The Corsair!*"[35]

Why did Kierkegaard respond to Møller's article in a way that eventually had momentous consequences? The review itself was the occasion, not the central issue. The most accentuated part of the review did indeed invade the personal Regine-Kierkegaard relation, which in *Stages* is transmuted into an aspect of the universally human. And that the model for Johannes the Seducer should do this, "that this morally depraved person, this conscienceless libertine, should dare to pose as morally offended . . . was too much for Søren Kierkegaard and awakened his deepest indignation."[36]

Møller's review, however, as the immediate occasion, and

[32] Brandes, II, pp. 376-77 (ed. tr.).
[33] See Supplement, p. 145.
[34] See pp. 38-46.
[35] See p. 46.
[36] Magnussen, p. 164 (ed. tr.).

Kierkegaard's response, as its immediate effect, are both only tokens of the more central and earlier issues and only the beginning of the extended series of consequences. In many journal entries from early 1846,[37] Kierkegaard declares that the action against Møller and *The Corsair* was not undeliberated: "For some time now, I have been aware of that paper and its insinuating misuse of the comic. It is not at all true that I got into all this by a rash step."[38] "Prior to that time nothing could be done; my work for my idea demanded all my time, every minute, and as undisturbed as possible."[39]

Kierkegaard's early criticism of *The Corsair*, because of Goldschmidt's misunderstanding of the comic, has been noted. Goldschmidt recounts a conversation (1842) in which Kierkegaard took exception to invasion of privacy and to anonymous writing.[40] On another occasion (1845), as they discussed a review praising Goldschmidt's recent book, Kierkegaard, according to Goldschmidt, said, "the point is that there are men who want to see in you the author of *En Jøde* but not the editor of *The Corsair*—*The Corsair* is P. L. Møller."[41] In response to *The Corsair*, no. 269, November 14, 1845, which declared that "Victor Eremita will never die,"[42] Victor Eremita (Kierkegaard) wrote "A Request to *The Corsair*," complaining that to "become immortal . . . through the testimonial of *The Corsair* . . . will be the death of me. . . . Oh, let me move you to compassion; stop your lofty, cruel mercy; slay me like all the others."[43] This piece, written, as Elias Bredsdorff says, "in *The Corsair*'s own style,"[44] was not published, but it was repeated in essence in Kierkegaard's December response to Møller's article in *Gæa*.

In December 1845, Kierkegaard had finished *Concluding*

[37] See Supplement, pp. 200, 207, 210, 218 (*Pap.* VII¹ B 69, 72, A 98, 214).
[38] See Supplement, p. 194 (*Pap.* VII¹ B 55).
[39] See Supplement, p. 208 (*Pap.* VII¹ A 98); see also Supplement, p. 204 (*Pap.* VII¹ B 71).
[40] Goldschmidt, *Erindringer*, I, p. 279.
[41] Ibid., I, pp. 371-72.   [42] See Supplement, p. 96.
[43] See Supplement, pp. 157-58 (*Pap.* VI B 192).
[44] Elias Bredsdorff, *Goldschmidts "Corsaren"* (Copenhagen: Sinistra-Klubben, 1962), p. 99 (ed. tr.).

Unscientific Postscript to the Philosophical Fragments. Not only was the work a postscript to an earlier work, but it was also supposed to be his *concluding* work as an author. Now he was ready to do something about certain things that concerned him and "in such a way that to be an author becomes a deed."[45] Møller's piece in *Gæa* provided him, according to journal entries from the time and later, with the occasion to make "a personal statement in costume," an "action-response in personal costume,"[46] with the following aims: (1) to test Goldschmidt; (2) to separate Møller and Goldschmidt; (3) to "snatch" Goldschmidt from *The Corsair*; (4) to do a service to others; and (5) to widen the distance between himself and his writings.

(1) "I had entertained the thought of becoming more involved with him [Goldschmidt]. But before that happened, there had to be a test."[47] Assuming Goldschmidt's admiration for him and his own high expectations for Goldschmidt and his developing talent, Kierkegaard saw that the test would reveal whether Goldschmidt had the "courage and self-respect to say: No, I will not attack him *or* I will attack the little article he has written but not the earlier books I have admired and immortalized and to which I really am deeply indebted. He did not stand the test. For me it became—if it must be called a punishment—a punishment for being the only person here at home who did Goldschmidt the wrong of having too much faith in him . . . ."

(2) Kierkegaard made a distinction between Goldschmidt as the editor of *The Corsair* and Goldschmidt as a writer and the "editor" of the book *En Jøde* (1845),[48] one who "deserves honor for having published a good book."[49] Kierkegaard's idea that Møller was a detrimental influence upon Goldschmidt was epitomized in a conversation that took place in early 1845, in which Kierkegaard stated to Goldschmidt that

---

[45] See Supplement, p. 208 (*Pap.* VII¹ A 98).
[46] See Supplement, pp. 178, 196 (*Pap.* VII¹ B 55, 57).
[47] See Supplement, p. 237 (*Pap.* X¹ A 123).
[48] See Supplement, pp. 143, 176 (*Pap.* VII¹ B 41).
[49] See p. 47.

"*The Corsair* is P. L. Møller."[50] Of course, Kierkegaard knew that Goldschmidt was the proprietary and editorial principal in a formal sense, but he accurately discerned that for Goldschmidt "Møller loomed up."[51] His hopes for Goldschmidt could be fulfilled only by driving "a wedge between the promising (despite everything) Goldschmidt and his evil spirit Møller."[52] If that had not been the case, the omission of Goldschmidt from Kierkegaard's attack on Møller and *The Corsair*[53] would be entirely inexplicable.

(3) Consonant with the aim of separating Møller and Goldschmidt was the aim of persuading Goldschmidt to give up *The Corsair*. "It was my desire to snatch, if possible, a talented man from being an instrument of rabble-barbarism . . . ."[54] "I told him that he perhaps had misunderstood all that I previously had pointed out to him, admonished him to give up the *Corsair* enterprise, and said that he even may have imagined that I was putting on a good face with him in order not to be exposed to his attack myself. Now surely he could see that the opposite was the case. I wanted earnestly to repeat what I had said to him. This I did. I urged upon him very earnestly that he must leave *The Corsair*."[55] The most amazing thing about the whole *Corsair* affair is that this particular aim was not only achieved but achieved very quickly,[56] yet not before other unforeseen consequences had emerged.

(4) Kierkegaard wanted not only to separate Goldschmidt from Møller and *The Corsair* but also to alter or to eliminate *The Corsair*, which he considered to be a social blight. As a satirical-political paper, it could have its place, particularly if the satire did not take a merely party line: "it was nonsense [for Goldschmidt] to be ironical and also a party man who merely attacked the government; irony must make a clean sweep—the very point of which was to indicate to him how

---

[50] See Supplement, p. 143. [51] See Supplement, p. 141.
[52] Toldberg, p. 220 (ed. tr.).
[53] See pp. 38-46; Supplement, p. 159 (*Pap.* VII^1 B 5).
[54] See Supplement, p. 213 (*Pap.* VII^1 A 99).
[55] See Supplement, p. 235 (*Pap.* X^1 A 98).
[56] See Supplement, pp. 149-50.

cowardly he was toward the public."[57] This was a remark, "dialectically thrown out and misunderstood, that had led Goldschmidt in the past to take a new direction, to attack everybody, while in another sense I did everything to save Goldschmidt from the whole stinking mess, but always *dialectically*, in order to give him the chance to become open."[58] To Kierkegaard, *The Corsair* actively represented a destructive misconception of satire, irony, and the comic. In *Two Ages* (1846), published during the *Corsair* affair, he wrote: "anyone who understands the comic readily sees that the comic does not consist at all in what the present age imagines it does and that satire in our day, if it is to be at all beneficial and not cause irreparable harm, must have the resource of a consistent and well-grounded ethical view, a sacrificial unselfishness, a highborn nobility that renounce the moment; otherwise the medicine becomes infinitely and incomparably worse than the sickness."[59] We are, he continues, "oblivious to the fact that in an era of negativity the authentic ironist is the hidden enthusiast (just as the hero is the manifest enthusiast in a positive era), that the authentic ironist is self-sacrificing, for, after all, that grand-master of irony ended by being punished with death."[60]

In a time of demoralization, an authentic ironist would be of great benefit. Goldschmidt and *The Corsair*, however, were not practitioners of authentic irony, because they lacked the presuppositions, as stated above. Nevertheless, Kierkegaard did not charge Goldschmidt with being the cause of the demoralization but rather with being a sign and an instrument of it.

What brought in a new government[61] was not wisdom, patriotism, and the like but an expression of this demoralization. And what will overthrow the new government will

---

[57] See Supplement, p. 224 (*Pap.* VIII¹ A 421).
[58] See Supplement, pp. 224, 233 (*Pap.* VIII¹ A 420; X¹ A 98).
[59] *Two Ages, KW* XIV, p. 74 (*SV* VIII 70).
[60] Ibid., p. 81 (*SV* VIII 76).
[61] See Supplement, p. 228, and note 449.

again be envy, caprice, pettiness, and the like; it is not the noble, the good, that triumphs—no, it is the same demoralization, which has given itself a new shape.

In this respect, Goldschmidt is not undistinguished. He is like a cholera fly to cholera; it cannot be said that it is he who produces the demoralization (and everybody else is good) but that he makes manifest that there must be demoralization. He is and remains the characterless instrument of envy and demoralization. He has nothing to lose, cannot be attacked, or envied, either; he is safeguarded by means of contemptibility—and then he gnaws and gnaws. And a good many representatives of the old regime think this is fine—because the new government is the victim. How tragic that there is no character at all, no reflection, no consistent point of view anywhere in Denmark, but everything is momentary passion.[62]

Another aspect of *The Corsair*, its anonymous, gossipy, and at times libellous invasion of privacy, made the journal feared more than its political satire and literary criticism. "It was clear to all of any importance in the intellectual world that this destructive influence had to be curtailed, but to do it oneself—no one had any desire to do that. On the other hand, there were many who gave him to understand that he, Kierkegaard, with an esteemed name as author and especially with an independent position in society, was the right one to undertake what was necessary. Consequently, here was a situation in which he felt himself in contact with the best and most important men in the country and in which they acknowledged that they had use precisely for him. . . . But the basis of his mode of approach lay deeper, namely, in the presuppositions of his entire authorship."[63]

(5) Besides hoping (4) "to benefit others by this step,"[64] Kierkegaard wrote in the spring of 1846: "It is expedient for my life as an author to be abused, and that is why I wished it

[62] See Supplement, pp. 228-29 (*Pap.* IX A 303).
[63] Magnussen, pp. 166-67 (ed. tr.).
[64] See Supplement, p. 213 (*Pap.* VII¹ A 99).

and asked for it as soon as I was finished, for by the time Frater Taciturnus wrote [the article against Møller and *The Corsair*], Johannes Climacus [*Postscript*] had already been delivered to the printer a few days before."[65] It is not clear to what extent this aim was important to Kierkegaard before writing the provocative article against Møller and *The Corsair*, but it was certainly consonant with the idea of pseudonymity from the outset, which Kierkegaard formulated in terms of the *Corair* affair: "it can serve the idea to have every possible lie and distortion and nonsense and gossip come out, confusing the reader and thus helping him to self-activity and preventing a direct relationship."[66]

Motivated by these five privately recorded aims, Kierkegaard used Møller's piece on *Stages* in *Gæa*[67] not only as the immediate occasion to respond[68] directly and publicly to Møller's discussion of *Stages* but also and primarily to create a situation in which the more central issues would be clarified and resolved. The sting comes at the end,[69] where Møller is linked with the *Corsair* but Goldschmidt is not mentioned. Møller's reply[70] came quickly in the form of a short piece in *Fædrelandet* (no. 2079, December 29, 1845) addressed "To Mr. Frater Taciturnus, Chief of Part Three of *Stages on Life's Way*," in accordance with Kierkegaard's article of December 27. Møller states that he finds "no reason to discuss the particular points," but he does wish to point out "a small factual inaccuracy" with regard to the participation of Carsten Hauch and to Hauch's house as the setting of the discussion reported in *Gæa*. At the same time, Møller wrote—in a quite different vein—a four-part piece[71] for *The Corsair*. The manuscript of this piece shows some signs of initial editing in another hand, presumably that of Goldschmidt, who did not use Møller's

---

[65] Ibid.
[66] See Supplement, p. 214 (*Pap.* VII^1 A 99). On Kierkegaard's theory of indirect communication, see *JP* I 617-81; *Postscript, KW* XII (*SV* VII 55-62, 203-11, [545-49]).
[67] See Supplement, pp. 96-104.   [68] See pp. 38-46.
[69] See p. 46.   [70] See Supplement, pp. 104-05.
[71] See Supplement, pp. 105-08.

piece but printed his own bantering, but at times incisive, fantasy on "How the Wandering Philosopher [Frater Taciturnus] Found the Wandering Actual Editor of *The Corsair*."[72]

The next piece in the exchange, written by Goldschmidt, appeared in *The Corsair* (no. 277) on January 9, 1846. Here the whole approach by way of pseudonyms, an approach that had also been maintained in the earlier conversations between Kierkegaard and Goldschmidt, is dropped, and Kierkegaard is considered by name.[73]

Frater Taciturnus's next and last published piece[74] (January 10) is an elaboration of a few sentences in the last paragraph of his earlier article. He again protests being immortalized in *The Corsair*. He also states a willingness to renounce, for ethical reasons, his old wish " 'always to have the laughter on my side,' the laughter of those who have a true sense of the comic [a reference to the "task" assigned to Goldschmidt by Kierkegaard], for to be abused on one's own order ["Would that I might only get into *The Corsair* soon," for it is hard to be "the only one who is not abused there"] is precisely that advantage, even though I took the step for the sake of others."[75] In the first paragraph, Goldschmidt is mentioned by name and also as being the editor of the financially profitable *Corsair*. In a confrontation of "the Terrible One" by irony, *The Corsair* may be "ruined by the dialectic of one person's order to be abused . . . ."[76] An analogy is made between *The Corsair* and a prostitute on the sidewalk. Reference is also made to the use of street-corner loafers as straw-men editors.

The series of *Corsair* pieces on Kierkegaard for the next six months is quite different from the first piece in no. 276. The new central elements are defamation of character by association and personal ridicule by caricature of external charac-

---

[72] See Supplement, pp. 108-12.

[73] *Berlingske Tidende* had already (May 6, 1845) linked Kierkegaard with some of the pseudonyms, and *The Corsair* had printed a piece on that attribution (see p. 24 and note 55). Møller's article in *Gæa* had made direct reference to Kierkegaard and *B.T.* (see Supplement, pp. 97-100, especially p. 99). See Supplement, pp. 112-15.

[74] See pp. 47-50.   [75] See p. 47.   [76] See p. 46.

teristics. On January 16 appeared the first[77] of the pieces identifying in a doubly brutal way Frater Taciturnus with Crazy Nathanson,[78] a well-known Copenhagen character. Victor Eremita and Frater Taciturnus are directly declared insane. On January 23 began the numerous references to and caricatures of Kierkegaard's external appearance, particularly his legs and trousers.

Goldschmidt initially felt that he had to do something when such a hard blow had been "struck against *The Corsair* .... What I wanted most of all at the moment was to show him that I had fulfilled the task he once had assigned to me: to do comic writing. In my opinion, even now, the task was successfully carried out in that I strictly limited the question and gave a sprightly account of the discovery at last of the secret editor of *The Corsair* . . .."[79] "The whole thing took an unexpected bitter turn. . . . After the replies, which I wrote myself, some accompanied by cartoons, my colleagues carried on, and thus the affair was constantly raked up, with side-cuts at him. To what extent this was distasteful to me, I cannot say."[80]

Thirty years later, Georg Brandes made this assessment of the affair:

It was unfortunate for Kierkegaard that he had placed his article in the newspaper *Fædrelandet*, which for long had looked askance at its younger and more successful fellow and which gladly would take an article against the more widely read *Corsair*.

But Goldschmidt's situation was far less enviable. It is stupid to abuse a man one has spontaneously praised earlier, and also on his order, and it is abominable to depict such a man in caricatures and to make peculiarities of his external appearance and of his dress the objects of ridicule by those who always laugh with the jokester and at intellectual-spiritual superiority.[81]

[77] See Supplement, pp. 117-23.
[78] See Supplement, p. 117, and note 121.
[79] See Supplement, p. 147.
[80] See Supplement, pp. 148-49.
[81] Brandes, II, p. 378 (ed. tr.).

Elias Bredsdorff, although generally holding both parties equally responsible for the negative aspects of the affair, concludes that "*The Corsair* hereby fell for the temptation to begin the ridiculing of Kierkegaard's external appearance, which justifiably came to wound Kierkegaard very much. . . . Although it must be acknowledged that *The Corsair* was rudely provoked, the paper should not have fallen for that temptation."[82]

By shifting the center of attention from Kierkegaard's works (as in *Gæa*) and from Møller's writing and *The Corsair* itself (as in Kierkegaard's two articles) to character assassination and visual caricature, *The Corsair* outflanked Kierkegaard. He wrote many long and short pieces for possible publication,[83] but they remained among the papers until 1872, when H. P. Barfod published them in *Af Søren Kierkegaards Efterladte Papirer*, five years before the appearance of Goldschmidt's autobiography. In caricaturing prose and drawings, *The Corsair* exploited the identification of Kierkegaard and Crazy Nathanson and made public property of Kierkegaard's legs and trousers. Kierkegaard was effectively silenced, because *The Corsair* made his person the object of ridicule. In *Two Ages* (1846) there are unspecified references to *The Corsair* and other references to journalism,[84] and in *On My Work as an Author* (1851) there is a footnote on the affair,[85] but that is all. Here and there in the journals there are retrospective summaries and analyses of the *Corsair* affair[86]—obvious indications of its significance for Kierkegaard, not only as something remembered but also as a crucial occasion for making new decisions about the last phase of his life.

One of Kierkegaard's pieces[87] for possible publication con-

---

[82] Bredsdorff, p. 107 (ed. tr.).
[83] See Supplement, pp. 157-208, for an extensive selection of pieces written for possible publication.
[84] *Two Ages*, pp. 61, 74, 81, 94-95, *KW* XIV (*SV* VIII 58, 70, 76, 88-89).
[85] *The Point of View*, *KW* XXII (*SV* XIII 498).
[86] See Supplement, pp. 208-41, for an extensive selection of journal entries on the *Corsair* affair.
[87] See Supplement, pp. 184, 196 (*Pap.* VII¹ B 55, 58).

tains a specific challenge to Goldschmidt to reply, agreeing or disagreeing, in a paper other than *The Corsair*. Although the piece was not printed, the challenge was given in a decisive, silent meeting of the two men on Myntergade in March 1846.[88] Goldschmidt recalls:

> But then he publicly named himself Victor Eremita, Frater Taciturnus,[89] etc., etc., and immediately thereafter he met me on Myntergade and passed me by with an intense, very bitter glance, without wanting to give a greeting or to be greeted. . . . There was something about that intense, wild glance that drew the curtain, as it were, away from the higher right[90] that Kierkegaard had asserted earlier and that I had not been able, rather, was unwilling, to see, although I did indeed suspect it. It accused and depressed me: *The Corsair* had won the battle, but I myself had acquired a false no. 1. Nevertheless, a protest also arose in my mind during that moment packed with meaning: I was not one to be looked down upon, and I could prove it. On my way home I decided that I would give up *The Corsair*, and when I told them at home that I was going to do it, they said, Praise God—so happy but so little surprised, as if they had known about it before I did. . . . *The Corsair* itself was actually not salable. As soon as I left it, anyone could take the name and continue it. But Flinch, the wood engraver, thought that if I would turn it over to him he could give me 1,500 rixdollars for it. Reitzel bought a volume of short stories I had written, and thus I gathered together around 4,000 rixdollars, which I divided, and with one-half I left the country "in order to be done with witticism and to learn something."[91]

---

[88] See Supplement, p. 149, and notes.
[89] "A First and Last Declaration," *Concluding Unscientific Postscript*. The official publication date was February 27, 1846. In a note (see Supplement, pp. 196-97; *Pap.* VII[1] B 59) added to the written challenge, Kierkegaard refers to a review of *Postscript* in *The Corsair*, no. 284, February 27, 1846. Therefore the silent meeting of the two men must have come shortly after the unpublished challenge was written.
[90] See Supplement, pp. 146, 148.   [91] See Supplement, pp. 149-50.

After editing the *Corsair* issue of October 2, 1846, Goldschmidt left Denmark for the Continent and did not return until the autumn of 1847. Thus one of Kierkegaard's aims was fulfilled: Goldschmidt was separated from *The Corsair*. Another aim was also fulfilled: *The Corsair* was never the same and in its last nine years was reduced to a rather insignificant paper. (In the photo-offset edition launched in 1977, the issues of the last nine years are omitted.)

A more tentative aim—the possibility that there might be a working relation between the two men—was, of course, not fulfilled. Another aim, however, Kierkegaard's expectations for Goldschmidt and for his talents, was in a measure fulfilled. Upon returning to Denmark, Goldschmidt founded *Nord og Syd*, a political-literary journal of a kind entirely different from *The Corsair*. He also wrote numerous novels and short stories, which, according to P. M. Mitchell, make him "the most significant forerunner of modern realism" in Danish literature.[92]

Goldschmidt's appraisal of the affair is summarized in a letter written in 1878: "as far as the *affair* itself is concerned, I think that K. understood *The Corsair* very well. To me a powerful testimony seems to be the fact that he advised me to produce 'comic writing' and gave me that as the task. . . . For me, S.K. was the first of the means to 'comic writing' and thereby, when I had practiced the art upon him, the great occasion for my casting the whole *Corsair* from me and for my achieving in a significant moment a painful ideality, which long afterwards has cast a kind of splendor in my mind."[93]

P. L. Møller, after being excluded by Goldschmidt from direct participation in *The Corsair*'s attacks upon Kierkegaard, devoted himself to writing, publication, and republication. On March 27 and 28, 1846, in *Kjøbenhavnsposten*, no. 73 and 74, a review by Møller of *Concluding Unscientific Postscript* appeared over the name Prosper naturalis de molinasky. In

---

[92] P. M. Mitchell, *A History of Danish Literature* (New York: American-Scandinavian Foundation, 1958), p. 166.

[93] Goldschmidt to Otto Borchsenius, December 25, 1878, *Breve fra og til Meïr Goldschmidt*, Letter 407, I, p. 219 (ed. tr.).

Historical Introduction xxv

1847, the review was reprinted in Møller's *Kritiske Skizzer* with an additional sentence: "Since in the meantime it has become apparent that this author belongs to the irritable species of the genus, I have decided this time to be satisfied with my own insignificant name, in order to calm his mind with the declaration that apart from the present article (and a postscript omitted here) I have had nothing printed pseudonymously or anonymously concerning the author and his writings."[94] In the style and tone of *The Corsair*—quite different from that of Møller's published reply[95] to Kierkegaard's first article[96]—Møller lightly treats of concepts such as "the absurd" and "the single individual." Before stating "some aphoristic observations that occurred to me during the reading,"[97] Møller makes the general observation that the French require that a book "shall be worked through organically, and there an author like our great Climacus, despite all his writings, would perhaps find a place under the rubric: chaotic literature—or not be recorded among the writers at all."[98] The only need is, "as it is put in *Either/Or* (I, p. 377), 'to place me astride a thought,' in order to get the most advantageous arrangement at the circus in Tivoli."[99] Kierkegaard offered no reply, but in his journal[100] he made passing note of the review. In addition to republishing the critical writings, Møller republished some poems, together with some new poems, in a volume entitled *Billeder og Sange* (1847).

When Goldschmidt returned to Denmark in October 1847, he started the journal *Nord og Syd* and published the first volume in December. "At that time Møller was about to travel."[101] They had not seen much of each other since the

[94] P. L. Møller, "Søren Kierkegaard," *Kritiske Skizzer fra Aarene 1840-47*, I–II (Copenhagen: 1847), II, pp. 254–55 (ed. tr.).
[95] See Supplement, pp. 104–05.
[96] See pp. 38–46.
[97] Møller, *Kritiske Skizzer*, II, p. 264.
[98] Ibid., p. 262.
[99] Ibid., pp. 263–64. See *Either/Or*, I, *KW* III (*SV* I 332).
[100] See Supplement, p. 203 (*Pap.* VII^1 B 71).
[101] See Supplement, p. 150. The year of Møller's departure is sometimes given as 1846. Goldschmidt's recollection conforms to his statement in *Nord*

evening when Goldschmidt had reported the conversation (early 1845) in which Kierkegaard had said "*The Corsair* is P. L. Møller."[102] Although their relationship had become cool and more distant, they did meet on occasion. During their last meeting before Møller's departure, Møller sarcastically congratulated Goldschmidt on the first issue of *Nord og Syd* as being quotable by Bishop Mynster. "It is difficult to defend oneself against such congratulations—that I had had to learn for myself during the *Corsair* period—and when I nevertheless tried, he said that nothing would help, that by giving up *The Corsair* I had betrayed myself; it was not natural for me to pursue some 'positive good' in public life here at home; the caustic Jewish nature demanded hate, and in hate I had and have my strength."[103] Goldschmidt shifted the conversation to Møller's attainments. "What have you yourself accomplished by not choosing something positive? What effect, if only literary, has your esthetics had on writing? Where is that for which we had once hoped?" He then went on to criticize Møller's poetry. "One word led to another, and we were a hair's breadth from becoming outright philistine enemies." Reminded of their pact that for the sake of truth in literature they would, if necessary, oppose each other, Møller said, " 'Well, let's fight, then! I can find occasion to say a lot on that score. Come on!' "[104]

Møller left Denmark in late December 1847 and never returned. Although he and Goldschmidt kept in touch through occasional letters and Goldschmidt's visits to the Continent, the ties had been cut and the relationship became more and more distant.

Møller's ambition had been to succeed the poet and dramatist Oehlenschläger as professor of esthetics at the University of Copenhagen. The post did not become vacant until 1850, four years after the *Corsair* affair, but, according to

---

og Syd, I, 1848, p. 172 (written in December 1847): "Mr. P. L. Møller has now officially announced that he will make a long foreign tour."

[102] See Supplement, p. 143.
[103] See Supplement, p. 151.
[104] See Supplement, pp. 151-52.

Goldschmidt, Møller had nourished the dream since he won the University gold medal in 1841 for an essay on French poetry. This dream, Goldschmidt states in a draft of his autobiography, explains "many things that are otherwise self-contradictory, his seeking after friendship and his reckless enmity."[105] But Møller was his own worst enemy. "I believe that the greatest error he committed was his continual desire to avoid suffering, for by fleeing from the consequences of the evil possibilities he had created for himself, he fled also from the good possibilities.... He demanded a miracle in the outer world, and therefore did not get it in the inner world."[106] This may sound like Judge William in *Either/Or*, but the words are Goldschmidt's about Møller the man.

Goldschmidt thought that Møller considered himself "to be a genius, and he did not have the enthusiasm required for him to be able to take upon himself the obligation of a genius; he would only demand the reward and the privileges of a genius, and on this he was broken, in this his fate was consummated."[107] Furthermore, in Goldschmidt's view, Møller's basic defects in the esthetic sphere were that "he was not a poet," that "no great vision passed by his 'inner eye,'"[108] that he lacked a "comprehensive theory of literature and poetry, and he had never developed any system in the sense of a view of life."[109] This may sound somewhat like Kierkegaard's criticism of H. C. Andersen in *From the Papers of One Still Living*, but the words are those of Goldschmidt on Møller the poet and esthetician.

Goldschmidt's retrospective assessment of Møller as poet and esthetician suggests that Møller was not qualified to be Oehlenschläger's successor. However, after Oehlenschläger's death, Goldschmidt sent a letter to Møller in which he said, "My ambition is to become professor of esthetics at the University of Copenhagen when you have been that and are dead.

---

[105] Goldschmidt, *Livs Erindringer og Resultater*, I–II, ed. Morten Borup (Copenhagen: 1965), I, p. 263 (ed. tr.).
[106] Ibid., p. 264.
[107] Ibid., p. 265.
[108] Ibid., p. 268. [109] Ibid., p. 255.

. . ."[110] Paul Rubow, however, judges that Møller's expectation was unjustified. Møller believed, "according to Goldschmidt," that because of Kierkegaard's linking of Møller and *The Corsair*[111] he "lost his chance to become Oehlenschläger's successor as professor of esthetics. He had none, and in 1850 he would scarcely be disqualified because of *The Corsair*."[112] Møller's productivity during the intervening four years—largely reprintings, letters to the editor, and editing the works of Johan Herman Wessel and Steen Steensen Blicher—contributed little to whatever chance he might have had.

An important issue related to Møller and the unattained professorship is the significance of the brief Latin phrase "*Ubi P. L. Møller, ibi The Corsair.*"[113] Just as Kierkegaard's relation to the pseudonymous writings was known or definitely suspected in literary and university circles[114] before Kierkegaard's declaration in *Concluding Unscientific Postscript* (1846), Møller's participation in *The Corsair* was also known and did not need merely to be suspected by those who had already read Møller's own bibliographical piece in Erslew's lexicon of authors.[115] Kierkegaard was aware of the piece,[116] which only confirmed what he already knew about the relation between Møller, Goldschmidt, and *The Corsair*.[117] If Møller's qualifications to become Oehlenschläger's successor four years later were in themselves dubious, and if his esthetic productivity during those four years was qualitatively inadequate, the statement in a short Latin line of what was already known in the pertinent inner circles could scarcely have

[110] *Breve fra og til Meïr Goldschmidt*, Letter 181, I, p. 296 (ed. tr.). The letter is dated May 1, 1851, five months and five days before the poet Carsten Hauch was named professor of esthetics.
[111] See Supplement, p. 46. [112] Rubow, p. 118 (ed. tr.).
[113] See Supplement, p. 46.
[114] See, for example, the review in *Berlingske Tidende* (May 6, 1845) and a sequel in *The Corsair* (May 23, 1845) in note 55, pp. 274-76. See also Supplement, pp. 95-96.
[115] See p. 46 and note 122.
[116] See Supplement, pp. 191,198-99, 207 (*Pap.* VII¹ B 55, 69, 72).
[117] See Supplement, pp. 143, 228 (*Pap.* IX A 92).

been an important factor in the appointment (1851) of the poet Carsten Hauch, rather than of Møller, as Oehlenschläger's successor.

As noted above, the consequences of the *Corsair* affair for Møller and Goldschmidt were quite different from what they had expected. For Kierkegaard, too, the consequences were, if not wholly different, more numerous and more incisive than he had anticipated. "Incidentally, it has happened here, as it frequently does, that despite all my deliberation, a something more eventuates . . . ."[118] Appropriate to all three men is the observation in the "Diapsalmata" that "sometimes a brisk little cause produces a colossal effect."[119]

Goldschmidt recalled his view of Kierkegaard and of Kierkegaard's probable response. "He belonged to a great illuminated world of thought; he carried within himself—in his head there was, so to speak, an Olympus—clear, blessed gods of thought; there was interest, probably not for the individual, but for all mankind; there was a special purity and consequently a special power, and when he stood before me in such a form, I perceived that for such persons one should go out of one's way with hat in hand, while one looks through chinks for their small weaknesses. And when I suddenly remembered that I myself had been led fatefully to attack his weaknesses, there was a veil, something both pleasant and unpleasant, in which I could wrap myself and hide myself from that thought: he himself took it so good-naturedly, was not hurt, did not suffer because of it."[120]

At the outset, Goldschmidt's characterization of Kierkegaard's response was appropriate. The first stage involved the unpleasantness of controversy, which Kierkegaard accepted as part of the enterprise. But with the shift of *The Corsair* from concern with Kierkegaard's two articles to attacks on Kierkegaard's person, there was a destruction of Kier-

---

[118] See Supplement, p. 208 (*Pap.* VII¹ A 98); also pp. 228, 236 (*Pap.* IX A 92; X¹ A 98).

[119] *Either/Or*, I, *KW* III (*SV* I 10).

[120] From a draft of Goldschmidt's autobiography, *Livs Erindringer og Resultater*, ed. Borup, I, pp. 272-73 (ed. tr.).

kegaard's environment.[121] The character assassination by way of identification of Kierkegaard with Crazy Nathanson and the incessant ridicule of his clothes and physical features made him the object of curiosity and taunting on the streets, where he had been Copenhagen's foremost peripatetic and conversationalist. "Søren" (as well as "Enten/Eller") became a street nickname and the name of ludicrous characters in plays.[122] Copenhagen was no longer the congenial place it had been for him. He felt that he was undergoing a "martyrdom of laughter,"[123] and in a journal entry from 1847 he wrote, "To be trampled to death by geese is a lingering death...."[124] Driven from the streets and the frequent company of ordinary people, he took numerous drives to wooded areas near Copenhagen in order to find simple solitude,[125] but even there curiosity followed him. For two weeks in May he visited Berlin, where he could walk again without molestation.

For all his emphasis on "the single individual," Kierkegaard was a sociable person. Despite his full awareness that he had taken the initiative against *The Corsair* and had to expect unpleasantness, he had not reckoned that the atmosphere would become "tainted for me."[126] Least of all had he expected that those who had urged him to engage *The Corsair* would give him the silent treatment publicly (although many thanked him privately) and regard the whole thing as a trifle.

In one sense, the affair did become an affair of trifles—Kierkegaard's clothes and physical appearance—and therefore Kierkegaard was silent after the two articles were published. But the immediate effect of the caricature and ridicule that altered the atmosphere was heightened by two things: the per-

[121] See Supplement, pp. 208-09, 217-18, 220, 222-23, 225-27, 229, 237-38 (*Pap.* VII^1 A 98, 107; VIII^1 A 99, 163, 175, 458, 544; IX A 64, 370; X^1 A 123, 177).
[122] See Supplement, pp. 237-38 (*Pap.* X^1 A 177), and note 480; *The Moment, KW* XXIII (*SV* XIII 108).
[123] *JP* II 2046; VI 6509 (*Pap.* X^5 A 121; X^2 101); see Supplement, p. 236 (*Pap* X^1 A 120).
[124] See Supplement, p. 220 (*Pap.* VIII^1 A 99).
[125] See Supplement, p. 222 (*Pap.* VIII^1 A 163), and note 436.
[126] Ibid.

vasive and devastating power of an unprecedented kind of journalism in a small city of 125,000 and the uncommon sensitivity of the object of the personal attack. Writing in retrospect about an earlier discussion among the *Corsair* editorial staff, Goldschmidt observed, "but accustomed as we are now [1877] to vehement and violent newspaper articles, one will have difficulty in understanding how it could sound in that anxious, quiet time [1846] and how dangerous it must appear if one like me had had his sensitivity sharpened a little."[127] In the late twentieth century, when journalists operate practically without even the restraint of libel laws, it is even more difficult to comprehend the sensational, tyrannizing effect of *The Corsair*. It may be said that the wounding inflicted by the ostracism of ridicule is in some degree a universal experience, but in the *Corsair* affair there was at least one difference—the sensitivity of a poet deeply interested in other persons.

Kierkegaard's hope that the distortions would increase the distance between him and the pseudonymous works, with the result that the reader would be alone with the works without the intrusion of an author,[128] went unfulfilled at the time. Besides being mocked with "Søren, Søren," Kierkegaard was taunted on the streets with "Enten/Eller," as is epitomized, for example, by the well-known contemporary drawing with the caption: "There comes Either/Or!—Psst! Psst!"[129]

However important the consequences of the *Corsair* affair were for Goldschmidt, Møller, and *The Corsair* itself, and however much Kierkegaard's aims were fulfilled, plus the unexpected tainting of the whole atmosphere, the most important consequence was wholly unexpected and unintended: the second phase of Kierkegaard's authorship.

Kierkegaard clearly intended *Concluding Unscientific Postscript* as the conclusion of his work as a writer. He thought an occasional long review would be possible, such as of Thomasine Gyllembourg's *Two Ages*, which he wrote in 1846, and of A. P. Adler's writings, which he drafted in 1847,

[127] Goldschmidt, *Erindringer* (1877), I, p. 255 (ed. tr.).
[128] See Supplement, pp. 209, 214 (*Pap.* VII¹ A 98, 99).
[129] By Johan Thomas Lundbye (1818-1848).

but his intention was to seek an appointment as a rural pastor or a post as a teacher. At the moment, December 27, 1845, after delivering the manuscript of *Postscript* to the printer, he wanted simply to perform an act on behalf of Goldschmidt in relation to Møller and *The Corsair* and on behalf of others in relation to *The Corsair*. Perhaps Kierkegaard could never have given up writing, even if the *Corsair* affair had not taken an unexpected turn with an unexpected consequence for him. In retrospect (1853) he wrote:

> I intended to finish writing as quickly as possible—and then become a rural pastor.
> With every new book I thought: Now you must stop.
> I felt this most strongly in connection with *Concluding Postscript*.
> At this point I meant to stop—then I wrote the lines about *The Corsair*.
> From that moment on, my idea of what it is to be an author changed. Now I believed that I ought to keep on as long as it was in any way possible; to be an author now, to be here, was such a burden to me that there was more asceticism involved in this than in going out in the country.[130]

The *Corsair* affair had been a crucial step in his "education and development."[131] In a sense driven out of his ordinary associations, he was driven to deeper reflection and higher vision. "Voluntarily exposing myself to attack by *The Corsair* is no doubt the most intensive thing along the order of genius that I have done. It will have results in all my writing, will be extremely important for my whole task with respect to Christianity and to my elucidation of Christianity, to casting it entirely into reflection.[132]

The result was the second phase of the authorship, not essentially unconnected with the earlier pseudonymous works,

---

[130] *JP* VI 6893 (*Pap.* X^5 A 146).
[131] *JP* VI 6548 (*Pap.* X^2 A 251); see Supplement, p. 228 (*Pap.* IX A 92).
[132] *JP* VI 6373 (*Pap.* X^1 A 187). See *On My Work as an Author, KW* XXII (*SV* XIII 495); *The Point of View, KW* XIII (*SV* XIII 539, 543, 578).

but more concentrated, different in form, with a decisive accent, and also with new pseudonyms: Anti-Climacus (above, not against, Johannes Climacus of *Fragments* and *Postscript*), author of *The Sickness unto Death* (1849) and *Practice in Christianity* (1850); H. H., author of *Two Minor Ethical-Religious Essays* (1849); and Inter et Inter, author of *The Crisis and a Crisis in the Life of an Actress* (1848). Besides those came the signed works: *Two Ages* (1846); *Upbuilding Discourses in Various Spirits* (1847); *Works of Love* (1847); *Christian Discourses* (1848); *The Point of View for My Work as an Author* (written in 1848, published posthumously in 1859); *Armed Neutrality* (written in 1848-1849 but not published); *The Lily of the Field and the Bird of the Air* (1849); *Three Discourses at the Communion on Fridays* (1849); *An Upbuilding Discourse* (1850); *Two Discourses at the Communion on Fridays* (1851); *On My Work as an Author* (1851); *For Self-Examination* (1851); *Judge for Yourselves!* (written in 1851-1852 but not published); various short pieces and *The Moment* (1854-1855); and, on September 3, 1855, *The Unchangeableness of God*.

On October 2, 1855, Kierkegaard entered Frederiks Hospital, and on November 11, 1855, he died. In one sense, he had been defeated in the *Corsair* affair "because the conflict was drawn into another sphere—the ridicule of his person."[133] With regard to Goldschmidt and the "others," he had accomplished his purposes. Most important of all, the affair was the occasion for his further education and the whole second phase of the authorship, without which his legacy would have been very important but would have lacked some of his greatest works. The *Corsair* affair, in its unexpected consequences, was indeed a *felix culpa*.

Because the present volume is somewhat different from the other volumes in the series *Kierkegaard's Writings*, a special word about the inclusion and arrangement of materials—and a suggestion about an order of reading—are in order. Part I (Articles) comprises early writings published by Kier-

[133] Magnussen, p. 163 (ed. tr.).

kegaard. Part II (Addenda) comprises articles of possible, but dubious, attribution to Kierkegaard. As newspaper articles they belong in kind to the *Corsair* affair. Except for the "Open Letter" to Rudelbach (1851), they belong chronologically to a period before and around the *Corsair* affair. The Supplement includes writings pertaining to the *Corsair* affair published by others, as well as unpublished pieces by Kierkegaard (journal entries and drafts of articles), and items from Kierkegaard's journals and papers pertaining to "An Open Letter." In approaching the *Corsair* affair, the reader is advised to observe the following order:

1. Early *Corsair* items on Kierkegaard's pseudonymous works (pp. 91-96).
2. Frater Taciturnus-Kierkegaard's unpublished open letter, written before Møller's article (pp. 157-58).
3. P. L. Møller's article in *Gæa* (pp. 96-104).
4. The piece by Frater Taciturnus-Kierkegaard in *Fædrelandet* (pp. 38-46).
5. P. L. Møller's published reply (pp. 104-05).
6. P. L. Møller's rejoinder, rejected by Goldschmidt (pp. 105-08).
7. Goldschmidt's first *Corsair* article in the attack (pp. 108-12).
8. Kierkegaard's second and last published piece in the affair (pp. 47-50).
9. The subsequent articles in *The Corsair* (pp. 112-37).
10. Kierkegaard's unpublished drafts of articles and journal entries (pp. 159-241).
11. Goldschmidt's retrospective observations (pp. 138-52).

If the present volume were an independent work and not part of *Kierkegaard's Writings* (published works plus supplementary material), the above order could have been used in arranging the various parts.

ARTICLES

The two articles related to the *Corsair* affair, "The Activity of a Traveling Esthetician" and "The Dialectical Result of a

Literary Police Action," overshadow the others in the volume because of the unique significance of that episode for Kierkegaard the man and the writer. The others have importance as elements akin to works within the authorship as a whole.[134]

Among the other articles, the first four and the one on *Don Giovanni* are directly related to the pseudonymous authorship and are part of Kierkegaard's intricate and ingenious indirect approach. "Public Confession" (1842) appeared eight months before the publication of *Either/Or* (February 20, 1843). In this elaborate disavowal of being the author of anything that might be credited to him, Kierkegaard requests that he should never be regarded "as an author of anything that does not bear my name."[135] The second piece, by A. F. (1843), on the author of *Either/Or*, and the next piece, by Victor Eremita, addressed to the literary critic J. L. Heiberg, are not of the same kind, yet both are again part of the mystification of pseudonymity and appeared shortly after the publication of *Either/Or*. "A Little Explanation" is, like "Public Confession," a signed disclaimer. "An Explanation and a Little More" (1845) is likewise a signed disclaimer but differs from the others in that it is a direct disclaimer occasioned by the first printed attribution of *Either/Or* and *Stages* to Kierkegaard.[136]

The serial article by A. on *Don Giovanni* (May 19-20, 1845) is also linked to *Either/Or* (1843) in particular and to the other

---

[134] Only an explanation of the presence of the letters and the article in the Addenda is necessary here. The Danish editors of *Kierkegaards Samlede Værker* state that the authorship is doubtful because the writing is not quite like Kierkegaard's. They included the pieces, however, because of the testimony of others. H. P. Barfod, the first editor of *Af Søren Kierkegaards Efterladte Papirer*, was convinced on internal grounds that the letters were by Kierkegaard and, for lack of other evidence, included them in an appendix (*Af Søren Kierkegaards Efterladte Papirer*, I-IX, ed. H. P. Barfod and H. Gottsched (Copenhagen: 1869-81), I (1833-43), pp. 364, 478-86. H. P. Holst, editor of *Ny Portefeuille*, was his authority for including "Literary Quicksilver" (ibid., pp. 364, 491-506). Kierkegaard does not include the letters or "Literary Quicksilver" in a list drawn up in 1848 (*JP* VI 6202; *Pap.* IX A 167). But the omission is not determinative, inasmuch as Victor Eremita's letter to Professor Heiberg is also omitted from that list.

[135] See p. 5.   [136] See p. 24 and note 55.

early pseudonymous works, but in a different way. In substance, it is clearly an extension of the brilliant discussion of Mozart's *Don Giovanni* in *Either/Or*.[137] Its special importance (which it shares with *The Crisis and a Crisis in the Life of an Actress*, 1848) is that its substance is more akin to the first phase of the authorship (pre–*Corsair* affair) and that the piece was written in the second phase. Kierkegaard's explanation of the significance of *The Crisis* holds also for the later piece on *Don Giovanni*: "The religious is present from the very beginning. Conversely, the esthetic is still present even in the last moment. After the publication of only religious works for two years, a little esthetic article follows. Therefore at the beginning and at the end there is assurance against explaining the phenomenon by saying that the writer is an esthetic author who in the course of time had changed and had become a religious author."[138]

With regard to the remaining articles, the polemical "Open Letter" to Dr. Rudelbach (January 31, 1851), published about six years after the two polemical pieces against *The Corsair*, is more significant in substance than the two pieces, but it did not have the important immediate consequences they had. It was, however, prophetic.

Andreas Gottlob Rudelbach (1792-1862) was the Danish son of a Saxon, J. H. Gottlob Rudelbach, and a Swede, Birgitte Østrom. In 1817 he won a University gold medal for a study of "The Nature and Value of Dithyrambic Poetry," and in 1822 he was granted a doctor's degree by the University of Copenhagen for his dissertation on the principles of ethics. The following year he traveled in Germany, Switzerland, and France. In 1825, together with N.F.S. Grundtvig, he began the publication of *Theologisk Maanedsskrift* (Theological Monthly); he continued it alone from Volume VI (1826) through Volume XIII (1828) because Grundtvig had been censured officially. The journal usually contained a polemic against the reigning rationalism. He impressed students, H. L.

---

[137] *Either/Or*, I, *KW* III (*SV* I 29-113).
[138] *The Point of View*, *KW* XXII (*SV* XIII 522).

Martensen in particular, by a "combination of earnestness and keenness but especially by his prodigious learning and his large library."[139] With little chance of getting an appointment in Denmark because of his Grundtvigianism and his opposition to dogmatic rationalism, Rudelbach accepted an appointment in Saxony as head pastor and councilor in Blauchau. After an active, influential, and scholarly career in Germany, he returned to Denmark in 1845. He broke with Grundtvig over interpretation of apostolic symbols as "the living word." H. N. Clausen and others were opposed to his appointment to the university divinity faculty, and after lecturing in 1847-1848 as *privat-docent*, Rudelbach gave up thought of an academic appointment and was named pastor of St. Mikkels in Slagelse, Denmark. A series of writings in Danish (essentially Grundtvigian and free church in outlook) included, in 1846, *Christelig Biographie* (Christian Biography), which Kierkegaard read and appreciated, and, in 1851, *Om det borgerlige Ægteskab* (On Civil Marriage), the occasion of Kierkegaard's "An Open Letter."

Three times in his life, Kierkegaard ventured into uncharacteristic direct controversy: with Meïr Goldschmidt and *The Corsair* on the issue of destructive anonymous journalism; with A. G. Rudelbach on the issue of politicizing reformation of the Church; and later (December 1854-1855) with H. L. Martensen and the established order on the main issue of the acculturized, emasculated Christianity of Christendom. In each case, the primary concern was an issue, not a person. Goldschmidt and Kierkegaard each had a certain respect for the other. Rudelbach and Kierkegaard were acquainted through visits and conversations in the remarkable home of M. P. Kierkegaard. Martensen had been Kierkegaard's teacher and was a scholar and professor of eminence. Furthermore, in all three instances, Kierkegaard initiated the battle because of the important issues at stake.

The three engagements became intertwined in "An Open

---

[139] Hans Lassen Martensen, *Af mit Levnet*, I–II (Copenhagen: 1883), I, pp. 23-24 (ed. tr.).

Letter." One strand was the politicizing and sectarianizing of Church reformation by Rudelbach. This involved Bishop Mynster (whom Martensen, an early admirer of Rudelbach, succeeded and called "a witness").[140] It also drew in Goldschmidt and the aftermath of the unresolved *Corsair* controversy because of Mynster's bland insensitivity to what was at stake in the *Corsair* controversy and in Kierkegaard's critique of Rudelbach. To Kierkegaard, this was a token of Mynster's obtuseness in trying to accommodate Christianity to the mediocre mentality of the age. Although he was deeply attached to Mynster personally, Kierkegaard reluctantly initiated an attack on the bishop's apostasy of accommodation after Martensen's "witness" eulogy. Although "An Open Letter" (January 31, 1851) was in one sense a defense of Mynster against sectarian, politicizing reformers, it was, together with *Practice in Christianity* (September 11, 1850) and *For Self-Examination* (September 10, 1851), the beginning of a direct critique of the establishment because of its "modifications" and devitalization of Christianity. Therefore, "An Open Letter" is important both as a direct declaration of Kierkegaard's position and as a signal bell of what was to come. Within eight months after "An Open Letter," only three small publications appeared, all under his own name, and for three years thereafter there was an unusual silence. Then came the terminating series of direct-action communications, culminating in the issues of *The Moment*.

Given the relationship of the seemingly disparate pieces and their essential relationship with the later writings, the present volume might well be summed up in a subtitle: "Kierkegaard: Pseudonymist and Polemicist, Practice and Preparation."

---

[140] Hans Lassen Martensen, *Leilighedstaler* (Copenhagen: 1844), p. 20 (ed. tr.).

CHRONOLOGY

* designates articles in Part I of this volume
** designates articles in Part II

1813
May 5   Søren Aabye Kierkegaard born at Nytorv 2 (now 27), Copenhagen, son of Michael Pedersen Kierkegaard and Ane Sørensdatter Lund Kierkegaard.

1814
Apr. 18   Peder Ludvig Møller born in Aalborg.

1819
Oct. 26   Meïr Aaron Goldschmidt born in Vordingborg.

1830
Autumn   Kierkegaard enters the University of Copenhagen.

1832
Autumn   Møller enters the University of Copenhagen.

1837
Between May 8 and May 12. On a visit to the Rørdams in Frederiksberg, Kierkegaard meets Regine Olsen for the first time.

Oct.   Goldschmidt assumes editorship of *Næstved Ugeblade*.

1838
                "The Battle between the Old and the New Soap-Cellar" (a philosophical comedy drafted but not completed or published; *Pap*. II B 1-21).

Sept. 7   Publication of *From the Papers of One Still Living*, published against his will, by S. Kjerkegaard [*sic*] (about H. C. Andersen as a novelist, with special reference to his latest work, *Only a Fiddler*).

—   Kierkegaard and Goldschmidt meet at the Rørdam residence in Frederiksberg.

1840

Sept. 10	Kierkegaard becomes engaged to Regine.
Oct. 8	First number of *Corsaren (The Corsair)* published by M. Goldschmidt.

1841

Spring	Møller wins University gold medal for essay on French poetry.
July 16	Kierkegaard's dissertation for the *Magister* degree, *The Concept of Irony, with Constant Reference to Socrates*, accepted.
—	Kierkegaard and Goldschmidt's discussion of comic writing.
—	Kierkegaard and Goldschmidt's discussion of *The Corsair*.
Aug. 11	Kierkegaard returns Regine Olsen's engagement ring.
Sept. 16	Dissertation printed.
Sept. 28	10 A.M.–2:00 P.M., 4:00–7:30 P.M. Kierkegaard defends his dissertation. (In 1854, *Magister* degrees came to be regarded and named officially as doctoral degrees.)
Oct. 8	Kierkegaard's public defense of his dissertation reported in *The Corsair*, no. 49.
Oct. 11	Engagement with Regine Olsen broken.
Oct. 22	Review of *The Concept of Irony* in *The Corsair*, no. 51.

1842

—	Conversation between Kierkegaard and Goldschmidt in which Kierkegaard took exception to anonymous writing in *The Corsair* and the invasion of privacy.
June 12	* "Public Confession," by S. Kierkegaard, published in *Fædrelandet*, no. 904.
Autumn	Goldschmidt and Møller begin their association.
—	*Johannes Climacus, or De omnibus dubitandum est* begun by Kierkegaard but not completed or published.

1843

Feb. 5	**"A Letter," anonymously published in *Berlingske Tidende*, no. 33.
Feb. 7	**"Another Letter," anonymously published in *Berlingske Tidende*, no. 35.
Feb. 8	**["A Letter"], anonymously published in *Fædrelandet*, no. 1143.
Feb. 12	**"Literary Quicksilver," anonymously published in *Ny Portefeuille*, I, 7, col. 198-216.
Feb. 13	Publication of fascicle 2 of Vol. II of Erslew's *Forfatter-Lexicon*, containing Møller's literary vita, including his writing for *The Corsair*.
Feb. 20	*Either/Or*, edited by Victor Eremita, published.
Feb. 27	*"Who Is the Author of *Either/Or*," by A. F....., published in *Fædrelandet*, no. 1162.
Mar. 5	*"A Word of Thanks to Professor Heiberg," by Victor Eremita, published in *Fædrelandet*, no. 1168.
—	Goldschmidt and Møller celebrate the publication of *Either/Or*. Victor Eremita invited as the guest of honor.
Mar. 10	Review of *Either/Or* in *The Corsair*, no. 129.
May 8	Kierkegaard leaves for short visit to Berlin.
May 16	*Two Upbuilding Discourses*, by S. Kierkegaard, published.
May 16	*"A Little Explanation," by S. Kierkegaard, published in *Fædrelandet*, no. 1236.
June	Møller in charge of *The Corsair* during Goldschmidt's visit to Sweden. Goldschmidt sentenced to "six times four days" imprisonment for violation of the press laws.
July	Kierkegaard learns of Regine's engagement to Johan Frederik Schlegel.
Autumn	Møller in charge of *The Corsair* during Goldschmidt's visit to Paris.
Oct. 16	*Repetition*, by Constantin Constantius, *Fear and Trembling*, by Johannes de Silentio, and *Three Upbuilding Discourses*, by S. Kierkegaard, published.

Dec. 6	*Four Upbuilding Discourses*, by S. Kierkegaard, published.

1844

Mar. 5	*Two Upbuilding Discourses*, by S. Kierkegaard, published.
June 8	*Three Upbuilding Discourses*, by S. Kierkegaard, published.
June 13	*Philosophical Fragments*, by Johannes Climacus, published.
June 17	*The Concept of Anxiety*, by Vigilius Haufniensis, and *Prefaces*, by Nicolaus Notabene, published.
Aug. 31	*Four Upbuilding Discourses*, by S. Kierkegaard, published.

1845

—	*En Jøde*, by Adolph Meyer, edited by M. Goldschmidt, published.
—	Kierkegaard and Goldschmidt's discussion of *En Jøde* and of Møller's relation to *The Corsair*.
Apr. 29	*Three Discourses on Imagined Occasions*, by S. Kierkegaard, published.
Apr. 30	*Stages on Life's Way*, edited by Hilarius Bogbinder [Bookbinder], published.
May 9	Allusion in *The Corsair*, no. 242, to disclosure in *Berlingske Tidende*, no. 108, of Kierkegaard as the author of *Either/Or* and *Stages*.
May 9	*"An Explanation and a Little More," by S. Kierkegaard, published in *Fædrelandet*, no. 1883.
May 13-24	Kierkegaard visits Berlin.
May 19-20	*"A Cursory Observation Concerning a Detail in *Don Giovanni*," by A., published in *Fædrelandet*, no. 1890-91.
May 23	Report in *The Corsair*, no. 245, of fictitious case of Kierkegaard vs. *Berlingske Tidende*.
May 29	*Eighteen Upbuilding Discourses* (from 1843-1844), by S. Kierkegaard, published.
July 4	Praise of Hilarius Bookbinder, editor of *Stages*, in *The Corsair*, no. 251.

Nov. 14	Praise of Victor Eremita, editor of *Either/Or*, in *The Corsair*, no. 269.
Dec.	Møller's "A Visit in Sorø," in *Gæa 1846*, published.
Dec. 27	*"The Activity of a Traveling Esthetician and How He Still Happened to Pay for the Dinner," by Frater Taciturnus, published in *Fædrelandet*, no. 2078.
Dec. 29	Møller's reply in *Fædrelandet*, no. 2079, to Frater Taciturnus's article of Dec. 27.
—	Møller writes four-part piece against Kierkegaard for *The Corsair*, rejected by Goldschmidt.
1846	
Jan. 2	First attack on Kierkegaard in *The Corsair*.
Jan. 9– Jan. 7, 1848	Nine issues of *The Corsair*, each with one to three pieces on Kierkegaard.
Jan. 10	Reply by Frater Taciturnus, *"The Dialectical Result of a Literary Police Action," in *Fædrelandet*, no. 9.
Feb. 7	Kierkegaard considers qualifying himself for ordination (*JP* V 5972; *Pap*. VII[1] A 4).
Feb. 27	*Concluding Unscientific Postscript*, by Johannes Climacus, published.
Mar. 27-28	Review by Prosper naturalis de molinasky (Møller) of *Postscript* in *Kjøbenhavnsposten*, no. 73-74.
—	Kierkegaard and Goldschmidt meet in silence on Myntergade. Goldschmidt decides to give up *The Corsair*.
Mar. 30	*Two Ages: The Age of Revolution and The Present Age. A Literary Review*, by S. Kierkegaard, published.
May 2-16	Kierkegaard visits Berlin.
Oct. 2	Goldschmidt sells *The Corsair* and resigns as editor.
Oct. 7	Goldschmidt travels to Germany and Italy.
1847	
Jan. 24	Kierkegaard writes: "God be praised that I was

	subject to the attack of the rabble. I have now had time to arrive at the conviction that it was a melancholy thought to want to live in a vicarage, doing penance in an out-of-the-way place, forgotten. I now have made up my mind quite otherwise" (*JP* V 5966; *Pap*. VII^1 A 229).
Mar. 13	*Upbuilding Discourses in Various Spirits*, by S. Kierkegaard, published.
Sept. 29	*Works of Love*, by S. Kierkegaard, published.
Oct.	Goldschmidt returns to Denmark and prepares for the publication of *Nord og Syd*.
—	*Kritiske Skizzer*, by P. L. Møller, published.
Dec.	Møller and Goldschmidt part on bad terms.
—	Møller leaves Denmark.
1848	
Apr. 26	*Christian Discourses*, by S. Kierkegaard, published.
July 24-27	*The Crisis and a Crisis in the Life of an Actress*, by Inter et Inter, published.
Nov.	*The Point of View for My Work as an Author* "as good as finished" (*JP* VI 6258; *Pap*. IX A 293); published posthumously in 1859 by S.K.'s brother, Peter Christian Kierkegaard.
	Armed Neutrality, by S. Kierkegaard, "written toward the end of 1848 and the beginning of 1849" (*Pap*. X^5 B 105-10) but not published.
1849	
May 14	Second edition of *Either/Or* and *The Lily of the Field and the Bird of the Air*, by S. Kierkegaard, published.
May 19	*Two Minor Ethical-Religious Essays*, by H. H., published.
July 30	*The Sickness unto Death*, by Anti-Climacus, published.
Nov. 13	*Three Discourses at the Communion on Fridays*, by S. Kierkegaard, published.
1850	
Sept. 27	*Practice in Christianity*, by Anti-Climacus, published.

Dec. 20	*An Upbuilding Discourse*, by S. Kierkegaard, published.
1851	
Jan. 31	*"An Open Letter . . . Dr. Rudelbach," by S. Kierkegaard, published in *Fædrelandet*, no. 26.
Aug. 7	*On My Work as an Author* and *Two Discourses at the Communion on Fridays*, by S. Kierkegaard, published.
Sept. 10	*For Self-Examination*, by S. Kierkegaard, published.
—	Carsten Hauch appointed professor of esthetics as Oehlenschläger's successor.
1851-52	
	Judge for Yourselves!, by S. Kierkegaard, written; published posthumously, 1876
1854	
Jan. 30	Bishop Mynster dies.
Apr. 15	H. Martensen named bishop.
Dec. 18	Kierkegaard begins polemic against Bishop Martensen in *Fædrelandet*.
1855	
Jan. - May	Polemic continues.
May 24	*This Must Be Said; So Let It Be Said*, by S. Kierkegaard, advertised as published.
	First number of *The Moment*.
June 16	*Christ's Judgment on Official Christianity*, by S. Kierkegaard, published.
Sept. 3	*The Unchangeableness of God. A Discourse*, by S. Kierkegaard, published.
Sept. 25	Ninth and last number of *The Moment* published; number 10 published posthumously. S. K. writes his last journal entry (*JP* VI 6969; *Pap.* XI^2 A 439).
Oct. 2	Kierkegaard enters Frederiks Hospital.
Nov. 11	Kierkegaard dies.
Nov. 18	Kierkegaard buried in Assistents Cemetery, Copenhagen.

I

Articles, 1842-1851

PUBLIC CONFESSION[1]

To be disparaged and belittled undeservedly certainly can make one outraged for a time, but the proud mind quickly bounces back again and regains its composure simply because the charge was not true. To be praised undeservedly, to be attributed a worth that a person does not feel he himself has, to be extolled for something he has not done, something he may not even be capable of doing or is too lazy to do—has a far more profound, painful, and humiliating effect; by and large it is a dangerous test for the weak human heart. The vain mind may be tempted to confirm people in this mistaken belief; awareness of one's own unworthiness does not promptly give a person the courage to admit to himself and others the truth of the matter. Yet the undeserved praise burns in the soul. Even though it was not his fault that he got what does not belong to him, he not only feels undeserving of the honor but also feels an indirect reproach that is all the more emphatic because it does not come in a hostile, infuriating form but as a kind and friendly approval that makes him feel his unworthiness ever more deeply.

All this is said primarily for my own sake and to provide the text on which I wish to speak to myself. Many times during the last four months, I have enjoyed the undeserved honor of being regarded and considered to be the author of a number of substantial, informative, and witty articles in various newspapers, of several fliers that were fliers only outwardly, since their contents were solid, weighty, and unpadded, assuring them much more than an ephemeral significance. For a time, I tried to conceal from myself how much indirect reproach there was in this, but the more frequently it was repeated, the more difficult it became for me. Finally, the accusing voice inside me became so loud that I tried in vain to escape its judgment. Four months have gone by again, it said, and what have you achieved in that time? Now if you really were the author of all that good men have ascribed to you, or even if this were an inordinate wish, so much more so since at times you were said to be the author of something altogether different—if you had written any part of it, what a splendid activity you would then have to look back upon. Not only would you have benefited by your work, but your example, as the pastor is wont to say, would have been an encouragement to others. Then your life would not have been consigned to well-deserved oblivion, for your work would have made it unforgettable. And not only that, it perhaps would be analyzed, set up as an example, perhaps in *Folkebladet*[2] or in *Naturen, Mennesket og Borgeren*.[3] It would be said of you: So young and yet such a hard worker. They would point at you and say: Look, there he goes, indefatigable at work. Though I grow old and the years wipe out most of my memory, that impression will never be erased. I was ashamed of myself, ashamed before the good people who had fostered and spread such prepossessing ideas about me. My humiliated soul rallied to a firm resolve. You must openly confess your weakness, your idleness,[4] or there is no hope of improvement for you. So here I stand, face to face with the reading public in this momentous moment: I acknowledge my frailty, I have not written anything, not one line; I confess my weakness, I have no part in the whole thing or any part of it—no part at all, not even the slightest. Be strong, my soul, I confess to not even having read some of it. They will severely condemn me as I deserve to be; they will give up the inflated opinions of me that they have fostered up until now—it is my just punishment. They will not tolerate my being considered the author of a single line and will let me stand completely stripped as a warning to the young—I feel the courage to be reconciled to this. But having borne my punishment, I beg my contemporaries on the basis of the moral courage I have demonstrated not to surrender hope for me completely. Someday I may live up to some of the expectations they once had for me. I do not doubt that my contemporaries will be good-natured enough to do this. Far from doubting their good nature, I rather fear it, fear that they will again regard me as an author, attribute to me an enormous capacity for work and collaboration in the service of the age. But this I cannot allow, for the sake of my own moral improvement I cannot tolerate it, and therefore I beg the good people who show an interest in me never to regard me as the author of anything that does not bear my name.[5]

But it is not only for my own sake and with my own moral improvement in mind that I openly and candidly admit and acknowledge my unworthiness of the honor intended for me; it is just as much for the sake of those to whom it is rightly due, even if their modesty bids them conceal their names. We live in a remarkable age. The prospect of an extraordinary yield of imperishable results is so positive that this age will be unforgettable to the coming ages, which will owe everything to it. How very plausible, then, that a grateful posterity will remember all the heroes who fought for the good cause. If, then, I did not hasten to explain, to my own derision, that I had no part in it, how very plausible that I, altogether undeservedly, would become immortal[6] instead of these men of distinction whose lives have made them worthy of it. Precisely because the age is so remarkable, silence on my part is all the more unforgivable. Here it is a question not only of the brief honor and glory that can fall to heroes in their lifetime but also of the immortal honor that will endure until the end of the world.

Yes, the age is truly remarkable. It is worth the trouble to heed the earnest, profound, significant signs, to heed the great forces stirring in literature everywhere in so many ways, to watch for the hints that everywhere point to the fullness of time. It is the system[7] toward which the age is directing its efforts. Prof. R. Nielsen[8] already has published twenty-one logical ¶¶* that constitute the first part of a logic that in turn constitutes the first part of an all-encompassing encyclopedia, as intimated on the jacket, although its size is not more explicitly given, presumably not to intimidate, since people

---

* Well, not actually twenty-one paragraphs in all, since the first ten are missing, but in recompense he has dramatically hurled us headlong into the system.

certainly will venture to conclude that it will be extremely large. An encyclopedia! I happen to have in my possession Diderot's and d'Alembert's *Encyclopedia*—as yet incomplete—I have only twenty-eight folio volumes.⁹ It has often been encouraging to me to think that Professor R. Nielsen is writing such a book. He already has written twenty-one ¶¶ and several years ago published a subscription prospectus for a systematic ethics that will amount to at least twenty-four printed sheets¹⁰ when it is finished. At least that was the word at one time, but since it is still not completed, it may turn out to be forty-eight sheets—when it is finished. Who has forgotten how much Bastholm¹¹ has lying in his high desk? Who failed to notice that Dr. Beck¹² has abolished religion in order to make room for the system? Yes, our age is remarkable, is profoundly stirred; it seems as if the system were already here. When I read some time ago that a young scholar had sent a sealed package to a scientific society¹³ to be placed in its archives, I thought: it is the system. Who knows, maybe it is the system; maybe we already have the system in a sealed package.

Everything indicates that the decisive moment is approaching. There are a yeastiness and ferment that cannot possibly fizzle out. There is a vigorous party spirit astir everywhere. This, of course, must not be interpreted to mean that we have only one party that is vigorous, for that, after all, would not be a vigorous party spirit but a vigorous spirit within the party. No, there is a vigorous party spirit in a variety of parties. We have Liberals, Ultra-Liberals, Conservatives, Ultra-Conservatives, *juste-milieu*. In politics we have every conceivable and inconceivable worthiness. We have Kantians, Schleiermacherians, and Hegelians; these in turn are divided into two large parties: the one party comprises those who have not worked their way into Hegel but nevertheless are Hegelians; the other comprises those who have gone beyond Hegel¹⁴ but nevertheless are Hegelians. The third party, the genuine Hegelians, is very small. We have five anti-infant Baptists, seven Baptists, nine Anabaptists. Among the Baptists there are three who think the adults should be baptized in salt water, two who think they ought to be baptized in fresh water, and one who mediates between the two factions and insists on brackish water. We have two Straussians. We have a tailor on Utterslev Heath who has formed a new sect consisting of himself and two tailor apprentices. For some time there was a lot of talk that he had gained a third disciple from another trade, but just as he was about to capture him there was a quarrel that caused the neophyte to forsake him and take one of the apprentices along, and the person from the other trade also came up with a new belief. Right now in Pistol Street someone is supposed to have retired into solitude to think up a new religion, and his conclusions are expectantly awaited in the neighboring streets, Christen Bernikov Street and Peder Madsen's Alley. Party spirit is stirring everywhere. Soon there will be insufficient manpower to have one person for each party. Our age is as important and significant as any previous age. That a man is a great man and as such amounts to something has been heard before, but that every man is a party is unheard of. (No wonder, then, that no one pays any attention to an experienced, earnest, stirring Right Reverend voice[15] when it speaks—if not daily, at least once a month—for it is only a great man who speaks, not a party; it is only a solitary voice, not a party voice.) But this is important in other respects as well. It is an enormous advancement, analogous in our day only to the police-court judge who traveled in Sjælland—he was not only the judge in the court but also the jury. And that is not all. Soon one may well have to represent several parties, just like that remarkable man who was mustered by Lippe-Detmold and Schaumburg-Lippe in the field as a company, who on one side represented Lippe-Detmold and on the other Schaumburg-Lippe, on the one side was an infantryman and on the other was a cavalryman.

It is a momentous age. If anyone is still unconvinced by my statements, if he does not feel the tremendous energy in every individual, to say nothing of the sum of them, then I will cite another feature. Carstensen[16] has gained importance not by virtue of the way he wears his hair, for on that point we all acknowledge him as master, but by virtue of his head; Professor Heiberg's importance has dwindled.[17] This is a gallant expression of the momentousness of the age, a bold thought; I almost swoon at the thought, and perhaps I shall be unable to bear it beyond the moment I write it down here.

Everyone agrees that it would be incomparably foolish to think that nothing is going to come of this prodigious movement, this tremendous effort. I am no prophet and willingly admit that I am the least competent in Troy, but I, too, spy the system: there it is—twenty-eight volumes and Bastholm's aphorisms![18] We cannot go backward; Hegel's *Logic* has stood the test of Prof. Nielsen's thought. The moment approaches; for the last time Stilling[19] has undertaken to administer extreme unction to us, to establish us in the proper point of view, and if we will only stay there, it will come, it will surely come. But when it comes, what is the future going to undertake? There is nothing for it to do; we have done it all.[20] It can blissfully rest in the system, it can read at leisure the twenty-eight volumes, which were no easy matter to write. But if posterity is going to be able to live so securely and carefreely in systematic contemplation,[21] it will also have time to remember how much effort was required to attain that state, and it will feel called upon never to forget what it owes to our age and its heroes. What worries such an attainment has cost our authors, and what peace and quiet at night it has cost the reading public! The reading public never did have peace, for it had to be ready at all times, because the system was supposed to come, the one and only saving truth.

Since it would be difficult to give a precise idea of this movement and the painstaking research involved, I would rather suggest what it required by relating an experience I once had. In my younger days, I liked to watch the National Guard drill at the parade grounds. During a royal review, it so happened that a major stood facing his battalion when he should have been facing the other way. An experienced army officer present, no doubt fearful that this mistake would not escape the late king's[22] sharp scrutiny, rode over to him and whispered softly: "Major, you are facing the wrong way. You must turn around." The major was no pighead. He willingly took the advice and in a loud voice shouted, "Battalion, all together, about-face!" making matters still worse. If that battalion were the reading public, one can imagine what it would suffer in having a new major make the same mistake every day. Still ringing in my ears are the hundreds upon hundreds of voices shouting to all of us: "Battalion, all together, about-face!" The battalion continues, as they say in the military, to mark time and yet does not make any headway, because it is constantly told: "Battalion, all together, about-face!"[23]

But why recall these tiresome impressions. Let us rather dwell on the cheerful prospect ahead of us, when the system will have been discovered and the future will commemorate every ever so minor hero in our age of heroes. But that is why each and every one must make his contribution, so that this honor does not fall upon the unworthy. I have contributed my bit by confessing that I have no part in the whole thing, not the slightest.

POSTSCRIPT

My thesis that undeserved praise has a far greater effect than criticism, even if the latter is deserved, has been demonstrated to be true in my own slight experience. In a review in *Fædrelandet*, Dr. Beck[24] has extricated my dissertation from oblivion in the reading world. My esteemed critic summarized the contents of the book, but I actually learned nothing new from it. He finally concludes that I deserve to be criticized because there are several allusions he does not understand. Well, admittedly he did not say it exactly that way; he said, in fact, that the majority do not understand them. But since I cannot possibly assume that Dr. Beck had the opportunity to poll the opinion of the majority, Dr. Beck no doubt is using this expression as a party man. It must, therefore, be regarded as a genuinely emotional party expression; "the majority" or "most" is the superlative of the word "many," which is ordinarily used. That being the case, it is entirely appropriate for me not to reflect on it but to limit myself to my first statement, that Dr. Beck has not understood them. The problem is to explain how Dr. Beck, who otherwise is a dialectician and an expert in categories, has not perceived that several other conclusions can be arrived at from the sentence presented. There are several allusions that Dr. Beck has not understood. From that Dr. Beck concludes that I deserve criticism. What if someone drew the conclusion that Dr. Beck deserves criticism? This conclusion is much closer to the point, because, after all, my treatise was not intended for Dr. Beck alone, whereas Dr. B. *proprio motu* [on his own initiative] has set himself up as my critic and thus may justifiably be asked to take the trouble to understand. The second conclusion could read: There are several allusions that Dr. Beck did not understand; therefore, the author deserves praise. A third conclusion could be set forth this way: There are several allusions that Dr. B. did not understand; therefore Dr. B. deserves praise—in other words, it indicates a laudable naiveté, but it by no means follows that the author deserves criticism. It is incredible that so much can be drawn from the fact that Dr. B. has not understood; would that one might conclude as much from what Dr. B. has understood.

My esteemed critic also believes that I deserve criticism. As far as is generally known of this writer, he hates everything that ordinarily is termed positive. Why then does he insist on positive punishments; why be so cruel to me as not to be satisfied with the natural punishment that Dr. B. does not understand me. Furthermore, I do not see how it can be done. I am past the age when a superior or a teacher is in a position to reprimand me; nor is it a political matter so that the police chief could censure me. The case cannot come before the consistory, either. Moreover, it is sufficient punishment for me that Dr. Beck has not understood me, and all the more so since it already was grievous enough for me that Dr. Beck believed that he had understood me in several passages. In the book[25] Herr Doktor recently published, I see that he has most incredibly thrust me in among the Straussians. In formation with *Strauss, Feuerbach, Vatke, Bruno Bauer*,[26] I must, whether I want to or not, keep step with them while Dr. B. counts: *ein, zwei, drei.* This is something all German noncommissioned officers (especially the systematically armed) are extraordinarily expert at doing, since he adds: "Just look to the right and watch the way I do it." It is grievous enough in itself, but a person has to put up with it if he does not belong to the systematic intelligentsia, who, to pass the time, call up for inspection not only the contemporary authors but all the authors of the world. If one is simply a poor renter who cultivates his little plot, he must come when the owner whistles and be assigned his place, now here, now there.

At the end, my esteemed critic adds that there are various things that have amused him—but not to my credit. This passage is very ambiguous and obscure, and I can do nothing but rejoice that what my critic produced in addition to an account of my dissertation—from which I learned that Herr Doktor has come quite close to having understood me—is limited to just a few sentences. It would have been too bad for me if the critic had written just a column of such ambiguous phrases. If the reviewer had said, for my benefit, that there were various things he was amused over, I would not have understood him, either. Herr Doktor must by no means attribute this to lack of good will. The book cost me 182 rix-dollars, 4 marks, and 8 shillings[27] to publish, and it is highly plausible that I wanted every legitimate benefit from it without becoming guilty of what for an author is an unworthy itching for advantage. But for the same reason that my critic's opinion would have been an enigma to me if he had expressed himself this way, it is an enigma to me why my critic has been amused by my book in such a way that it is not to my benefit, or, in other words, is to my detriment. Since I am not a party-liner, I am unable to say, as my esteemed critic is able to say, that several, or maybe even the majority, have found it to be just as much an enigma. Since I am unable to impress him with a majority, I have done my utmost to find an explanation, the only one I can find. The critic perhaps has bought a copy of my dissertation, has not been satisfied with it, and now has returned it to the publisher and demanded his money back. I do not know if it is customary for the publisher to return the money—if so, then the critic has caused me an additional loss of 9 marks. I do not deny that it is a loss, but yet it is not quite 9 marks. If the publisher is humane enough to share the loss, perhaps a secondhand book dealer will buy the used copy, perhaps he will pay 3 marks, 8 shillings for it, and in all human probability the loss will then be approximately 3 marks. If that is the way it turns out, then the critic is right—he has caused me a loss, and it really has not been to my advantage that he has been amused.

S. KIERKEGAARD

WHO IS THE AUTHOR OF EITHER/OR[28]

This question has already engaged a portion of the reading public for some days. Despite all the acumen applied, there is no certainty or agreement concerning the clues. So the matter is still *adhuc sub judice* [before the court][29] and perhaps will never go further unless on the occasion of this authorship they complain that the legal right to use flogging during inquiry has been abolished and are able to get it reinstated. In that case, I would not be the sinner against whom they have sufficient moral evidence; even less would I be his back. But the legal right to use flogging during inquiry certainly remains a *pium desiderium* [pious wish], which in fact every friend of literature must desire, for it would, after all, be a very rigorous way to discover who the authors are.

Far from making so bold as to venture to bring the question closer to solution by this article, I shall merely summarize historically the various investigations that have been made into it. The investigators may be conveniently divided into two classes. Some try to pick up the trail by means of *external* evidence, others by *internal* evidence.

1. The External Evidence

Actually, there is but one bit of external evidence—that the book has no publisher but in all probability has been published by the author. Of course, this unity[30] conceals in itself a host of clues to estimates of the cost of publishing. A thrifty, hard-working citizen here in the city maintains that publishing a book like this must cost 30,000 to 40,000 rix-dollars.[31] He reasons as follows. It is very expensive to have anything printed. The only thing he has had printed was an advertisement in *Adresseavisen*, which was only four lines and still cost three marks. He no doubt thinks that it must be taken into account that the cost is on a sliding scale according to the number of lines, but he nevertheless assumes that a book with thirty-six lines per page and over 800 pages in length must cost 30,000 to 40,000 rix-dollars. He is therefore convinced that no local person is in a position to write such a book. His guess is Donner[32] in Altona. As far as I know, this citizen is the only one who holds exclusively to external clues; given the certainty that the expenses are so great, he does not pay any attention at all to the internal clues.

Others who know more about printing costs estimate the expenditure lower and thereby are already on the way to following the internal clues. The lower the estimate, the more clues there are. They scrutinize people they know who have a nice little fortune or who have such good prospects that they could easily float a loan. Then, when they find someone who fits these financial criteria, there is nothing to prevent them from assuming that this or that person could write such a big book. In this respect, it is desirable to find out very quickly who the author is, for a situation such as the present one is highly irksome to anyone with money. It is a well-known fact that anyone who owns anything usually makes a secret of how much he owns, but in these times people are on one another's backs, brother rises up against brother,[33] and this may even have unpleasant financial consequences. The city council will have occasion to get a quite different perspective on people's assets than it had previously, which can have the result that many who have paid only a 3% trade tax[34] will now have to pay 5%, that the church rates[35] will be raised, etc.

As a fitting philosophical transition to discussing the researchers who are attempting to ferret out the author by means of internal evidence, I will mention an opinion that contrasts paradoxically with the first one. A government official believes that no attention should be paid to the external evidence at all, since it does not cost anything to get something printed in Denmark. He offers as argument his many years of experience as a public official. But I offer this opinion only to make a philosophical transition. It belongs neither in the section on external evidence nor in the section on internal evidence nor in actuality—actually, it is merely a transition.

2. The Internal Evidence

It is difficult to summarize the efforts of the many investigators along these lines, but we shall attempt to do it.

The book has two parts. Some read only the first part, others only the second. Since they are significantly different, various readers arrive at contrasting suspicions, depending upon whether they judge the whole book on the basis of the first or second part.

Some read neither the first nor the second part but devote themselves entirely to pondering the interesting question: Who can be the author? From the honest zeal with which they go at the matter, one would think they would quickly discover the secret. But that is not the case. Instead of withdrawing silently and, without reading the book, speculating purely objectively on who the author is, they have committed the indiscretion of consulting others. By this contact they have become a mediation of the earlier differences. Despite their honesty, they arrive at the most ridiculous conclusions, depending on whether they talk with someone who judges the whole book on the basis of the first part or with someone who judges it on the basis of the second part. Just to have an opinion, they assume that there are two authors, all the more so since Councilor Fribert[36] has let the matter remain undecided.

On the basis of statements made by many who have read just the preface and say it is very different from the rest of the book, a few people assume that there are three authors. This circumstance has prompted a small group to outdo one another in bold hypotheses related to numbers. This band also finds itself in a position to solve the problem of printing costs, since it assumes so many authors that the whole thing perhaps will amount to five rix-dollars per man.

Those who probe more deeply into the work try primarily to ascertain the author's personality from the style of writing and to ferret him out in that way. *Et hic diversi abeunt interpretes* [Here, too, the interpreters take different positions]. Some assume that he is a young man, others that he is an old man;

XIII
410

some that he is a profligate, others that he is a man of integrity; some think him a casual, unemployed man, others think him a public official; some that he is a bachelor, others that he is a married man.

Some pay more attention to the externalities in style, and, being more sensitive observers, they take special notice of the minute details, since they are sharp enough to see that the author has tried to conceal his identity. A theologian, for example, thinks he has detected that the book betrays too much philological education to be a theologian. A philologist thinks he has detected that the philological training is just what can be expected from a theologian, for a philologist would accent the Greek more accurately.

A few—these are the most clever of all—are attentive to a very specific word. They use it in many subtle ways when they are speaking with persons they suspect and watch very sharply to see what effect it has. They no doubt will succeed by using this method, and, as far as I know, they already have had extraordinary luck, for with one single word one of them has trapped fifty authors of the book.

Most people, including the author of this article, think it is not worth the trouble to be concerned about who the author is. They are happy not to know his identity, for then they have only the book to deal with, without being bothered or distracted by his personality.[37]

A. F. . . . .

A WORD OF THANKS TO PROFESSOR HEIBERG[38]

That a "one"[39] so numerous that the only contrary term is "some" could actually behave as irresponsibly as you describe in your most recent number of *Intelligensblade* with respect to the reading of *Either/Or*—I would not believe if it were not you, Professor, who said it! If it were someone else, anyone else, I would have argued on the basis of my own personal experience, I would have risked a dispute with one who thus attacked a public that no doubt would have witnessed with approval that an editor, although distantly related to the author, was the calm one, not the irritated one. But it is you who say it. I believe you, I do not risk a dispute; if there is to be any mention of a dispute, it must come from "one" himself, a "one" who, indeed, by your own statement, has manly vigor.

But is it actually true that, without even having sniffed around in the first part, "one" judges a work and its several parts, judges with the stridency echoed in *Intelligensblade*? Alas, yes, God keep us, the times are evil! Now you, Professor, have worked for some years at educating the public, and yet you have to experience something like this. Just to read about it so broke my heart that it could not be consoled even though consolation was offered, for, strange to say, in another part of the city this supposedly is not the case. There, when one sees such a big book come out, one smiles for a moment, at the same time reflecting that one is not smiling at the book but at the order of things that makes a big book a monster.[40] There, when one sees that an editor risks what perhaps no publisher would risk, one smiles, at the same time reflecting: No doubt there are plenty who try to make money by writing; it is beautiful of the editor not to want to peddle his book. Neither does one immediately ponder some peculiar means by which an editor can make money, because one has no time for it since one is kind enough to realize with pleasure that the editor is more than protected in a simple and ingenuous manner—namely, that one has bought the book. There, when one is amazed at the sudden appearance of such a large book, one thinks, "It is like a stroke of lightning in a clear sky," at the same time saying: But it is a change—subscription plans and promises of big books are no longer surprising. There, when one sees that the sheets are "closely printed," one praises the editor's courtesy and integrity for not presuming to use lapidary style or disgracing himself by printing for the market. There, when one, like your "one," finds "unusual brilliance, learning, and stylistic facility" in the first part of a book, one thinks: But it is always something, especially in our meager times; it is always sufficient to move on steadily and suppress one's urge to go in leaps, as one is accustomed to do when reading a newspaper. There, when one finds a preface to a work, one reads it. When in it one reads, "A.'s papers contain a variety of approaches to an esthetic view of life" (see p. xviii),[41] one does not become self-important by discovering that the various portions of the first part are fragmentary; neither does one sense by paging through the second part a capacity for organization, for one does not forget that the preface has modestly and decorously and adequately said it. There, when one sees an epigraph in the first volume, one reads it. When one reads these words, "Is reason then alone baptized, are the passions pagans?"[42] one does not promptly forget them but sees depicted a passion that is not supposed to captivate but to vex and incite. And although one has infinitely much more time than the hastening "one" in *Intelligensblade*, one still does not have time to fantasize about the author's individuality. There, when one, just like the "one" in *Intelligensblade*, "encounters many intriguing reflections and does not know whether some of them are perhaps profound,"[43] one suspends judgment, for, after all, there is no haste. When one sees how the particular passion in particular portions of the first part is always brought to the point where it seems about to make a leap and become something else, then one has a sense of the machinery. In short, when one gets a book there, one is in a hurry to read

A Word of Thanks to Professor Heiberg

it and slow to judge.⁴⁴—And yet, what good is it that this is the case, that it actually is the case? I dare not believe it; my heart is crushed, my soul full of doubt. It is you, Professor Heiberg, who have said that "one" behaves altogether differently; it is you who have robbed me of my faith, but it is also you who heal my sick mind—it is Professor Heiberg who has undertaken to put "one" right.

That you would be the only man in the kingdom one could think of to do this, if anything like this should be necessary, I do not need to tell you. I do not need to tell anyone at all, for in this respect every man in the kingdom knows what you know. How mighty your influence is, I have already learned from experience. I made an experiment [*Forsøg*] with an ex-reader who had completed his rash and precipitous judgment on *Either/Or* with the greatest haste. I simply looked at him and said: "You no doubt belong to the 'one' Professor Heiberg speaks about." I myself on this occasion learned the truth of what I always have known, that it is an incalculable advantage to dare to quote you, since one can assume that everyone has read what you write, has read it all the way through, word for word, without your needing to admonish the reader by an either/or, for example, a preface, etc. not to be too hasty. Now, then, the ex-reader, what did he do? He was put to shame, went away, and was converted. Soon no one will be "one" any longer. Some have never been so inclined, because they assume that to be "one" is in a sense much more than being one single person, in another sense much less. Yet this does not concern me—but what I venture to be certain about is that, with respect to *Either/Or*, no one will ever again be "one" after you have so suggestively explained what one is to understand by "one," that one is thereby to understand everyone who does not prove to be "a careful and conscientious reader," does not distinguish oneself as the "some" in *Intelligensblade*, but everyone who conducts oneself—well, I do not feel like saying more—conducts oneself as "one" in *Intelligensblade*.

How much, then, do I not have to thank you for? I thank you that I found out how "one" treats *Either/Or*, found out that A. was almost a prophet when, without concerning himself about B.'s papers, only his own, he said in the preface: "Read them or do not read them, you will regret both."[45] I thank you that it probably will be fulfilled, the modest wish B. made in the preface about the whole book, "that it may visit an individual reader in a sympathetic hour,"[46] a reader who will have sufficient patience and indulgence to read the whole book, enough good will to accommodate his pace somewhat to the author's. I thank you that, according to the advice of *Intelligensblade*, an individual may possibly judge as favorably of "Or" as the individual who in *Intelligensblade* is depicted as an ordinarily conscientious reader, all the more so since it is inexplicable to me that by reading only "Or" anyone can grasp the contrast as completely as he will after reading the first volume. I by no means think that every careful and conscientious reader will judge the book as favorably, indeed not; even less do I believe that if an individual judged just as favorably he then would be able to make his judgment in such choice phrases, or if he used exactly the same words that his judgment then could in any way have the meaning, the weight, the fascination, the seductive sweetness as that which, for me at least, simply through being attributed to Prof. Heiberg is just as absolute for me as a royal command for a civil servant, just as reliable as a check on a bank for a financier. I thank you for presumably having prevented the arousing of tumult and uproar and hullabaloo and gossip, not even in the ambiguous form of "one," so that "one" does not get *vapeurs*, nausea, etc., because no one wants to be "one."

For all this I thank you, Professor! I rejoice that learning is so swiftly imitated. I thank you for wanting to communicate it so quickly. If I were to choose the person in literature whom I would thank first of all, I would choose you, Professor! And if I were to choose what I would thank him for first of all, I would choose what you have done for me in *Intelligensblade*, what one word is too little and two words are too much to express, that you through "the category of winter grain"[47] have helped *Either/Or* to a happy sprouting and flourishing in literature.

In conclusion, just one wish, that my expression of gratitude may stand in the proper concordant relation to and with the magnanimity with which you came to the assistance of a stranger, for only in this way can both you, Professor, and I have the joy of your magnanimity.

VICTOR EREMITA

A LITTLE EXPLANATION[48]

A fairly widespread and persistent rumor that makes me out to be the author of an earlier published sermon is the inspiring summons that elicits the following little explanation. In the winter of '41-'42, I studied at the pastoral seminary, and when my turn came—as far as I recall it was in January—I gave a sermon[49] on a text prescribed by the reverend superior, namely, Philippians 1:19-25. The theological apprentice scarcely dreamed of what now has utterly astonished him—that among those present there must have been the wide-awake, attentive listener who after fifteen months was able to recognize my sermon instantly in the sermon that concludes a recently published book.[50] It is incredible that he could recognize it, since it is not the same, amazing that he could do it instantly, since the two sermons do not have even the most fleeting resemblance. Does the one who first started the rumor perhaps assume with Leucippus[51] that a comedy and a tragedy are the same since the letters are the same and only the order in which they appear is different? In that case, he could readily have conceded that in an imperfect and more popular sense they are different. Yet he seems to believe that empirically, factually, and in an ordinary human sense these two sermons are the same. If that is so, then it certainly is a risky matter to try to explain his statement. But I will take the risk. The inventor of that rumor has neither heard my sermon nor read it in print but knows that I once gave a sermon at the seminary. He probably thought something like this: "In that book (in 868 closely printed pages) there is a sermon (about 14 pages). Candidate Kierkegaard has given a sermon at the seminary—*ergo* the book is by Kierkegaard, *ergo* the sermon is by Kierkegaard, *ergo* it is the same sermon he gave at the seminary—*ergo* the book is by Kierkegaard, *ergo* the sermon is obliging rumor does not get wind of my having published two discourses.[52] He just might be indefatigable enough to foster a new misunderstanding by presuming to assert, without inspection (this word is used to indicate properly how positive he is about this), that these two discourses are the same single sermon I gave at the seminary. Perhaps, *tenax propositi* [tenacious of his purpose],[53] he would be consistent enough during all these rotations to remain the same, one who always says the same thing, not Socratically about the same thing[54] but about things that are different—that they are the same. Well, it all gets to be the same.

S. KIERKEGAARD

AN EXPLANATION AND A LITTLE MORE[55]

Because it is fairly easy even for a merely passable dialectical resourcefulness to produce continuous confusion in the sphere of pseudonymity and anonymity, and because I always must fear being linked with the pseudonymous and the anonymous,[56] it perhaps is not superfluous for me most emphatically to disavow the authorship and knowledge of an anonymous article in the *Berlingske Tidende*, no. 108,* which, with the aid of an imaginative colon right at the beginning and a confusing pronoun[57] a little further on, puts me, almost as if by decision, in a very close relation to the authorship of several pseudonymous books. I assume that what is said here is sufficient. Anyone who thinks at all will easily understand the following. If I am not the author of these books, then the rumor is a falsehood. However, if I am the author, then I am the only one authorized to say that I am that. Any other attempt is, according to the last assumption, unauthorized and as rumor is again a falsehood. In the one case the rumor is false, and in the other case the falsity is that it cannot be anything but a rumor. Furthermore, an unwarranted attempt of that sort is only poorly justified by a little hairsplitting, for to put up as a defense that one has said only what the rumor says (yet more decisively both in form and by its being said in print) is nothing less than a self-declaration betraying that one is aware of doing something forbidden. And, finally, when such an unwarranted attempt is first made now, that is, long, long afterwards, now when not even the most official certainty would be of any interest, the attempt is a tiresome blunder and entirely out of place when done with clever phrasing and out of a desire to make oneself interesting in a

---

* The article is marked: –n. Thus it does not come from this newspaper's very respected editorial staff.[58]

newspaper. Assuredly, if I were the author, I certainly would guard against bothering the literary world in such a boring way with such name-declaring at this time, when no one is curious any more and all were tired of guessing long ago.

So far my explanation. The honored pseudonymous authors (one could almost say the Messrs. pseudonymous authors, for the reviewer does not make it very clear how many he means) are handed the flattering recognition that falls to their lot in that one column by Mr. *–n*. They probably do not agree how to share the booty. At least my thought runs along such lines. Yet what I think makes no difference in the case at hand. And yet perhaps the pseudonymous authors think the same, and perhaps I may even do them a service by relieving them of the trouble of saying something themselves. If so, I would also wish that what I now write may be somewhat more entertaining and may redeem what I may have wasted for the readers by the tiresome explanation and a tiresome mention of my name, a tiresome result of a blunderer's attempt. So my thought runs along these lines. To be called before the front line of the reading public to be commended—ah, yes! But then it must be the general who does it. If the summoner, for example, is the driver of an ammunition wagon, then both become ridiculous. —To be assigned to a particular category, even the distinguished post of honor[59] in literature, over and above all one's contemporaries—ah, yes! But then it must be done by a person who himself is not on the outside. For the sake of impartiality, as they say, it may at times be good to be on the outside, but with respect to such a flattering invitation it would be best for the inviter to be on the inside, lest it end with both the inviter and the invited being on the outside and the show of honor becoming a counterpart of the transaction in which the two rogues sell and Studenstrup buys the town hall and courthouse.[60]

For a newcomer in literature to be received hospitably, yes, almost ceremoniously received, by someone rushing to welcome him—God forbid! But then this must be an authorized person, lest the poor, deceived author, when he comes sailing

XIII
420

along in procession, arm in arm with that noble representative of hospitality (alas, his hope for the future and source of his happiness), discover to his shame that he is in the company of a deceiver, that he has drunk Du's with the executioner.[61]

To be encouraged to try other directions—how flattering! But then the encourager must be the chief figure in literature. If, however, the beckoning guide disappears like a sneeze, what then? —To hear the seductive words, the royal applause, which benevolently signify that an author should continue his efforts—ah, yes! But then it must be a Maecenas[62] who speaks. But suppose that it was only a voting member of literature.

Since, as a matter of fact, that reviewer (what shall one quickly call a person who writes something in a newspaper about a book) is anonymous and thus divested of the trustworthiness of authority, since even in the article he does not project himself as a real general, a grand master, a Maecenas, then it is truly droll for an anonymity like that to give himself such lofty airs in one column and do nothing else. Perhaps there is someone who would find it more difficult to forgive him this puffery than the prolixity he so overbearingly forgives the pseudonymous writers.

So I find myself thinking as follows. Unwarranted recognition is just as objectionable as an unwarranted attack. Especially today, the former is so dangerous because attempts are made in so many ways to wrest from individual men of distinction, of whom our country can be proud, renown's right, earned by rare excellence over a period of years, to enjoy a younger generation's deference and the authority to assign beginners a place in literature, to encourage them with a beckoning call. Yes! When it is the legitimate leader in Danish literature, Professor Heiberg,[63] for example, who speaks, when it is a scholar of continental stature such as Professor Madvig[64] who speaks, when it is that masterful, most reverend writer under the pseudonym Kts.[65] who speaks—well, then a beckoning has meaning, then an encouraging word has validity, then a kind literary greeting is a joy. At least I do not feel older, and perhaps the pseudonymous authors feel just as I do, that it is by keeping up the price of recognition that a person protects himself from becoming ridiculous and honestly does his bit so that the lawful credit due to the older author is not changed into nonsense.

S. KIERKEGAARD

A CURSORY OBSERVATION CONCERNING A DETAIL IN DON GIOVANNI[66]

Mozart's *Don Giovanni* is being performed once again.[67] Compared with many another warmed-over, delicate, and unnourishing piece, in this opera the theater has what in household language is called good solid food that sticks to one's ribs, and the public is already happy to know that it can be presented, even though it is rarely produced. —The newspapers have already passed their verdict on the performance as a whole and in part. I shall not venture an opinion so quickly, not even of the newspapers' evaluation business. There is the beautiful ancient rule of the departed Socrates:[68] to reason modestly from the little that one understands of something to the much that one does not understand. The theater criticism in the newspapers always constrains me to extreme modesty and ascetic abstinence from any conclusion.

Concerning Mr. Hansen's[69] performance, much is said with general omnivalidity and a most admirable facility that is finished in an instant, overall judgment. There is, however, one particular detail of which I have become aware and on which I wish to dwell for a moment, requesting a reader's interest, for I do not wish to delay anyone who is in a hurry or to waste the time of businessmen. I much prefer to dwell on this particular detail since I do not regard it as an [exceptional] high point in Mr. Hansen's interpretation and rendering, on which I do not have any overall opinion, but rather regard it as a high point independent of whether this actor performs just as well in the whole opera (which, after all, cannot obscure the genuine brilliance of a specific part) or he does not perform as well in other parts (which could in fact make the high point relatively more conspicuous). This point is the duet with Zerlina in the first act, which must be regarded as the absolute prize, even though one may otherwise have a different opinion about the importance of the recitatives for performance on our stage.

A Cursory Observation

The first requirement for a singer is voice, then delivery, which is a unity of voice and mood and is different from vocal flexibility in coloratura and runs, since as possibility it is the mutual compatibility of the two and as actuality the harmony of voice and mood in the delivery. The final requirement for a singer is that the mood suit the situation and the poetic character. If the singer has voice and joins it with mood, he has artistic passion. If he is also an actor, by means of miming he will even be able to encompass contrasts at the same time. The more reflective he is and the more skilled at managing his voice on the pianoforte of mood, the more combinations he will have at his disposal and thus be able to do full justice to the composer's demands, if, of course, the composer's work knows how to make demands on the singer's delivery and is not one of the unendurable and unperformable operas. If he is less reflective, he will not have such a great range in mood and character. But there is still one more thing: all the more universal foundations of mood, the ability to infuse voice with imagination, to be able to sing with imagination. This is the kind of delivery I have admired in Mr. H. in this particular part.

For the duet with Zerlina, one involuntarily has great expectations. The first scene with Anna[70] is too stormy for one to identify Don Giovanni clearly, but here everything is set in order, the surroundings minimized, the attention focused on how he is going to respond to his first challenge, and we think: Here we will see whether Don Giovanni is a fop and a dandy, a windbag (which a person becomes when he wants to be a Don Giovanni) who has a gullible trumpeter in Leporello and an impotent troubadour in Mozart, or whether he is that celebrity and that celebrity's most famous work.

The composer fulfills his obligation. The accompaniment is charming and eloquent. Like the murmuring repetition of the brook, it recurs enchantingly, because the orchestra takes care of itself and goes on and cannot come to an end. It has a dreaming yet captivating effect, overpowering like the fragrance of flowers; it ushers one into the infinite, not with the energy of passionate desire but with quiet yearning. Mozart certainly knows what he is doing, and a Zerlina is deemed not to have the qualifications of individuality that define a different conception, such as, for example, a violent flaming passion in a shared desire, in which feminine concupiscence almost matches Giovanni's natural force in energy and daring, or a feminine absorption in Giovanni to which an infinite feminine kingdom is devoted, or an overcome resistance that subsides with pride, or that noble simplicity which is deceived, or that elevated purity which is defiled, or that humble ardor which once outraged is outraged for life, or that profound naiveté which once victimized is victimized forever, or the holy passion of infinity that is led astray to damnation, or a feminine rashness that amounts to nothing, etc. Zerlina's seduction is a quiet marriage that goes off without any fuss.

The situation is essentially this: she did not know how it happened,[71] but it did, and so she was seduced;* and the result of Zerlina's most strenuous mental exercise is this: It cannot be explained. This is very important for an understanding of Zerlina. Therefore, it was a mistake for an otherwise fine actress, Madame Kragh,[72] to sing the line "No, I will not"[73] with force, as if it were a resolve fermenting in Zerlina. Far from it. She is confused, dazed, and perplexed from the start. If reflection is attributed to her at this point, the whole opera is a failure.** The same is true of the line following: "Masetto's

---

* This is why Leporello and Zerlina would be able to talk together very well if he were to say to her of Don Giovanni what he said to Elvira in the old days[74] and what shocked her most of all: "Yes, oh, yes, how strange! Here today, gone tomorrow." And then Zerlina would say: "Isn't it true what I say—that no one knows at all how it happens."

** In that case the structure is altered: what is so profound and so Greek,[75] that Don Giovanni stumbles over a straw, over a little Zerlina, while he falls beneath entirely different forces. The total effect and total unity are disturbed. Anna's passion, the murder of the Commendatore, the reunion with Elvira, everything goes against Don Giovanni; he is on the point of being stopped, and for the first time in his life he gasps for breath. All this happens so early, in the first two scenes, so the opera is still just beginning. What kind of seduction is this supposed to be that takes place in the opera? There are two alternatives: either a seduction so difficult and dangerous that the incitement of tension fans his most intense desire and utmost energy (which, however, will weaken the effect and is weakened by the effect of Anna and Elvira) or

soul will bleed." If this sympathy is distinctive, the whole thing will not pass muster. Therefore, the line must not signify more and must not be sung otherwise than is appropriate for its being *au niveau* [on the same level] with spontaneous gestures, for example, clutching her apron or repulsing Don Giovanni's embrace. Precisely this makes her beautiful and adorable, her relation to Masetto just right. To hear an act of reconciliation in the aria "*batti, batti*"[76] is completely wrong. She has not even attained her meager presence of mind, which is quite adequate in Masetto's household but not in Don Giovanni's trap. She sees that Masetto is angry, and so there is nothing to do but to speak a good word for herself to him and to herself, for she is unclear about the whole thing, and to her in her innocence, her innocence is altogether unquestionable. She must be maintained in this naiveté; she cannot even make out why Masetto became so angry. Therefore, the reconciliation must have no essential character to it, as if now she were saved. By no means. As soon as she sees Don Giovanni, it begins all over again, and then she must once again go and whimper a little to Masetto,[77] and then she comforts him, and then finally she believes that it is Don Giovanni and Masetto who have become enemies, God knows why, and she is the one who is to mediate between them. Let a few years go by, and then pay a visit to Madame Masetto. You will find Zerlina essentially unchanged. Just as she dillydallies and whiles away the time in the opera, she scurries about her house, sweet, utterly charming, etc. If you were to say to her, "But how was it with that character Don Giovanni," she will answer: "Well, it was strange, a strange wedding day, such a hullabaloo, and I had to be on the go everywhere; now it was

---

the seduction of a sweet little peasant girl with a natural archness and childlikeness, a feminine manifestation that is found only approximately in the north and for which the Catholic Church has a mixed category. Don Giovanni is certainly in his element, but the effect of the others in the opera is not diminished. This is Mozart's idea, and in the idea the piece has its beautiful unity and Mozart his felicitous task. Don Giovanni and Zerlina are related spontaneously to each other as a natural force to a condition of nature, a purely musical relation.

Masetto who grumbled, then Don Giovanni wanted to talk with me, and I am positive that if I had not been there they would have killed each other."

This character must be sustained to distinguish her in her femininity from Anna and Elvira. Anna is relatively far less guilty than Zerlina. She has mistaken Giovanni for Ottavio, nothing more. But because she is essentially developed, this is sufficient to disturb her for perhaps the rest of her life. She suppresses it as long as possible and then is beside herself with revenge.[78] But Zerlina is undaunted and undismayed, goes blithely away both to the dance with Don Giovanni and to confession with Masetto; it is all wonderful and to each of the interested gentlemen is good enough in turn. She joins in everything, feels that she is associating with fine ladies and is just as important as any of the others. She takes part in capturing Don Giovanni, not because he has seduced her but because he has struck Masetto (it is clear that she confuses the physical and the moral), and she therefore considers Leporello just as guilty because he also has struck Masetto,[79] her own little Masetto of whom she is so fond and to whom the others are so mean.

Elvira is a tremendous feminine character, with the essential passion to know what it means to be seduced. She does not want to salvage one shred of honor from the world; she wants to stop Don Giovanni, with the reservation, of course, that if Don Giovanni will be faithful to her, then she will give up the itinerant activity of the mission—but in that case he is in fact stopped. It is genuinely feminine, a splendid invention. Yet, regarded as a woman, she with her mission is in a way *auszer sich* [beside herself] and therefore in all consistency must appear comic. I am not thinking of that deeply tragic situation in the second act,[80] where she mistakes Leporello for Don Giovanni, a scene that an author[81] has called almost brutal, but of something else. She herself has been seduced and now wants to save others without considering that such an enterprise takes preliminary study and much examination whereby one gains the competence to identify with others.

That she is utterly unable to do. This also explains why she cannot make herself understandable to Zerlina. Here Elvira becomes comic. She transfers all her pathos to Zerlina, and in the end Zerlina is better able to understand Don Giovanni than to comprehend Elvira. Therefore, an actress who portrays Zerlina must not—as was done when the opera was given in the past—be shocked, gripped by anxiety, because of Elvira's speech—that is much too much. She should be astonished at the new surprise, and so astonished that a good spectator almost smiles at the situation while at the same time he grasps the tragic in Elvira.

(To be concluded tomorrow.)

(Conclusion)

Now to Don Giovanni.[82] If the singer combines imagination with voice and uses this delivery as an accessory, what then? Then the situation becomes a situation of seduction. Perhaps, but not in an opera—on the contrary, this occurs in a drama, where a seducer does not sing *to* the girl but *for* the girl, using this means to stimulate her imagination. I shall sketch such a situation. The girl is no peasant maid but a donna, a mature young lady with impressive qualifications. The seducer has a good voice and knows how to combine imagination with it. So he sometimes sings for her what she wants to hear. One day, quite by chance, as they say, he chooses this number by Don Giovanni. He delivers it with all imaginative inspiration. He, of course, does not look at her, not one glance, not one desiring look, for then all is lost. He looks straight ahead, and his voice quickens in mood and imaginative seductiveness. The donna listens and feels safe, and since she knows that he is not singing *to* her, that the song does not pertain to her, she surrenders to infatuation, and since they are assumed to be equally strong, the seducer has to create the first tryst in her imagination and in the fleeting face-to-face encounter of imaginative intuitions and presentiments. If this is depicted, then it is not essentially an opera, but in a drama or narrative the transition is formed from this situation to the reflected actuality of the seduction.

Now if Mr. Hansen's task were to lay the groundwork for that situation in a drama, then his performance was *omnibus numeris absoluta* [perfect in every respect], and anyone who has a flair for such observations certainly will not deny that it is astonishing to hear such superb delivery. Calm, yet insinuating in tone, dreamy and full of longing, yet distinct in phrasing, with every letter so articulated that nothing is lost or wasted, he achieves a rare effect. But if it is an opera, and it is here that the battle is to be fought, then this excellent delivery is not in the right place, is not a golden apple in a silver bowl.[83] Don Giovanni is no mawkish zither player nor a seducer[84] who uses such a disguise at the outset. Taking another part of the opera, for example, the guitar aria,[85] or Don Giovanni's intervention in Elvira's first solo, "*Poverina, poverina*" [Poor girl],[86] then, specifically in the second instance, I would say that here such a delivery ought to be used. Essentially, this outburst is not addressed to anyone— it is Don Giovanni standing there pondering and anticipating pleasure. Therefore, imagination must be combined with the voice, and the irony must not arise in Don Giovanni's reflecting on the relationship but must be in the mind of the spectator, who understands Don Giovanni. Therefore, the actor ought to see to it that he is calm and collected at that moment, although it is quite right for him to pace back and forth in a kind of tension during the aria. But, above all, he must not come up front while singing these words, for Elvira is not supposed to hear them. Nor is he to sing them to Leporello, as he does in the rest of the aria. Essentially, they signify only that Don Giovanni is in good humor. The matchless effect of the situation must not result from Don Giovanni's reflection or planning but is to be sought in the total effect, as a writer[87] has pointed out.

In the duet with Zerlina, Don Giovanni sings to Zerlina. It is *Don Giovanni*, and Zerlina is an adorable little peasant girl.

In the imaginary situation with the donna, it was necessary for it to begin as it did, because it did not start with desire. Thus it began in an innocent dreaming; in all seduction it holds true: too speedy a plunge and all is lost. Just because Zerlina is a peasant girl, it does not necessarily follow that Don Giovanni should begin crudely; Don Giovanni never does that. Not through reflection but like a force of nature, he always has decorum and grace. The recitatives before the duet are even languorous in the best sense of the word. It is absolutely proper, for Don Giovanni is not reflective, and to portray a peasant girl in an idealizing cloak in such a capacious imaginative setting, when someone like Don Giovanni is sure that she has enough to do just to behold and admire him, the beautiful man, is perfect for making her bedazzled and confused. A fast, palpably obvious fellow would be understood by Zerlina too quickly and would make her alert, because in all her naiveté Zerlina is chaste and does not understand at all. Meanwhile, and as a decidedly important commentary on the text, we also see Don Giovanni's superiority, see him catching flies with sweets, see that in a certain sense he is right when he says to Elvira: "It was only for amusement."[88] This line is neither malicious nor ironic; it is spontaneous and direct. Don Giovanni regards Elvira as too strong to be affected by a little affair with a little Zerlina: she the seduced κατ' ἐξοχὴν [par excellence] and Zerlina! It is easy to endow Don Giovanni with a little reflection, but in the opera the art is precisely to keep it out so that Don Giovanni does not become an ordinary character and the opera structurally flawed. The actor has to use bearing, facial expression, gestures, personal presence, the full authenticity of the character to project his superiority.

The duet begins. The dreaming generality of the accompaniment (because music is a more generalized medium)[89] is audibly clear in Don Giovanni's performance, in his gripping Zerlina with his own natural power and that of the musical accompaniment. As he stands, incomparable, and sees her confused and perceives that her unwillingness is a camouflaged surrender, he concentrates all his superiority in an almost commanding omnipotence. It is the egotism of natural vigor and virility. Therefore, the accompaniment to the first "Be mine"[90] is not ingratiating but energetic and decisive. Now she surrenders. Don Giovanni, of course, does not do it that way. Here again his superiority may be seen. With respect to Anna, Elvira, and their kind, it is not inconceivable that Don Giovanni in the moment of victory relishes the desire so strongly that he seems like a lover who gives as much as he takes and is the seducer only in the next moment. But Zerlina is captured and treated in another manner. Here the amusing game is itself the enjoyment, and Don Giovanni, immediate and purely musical, is in his element. To him Zerlina is no less than any other woman, but is different from Elvira or Anna, and in her own way just as desirable and just as engaging to him. I repeat, therefore, that Zerlina must be projected in such a way that when she is seen and heard with Don Giovanni she will produce a certain feeling of elation in the viewer, because he will try in vain to apply the earnest category to her. And when she is seen with Masetto, she will elicit a smile, because essentially Zerlina is neither seduced nor saved but is continually in trouble.

Perhaps some, even the majority, feel that this whole thing is of no importance, since in fact one almost never sees Zerlina made an object of esthetic interpretation. I myself am inclined to regard it as unimportant and therefore feel obliged to beg Mr. Hansen's pardon, inasmuch as upon seeing his name mentioned he may take the trouble to read the article, and I beg the forgiveness of *Fædrelandet* for burdening it with such a contribution, whose defect, curiously enough, is that it is not sufficiently weighty. Mr. Hansen can easily forgive me. How fortunate for someone who has the desire and has made his choice in life to have the singing voice he has, how fortunate for someone who has the desire and has chosen his profession and then has all the fine qualifications for an actor that he actually has. When one has been given so much and has also acquired something, I daresay one could squander a little time practicing how to walk and how to stand. I really do not believe that my legs[91] or my gait have any connection with my interpretation of the most immortal opera; then I would have to get other legs for walking.

A.[92]

THE ACTIVITY OF A TRAVELING ESTHETICIAN AND HOW HE STILL HAPPENED TO PAY FOR THE DINNER[93]

Although New Year's Day callers are extending more and more the time for their courtesy calls, which properly were limited to New Year's Day, these calls still are more or less limited to a period of eight days. It is quite otherwise with our enterprising and venturesome man of letters, Mr. P. L. Møller, playing the role of the New Year's well-wisher. Long in advance, he begins going around paying courtesy calls and gathering charitable donations to his splendid New Year's gift (*Gæa*); yes, he even travels out in the country. If he does not collect anything or just a little, or if the paucity of copious and weighty contributions by the renowned indicates that his New Year's gift is lacking in plenitude, he fills it out with conversations he has had in his travels out in the country. Basically, it is a very economical way to travel, one that never occurred to me, having always regarded traveling as very expensive, and perhaps one that would not occur to many others besides Mr. P. L. Møller, for, after all, thriftiness, too, can be carried too far. One takes a trip to Sorø, as Mr. P.L.M. did (according to *Gæa 1846*), visits Prof. Hauch,[94] is received by the distinguished poet with Danish hospitality. One helps oneself to the dishes served, and although very stingy people generally pinch a little food, a piece of meat in the pocket and some cake in the hat, Mr. P.L.M. is so voracious that he takes along the whole conversation and has it printed—thus it is paid for, yes, more than paid for, and since the repast did not cost anything, it is clear profit. If Trop[95] had known about this way of traveling, he would not have suffered so much from want, for even if he had been given the brushoff in the famous man's waiting room, he still could have made a little by having the famous man's words printed. No sponging traveling salesman can travel so lucratively, for he can take away only the orders; yes, no gluttonous tithe collector can do it more advantageously—Mr. P.L.M. has the advantage that not a word is wasted: it all comes out in the New Year's gift.

In the conversation our traveling esthetician had down there, my writing[96] also became a subject for discussion. In that way, I, too, contributed my bit to the New Year's gift by providing him the occasion for some effusions after dinner. Let him have it. After all, my contribution is very figurative, for, since everything he says is not only a confusion (a rephrasing of the difficulty of the task, which the book itself far more strongly emphasized, into an objection to the way the task was dealt with)* but even abounds in factual untruths on

---

* In itself the confusion is quite amusing, and since it is not so dialectically difficult that it cannot easily and entertainingly be portrayed on one page, I shall do it here. An imaginative constructor [*Experimentator*] says: In order to become properly aware of what is decisive in the religious existence-categories, since religiousness is very often confused with all sorts of things and with apathy, I shall imaginatively construct [*experimentere*] a character who lives in a final and extreme approximation of madness but tends toward the religious. The imaginative constructor himself says that the point of view of the imaginatively constructed character [*Experimenterede*] is a deviation but adds that he is doing the whole imaginary construction [*Experiment*] in order to study normality by means of the passion of deviation (p. 309).[97] He himself declares that it is a very strenuous task to hold the imaginatively constructed character [*Experimenterede*] at this extremity while he himself supervises imaginatively constructively. The difficulty is to keep the imaginatively constructed character at the terminal point where it never becomes madness but is constantly on the brink. Now comes Mr. P. L. Møller's charge: "It is almost insanity, it is the preliminary stage of madness."[98] Reply: Absolutely right, that is precisely the difficulty of the task. Consequently, the charge is an acknowledgment, which I do not deny is slight, for, after all, it is Mr. P. L. Møller's, but on the other hand it perhaps is Mr. P.L.M.'s maximum. Presumably he will be capable of appreciating a dialectical work that is as crucial and decisive as my imaginary construction only when he himself is unaware that he is doing it, when after dinner he blissfully imagines that he is attacking it. After dinner—for I certainly assume that the same will happen to him after reading it, but nevertheless I hold to the given fact that it was after dinner; this stipulation is less indefinite and completely reliable. After dinner he attacks the imaginary construction, he charges it with bordering on insanity, but that was just exactly what the imaginary construction intended. Consequently, his attack is the defense, which I do not deny is insignificant, for, after all, it comes from Mr. P. L. Møller, but for him the precarious maximum of the vehemence of an attack is always that it becomes a defense.

the most crucial points, I actually am unable to say that it is my book he is talking about, except insofar as he mentions its title and in fulfillment reminds me of its prophetic motto: "Solche Wercke sind Spiegel; wenn ein Affe hineinguckt, kann kein Apostel heraussehen" [Such works are mirrors: when an ape looks in, no apostle can look out] (Lichtenberg).[99]

If there is anything distasteful in Mr. P. L. Møller's enterprise, it is more the affront to a poet like Prof. Hauch and his private life. The fact that the scene takes place in the house of Prof. Hauch and he takes part in the conversation naturally gives this interest. But it still seems somewhat offensive to make recompense in this way for—yes, for what?—for being received with hospitality by a famous man. Fortunately, there is in it not one single comment from Prof. Hauch[100] about my writing, which pleases me just as much for the professor's sake as for my own. Be it positive or negative, a comment from him always carries weight, as does every legitimate authority's. It must and ought not be weakened and rendered dubious by ambiguity so that one cannot know which is which, because Prof. Hauch may well have said it but did not say it in *Gæa*, and P. L. Møller probably said it but yet did not say it, since in *Gæa* he said only that Prof. Hauch had said it in his living room. What a twisted misrelation between the judgment of an authority and this irresponsibility!

Now, however, everything is in order. I certainly have no objection to make, either against Mr. P.L.M.'s actually having said that, for, after all, he himself must know that best, or against the comment being his actual opinion, about which I am not one bit curious. If the defense is that what Mr. P.L.M. really meant and was talking about was a work dealing with the double-dialectic of religiousness on the edge of a transi-

---

He has finished the imaginary construction; in fact, he judges it, and what is his judgment? That it borders on insanity. But that was precisely the task; so he is back at the beginning. And what does his judgment signify? Well, at most it means: It is a very difficult task. Reply: Without a doubt, Mr. P. L. Møller, and since it is after dinner and you no doubt already have thanked Professor Hauch for the food, I shall wish you: *velbekomme*.[101]

tional crisis, then I shall be always satisfied. A retraction of his opinion could not have as much significance to me as a solemn assurance that he really has an especially negative opinion.

The conversation about my writing is carried on between Mr. P.L.M. and, curiously enough, "a reasonable man." It really cannot be called a conversation but rather two lectures. One could almost suppose that Mr. P.L.M. had prepared the discourse he intended to deliver, for in a conversation it is somewhat stiff and formal to talk three pages running.[102] If this is assumed, then his journey is to be considered less remunerative. Perhaps he himself considers it a sacrifice to have traveled down to Sorø and competed esthetically with "a reasonable man" "after dinner" in Prof. Hauch's house. Perhaps he regards his speech as a remuneration, something that would have been more obvious had it come a bit earlier, namely, if Mr. P.L.M. had undertaken to read it as an expression of thanks at the table. But it always pays somehow. Let us assume that a man of no importance whatsoever had the honor of speaking with the emperor of Russia. God knows that what he said was something foolish, yet it inevitably acquires a certain interest by having been said during an audience at the emperor's palace. It is the same with Mr. P.L.M.'s speech. Its interest is due simply and solely to Prof. Hauch's house. If Mr. P.L.M. had delivered the same speech in the stagecoach to the driver, it would not have been at all interesting. The interest lies in the place; what is interesting is the contrast between the importance of the place and the unimportance of the speech. If delivered to the coachmen, consequently at the right place, the interest and the interesting disappear. As Mr. P.L.M.'s actual opinion, it is his actual opinion—and nothing more. "The reasonable man" is not much help, and, curiously enough, his speech ends with the words "At least this is how it seems to me," which seems to be very strange coming from the mouth of "a reasonable man." That is, it is not strange when, for example, Mr. Petersen, a reasonable man, says something like that, but when one is nothing but a purely *abstract* "reasonable man," a reasonable man between quotation marks, it is difficult to fit it in, it seems to me, since this phrase assumably affirms *individual* idiosyncrasy.

Thus the affair is altogether unimportant, unpleasant only for Prof. Hauch, because in an unseemly way a distinguished man is placed in an unworthy setting. But for me it has almost an advantageous side, as I shall bring out, because I do not believe it too dialectical to be read easily on one page. When an imaginative constructor, who, as a rule, thank God, feels very well,* lives in an age when all have doubted everything, overcome doubt,[103] made their way through reflection, found mediation,[104] left religion behind as surmounted presumably by leaving out its terrors, he pricks up his ears and thinks there must be trouble in the wind. And what does he do then? Well, he keeps himself healthy, cheerful; he eats, drinks, rides, travels, is a friend of jest and gaiety, for otherwise he would be unsuited for imaginative constructing. Collaterally, he writes an imaginary construction similar to the one I have just written, in which he taxes his reflection a bit. He does not care for reviews and understands this quite literally, just as he says in the book,[105] for this must mean literally that reviews are supposed to help him to understand his own imaginary construction. But, on the other hand, he may psychologically

---

*Only the person who carelessly confuses him with the *quidam* [someone][106] of the imaginary construction or has turned the page where he begins, without a new title page, to be sure, and with a totally different style, can think anything else, which is like confusing physician and patient, Jean Paul and Schmelzle,[107] Cervantes and the licentiate.[108] Only a completely worldly person utterly devoid of a concept of religiousness, virtually admiring Johannes the Seducer,[109] and with an arrogant notion of what it is to be healthy, can suppose that even *quidam*'s suffering is a blasé state of mind. And only a person who carelessly pages through a book can think that the *quædam*[110] of the imaginary construction is being used to be spun into a dialectical web, since the whole imaginary construction revolves around spinning her out and ends with her complete *restitutio in integrum* [restitution to the original state][111] under absolutely the most favorable conditions. All this is in my interest, the imaginative constructor's, who therefore points out again and again that if the relation is regarded for one single moment from the standpoint of egotism, it vanishes, and the imaginary construction is impossible.

The Activity of a Traveling Esthetician 43

welcome remarks, not just for the sake of comment itself but for the opportunity it gives him to get a little insight into whether he has wronged men by not believing that they actually have made their way through reflection, for if they have, then such an exertion in reflecting will be as simple as bread and butter, or it is as he supposes. Now Mr. P. L. Møller offers his comments. But an imaginative constructor is a calm and imperturbable man. However pleased he is over a possibly desired outcome, he looks first of all to the state of the one who is to divulge something by his comments—lest the significance of the imaginary construction be weakened. Now as to Mr. P. L. Møller—he is found to be in good physical condition, he has traveled by stagecoach down to Sorø, is refreshed and invigorated by the country air. To go on— might he be hungry and starving, on the verge of fainting? No, he has eaten well at Prof. Hauch's. Well, then, everything is fine. But might he have eaten too much? No, after all, he had to be alert to the conversation so that he could print it. Thus it was to his own interest as a guest not to eat too much or overload his stomach this time. So, then, everything is as it should be. What happens? The very thought of the book (he does not have it in his hands; it is down in Sorø), the very thought of the book, or perhaps even the thought of having had the book in his hands, makes him nervous. He feels sick, and in his distraught state he says something he himself almost fears "is saying too much."[112] By no means, Mr. P. L. Møller. All these are completely normal phenomena; the only abnormality is that the patient does not speak in the name of all humanity. To proceed, there are in fact circumstances present that could help the sufferer to persevere. He is in the company of others, it is after dinner, when anyone else, even a circumspect imaginative constructor who knows for sure and knows the reason why Mr. P.L.M. cannot be assumed to have eaten too much, could easily explain the belch some other way. But, no, he feels sick. The imaginative constructor's report would put it this way: This man has not made his way through reflection; if he nevertheless were to give the appearance of it and boast about mediation, I would know it.

XIII
428

XIII
429

If only Mr. P. L. Møller had been a somewhat more significant person and it really was certain that he had read the book, I would have turned the phenomena to account and argued on that basis.

An author with an awareness of the dialectical difficulty and strenuousness of his task expects, of course, very few readers and wants it that way as well, although he does not pretentiously and wantonly express it in a preface but acknowledges it in his own being and therefore even uses his own *I*, not exactly *à la* Andersen,[113] but rather a little Socratically, in order teasingly to thrust people away. He is contented with a few readers, with one; he is contented with fewer, for he is contented to be an author, enchanted by the contradiction of the infinite: *to be contented* with the divine pleasure of thinking. Existential dialectic, especially in the form of double-reflection,[114] cannot be communicated directly. If it so pleased me to declare everything I wrote to be nonsense, the person who is to be my reader must be able to let himself not be disturbed by it but see to it that he reproduces the dialectical movements himself. He must not be disturbed, either, if it pleased the whole world to declare it to be nonsense, no more than I would be; he must make that decision for himself. For this reason, that sort of author cannot object if a garrulous dinner guest prints his speech and thereby possibly contributes to repelling readers. Far from it—on the contrary, it is good. This is why I have not replied to him, either.

The person whose head can take the dialectical exertion can easily remain calm and undisturbed. In connection with a book that by reason of its dialectical character generally can have but few readers, a garrulous fellow always has an advantage when the matter is to be taken to the public at large, that is, if something that is an advantage only as a falsehood can truly be called an advantage. One learns much from Holberg.[115] One learns, for example, that the defect in Erasmus Montanus is not really a lack of capability but a lack of self-control to keep him from talking with Per Degn and from himself giving onlookers the impression that these two are discussing together learned and extraordinary matters that can concern only an Erasmus Montanus. You see, I refuse to give the impression that I am discussing the imaginary construction and its dialectic with Mr. P. L. Møller. No, we two talk about utterly different matters, about the trip to Sorø, the stagecoach, the driver, the meals and the drinks, the pack-asses,[116] and other such popular subjects that do not exceed Mr. P. L. Møller's powers of comprehension. The real reader of the imaginary construction will readily discover that what I have written here is of a different nature and can be read right away by anyone. Therefore, I am not insulting any newspaper reader by leading him into inquiries that cannot interest him and that cannot be dealt with in a newspaper. An interpretation of Mr. P. L. Møller's journey to Sorø should not be dialectically difficult; neither should one ponder too profoundly, for that is the very way to a misunderstanding. But however much I find the joy of infinity in the occupation of thought and know that my joy is due to my being contented with it, even if no one shares my joy, I still have not given up psychological familiarity with actual people. Such an actual person is Mr. P. L. Møller. But obtrusive as he is and known to many, I thought that a little interpretation like this would not be wholly devoid of interest to readers of a newspaper. I really believed, too, that I would be doing some people a service[117] thereby, but I do not insist that this service be appreciated, least of all by someone who for that reason would read a little in my book or buy a copy. For what I said in my note to the reader (p. 309),[118] "One does not buy admission to these performances for a lump sum," I repeat here without danger. After all, why should he be angry who has found his desire for the infinite satisfied, found what will occupy him day and night, even if it pleased God to increase the length of the day another 12 hours! He who is captivated by what captivates him eternally, even though he has much left to gain, is not disturbed, and I repeat unaltered the words of farewell (p. 77):[119] "Satisfied with the lesser, hoping that possibly sometime the greater will be granted me, I am happy in existence, happy in the little world that surrounds me." When I wrote that, I knew very well that there are such as Mr. P. L. Møller and *The Corsair*, and, indeed, I knew very well what I wrote. Such persons are not part of my environment, and no matter how obtrusive and rude they are, it makes no difference; this does not disturb my joy over the little world that constitutes my surroundings. On the contrary, the obtrusiveness helps me to enjoy my surroundings more deeply.

Would that I might only get into *The Corsair* soon. It is really hard for a poor author to be so singled out in Danish literature that he (assuming that we pseudonyms are one) is the only one who is not abused there. My superior, Hilarius Bookbinder, has been flattered in *The Corsair*,[120] if I am not mistaken; Victor Eremita has even had to experience the disgrace of being immortalized[121]—in *The Corsair*! And yet, I have already been there, for *ubi spiritus, ibi ecclesia* [where the spirit is, there is the Church]: *ubi* P. L. Møller, *ibi The Corsair*.[122] Therefore our vagabond quite properly ends his "Visit to Sorø" with one of those loathesome *Corsair* attacks on peaceable, respectable men,[123] each of whom in honest obscurity does his work in the service of the state, on men of distinction who have made themselves worthy in much and ridiculous in nothing, for as public figures authors have to put up with a great deal, including the imputation of a relation to people who by having something printed are also authors.

FRATER TACITURNUS
Chief of Part Three of
Stages on Life's Way

THE DIALECTICAL RESULT OF A LITERARY POLICE ACTION[124]

With a paper like *The Corsair*, which hitherto has been read by many and all kinds of people and *essentially* has enjoyed the recognition of being ignored, despised, and never answered, the only thing to be done in writing in order to express the literary, moral order of things—reflected in the inversion that this paper with meager competence and extreme effort has sought to bring about—was for someone praised and immortalized in this paper to make application to be abused by the same paper. I assume this was successful. The fact that the same Mr. Goldschmidt,[125] who deserves honor for having published a good book[126] (and in all events it is my wish that appreciation—sympathetic and abundant and encouraging—may come his way), makes money as editor of *The Corsair* does not alter the paper's situation. On the other hand, the situation is esthetically favorable for what I otherwise would gladly renounce ethically here and now, the fulfillment of my old wish "always to have the laughter on my side,"[127] the laughter of those who have a true sense of the comic, for to be abused on one's own order is precisely that advantage, even though I took the step for the sake of others.[128] So *The Corsair* can be hired to abuse just as a hand organ can be hired to make music. Perhaps it has already been used that way more than once, but with the difference that someone in bitterness and spite, bringing irony upon his own head, has hired *The Corsair* to abuse someone else.

I cannot do any more for others than to request to be abused myself.[129] *The Corsair*'s corrupt cleverness, along with its hidden helpers—producers and peddlers of pandering witticisms—must and should be ignored literarily just as public prostitutes should be ignored civically. As far as I am concerned, although I cannot be said to have done anything great, with that article I may be assumed to have made such a large contribution, as they say of charitable institutions, to *The Cor-*

sair's Demolition and Defamation Institute that it will feel duty-bound to exert itself to the utmost to fulfill its *præstanda* [obligation], perhaps for my whole life, or at least for a long time,[130] until a new contribution is made necessary by a new insulting attack—that is, by once again being praised by *The Corsair*, a paper that gives to him who is praised only the trouble of having to read and of having to protest. I say for my whole life, or at least for a long time—unless *The Corsair* is ruined[131] by the dialectic of one person's order to be abused or of a number of such orders.

At least something similar happened to a tailor whose story I shall now tell. He lived in a market town and had a fair little livelihood (in that respect his case is different from *The Corsair*'s) altering old clothes and doing other similar work. The way things go in the world, one ought not challenge the gods with foolish wishes lest they mock one—not by denying the wish but by fulfilling it. So it went with the tailor. As he sat at his bench he often sighed to the gods, "Would that I might get many customers, still more orders, so that I might become rich, and then still more so that I might become very rich. When I have become very rich, I will buy myself a kingdom and quit my trade." As he sat at his tailor's bench one morning after fortifying his soul with this foolish morning prayer, what happens? Suddenly a messenger arrives from a prosperous man with a big business who is ordering new uniforms for all his workers. Sad to say, it was an order for *new* garments, and the tailor only knew how to work with old clothes, alter and patch and so on. And yet this was his dream come true! What then? Well, it is a sad story and cannot be told without tears: indeed, they had to carry the tailor to bed, and he was never himself again. Maybe human beings would have punished the tailor for his foolish prayer by canceling his old orders, but the gods punished him ironically by fulfilling his wish. —So it is also when the person who carries on the contemptible trade of vilification perhaps time and again offends the gods with his prayer that his business may flourish, that there may always be more and more people to vilify, more and more active assistants of irascibility and spite on the paper, when in the work of his trade he indulges and enjoys himself in the delusion of impotence and bad temper—namely, that it is dreadful to be the object of his abuse—until he insanely goes so far as even to believe that others are living in the same delusion; and because he never gets an answer and always has the last word, he believes that people are afraid of him, just as in ordinary life no one is as sure to claim the right of way on the sidewalk as a public prostitute is. While he sits busy at work in his workshop, protected against legal punishment by a staff of street-corner loafers standing in for him,[132] protected from literary polemic by the paper's contemptibleness—then suddenly one day comes an order from a reputable man (but I am not sure of that), in any case, from one whom the vilifier himself has praised and immortalized[133] (perhaps to be able to vilify others all the more by praising someone), an order to be vilified: this, then, is a new kind of work, involving a very special kind of dialectical problem. How did it go with the master tailor and the new work and the secret wish that was granted ironically? And vilifying is even more dialectical than simply being able to remodel old clothes. He whose praise the self-respecting person refuses to accept and honor—his vilifying becomes a matter of personal honor. He whose abuse and whose abortive witty attack no one has ever answered, whereas the first answer he got was a protest against his praise by the one he praised—his vilifying is shown by this response to immortalizing to be what silence about the attack judged it to be. Being afraid is dialectically different from patching together, because a man avoided by respectable literary figures does not have power but is impotent. Maybe the civil authorities would like to put him out of business by preventing him from vilifying in the paper. Irony encourages the business by asking to be maligned; irony promotes the business by demanding to be abused. The civil authorities perhaps wanted to use force against the presumed Terrible One and yet made allowances for him. Irony calmly confronts the Terrible One—and thereby demonstrates that he is not terrifying.

The way is open, and as it says in the pseudonymous

books:[134] the method is changed. Anyone who is insulted by being praised by this paper—if he happens to find out about it—will protest if he so pleases and thereby confirm the judgment of decent literature upon *The Corsair*: it is to be permitted to continue its trade of attacking and vilifying at will, but if it has the nerve to praise, it must on this occasion encounter the brief protest: May I ask to be abused—the personal injury of being immortalized by *The Corsair* is just too much. The inconvenience will not be great, as if one now had to read *The Corsair* in order to see if one has been praised. Not at all. No doubt it will not happen frequently, and if one somehow does not find out about it, failing to protest is no great misfortune. Moreover, I do not doubt that the police superintendent, Councilor Reiersen,[135] who as a matter of fact is obliged to take the trouble of reading the paper through, will, if asked, do the favor of briefly informing a person that he has been praised. The reply to be given is very brief, and I have in fact offered a formula suitable for use. The variations will come at the end, where, instead of "immortalized," according to the factual circumstances the reply might read: "praised," "recognized," "admired," "singled out for distinction," "recommended," "cited," "shown to the place of honor," etc.

FRATER TACITURNUS

AN OPEN LETTER

PROMPTED BY A REFERENCE TO ME BY
DR. RUDELBACH[136]

The reference is on page 70 [of Dr. Rudelbach's *Om det borgerlige Ægteskab*].

The text reads: "Surely the deepest and highest interest of the Church in our day is . . . . . to become emancipated particularly from what is rightly called *habitual* and *state* Christianity."

The footnote reads: "This is the same point that one of our outstanding contemporary writers, Søren Kierkegaard, has sought to inculcate, to impress, and, as Luther says, to drive home to all those who will listen."

Then the text continues immediately with the following sentence: "But for this emancipation civil marriage is an important, perhaps indispensable, instrument, a necessary link in the marshaling of all the measures that signify and condition the ushering in of religious freedom."

Consequently, all those numerous, qualitatively different pseudonymous works all the way from *Either/Or*, and, in addition, all my variegated upbuilding works, all these are packed together under one heading and called: Søren Kierkegaard.[137]

But now to the statement itself. The idiom "It is just a half-truth" fits it fairly accurately—that is, the first half, taken literally, is true, and the second half is false.*

* Yet even in the first half (about "habitual Christianity") the expression "emancipate" must not be stressed, lest it be thought that in my activity I meant to employ external means or proposed their use, nor must the word "Church" be stressed, lest it be forgotten that I have been concerned only with "the single individual" [*den Enkelte*]; otherwise this half also becomes untrue. This is why I say the idiom "It is just a half-truth" fits "fairly accurately," for taken strictly the statement is not even half true.

I am a hater of "habitual Christianity." This is true. I hate habitual Christianity in whatever form it appears. I would like particular notice to be made of this "in whatever form," for habitual Christianity can indeed have many forms. And if there were no other choice, if the choice were only between the sort of habitual Christianity that is a secular-minded thoughtlessness that nonchalantly goes on living in the illusion of being Christian, perhaps without ever having any impression of Christianity, and the kind of habitual Christianity that is found in the sects, the enthusiasts, the superorthodox, the schismatics[138]—if worse came to worst, I would choose the first. The first kind has still taken Christianity in vain only in a thoughtless and negative way, if on the whole it may be judged even that rigorously. The second kind has taken Christianity in vain perhaps out of spiritual pride, but in any case in a positive way. One could almost be tempted to smile at the first kind, because there is hope; the second makes one shudder. But, as stated, it is true that I am a hater of habitual Christianity. Therefore, I can have no objection if our learned theologian, Dr. Rudelbach, says something like this; on the contrary, I would even thank him for it, all the more since I became acquainted with this man in my father's house and am convinced that he is genuinely well disposed toward me. Nor do I object if in the future Dr. R. privately includes me in his prayers, that I may unto the end maintain this hatred of all habitual Christianity, which I trust and hope Dr. R. also will keep, even though I perhaps am aware of forms of habitual Christianity that have come less to his attention. The only thing I wish in this matter is that in the future he would not associate that misleading term "emancipation" with my efforts, and the only thing I might fear is that, after I have said this myself, it will become a literary cliché to write that I am a hater of all habitual Christianity.

Now to the second half of the statement. I am supposed to have taken a position against "state Christianity." Yes, this Søren Kierkegaard's whole intention is supposed to be to attack established Christianity—more specifically, to fight for

An Open Letter

the emancipation of the Church from the state, or at least "to inculcate, to impress, to drive this home."

In Ursin's *Arithmetic*,[139] which was used in my school days, a reward was offered to anyone who could find a miscalculation in the book. I also promise a reward to anyone who can point out in these numerous books a single proposal for external change, or the slightest suggestion of such a proposal, or even anything that in the remotest way even for the most nearsighted person at the greatest distance could resemble an intimation of such a proposal or of a belief that the problem is lodged in externalities, that external change is what is needed, that external change is what will help us.

In proportion to the capacities granted to me and also with various self-sacrifices, I have diligently and honestly worked for the inward deepening of Christianity in myself and in others insofar as they are willing to be influenced. But simply because I have from the beginning understood Christianity to be inwardness and my task to be the inward deepening of Christianity, I have overscrupulously seen to it that not a passage, not a sentence, not a line, not a word, not a letter has slipped in suggesting a proposal for external change or suggesting a belief that the problem is lodged in externalities, that external change is what is needed, that external change is what will help us.

There is nothing about which I have greater misgivings than about all that even slightly tastes of this disastrous confusion of politics and Christianity, a confusion that can very easily bring about a new kind and mode of Church reformation, a reverse reformation that in the name of reformation puts something new and worse in place of something old and better, although it is still supposed to be an honest-to-goodness reformation, which is then celebrated by illuminating the entire city.

Christianity is inwardness, inward deepening. If at a given time the forms under which one has to live are not the most perfect, if they can be improved, in God's name do so. But *essentially* Christianity is inwardness. Just as man's advantage over animals is to be able to live in any climate, so also Christianity's perfection, simply because it is inwardness, is to be able to live, according to its vigor, under the most imperfect conditions and forms, if such be the case. Politics is the external system, this Tantalus-like[140] busyness about external change.

It is apparent from his latest work that Dr. R. believes that Christianity and the Church are to be saved by "the free institutions." If this faith in the saving power of politically achieved free institutions belongs to true Christianity, then I am no Christian, or, even worse, I am a regular child of Satan, because, frankly, I am indeed suspicious of these politically achieved free institutions, especially of their saving, renewing power. Such is my Christianity [*Christendom*], or so Christian-dumb [*Christendum*] am I, who, incidentally, have had nothing to do with "Church" and "state"—this is much too immense for me. Altogether different prophets are needed for this, or, quite simply, this task ought to be entrusted to those who are regularly appointed and trained for such things. I have not fought for the emancipation of "the Church" any more than I have fought for the emancipation of Greenland commerce, of women, of the Jews, or of anyone else. With my sights upon "the single individual," aiming at inward deepening in Christianity in "the single individual," with the weapons of the spirit, simply and solely with the weapons of the spirit, I have, as an individual, consistently fought to make the single individual aware of the "illusion" and to alert him against letting himself be deceived by it. Just as I regard it as an illusion for someone to imagine that it is external conditions and forms that hinder him in becoming a Christian, so is it also the same illusion if someone imagines that external conditions and forms will help him to become a Christian.

I can understand why a politician counts on free institutions as an aid to the state, for politics is externality, which by its very nature has no life in itself but must borrow it from the forms, hence this faith in forms. But that Christianity, which has life in itself, is supposed to be aided by the free institutions—this, according to my understanding, is a complete misconception of Christianity, which, where it is true in true inwardness, is infinitely higher and infinitely freer than all institutions, constitutions, etc. Christianity will not be helped from the outside by institutions and constitutions, and least of all if these are not won through suffering by martyrs in the old-fashioned Christian way but are won in a social and amicable political way, by elections or by a lottery of numbers. On the contrary, to be aided in this way is the downfall of Christianity. Christianity is victorious inwardness. This is what should be worked for, that this victorious inwardness may be in every person, if possible, that "the single individual" may become more and more truly a Christian. This is what should be done: self-concern must be awakened in "the single individual," the self-concern that infinitely gives him something other to think about than external forms, the self-concern that is transmuted under a higher influence into that victorious inwardness when it has turned a person inward in this way, although the self-concern still remains to protect him against becoming externalized again. Therefore, personally concerned, wounded by ideals, and yet unspeakably joyful and grateful for this fact, I have fought for the ideals against "the illusions" in order to awaken this self-concern in "the single individual" by means of the vision of the ideals.

The difference between Dr. R. and me is quite obvious; this difference I must assert most definitely. There is also another obvious difference between us that I wish to stress. Dr. R. possesses amazing learning; as far as I know, he is probably the most learned man in Denmark, and in my opinion we all ought to be happy to have such a learned man among us. On the other hand, in learning and scholarship I am, especially by comparison, a poor bungler who knows enough arithmetic for household use. But I cannot remain silent about an *appreciatory*—and such an extravagantly appreciatory—asseveration of the significance of my activity as an author. I am really afraid that, brief though it is, it might manage, "as Luther says, to drive home" this misunderstanding "to all those who will listen." And I have considered it my present duty precisely at this time to oppose—something that otherwise would hardly have occurred to me, and somewhat more specifically than would otherwise have occurred to me—to oppose this misunderstanding, and also to keep any particular party, perhaps misled by Dr. R.'s words, from "the habit" of automatically enrolling me in the party.

S. Kierkegaard

Permit me to add the following, lest what I say be misunderstood, as if it were my view that Christianity consists purely and simply of putting up with everything in regard to external forms, without doing anything at all, as if Christianity did not know very well what is to be done—if worse comes to worst. But my entire activity as an author has had nothing to do with such an eventuality. I have only provided, poetically, what may be called an existential-corrective to the established order, oriented toward inward deepening in "the single individual"—that is, I am positive that I have never directed one word against the teaching and the organization of the established order, but I have worked to make this teaching more and more the truth in "the single individual." And in order to prevent any misunderstanding, I have aimed polemically throughout this whole undertaking at "the crowd," the numerical, also at the besetting sin of our time, self-appointed reformation and the falsifications along this line.

In Acts[141] we read: We ought to obey God rather than men. There are situations, therefore, in which an established order can be of such a nature that the Christian ought not put up with it, ought not say that Christianity means precisely this indifference to the external.

But now let us see how the apostles did not act, for everyone pretty well knows how those venerable ones did act.

The apostles did not go around talking among themselves, saying: "It is intolerable that the Sanhedrin makes preaching the Word punishable; it is a matter of conscience. What should we do about it? Should we not form a group and send an appeal to the Sanhedrin—or should we take it up at a synodical meeting? It is just possible that by combining with those who otherwise are our enemies we can manage a majority vote so that we can obtain freedom of conscience to proclaim the Word." Good Lord! Forgive me, venerable sirs, forgive me for having to speak this way. It was necessary.

On the contrary, how did they act?—for no doubt a good many have forgotten. Essentially, "the apostle" is a solitary man. Among apostles there is no party solidarity, not even theoretically; one apostle does not look at another apostle to see what he should do; each one is personally bound to God as a single individual. Thus the apostle confers and consults with God and with his conscience. Thereafter he opens the door, as it were, the door of his solitary inclosure, and goes, *mir nichts und dir nichts* [without asking anyone's leave], with God out into the streets—in order to proclaim the Word. Suppose that someone meets him and says: Do you know that the Sanhedrin has stipulated flogging as punishment for preaching the Word? The apostle replies: Well, if the Sanhedrin has done that, then I shall be flogged. The next day the Sanhedrin imposes the death penalty. The apostle answers: Well, if the Sanhedrin has done that, then I shall be executed. He lets the established order stand—not a word, not a syllable, not a letter directed toward an external change, not the fleetingest thought in his head, not a blink of the eyelid, not a flicker of the countenance in this direction. "No," says the apostle, "just let the established order stand unshakably firm, for by the help of God it also stands unshakably firm that today I am flogged and tomorrow executed or—it amounts to the same thing—that today I proclaim the Word and tomorrow, Amen." Thank you, thank you, that you acted in this way. If you had acted as modern Christians do, Christianity would never have entered the world!

And here a Christian memento. Christianity within "Christendom" properly means: in self-concern an indifference to externals. But if someone collides with the established order in such a way that he could imagine it to be a question of conscience—good God, a question of conscience!—and he dares to say it, then he has to be a solitary person in order to strive through suffering, in order to choose martyrdom. Conscience and a matter of conscience can be represented only through action by a solitary person and in character, by action,* not by prompting a discussion that is concluded by voting—this is eternally certain and is rooted in the nature of the case. Everything that is partisan and wants to function as a

---

* Luther's marriage to Katharina von Bora can serve as an example—for with Luther there never was, no, with Luther there never was any nonsense.

How did he act? He counseled with God and with his conscience. After frightful struggling and spiritual trials [*Anfægtelser*] he came to this conclusion: At this point an intensive action must be ventured. This was a matter of conscience! He was silent. Although resolved, he remained silent. Then came the moment to act—he married. "A priest?!" Yes, in spite of the Pope. "With a nun?!" Yes, in spite of all public opinion. —Thank you. Do not disdain a grateful congratulatory message on your marriage—on that day you were hardly overwhelmed by congratulations! Do not disdain a congratulatory message because it is from a single man—it would perhaps be too much if you were to receive congratulations today from all the "married priests."

On the other hand, how did he *not* act? He did not go around with hearty nonsense to every Tom, Dick, and Harry, friends and acquaintances, casting a world-historical glance at the Church's past and ditto at its future. Nor did he talk to those "many friends" in this way: "The question of priests' marrying is a matter of conscience. But what are we to do? Let's get together, try to get a few more, and then I shall come out with a petition. Let's go to parliament. It is true that the matter concerns me on religious grounds, but there is a substantial party interested in the same thing for secular reasons. If we get together with them in the voting, according to my exact knowledge of numerical ratios (knowledge of numerical ratios—fix this in your memory, preserve it for the historian, for this phrase is the secret of my life—knowledge of numerical ratios is really what makes "the reformer"), it is not impossible, it is not impossible that we can squeeze a few points from the opposition and squeeze our way through—to freedom of conscience!—by a very scant simple majority. According to what I know about numerical ratios, this is not at all impossible. And if it should develop that this cannot be achieved, we can withdraw the petition; therefore the matter is not dangerous at all." No, the matter certainly is not dangerous. —Forgive me, dear Luther, you man of God and man of spiritual trials, but I believe that however reluctant you would be to see such deportment, you would nevertheless agree with me that there is really nothing more to do than to say: The matter certainly is not dangerous. The only danger—and this would be very dangerous—the only danger would be that such a thing might be called reformation and earnestness.

party, perhaps even by intrigue—if it wants to appeal to "conscience" against an established order—is guilty of an untruth.

If it is a matter of conscience, it must be fought out in this way. If it is not a matter of conscience, then it becomes something entirely different. Christianity means precisely this: in self-concern to develop an indifference toward externals. However, if there is some change or other that a weaker person might desire (for, understood in this way, the stronger person is the very one who in self-concern has the greatest indifference), he then expresses this desire by saying, I could wish—but he does not speak of a matter of conscience, and he shudders at the thought that this should become "a habit" for him. This is my understanding, for I am a hater of "habitual Christianity."

II

Addenda[1]

1.²

A LETTER³

I hasten to inform you, dear friend, of an event that occurred in the house where I live and that will show you how perfectly right I have been when I so frequently declared that there is no reliable legal system here in our country and that our most sacred personal rights are stripped of every guarantee. I can almost rejoice in this fact, for it finally must open the eyes of these crass lawyers who always speak as if among us there were a well-ordered judicial administration, a secure legal system. Righteous heavens! A secure legal system where such a thing can happen! Can any man in all honesty maintain this? It really is high time that someone rises up in protest against this; it is high time to show that this old fable about Denmark's having such an excellent legal system is only a fable. I know well that many good-natured, superstitious people of most varied classes have believed this for many years, but what is there that such people do not believe? So it goes with this as with so much else that is also presented as good and worthy of imitation here in our country but vanishes upon closer inspection, for one thing is always lacking: the great guaranteeing forms, those all-securing norms of law, the first and only condition for our most sacred rights, without which guarantees everything else counts as nothing. Therefore, it is of utmost importance that this superstition, which has prevailed in this country so long, be eradicated; this is doubly necessary since it can find far too much sustenance by trafficking in names like *Stampe*,⁴ *Colbjørnsen*,⁵ and *Ørsted*,⁶ these no doubt intrinsically estimable men, but nevertheless, no one will assert that they have done anything worth mentioning to protect the personal security of citizens and the legal system here in our country. Consequently, this dangerous misconception that an excellent legal system exists here in the kingdom ought to be and must be eradicated. It is a cause around which all good citizens ought to unite; it is a genuine *natural* concern. Everyone who is well intentioned toward the oppressed ought to make his contribution toward eradicating this pernicious superstition. The more widely he can publicize this beneficial truth, the further he can reach down with this throughout the people, the more thoroughly he can destroy in the simple, unenlightened man this disastrous notion that there exists a good legal system in the country, the greater will be his service. Do not fear the consequences of this; do not speak of the danger of enlightening people on certain points. This, too, is part and parcel of the superstition that has to be eradicated. Believe me, my friend, *truthful, correct information* can never be anything but beneficial, and in order to publicize it, I consider it extremely important that a small, but very typical, contribution to a description of our legal system, something that occurred here recently, become as well known as possible.

This is the story. In the same building in which I live, there is a merchant by the name of Poulsen. The day before yesterday, he sends his servant to the bank to withdraw 1,000 rix-dollars.[7] My servant, who is together with him a great deal, goes along with him, and they leave the bank together. On the way home they stop at a restaurant run by a man named Ulrichsen, and there they meet two other acquaintances and have a schnaps and sandwich. Poulsen's servant takes out his billfold containing the 1,000 rix-dollars and pays for the lunch. There is comment about his carrying so much money. All four of them leave together, but immediately afterward my servant leaves them, while the other two accompany Poulsen's servant home, go up to his room with him, and spend a half-hour there while he shaves and in the meantime takes off his coat with the billfold in it and hangs it on a chair. When he goes down to his master and puts his hand in his pocket, the billfold is gone. You can imagine his shock! What is he to think? What should he do? He searches his room; no billfold to be found. He runs to Ulrichsen's restaurant; he searches every nook and corner—no billfold! His employer does what any one of us most likely would have done, he reports the matter to the police. But what do the police do?

Would you believe it possible? Can you imagine anything more irresponsible? Can you visualize a more indefensible toying with the legal system, a more corrupt use of legal power? A criminal investigation is held on the matter. My servant, the two other servants, the restaurant owner Ulrichsen, all are required to meet to give evidence to the appropriate police-court judge concerning any information they might have in the case. The hearings are fruitless, and for good reason. On the evening of the interrogation, when Poulsen's servant is undressing, he finds the billfold, with all the money, which had slipped through a hole in the lining of his coat. "Can something like this," I justifiably ask, "happen in any other civilized country where there is any guarantee of personal rights? Is this a legal climate to be desired, one in which a criminal interrogation is made although there is not a shred of evidence that any offense, to say nothing of a crime, has taken place? Cannot this legal system be called totally devoid of guarantees, and cannot men's most sacred rights be said to be improperly safeguarded in any sense, when a high-ranking person's unverified and, as we learn, unverifiable and unjust charge is sufficient to bring down upon a poor, simple man a criminal interrogation with all its consequences? And yet we are supposed to listen to big Danish lawyers and their parrots saying that we have a desirable legal system. We are forced to believe that such persons either do not know what a well-ordered legal system is or that they are speaking contrary to their better judgment."

2.
ANOTHER LETTER[8]

Dear Friend, a little inaccuracy slipped into my last letter, which I hasten to correct. I wrote that the billfold was found in the lining of the servant's coat, but I was later informed that it had fallen through a hole in the lining onto the street and was brought to the police station by the honest finder on the evening of the same day the interrogation ended. But you will easily perceive that this does not change the case itself. "The police's unwarrantable, yes, indefensible, conduct on this occasion consists in its HAVING NEGLECTED TO MAKE SURE THAT A CRIME HAD BEEN COMMITTED BEFORE INSTITUTING AN INTERROGATION."* This ought to have been done just the same, in either case, as the facts have now proved to be or if the billfold had been found in the lining of the servant's coat. The police should have been sent out into all the streets where Poulsen's servant had been; they should have stopped at all the houses along the way and asked if any such billfold had been seen, and when nothing came to light on the matter, they should not have interrogated any of the persons whose testimony possibly could lead to any clue, for they had no positive proof that any crime had been committed. And for the sake of the legal system, this must be definitely and decisively upheld, for otherwise our most sacred personal rights will never be safe. Without a doubt the police should have searched the servant's coat first of all, but when the billfold was not found in it, they should not for that reason have resorted to any provisional interrogation of any person, because there was no positive proof that any crime had been committed. *This must always be established first before any investigation by the police may be made.* This is precisely "THE POINT" in the whole affair. That fre-

* The author of this letter is happy to see in yesterday's number of *Fædrelandet* that this newspaper, which circulates so many beneficial truths among the people, has gone to the heart of the matter in the above words, which have been stressed in capital letters.

quently it cannot be known at the time the investigation begins whether there is a crime, that often precisely this has to be brought to light through the testimony of the persons involved, that personal and property security would be exposed to obvious dangers if no preliminary investigations may be initiated by the police unless it was first established that a crime had been committed, that a most detailed investigation of the case is in the interest of persons who otherwise could innocently fall under suspicion, that a person is not charged with thievery simply because he is asked for information he might have about a case in hand, that it is neither an "injury nor a disgrace" to provide information for examining magistrates but on the contrary that this is something to which every good citizen will submit in order to add his bit to the maintenance of law and order—all these are nothing but legal subtleties, these idle quibbles, these meaningless assertions that we ever and forever have to hear from our ultra-Danish lawyers who slavishly walk in the footsteps of Stampe, Colbjørnsen, and Ørsted.⁹ Why in the world do we have a police force if it cannot know whether or not a crime has been committed without first holding an interrogation? Is it not the plain duty of the police as police to know this? Why are the police paid, may I ask, if they are not even capable of knowing that much? I hear that a fellow from Nørrebro was found drowned in Ladegaard River early one morning. What do the police do? Is it not indefensible? Is it not shocking? Are not our most sacred personal rights in jeopardy? Instead of first of all making sure that a crime has been committed, the police resort to taking testimony from all the people in the neighborhood. In my opinion, it was the police's absolute duty to know that the dead man had gotten drunk the night before and in his drunken state had fallen into the water. Why do we have police if they cannot know in advance even such a simple thing without first taking testimony from people in order to gather information? Why? Answer me if you can. Likewise, I hear that a short time ago in a rural district—for you must not believe, my friend, that this evil is limited to Copenhagen; no, unfortunately it is spread over the whole country—a mill burned down. The police made detailed investigations, and testimony was taken from a great many people, until finally it became as clear as two plus two equals four that the mill had caught on fire by spontaneous combustion. Is the spontaneous combustion of a mill a crime? Have you ever heard anything like it? Should not the police have made sure in advance that a crime existed "before it charged innocent people with arson"? Do those fellows not know the difference between *dolus, culpa*, and *casus* [deceit, guilt, and accident]?[10] Do they not know that there is no such thing as an *accidental* crime? How did they study their law, if they do not know such a simple thing, and as vigilant and zealous policemen should they not, as is becoming and suitable to zealous and vigilant police, know in advance whether this was *dolus* or *culpa* or merely *casus*? *Quos ego* [I will teach them]![11] Therefore, the statement that *Fædrelandet* makes is as solid and fixed as the Round Tower [Rundetaarn]:[12] *The police must not institute any inquiry before it has positive proof that a crime has been committed.* If the police can do that, then the guarantee of rights is done for; then, as we have said, it is an old fable in which only good-natured, superstitious people believe, that there is a good legal system here in this country, and, as *Fædrelandet* so truthfully and correctly expresses it, "men's most sacred rights can then in no way be said to be properly protected."

3.
[A LETTER]¹³

Gentlemen!

I have gotten into a very awkward situation, and I hope you will be kind enough to help me out of it. As you know, I was deeply disturbed by a story reported in the Saturday issue of your paper¹⁴ about a criminal interrogation of court bailiffs, and I wrote the editor of the *Berlingske Tidende* "a letter" that was printed there in the Sunday issue.¹⁵ In that letter, I used your comments in the first instance as pertinent to another story about a billfold regarded as lost but later found in the lining of the loser's coat, a story you were so kind as to consider in your Monday paper,¹⁶ accompanied by several remarks, some of which, it is true, were very flattering to me, but which, on the other hand, made me fear for myself. From these remarks I learned something that I must not have understood clearly when I wrote my letter, that I had accused the police of extreme irresponsibility when I related that the criminal inquiry into the presumed theft was instituted *without having made a search of Mr. Poulsen's servant's coat,* in whose pocket the aforementioned billfold had been put. Since I am somewhat loath to incur, because of my insults to public officials, rebuke and a fine etc., which, after all, are the honorarium easiest for frank and truth-loving people to obtain in this country (if you find this statement too bitter, I beg you for God's sake to strike it from the manuscript), and for certain private reasons I would rather not run afoul of the police, so as soon as I had read your respected paper for Monday, I hurried to gather more information about the story I had related, hoping to make it look less serious for the police. I did actually manage to find such information, and I made haste to correct in "Another Letter,"¹⁷ printed in yesterday's issue of *Berlingske Tidende,* the "little inaccuracy" it contained, namely, that the billfold had not, as I reported, been found in the lining of the servant's coat but "had fallen through a hole in the lining onto the street and was brought to the police station by the honest finder on the evening of the same day the interrogation ended." But, although the element in the story that I corrected or changed is very important, and although the whole story is altered by this correction and has become different from the report given in my first letter, you will still readily perceive—all of which I pointed out yesterday in the *Berlingske Tidende*, but, regrettably, when I wrote the comment I did not comprehend how pertinent it was in every respect—"*that this does not change anything in the case itself.*" A good friend of mine who is very interested in me and what I do came running over to me last evening an hour after my second ill-starred letter had come out into the world and called my attention to the fact that the insult to the police in the story was by no means removed or appreciably diminished by my ingenious correction. "For," he said, "in the first place, the facts as you first related them do not change the case; it was just as much the police's duty to search Poulsen's servant's coat before instituting a criminal interrogation, because in all great likelihood it would then have been disclosed that the billfold had not been stolen but had been lost on the street, inasmuch as the pocket and the coat lining were found to have burst their seams, making the probability of discovering a crime by means of a criminal hearing very poor, and, as a result, they undoubtedly would have waited a few days for some finder to come forward and also have advertised the billfold in *Adresseavisen* before taking further steps. So you see that the irresponsibility of which you accuse the police remains just about as great whether the billfold is found in the lining of the coat or on the street, provided it remains fixed that no search of the coat was made, *because, given that omission, the irresponsibility stands.* In the second place, you said in your first letter that the 'criminal interrogation' was instituted by 'a police-court judge,' thereby making your charge of police irresponsibility even more serious. The usual procedure is as follows: when someone reports that he suspects a crime has been committed, the police assign a couple of their officers or, in more important cases, a lieutenant or a captain

[*A Letter*] 71

to gather preliminary evidence from all the persons who may be assumed capable of giving any information on the case, and they give their report to the police chief. If this report shows proof or a high degree of probability that a crime was committed, he refers the case, according to its nature, either to a court or through the bailiff to the criminal court. When you said that a police judge had instituted the criminal interrogation in this case, you thereby declared that proof or at least the probability of the presence of a crime had been procured. Thus you declared that the police chief had instituted a court case, and although it certainly was the police officers' or the police lieutenant's or the police captain's duty to search the servant's coat before making their report, you nevertheless do see that it was far more excusable for them to have omitted this than for the police chief, as you said, to refer the case to the police court without undertaking the most preliminary of all preliminary investigations—therefore, it is the chief of police whom you have harshly attacked; he is the one you have charged with serious misconduct."

You can well imagine that my friend's words, the well-founded truth of which I dare not doubt for a moment, agitated me greatly, for now I saw that my correction did not correct what I wished to correct but that my wretched story contained an even grosser insult to the police and that I therefore could expect unpleasantness to arise from it very soon. After a bad night, I have been out this morning looking for new and better information on the true shape of the case. Thank God, I was fortunate enough to find what I was searching for, and although I know that the *Berlingske Tidende* has nothing against repeated corrections of the same mistake in other newspapers, I dare not assume that it is equally willing to correct a second time one of its own mistakes. So I beg you, who in fact have indicated your interest in the case by the praise you have conferred on me, to correct one more "little inaccuracy" in my letter.

As I said in yesterday's correction, the billfold did fall through a hole in the lining of the servant's coat onto the street and was delivered to the police station by the honest

XIII
470

finder—but not, as I wrote yesterday, on the evening of the same day the criminal interrogation ended, *but on the morning before the criminal interrogation was held*, with the result that no judge had held any interrogation. Consequently the story, as I now—and I hope for the last time—correct it, is briefly this: A servant lost a billfold on the street; it was found, taken to the police station, and returned to the rightful owner. It is easy to see that the remaining similarity between my corrected story and the one reported on Saturday by you is only very meager, but also that my unmistakably good intentions must all be sufficient excuse for the inaccuracies that slipped in. Therefore, I must continue without the slightest change or correction to insist on one of the opinions expressed in both letters, that Stampe, Colbjørnsen, and Ørsted[18] are great jurists, lawyers, and I think it is good that this has been stated. I further add the perhaps unnecessary assurance that I myself am no lawyer but a job-holding citizen who honestly supports himself by molding candles, but I am very sorry that the last thing I molded is held by the *Berlingske Tidende*.

I have the honor to be
The Writer of the Letter

LITERARY QUICKSILVER[19]

Or
A VENTURE [*FORSØG*] IN THE HIGHER LUNACY[20]
WITH
LUCIDA INTERVALLA[21]

> I will not sing along in harmony
> But grate as a strange dissonance.
>
> OEHLENSCHLÆGER'S *Dina*[22]

There is a saying that goes like this: To him whom God gives official position he also gives understanding. It presupposes, therefore, that the person concerned has no understanding beforehand; and since being an author actually is no official position, and furthermore, since authors are by no means always public officials, it is easy to see how unreasonable it would be to require an author to have understanding. I am not speaking only about poets, who, after all, always have had the privilege of being mad;* I speak of authors in general. And to justify even more this lack of understanding, I will cite another proverb that says *Quem Deus perdere vult, prius dementat*,[23] which interpreted is: Him to whom God is going to bring misfortune he first deprives of sanity. In other words, how could God bring greater misfortune upon anyone than by making him an author? Accordingly, it is quite all right for an author, with or without public office, to have no understanding. And, in any case, it is no concern of the public whether an author has understanding or not if only he is original. As one drives along a country road, especially in certain regions, it not infrequently happens that a ragged urchin suddenly leaps over

* *Non est poeta sine furore* [There is no poet without madness].[24]

the hedge from the field into the middle of the road, stands on his head right in front of the horses, rolls his eyes at the travelers, and, without paying any particular attention to the danger of being run over, waves his bare legs in the air. If a driver does not want to run him down, he has to halt and honor him with some coins or with a few raps with the whip, as the case may be, which is somewhat like an author's position with the public. An author is supposed to be the public's fool; more is not required. If eventually he wants to acquit himself with distinction, he must—to continue the metaphor—do his best to create the rolling-eye look with which he regards the travelers while standing on his head, an expression so curious, together with so curious a way of waving his legs in the air, that all those who drive and ride and walk along the public highways of literature come to believe that he alone has the proper posture and that it is they themselves who are askew. Then, to get in proper line again, they promptly begin to attack coal bins, knock down windmills and other such things, thereby letting the world know that the author has made an impression on them, that he is original, that he is creating an epoch, that a completely new order of things is beginning with him. —You no doubt are familiar with the name Lucretius,[25] a Roman poet who was mad but had his more luminous moments and devoted these very moments to his poem *De rerum natura*. I will not quarrel with anyone over the extent to which he was justified in doing that and whether he should rather have forged while the iron was hot, that is, written his poetry while he was mad. As far as I am concerned, in order in one way or another to hit it right, I have written both in and out of season, and for the same reason I let my "A Venture [*Forsøg*] in the Higher Lunacy" stand peacefully along with my *lucida intervalla*, and I am also positive that it will be hard to distinguish the one from the other.

Note. Life = a highway is a fairly trite metaphor, but literature = a highway is a completely new metaphor, and whether it pleases or displeases, I take it upon my conscience all the same. The above is perhaps a bit prolix; you will, for example, find it conceivable to imagine both carriage passengers and riders attacking coal bins and knocking down windmills. On that point, allow me to suggest that the closest illustration of the highway of literature is the Old King's Highway [Gamle Kongevej],[26] with its daily traffic, which indicates that in certain ways it is very difficult to distinguish between those who ride in carriages, ride on horses, or walk, whereas it is a small matter to subsume them under a common point of view. For instance, on the Old King's Highway there is a separate footpath with a sign giving "pedestrians" the exclusive right to use it; but by "pedestrians" is meant not only human beings who walk on two feet but also other living creatures that walk on four, such as cows, bulls, sheep, and pigs, also horses with riders on them, by reason of the fact that although the rider, it is true, is on the horse, the horse is still on foot and consequently belongs among the "pedestrians." Ultimately, especially when the road is very muddy, this also includes carriages drawn by horses, according to the principle that need breaks all laws, or according to the German usage that also allows both carriages and horses on footpaths.

. . .

It is already far into autumn, but I still have not been able to decide to leave my beloved country place. Nature still has too much that is fascinating to me for me to tear myself from it so precipitously. I am not aware of autumn's so frequently mentioned melancholy; I constantly see in nature only the eternally blooming but roguish maiden who throughout the autumn and winter shows herself to us in the oddest clothing merely to tease her adorers. It amuses her to be able to make herself almost unrecognizable to them, over whose sighs and laments over her faded beauty and dull-hued loveliness she secretly gloats, until, tired of this northern masquerade party, she throws off the sallow covering, divests herself of the whole illusory masquerade costume, and, lovely as before, beckons us to her swelling, flower-decorated bosom, to her tender, fond, refreshing embrace, and asks with a smile: "Do you not know me any more? My shape was disguised and my voice counterfeited in the rustling leaves, in the ringing frost, in the whining wind; but how did it happen that not even the twittering of the birds on the naked branches disclosed me?"

As to my country place, one wing of the house overlooks the garden. It certainly does not have any more charms. But, yes, it does; in the garden there is a pond, and in the pond there are carp. Carp are rarely seen at this time of the year; it is only in the summer that the sun can lure them closer to the surface of the water, where one sees them splashing about animatedly and snapping up the crust of bread thrown out to them. Now, however, they stay down deep at the bottom, and I would almost wager that the pond is still not deep enough for them, for the higher the sun is in the sky, the deeper is its reflection, and I suppose that is what the silly fish go after. Generally, it is a beautiful sight when the sun is reflected in the pond, far more beautiful than in the summer, for then the water is often muddy because the ducks do their swimming exercises there. It is not very nice of the ducks; they could just as well let the carp have the pond in the garden and be satisfied with the pond in the field bordering the garden, which would be so much more reasonable, since the latter pond is both bigger and also completely overgrown with duckweed. Apropos of duckweed, viewed singly it is a lovely little plant, but in a mass it is somewhat disagreeable. Steffens[27] makes a similar remark about the so-called lemming, a kind of traveling mouse.* Ultimately, the same is also true of the fair sex: if one considers a single girl at a time, one cannot look enough at such a lovely little lass, with her wise, saucy, affectionate eyes; but a whole school of girls—well, I will not say another word.

The other wing of the house looks out on the farmyard. In the middle of the farmyard there is a manure pile, and on top of the manure pile struts the proud rooster, like an ancient king in parliament, and proclaims by its crowing that it is aware of its exalted position. The hens flock around it; undauntedly they scratch in the manure with their bustling feet, and many a tasty kernel rewards their domestic efforts. Small,

* Malkolm. Eine norwegische Novelle, I, p. 27.

nimble gray sparrows mingle with them, not to scratch but only to snatch away a kernel or two that the hens have taken the trouble to unearth; meanwhile, the hens are too generous and hospitable to chase their little sponging guests away. Here and there a single stem of grass thrusts upward from this rich and wonderful earth, defying the autumn cold with its fresh green color. When I stand at my window and look at all this, I feel more deeply than ever the truth of our philosopher's statement about nature and its meaning. "It is essentially a part of nature to exist for the other, and this other for which it exists is spirit."[28] Thus this manure pile exists for the chickens, the sparrows, and the grass; but the manure pile, the hens, the sparrows, and the grass in turn exist for spirit—for me. Oh! I feel my significance as spirit! Compared with the immortal Shakespeare, I suppose I am no more than a fly, and compared with his worse inspirations, my best inspirations are to be considered only as a pack of dogs;[29] but, in turn, compared with my worst inspirations, the sun in all its brightness is only a half-shilling compared with a hundred-dollar note.* So bow down, proud sun, before our wide-awake glory as you in the past bowed down before the dreaming Joseph![30] Moreover, be assured of our good graces! Look, we personally stretch our big foot out of this open window and allow you to kiss our slipper with your obsequious beams. Fie, you little slobberer! Could you not have first wiped the wet autumn cloud from your mouth? Well, never mind, this time we shall not be ungracious about your dampness.

But back to the manure pile! This manure pile represents literature, for just as the manure pile fertilizes the earth and makes it fruitful, so literature fertilizes and stimulates our immortal spirit. The diligent and careful readers, the indefatigable scholars, the painstaking researchers—the scratching hens give us a very edifying metaphor for them. But the gray sparrows are the modern esthetic *Bel-Esprits* who only appropriate the general achievements of the scholarly efforts, and

* Hegel's *Æsthetik, Werke,* X, 1, p. 4.[31]

the blades of grass are the writers by trade, for just as the grass strikes roots in the manure, so they stand rooted in the earth of literature and flourish—and it is a delight to see. Finally, the rooster symbolizes that other for whom everything exists—namely, the watching spirit.

* * *

How avid the sun is to see its reflection! It sees itself in the clear water, it sees itself in the muddy horse pond, it sees itself anywhere with the same pleasure. And yet—what self-will! Yet it does make one exception of your blue eyes, most beautiful Amanda! It will not reflect itself in them in any way. Do you remember our argument the other day, Amanda, when we stood together out on the lawn in the garden and I told you that there were spots on the sun? You refused to believe it, and what happened then when you were going to look at the sun more closely? Then my pretty Amanda* had to look down and shade her eyes with her hand and counteract the strong light with a little darkness. Can you see that I was right? There are spots on the sun, it is certain; or if its face were as spot-free as your angelic countenance, what would motivate it to avoid your gracious glance? No, you can believe that the sun has a bad conscience on behalf of its beauty; that is why it refuses such an incomparable mirror as Amanda's eyes and makes shift with the horse pond. —Yes, heavenly Amanda! In loveliness you surpass the sun, for your beauty has no spots. Alas, but in self-will you are just alike. You have forgotten it, I suppose, but I remember very well that the very moment we stood there talking, Pluto came leaping, the big fat mongrel, and placed its front paws on your breast and wagged its tail for you, and I had to watch you print a kiss on its shaggy forehead while you clasped its long ears, just as if this detestable mutt-mug were a bliss superior to a certain man's face, which, to be sure, far from belonging to an Adonis, yet shone with the clear flaming brilliance of love, in the dawn of first love, and on whose lan-

---

* May I not call you *mine*—"Wenn ich Dich lieb habe, was geht's Dich an?" [If I love you, what does that matter to you?].[32]

guishing lips there in any case dwelt more eloquence than in a dog's drowsy eyes and wagging tail.

* * *

"Das Aeuszere ist das Innere, und das Innere ist das Aeuszere" [The outer is the inner, and the inner is the outer], say the Hegelians.[33] Who would have thought that the Hegelians were so naive? One has only to compare it with Talleyrand's[34] well-known saying: *"L'homme a reçu le language pour cacher ses pensées"* [Man has received language in order to conceal his thoughts].

* * *

Now I have to laugh, said the German, and then he cried. In that way we are practically all Germans.

* * *

Good evening, Madame! You can hardly guess where I have been this evening. —"Heavens, no, I would have a hard time doing that." —Then I will tell you. I have been to a comedy. —"To a comedy? You? An avowed enemy of the theater, a professed hater of all *sham*, as you like to call what takes place on the stage?" —Yes, I, and for that very reason. I sought and found on the stage what one looks for in vain in life: actuality, naturalness, the true and perfect harmony between the outer and the inner. There was one scene that I liked very much. The hero of the play vented himself in the most violent expressions; he clenched his fists and stomped his feet on the floor—in short, his whole conduct showed quite clearly that he was angry. His beloved wrung her hands and hid her face in her handkerchief. I suspected at once that she was sad, and her lines completely confirmed this. Her lover had wrongly suspected her of unfaithfulness. When and where in daily life does one see such a natural outburst of indignation, such a striking indication of pain?—When the play was over, I went to a restaurant, where I met Justus Berner. God knows what ails him; he was so unusually elated this evening. Rejoice with those who weep and weep with those who rejoice[35]—isn't that the way the saying goes?—Tomorrow I plan to go to the vaudeville theater; there one sees nothing but pantomime and hears not a word. Yes, I must go there to be reminded that there was a time when men's external conduct corresponded to the motions within them, and that it was a very long time ago, and that men who lived then are now but dead shadows who cannot talk but have kept only the gestures!—

"Are you soon finished, Mr. Misanthrope? If you do not stop talking in that tone this minute, I will show you that I at least can get angry in earnest, so angry that I am able to drive you out the door with my fire tongs." —

Excellent, Madame! You really ought to go to the theater!

. . .

Whew, but this city air is stuffy! It is not enough that Cain[36] was the first fratricide, no, he was also the first to build a city,[37] and consequently from him came the desperate idea to pack people together in huge cities like dead herring in barrels. Cain, Cain, what have you done![38] —But there is the organ grinder.[39] Now we shall have music. How magnificent! Every time I look out my window and see the organ grinder coming, I am so happy, happy—I almost feel like joining the ragged boys who follow him from house to house and with pricked ears and wide-open mouths catch the tones of his organ. How heavily the organ hangs upon his shoulders! He almost sinks under its weight—but it does also keep him warm—see how he sets it down and is shivering with cold. He is in the service of sorrow; his furrowed brow and his deep-set eyes tell us that. It is *sorrow* that has driven him from home and bids him go around and *cheer up* the whole world. Yes, so it should be! Life parodies itself and does it with an esthetic thoroughness that puts every Aristophanes to shame. Hey there, you jolly folk! Do you see the organ grinder? Does he not look hungry, frozen, and sad enough to make all of you mad with joy? — —

> Master Peder threw runes over the bridge
> That Little Helga . . . . .

What is that? Ah! Svend Dyring's house.[40] Apple, apple! Do you see that? There it flies through the air with strong runes

Literary Quicksilver

deepy engraved in its juice—do you see how blind chance gives the sacred Forsete*[41] a good-day and plays shuttlecock with the knight's love! Ha! That is a gay comedy. The apple travels at devilish speed—now it is falling—look out!—it is falling for sure onto the lap of an old, shriveled crone, Mother Elle,[42] up at daybreak, she who forced Thor to his knees at Utgardi-Loke's—her *hate* would be cruel enough to bear, but her *love*—O ye good gods! —How cross the old woman will be—how she will stare before her with a frenzied look—stare at the knight—after him—after him—ha, ha, ha! —Love's strokes of genius[43]—no, it fell onto Ragnhild's lap—aha, so it is a tragedy! It veered about so strangely. —

> Gentle love!
> Your rapture I do not know . . . . .[44]

Well, my good organ grinder, that is enough for this time. Look, a whole mark—yes, that is enough to take your hat off for. He understands me perfectly—the hand organ on his shoulders—and off he goes. Farewell, you model for all musicians! You who also know the rare art of stopping at the right time—our dabblers in poetry could learn something from you. But, of course, you are also paid to stop when people are tired of listening to you. The poor devils on Parnassus, no one gives them anything to make them pipe down. No, they had another view of such things in Greece. Orators in Athens[45] were paid both to talk and to be silent. What if a fund were established to support certain indigent writers on the condition that they would not write?

· · ·

The piano is open and no one is in the room—fine, I sit down in the young lady's place and fantasize a bit in solitude. Oh, how stupid of me not to have learned to play! In vain do I hear the music of the spheres, in vain do their harmonies echo within me—the damned keys, these foolish, dull, and sluggish wooden sticks or ebony stumps, whatever they are, will not obey me. Well, then, I shall sing the scale; to that I can strum an accompaniment. Do, re, mi, fa, sol, la, ti—do, re, mi, fa,

* Providence.

sol, la, ti—so these seven basic notes make up the whole musical corps. With this army, seven men strong, all the innumerable maneuvers are executed, but under the names of sonatas, overtures, etc. such a big fuss is made. Hmn! Very strange! The tactic that composers and musicians use is practically the same as that of Tordenskjold,[46] who in trying to scare a fortress into surrendering marched the same troops up and down different streets, or that of Hamlet,* who in trying to give the enemy a scare continually propped up the fallen in battle order. Always the same notes, only that the order is now this, now that; now the army draws up in a major, now in a minor; now they dash forward in one tempo, now they march in a second, now they creep in a third. And these perpetual seven basic notes create an aural illusion of an infinite variety of harmonies; the soul is snared in the same illusion, and the mouth falls in line and blabbers about the hosts of notes, about a sea of sound with ceaseless fluctuations. —Ha! A ridiculous delusion, and yet so salutary! A delusion, and yet so enchanting! A frustrating dream, and yet so blissful! — —

When Odysseus[47] sailed past the coast of the Sirens, he stopped the ears of his crew with cotton but had himself just tied securely to the mast, letting the Sirens' voluptuous notes flow into his open ears, and he sailed on unscathed.

Look at your reflection in this ingenious. hero, gentle, romantic youth! Do not be afraid of capsizing in the waters of life or of stranding on the reefs of poetry, even if your ears are listening to spellbinding voices from an invisible world; they will not be able to harm you if you are securely bound with the rope of prose to the mast of actuality!

And you, my sagacious philosopher! You must not become a martyr, either. You must by no means stop your ears with cotton, even if you believe a thousand times that you notice a profusion of melodies; you must not put out your eyes, either, no matter how often you imagine that you are seeing numerous glowing colors, be it in nature or on the artist's canvas; you must in no way mutilate yourself but merely remember that neither the eye nor the ear is the organ for your

---

* According to *Saxo Grammaticus*, IV.[48]

study, but that all your wisdom sits in your finger tips. You must make up your mind that you know—or at least can count on your fingers—that there are only seven basic notes, seven basic colors, and probably only seven ideas, thus the wealth of ideas in which some people take great pride is a lot of nonsense. Greece did not have more than seven wise men.

• • •

Julius Caesar is supposed to have said that he did not see how an augur or priest could look at another priest without both of them bursting into laughter.[49] What a smart man this Caesar must have been! I happen to have a hard time understanding even how two men can look at each other at all and keep from laughing; and what I comprehend least of all is how one author can look at another author without both of them splitting their sides with laughter.

• • •

Here I stand washing my hands. This is no symbolic act such as Pilate's,[50] but neither is it an idle statement. It is neither more nor less than a true report about the simple fact that I am washing my hands. It would never occur to a sensible layman to report such a thing, and if he did, he would be laughed at because it is an all too everyday event. But for me it is quite another matter; I am an author, and what such a public person does is always important, even if it is intrinsically insignificant. The public knows how to invest it with significance all the same. Therefore, I herewith once again inform each and all: I am washing my hands!

XIII
482

I wonder what this wash basin would say if it could speak? I dare say it would tell me its story and among other things try to dupe me into believing that it had descended from that famous golden wash basin that the Egyptian King Amasis[51] had recast into a golden image for the purpose of divine worship. Well, if that is so, my good wash basin, then you have not reminded me of King Amasis in vain. That worthy man was a great admirer of the Greeks. I go along with that, and because of my profound respect for them, I transform you by a hefty heave at the floor into a multitude of little pieces of porcelain. Look now, lie there now and listen to what I say; now I shall teach you Greek. Do you know what *ostracism*[52] is? It is like this. The Athenian rabble scratch names on potsherds and thereby drive the leaders, the real Athens, into exile. Do you hear? The Athenian rabble drive Athens into exile. And I, what do I do? I strew Attic salt[53] on both Athens and its rabble. I can easily salt—would that I might have a misfortune if I did not have both fists full of genuine Attic salt. Yes, by the three-headed hound of hell! And it amazingly comes at the right moment for me, because Athens is like a leech whose dead treasures have occupied my best energies! That is why I sprinkle salt on this leech, and then it ejects the blood again—my blood—and so everyone gets his own. The Athenian rabble can easily scratch names on potsherds, for they have Athenian citizenship; *ergo,* they scratch. Moreover, one can turn the proposition about and say: they scratch; *ergo,* they have citizenship. I, too, am a citizen; I am a citizen of the world, a cosmopolite; *ergo,* I establish a universal ostracism and drive the whole world into exile by scratching its name on this broken piece of my wash basin. Believe me, it will be a joke when I wake up tomorrow morning and look around and discover the whole world is gone. Where in the world has the world gone? I will say to myself. Away! I myself, in fact, have driven it into exile. Poor world! In a way, I am sorry for it. It will not shut its eyes all night, busy with packing and moving. The whole Atlantic Ocean will be filled up with bedstraw, and, just as in the days of Noah's flood the wet inundated the dry, so now the dry will inundate the wet. "You get your just deserts," the solid element will say to the fluid. "You humiliated me in sainted Noah's day." —"But vengeance is mine,"[54] objects fire. "It is I who shall burn up the earth." "Yes, where it is shallow!" says the air, "but we shall see whether you are the fellow to burn up the ocean." Very likely this is the kind of small talk the elements will carry on together. Yes, it will be an awful hullabaloo; but it will not help. Everything will happen only for the world's own good, and as soon as I perceive that it is behaving itself fairly well, I shall promptly call it back again. The fair sex will benefit especially from this exile; it will learn to appreciate me more, for a woman told me that I look splendid from a distance. —Is there anyone at all I would like to keep? No, it would be unjust if I used the occasion to discriminate among people. —Sh! I hope no one hears or sees me—if I am found out, will I not surely be considered crazy? After all, it will not mean much more than belonging to the minority in the committee appointed by our Lord. Am I not allowed to belong to the minority? Am I not allowed to be—crazy, preferably alone? Does not Jean Paul say that in solitude every man is an "eccentric" [*Sonderling*]?

But careful! A mortal being is actually staggering up the dark stairway. Trip, trip, trip, trip—. I wonder who is out so late in the evening? Well, it is not important! Just so Nicodemus[55] has not been eavesdropping on the stairs. For safety's sake I will drop a few sensible remarks so no one smells a rat, for example, that the earth is round.[56] But I say! The wash basin — — —

Ah, is it you, Albert? How are things out there on our *round earth*?

"Well enough, Monsoor, as Arv[57] says, but things are in a bad way in here. Someone has smashed the wash basin."

Yes, one does what one can. The destructive tendency of our day leads to such things, I tell you.

"Yes, I think I understand what you mean; you are of the same opinion as my wife."

What does she think?

"She believes that when maidservants start breaking things, it doesn't stop with one plate or one glass. Bad luck seldom comes singly, she says. But come, let us pick up the pieces. I don't want to step on them and get them in my cork soles."

Oh, it isn't worth the trouble. Sit here on the sofa and you will be safe enough from the pieces.

"Speaking bluntly, no, thank you! I must leave at once; it is not at all cozy here with you this evening—besides it is very late. Bah, my watch has stopped."

My watch has stopped—now that is a hackneyed phrase,

XIII
484

Albert. How do you suppose it is going to go with us at the judgment seat of esthetics when we have to account for every useless word we have spoken?⁵⁸ Couldn't you easily have thought of another way to say it, for example: My watch has accepted the Copernican system?

"What in the world is the matter with you? God forgive me, but I believe you are not all there. Good night, and do get well."

Thank you, Albert; the same to you! —— ——

So he left. Well, it is probably high time the world comes out and gets to look around a bit; finally, it gets too boring to have to stay home all the time this way. Consequently, next day—*à bas tout le monde* [down with the whole world]! —But wait, I first have to consider whether the world is in fact *good enough* to be sent into exile this way. *In Athens*, only *worthy* men were exiled this way; ostracism became obsolete because eventually it came to be practiced against a good-for-nothing.⁵⁹ When all is said and done, the world is not much better than this good-for-nothing; therefore, I think I shall spare it and let it stay where it is.

SUPPLEMENT

Key to References
88

P. L. Møller, M. Goldschmidt, *The Corsair*,
and Related Publications, 1841-1848
91

Selected Entries from Kierkegaard's
Journals and Papers Pertaining to Articles, the *Corsair*
Affair, and "An Open Letter"
153

KEY TO REFERENCES

Marginal references alongside the text are to volume and page [VIII 100] in *Søren Kierkegaards Samlede Værker*, I–XIV, edited by A. B. Drachman, J. L. Heiberg, and H. O. Lange (1 ed., Copenhagen: Gyldendal, 1901-06). The same marginal references are used in Sören Kierkegaard, *Gesammelte Werke*, Abt. 1-36 (Düsseldorf: Diederichs Verlag, 1952-69). References to Kierkegaard's works in English are to this edition, *Kierkegaard's Writings* [*KW*], I–XXV (Princeton: Princeton University Press, 1978–). Specific references to the *Writings* are given by English title and the standard Danish pagination referred to above [*Either/Or*, I, *KW* III (*SV* I 100)].

References to the *Papirer* [*Pap.* I A 100; note the differentiating letter A, B, or C, used only in references to the *Papirer*] are to *Søren Kierkegaards Papirer*, I–XI³, edited by P. A. Heiberg, V. Kuhr, and E. Torsting (1 ed., Copenhagen: Gyldendal, 1909-48), and 2 ed., photo-offset with two supplemental volumes, I–XIII, edited by Niels Thulstrup (Copenhagen: Gyldendal, 1968-70), and with index, XIV–XVI (1975-78), edited by Niels Jørgen Cappelørn. References to the *Papirer* in English [*JP* II 1500] are to volume and serial entry number in *Søren Kierkegaard's Journals and Papers*, I–VII, edited and translated by Howard V. Hong and Edna H. Hong, assisted by Gregor Malantschuk (Bloomington: Indiana University Press, 1967-78).

References to correspondence are to the serial numbers in *Breve og Aktstykker vedrørende Søren Kierkegaard*, I–II, edited by Niels Thulstrup (Copenhagen: Munksgaard, 1953-54), and to the corresponding serial numbers in *Kierkegaard: Letters and Documents*, translated by Henrik Rosenmeier, *Kierkegaard's Writings*, XXV [*Letters, KW* XXV, Letter 100].

References to books in Kierkegaard's own library [*ASKB* 100] are based on the serial numbering system of *Auktionsprotokol over Søren Kierkegaards Bogsamling* (Auction-catalog of Søren Kierkegaard's Book-collection), edited by H. P. Rohde (Copenhagen: Royal Library, 1967).

In the Supplement, references to page and lines in the text are given as: 100:10-20.

In the notes, internal references to the present work are given as: see p. 100.

Three periods indicate an omission by the editors; five periods indicate a hiatus or fragmentariness in the text.

P. L. MØLLER, M. GOLDSCHMIDT, *THE CORSAIR*, AND RELATED PUBLICATIONS, 1841-1848

FROM *THE CORSAIR, GÆA*, AND *FÆDRELANDET*, 1841-1845

The Corsair, no. 49, October 8, 1841, col. [9-10]:

Charivari . . .

Today, Friday, October 8, is *The Corsair*'s birthday. All those who present themselves outside its office and shout "Hurrah!" will be royally regaled. . . .

On the occasion of this festive day the editorial staff is holding a celebration with the following

Program

Friday at 11:02 A.M. . . .

At 3:00 P.M., in the University auditorium, there will be a great public defense of a dissertation. In order that it may be as brief as possible, the subject will be "Irony in Kierkegaard."[1] One respondent, two regular opponents, and one outside opponent have been appointed. The prize for the dissertation is a bottle of champagne, and as proof that the author here, as in all disputations, is to have the prize whether he wins in the public defense or not, he has drunk it in advance. . . .

The day's festivities will conclude with a great banquet at which, together with many more things, toasts will be given to all those who in the past year have shown their good will toward *The Corsair* by giving it material for its consideration. . . .[2]

The Corsair, no. 51, October 22, 1841, col. 7-8:

Literature
**The Concept of Irony
with Constant Reference
to Socrates**[3]
*by S. Kierkegaard
Philipsen Publishing House*

That we were present at Mr. Kierkegaard's public oral defense of his dissertation on irony (both a public defense on irony and, like all other University public defenses, irony on the University) and what delight we had in being there, we have already tried to indicate briefly in a previous number [no. 49, October 8, 1841]. Now, having read through the dissertation, we will try to relieve our hearts of the almost overwhelming gratitude that has seized us by a salute of thanks to Mr. Kierkegaard, in which we—all the more to honor him—retain his own phrases and idioms, thus contributing to his own fame and glory as well as to our own. —Consequently:

Thank you, beloved Kierkegaard, for your irony! You have not made your appearance *ad modum* Peder Erik Madsen, wearing white gloves (p. 264)[4]—no, you have exceeded our boldest expectations! For while the crowd's investigations begin and end in a stagnating village pond (p. 12),[5] while the pre-Kierkegaardian scholarly professional mourners (p. 175),[6] massed like blindman's buffs, groped for the idea (p. 47)[7] and the lachrymose humanitarians filled the centuries with their blubbering and sighing (175),[8] while they, following the blending of everything together[9] by Xenophon (189), whose expositions are quite in the same taste as the profundities of our *Folkeblad* or a nature-worshiping seminarian's heavenly parish caterwauling (p. 15),[10] portrayed Socrates as a kindly, garrulous, quaint patron saint who is so fervently well-intentioned toward the whole world if it will only listen to his slipshod nonsense—a good-natured bourgeois who moves around down below in empiricism's bad infinity (p. 19),[11] an officious bagman for mediocrity (p. 132)[12]—then you, O Kierkegaard, just like Plato, have used an enormous lever and tilted Socrates up into the air in a really lively toss-in-the-blanket so that we may see how funny he looks in such a hurly-burly (p. 58);[13] you have let us see the divine underside in the midst of the braying of the pack-asses (p. 13)[14] so that our sensitive contemplation need no longer wander about in difficulties (p. 17).[15] And you have not let us remain fasting witnesses to how you, storklike, drank deeply from the long-necked bottle (p. 147),[16] but you have shown us how Protagoras and Socrates weigh salt with each other (p. 57).[17]

For all this, O Kierkegaard, with the first name of Søren, accept our thanks.

P.S.[18] In appending the acknowledgment that Mr. Kierkegaard's treatise, despite its amazing language, will be of interest to those who have the patience to read it through, we presumably by our admission—when it is placed, please note, together with the above—give Mr. K. all the justice due him.

The Corsair, no. 129, March 10, 1843, col. 1-3:

"Either/Or"[19]
by Victor Eremita

The first thing we heard about this book, and keep on hearing every day, was that it was so thick. The press, from *Dagen* to *Aftenbladet*, from *Berlingske* to *Intelligensbladene*, raised a cry of surprise—did say, to be sure, a few words about it, but began and ended with: How thick it is! A few of them did also review it, as if it were the thinnest book in the world—that is, as if they had been able to read it through in one day (it is 864 pages in two volumes). Almost immediately after its publication, they pronounced panegyrics upon it, they praised it as a marvel; from the contents, *Dagen* had already inferred the author's name, which it seems to want to suggest by saying that the book is a work by one of our truly philosophical geniuses etc.

We became curious to find out what had aroused in the offices of *Dagen* and in the offices of its colleagues a hullabaloo such as occurs when a huge head is thrust through the shutter opening of a cowshed and obscures the horizon of the occupants. We took the book and read it, and right away at the beginning a light dawned on us.

This author is a mighty intellect, he is an aristocrat of the mind; he mocks the whole human race and shows its wretchedness, but he is justified in doing this, for he is a rare and exceptional mind. The others saw him standing there, pointing at the crowd they were in and saying, "What wretched men!" and promptly, with the help of their ready access to the press, ran up to him, leaned intimately on his shoulder, and said, "Damned right, it's a wretched bunch." Now they stood alongside him and did not belong to the crowd!

Now there really is nothing as heroic as scoffing at the crowd. Those proud people (one of these heroes is Prof. Heiberg,[20] who so gallantly took to the field against the whole "public") do indeed speak contemptuously of the anonymous writers and say that they are cowardly in their attacks, but we are unable to see especially great courage in those who vociferously attack a mass from which each one feels himself excepted, and consequently no one defends himself. Don Quixote showed more courage when in coat of mail he attacked the flock of sheep, for, after all, he believed that it was the enemy; but these people feel safe and secure in their attack and let themselves be admired for their courage in engaging single-handedly, like a Samson, a host of Philistines. As we said, no one of the crowd believes himself to be a Philistine. Prof. Heiberg certainly had some such feeling, for he eventually declared that he was going to mention by name every individual in the public who was guilty of transgressing his law, but the minute he sensed that this time he had struck at flesh and blood and not a mirage, he promptly stopped. (We do not doubt that Prof. Heiberg has courage in other respects, but we are unable to conclude it from this.)

However, the human race, which Mr. Victor Eremita takes to task, is a far more inclusive circle, and therefore it is something quite different. For one thing, the "human race" is a far more definite concept than "the public" in that everyone understands it, whereas no one knows who really constitutes "the public"; for another, everyone can determine for oneself whether what is said of the human race is true, whereas one has to feel oneself absolutely a part of "the public" under discussion in order to know the same.

This author, therefore, is a rare and exceptional mind, but what is most rare and exceptional is that he also has a rare and exceptional body as far as authorship goes; at his own expense he has published his voluminous work.[21] Some have taken this circumstance as an occasion to bemoan the pecuniary condition of our literature and have called on the public to compensate the author by buying the book. From the conclusions we have drawn about the author, we feel it would be doing him a greater service to request the opposite of the public. He is, as we have twice said, an extremely rare phenomenon, and we believe that he attaches such great value to this exceptionality that it is his vanity. To write an outstanding book and get it marketed is so common that almost anyone could do it; but to write such a book and have to pay for it oneself, to have good reason to bemoan an injustice such as this, to have something on which one in fairness can vent one's spleen—this is a most exceptional pleasure—for the person who has the means to procure it.

Incidentally, what we find to be more amusing or more entertaining is the review this book will have. A review of this big 864-page book can scarcely be less than 872 pages, and what delights us most of all is that the reviewer will also have to bear the cost of it.

The Corsair, no. 242, May 9, 1845, col. 11:

Since *Berlingske* has found it appropriate to disclose the name of the unknown author of *Either/Or* and *Life's Stages*,[22] we must also be allowed to name the author of *Kjærlighed i Valby*, of *Nytaarsgave, tilegnet Danmarks smukke Kjøn*, as well as of *Et Eventyr: Fastelavn*. It is, namely, Mr. Wholesaler

Nathanson.[23] The same gentleman is also the author of the next piece that will be booed at the Royal Theater.

The Corsair, no. 251, July 4, 1845, col. 3:

 . . . The thought-experiment,[24] whether it would not be more enjoyable, for example, to eat dry bread and drink water with Hilarius Bookbinder[25] than to drink champagne with Mr. Böotius)[26]. . . .

The Corsair, no. 269, November 14, 1845, col. 14:

 . . . Lehman[27] will die and be forgotten, but Victor Eremita[28] will never die . . . .

Gæa, ed. P. L. Møller (Copenhagen: 1846), pp. 144-87:

A Visit in Sorø
Miscellany
by
P. L. Møller[29]

Sorø[30] is the only place in Denmark where there are famous men.

Since to some this may seem to be a strange and paradoxical thought, I shall do the easiest thing in the world—prove that this not only is true but by the very nature of the case cannot be otherwise.

The first condition for being a famous man is that there be people capable of appreciating him beyond the locality where he is living. For just as in the days when there were prophets, a prophet was not honored in his native land, so in our day a great man can never be appreciated in the locality where he lives, where everyone knows what he looks like, how he dresses,[31] what he eats and drinks, how many children he has, what foolish blunders he may have made because of his genius, etc.

Now it is a fact that as far as famous men are concerned,

Denmark is not Denmark but Denmark is Copenhagen, for only there can fame become real fame or find a chorus of thousands of tongues. Consequently, to become famous in Denmark one must live outside of Copenhagen, which is Denmark. Not until fame is certified and registered here does it receive permission to emigrate to the country; therefore, men of distinction who find themselves in Copenhagen do not really reap the advantages of Danish fame unless they move away from this fame's Denmark, that is, Copenhagen. But at present Sorø is the only place in Denmark outside of fame's Denmark, or Copenhagen, where several men who qualify as famous have settled down to live. Thus it is inevitable that Sorø is not the only place in Denmark (geographically speaking) where there are famous men but the only place where there are men who are famous in Denmark....

My first visit was to Hauch.[32] His latest novel,[33] which I had just read, had heightened my interest in him personally. He lives in a low, modest house, and I entered not without some of the nervousness one experiences when about to stand face to face with a famous man. This feeling disappeared with the immediate discovery that Hauch is the author not only of some of our literature's most noble flowers but also of a flowering flock of children. A flock of children such as that is like a bridge or ladder that promotes communication between the profane world and the ideal heights of the poet. There is a very impressive harmony between Hauch's conduct in life and his poetic personality. I for my part prefer a brilliant man who does not feel compelled to be aloof or trivial when he does not happen to be sitting on his Pegasus. In the evening, I was in a little group in which very intelligent things were said on various subjects, some of which I shall try to repeat. After some jovial remarks about the weather and its influence on the year's productivity, the talk turned to books....

"All this is no doubt quite correct," remarked our host.... "But to go on to something completely the opposite, have any of you gentlemen read the latest volume by the philosopher with the many names—'Hilarius Bookbinder,'[34] I think he calls himself this time, or Peregrinus Proteus, as I call him?

He cannot possibly expect anyone with anything else to do to be able to remember all the barbaric names[35] he puts to his many books."

The reasonable man from the country and I answered in the affirmative.

"There is a fellow who beats all our Danish and most of the German philosophers, don't you think so?"

"He certainly has not had a warmer admirer than I,"[36] I stated, "but at the same time I am all the more annoyed at the barren and pernicious use he sometimes makes of his remarkable gifts, which reaches a peak particularly in his last chapter of *Stages on Life's Way*.[37] Already in *Either/Or*, interest was aroused by this double personality who with the passion of genius penetrated the mysteries of metaphysics and esthetics and simultaneously relinquished these glories to seek rest in an ethical, not entirely unbourgeois, life. This determines the different literary merits of the first and second part. In the first, we see the master who has a grasp of his material and therefore almost always finds a proper, often a felicitous, form, only now and then disturbed by the skeptical dissonance of the demons he has tried to curb in his later writing. But in the second part, one sees the neophyte, the searching and developing personality whose discourse constantly 'gads about in all directions' because he is not communicating mastered and organized material but only develops his ethical ego—by writing. As an esthetic practitioner and experimenter, he can be said to have perfected his development; as a moral personality, he is still a possibility. Therefore, despite its interest in the application of dialectics to social life, despite all the occasional flashes of beauty and spirit, the second part is less a literary work than a collection of material."

"Yes, that's just it," said another. "What I have against all these books (which in form and content adequately betray a common source) is that every time one feels able to surrender to pure literary enjoyment the author gets in the way with his own personal ethical and religious development, which no one actually is asking about, which privately may be very respectable but does not have the mark of detachment of the

Langelinie[38] of objective literature; he commits the same error for which the poet Andersen[39] has been taken to task, for exposing his whole inner development to the public eye. Such writing can be interesting only when the discourse rises to genuine lyrical or evocative pathos, and for that reason, of all these books, I rate *Fear and Trembling* highest as a literary work. Here a certain unity of elemental tone and expression is maintained throughout, and although a sick nature, both physically and morally, expresses itself in this convulsive battle to gain faith 'by virtue of the absurd,'[40] the form still permits the grief and passion to be regarded as a lyrical mood. In my opinion, this book occupies a high place in modern literature as a lyrical poem and rates with Byron, Pushkin, and *die ungöttliche Comedie.**[41] What I most admire among the various aspects of this author is his brilliant wit and the genuine humor whereby he uses everyday trivialities as the basis for the most exalted thoughts. To this sphere belongs the polemic against Heiberg in *Prefaces*,[42] which is not only some of the wittiest but unconditionally the most elegant of what has been written against Heiberg; yes, indeed, except for Lehmann's (?) article on the Houguemont farm and a *Corsair* piece about Lehmann,[43] I do not remember any polemical writing in Danish as excellent. Mr. S. Kierkegaard should have taken this author for his model when he recently polemicized in *Fædrelandet*[44] against a reviewer in *Berlingske*."

Taking the lead again, I said, "I think the easiest way to summarize the various directions in this author is to distinguish between his negative and positive sides. In the latter, I consider his individual religious drive, his passionate urge to reconcile philosophy and actuality (which he in fact has worked through experimentally in its most substantive ramifications) with faith. This aspect is rhapsodically manifest in many passages in his writing, and with an amazing abundance of thought and feeling, often a poetic fervor, and a richness and eloquence of language one rarely finds equaled. His discourse is sometimes reminiscent of Rousseau and Chateau-

---

* By a Polish poet.

briand, although in substance it gives much more, in form much less. Should he ever succeed in clarifying from this rhapsodic ferment an organic vitality, he will become a writer of top quality, a real literary genius, but I hardly believe that this will happen. As far as his negative side is concerned, the dialectical-critical-analytical aspect, there he is completely finished (in both meanings of the word), and any further movement on his part will inevitably lead either to mannered self-repetition or to desperation. His performance in this area is extraordinary and manifests authentic genius. With the exception of Sibbern,[45] no Danish philosopher has so comprehensively and exhaustively devoted himself to such a great variety of subjects, and in his analysis of esthetic problems he often emerges as a creative poet. His greatest service to scholarship, a new and invaluable dividend, I consider to be the lines he has drawn in 'The Seducer's Diary'[46] for a philosophy of *womanliness*, a subject that, rich and fascinating though it is, has scarcely been treated before. But when I picked up his latest big book, *Stages on Life's Way*, I had an almost uncomfortable feeling. Such an exaggerated, indeed, such an unnatural productivity may be healthy for an author, but for literature and the reader—never. Writing and producing seem to have become a physical need for him, or he uses it as medicine, just as in certain illnesses one uses bloodletting, cupping, steam baths, emetics, and the like. Just as a healthy person rests by sleeping, he seems to rest by letting his pen run; instead of eating and drinking, he satiates himself by writing; instead of reproducing himself with a fetus a year as an ordinary human being, he seems to have a fish nature and spawns. As it happened, I began with the 'Psychological Experiment— "Guilty?" / "Not-Guilty?" '[47]—which fills the last 242 closely printed pages. Here, as I feared, he had gone astray. Here are repetitions, self-disburdening, flashes of brilliant genius, and the preliminary stage of madness;[48] the earlier fulfillment has finally become nothing more than facility, and method has become static technique that anyone can spot. He does not care about the reader, for he writes for his own comfort; he is not concerned about being known as a classic author, for he writes without form. He moves about in the language as an English clown, walking on his hands and turning somersaults in it, but he has no style, for he uses superfluous words and says everything that comes to his head. The content in this Danaidean vessel of reflection is the account in diary form of a love affair, an engagement and a broken engagement. Every section has the stilted beginning, 'A year ago today.' Here one meets a masculine individual who has lost everything that constitutes personality. Feeling, understanding, will, resolution, action, backbone, nerve, and muscle power—all are dissolved in dialectic, in a barren dialectic that swirls around an indefinite center, uncertain as to whether it proceeds as a result of centrifugal or centripetal force, until it eventually, slowly vanishes. He has become transparent to himself, like the licentiate (in Cervantes's story)[49] who believed he was made of glass and had himself packed in straw like a bottle lest he break into pieces. Indeed, the comparison can be carried even further, for the transparency in our author seems to be a result of poisoning. And, of course, the feminine nature placed on the experimental rack turns into dialectic in the book and vanishes, but in actual life she inevitably must go mad or into Peblinge Lake. The thought process may be briefly reconstructed something like this:

> A year ago today. So now I am engaged. Lovely she is, to be sure, but a little miss like that can be a big nuisance; she cannot comprehend that I both want to be engaged and also want to break the engagement, that I want both to break the engagement and not break it, want both to marry and not marry. She does not comprehend that my engagement is dialectical—that is, it signifies both love and lack of love, that I intend to call it quits and also keep myself forever at the peak of desire. —A year ago today. The method is no good; it must be changed. She lacks the religious presuppositions; we are not compatible, and if she approaches the religious, she is also lost to me as well; she must be made free, for only then will she belong to me, and she can then become engaged and married to whomever she will, but she is married to me just the same, and so on *ad infinitum*.

"If ordinary common sense may be permitted to intervene here, it perhaps would say in elemental immediacy: If you regard life as a dissecting laboratory and yourself as a cadaver, then go ahead, lacerate yourself as much as you want to; as long as you do not harm anyone else, the police will not disturb your activity. But to spin another creature into your spider web, dissect it alive or torture the soul out of it drop by drop by means of experimentation—that is not allowed, except with insects, and is there not something horrible and revolting to the healthy human mind even in this idea? —And yet I have persevered in following this mental gantlet-run, this inquisition that does not let its victim go before every possible degree of mental torture has been experienced; at times I have even been fascinated by this agony of soul, because the dialectical executioner breathes now and then and there are oases in this desert, beautiful, flowering, refreshing oases, such as the reminiscences of the Latin school[50] and the description of the bookkeeper[51] in Christianshavn. These and many other separate passages are not only worthy of a true poet but also presuppose a true poet. But perhaps I am going too far.[52] What do you think, Mr. N.? Have you read the book, too?"

"There must be some truth in what you say," said the reasonable man from the country, "for I have felt and thought just about the same; it actually took a good deal of effort to finish reading the book, and it is easy to see that the person writing such books is not counting on many readers. No one can deny this author an extraordinary depth, keen discernment, and a comprehensive power of reflection. The dialectical talent that he has developed by studying Plato in particular seems to me so great that I know no one who can measure up to him; but—for I really have an important BUT to add to this. But I must first of all make the comment that the banquet in the beginning ('*In vino veritas*')[53] and the dialectical contrast to it (for with this author everything is dialectical, even though it is not satisfactorily resolved into a higher unity), a married man's journal,[54] are written with unusual subtlety and delicateness and display an extraordinarily mature talent. But the abstract esthetics, which absolutely must not take its stand on ethics and thus hovers in the air like a cloud, is nothing, actually, but Epicureanism decked out with poetic flowers, just as its opposite, the ethical, married happiness, divorced from the poetic, borders on philistinism—these two contrasts, which the author most anxiously believes ought to be kept apart, I must certainly declare to be excesses on both sides. I do not believe it possible to be poetically effective in earnest without respecting the requirements of ethics, nor do I believe that one can have a genuine and true marriage if the esthetic is brushed off and the relation is purely ethical. —The real nucleus of the whole thing (the engagement and the account of breaking the engagement) seems to me to have been written solely in order that the author could have the opportunity to spin out in as thin and long a thread as possible the dialectical difficulties posed by a mind abandoned to reflection. I have heard this kind of dialectic used by very hypochondriacal men almost completely under the sway of a fixed idea. I must admit that I never believed it possible to annihilate one's immediate nature as he demonstrates he has done (in this collection of letters, at least); nothing is fresh and direct, everything has to be reflected on. I wonder that he is even able to sleep, eat, etc., for actually he ought to weigh the reasons for and against so long that he would die of hunger or sleeplessness. To me his reflections are like daguerreotypes in which not only the most important and characteristic features are depicted, as in regular painting, but everything possible is caught so that the whole thing becomes a confused network and a trackless labyrinth. Despite all his intelligence, reflection for him has become a severe sickness; his religiousness, which renounces the whole world in order to be occupied with itself and which incessantly believes it is lying out 'in the depths of 70,000 fathoms,'[55] appears to me to be a pusillanimity at which our Lord and his angels must laugh. A religious person like that, who cannot make up his mind and does not dare to take a step without first weighing all the sins he could possibly fall into along the way and always stays on the same spot shivering and shaking, is a nonentity who can find a place neither in heaven nor in hell but only in the thin air of reflection, where no creature can live. He resembles Pastor Schmelzle in Jean Paul,[56] who did not dare to move from the spot because he feared a spring-gun would go off and kill him at any moment. Can such extreme cowardice be truly religious? Meanwhile, I am glad to acknowledge him as an intellectually gifted author, but he appears to me to be a decrepit old man, or, more correctly, an unusually intelligent man with a sick imagination; to me he seems very blasé. If he had lived under conditions that forced him to concern himself with something other than his own whims, he no doubt would have developed his talents to a higher degree; but now he stands like an ironization of irony. At least this is how it seems to me." . . .

Fædrelandet, no. 2079, December 29, 1845, col. 16665:

> To Mr. Frater Taciturnus, Chief of Part Three of
> **Stages on Life's Way**

Although I thank you very much for the kindness shown by such a prompt review[57] of an article by me in *Gæa* for 1846, I must nevertheless allow myself to add a brief, respectful observation. Inasmuch as the "conversation" in *Gæa* that you have reviewed contains a *general* consideration of certain literary works, I find no reason to discuss the particular points there to which you have directed your observations; the article must stand or fall as a self-contained whole. Of course, criticism cannot have anything to do with a writer's wish not to be criticized, and it cannot make a one-time exception of Mr. Frater Taciturnus. You will hardly find any way of disarming the criticism other than—not to have your writings printed, whereby you will obtain what you seem to prize so highly, namely, to have only "one reader."[58]

What I have to point out is a small factual inaccuracy that has crept into your account—presumably because of very hurried reading—where, in connection with this conversation, you say "that the scene takes place in the house of Prof.

Hauch and he himself takes part in the conversation"[59] etc. This, which you even repeat in various forms, is curiously enough a downright error, and there is not a single word about such a thing in *Gæa*, which anyone can ascertain by checking the appropriate passage.[60] Not a single one of the persons in the conversation is mentioned by name, which would have been very difficult, since the conversation did not actually take place (which a calm reader will easily be able to agree with) but is only a fictional form for some critical observations, not all of which seem to have pleased you.

I confess that to have to give such an explanation is not the most pleasant thing for a writer; nevertheless, in this case it seems to me to be necessary, since possibly not everyone would realize that your whole article is irony, which I first realized when I came to the end and saw that you call yourself "Frater Taciturnus" and, at the same time, in more than five closely printed columns (excluding the notes), you have discussed yourself and

Your most respectful
P. L. Møller[61]

FROM *THE CORSAIR*, 1846-1848

Draft of article by P. L. Møller for The Corsair:[62]

Frater Taciturnus
or
The Story of the "Silent Brother" Who
Could Not Keep Quiet
I.

In the beginning, Frater Taciturnus created many books and upbuilding discourses. The books were mighty and thick, and darkness brooded over the contents of the books, because Frater Taciturnus's spirit hovered over the *waters*.

Then the Brother found "infinite joy in the occupation of thought," and he was silent and thought: "If there are thousands and again thousands of readers! And there was— one reader."[63] And our Brother saw that one reader was already a great thing, and he "was contented with this," and he "was contented with less than one reader," and he was very contented.

And he separated this one reader from all the others and called this one "his little world," and "he was happy with these surroundings." But all the others [*preceding four words crossed out and changed to:*] On one occasion he lumped them together and called them "P. L. Møller" or "The Corsair." For he made experiments[64] and conducted this experiment—Ubi *spiritus*, ibi ecclesia: ubi *P. L. Møller*, ibi "The Corsair" [Where the *Spirit* is, there is the Church: where *P. L. Møller* is, there is "The Corsair"].[65] Thereupon he "was enchanted by the contradiction of the infinite"[66] in the morning in Gammeltorv and "was enchanted by the contradiction of the infinite" in the evening in the office of *Fædrelandet*.

That was the first thought-experiment.

II.

Then the silent Frater said: I am a "chief"![67] Therefore, let me make five columns of balderdash in the *Fædrelandet* as a tedious experiment and as a deadly boring firmament between P. L. Møller and the waters that are my philosophy.

And the Frater did it in this wise: for he separated his water and mixed P. L. Møller and the stagecoach[68] and *Gæa* and Hauch[69] and *The Corsair* and his dinner together in the infinite and "thereby satisfied his desire for the infinite."[70]

And the waters in his philosophy he called "the divine enjoyment of thinking,"[71] and P. L. Møller he called *The Corsair*, and it was so.

And "he was well aware of what he wrote"[72] in the morning, but in the evening he could not make anything out of it, and P. L. Møller was not *The Corsair*—it was indeed an experiment.

III.

Thereupon said Frater Hilarius[73] (i.e., the Frater to laugh at): Gather all my experiments that I have made in *Fædrelandet* and elsewhere in one place outside *The Corsair* so that I may get into *The Corsair* soon in order that "the laughter may be on my side,"⁷⁴ i.e., so that people can laugh at me!

Et voila, et fuit ita, and it happened jolly well just as he had said, for he came there and it was very much after his likeness, and people laughed at him.—

Then the Frater called *The Corsair* a loathsome paper, and he called it *ecclesia*, and, furthermore, he called it "P. L. Møller," and on the other hand he called himself a "peaceful" and "respectable" male and an "honest obscurity."⁷⁵ And the Frater with a plaster on his mouth, the silent Frater, saw that the experiment had failed, for he had jolly well come bodily into the paper.

Then there came over him a peevishness, a very illtempered peevishness, and he thought: devil take it! And he went and had his mouth covered with pitch plaster and was silent and was a philosopher, and then he thought: My philosophy bears fruit that has seeds, material for laughter and cartoons, and my peevishness eases itself, after its kind. And he looked into the mirror and saw that it was very good. And his philosophy was married to peevishness in the morning, and in the evening his peevishness came into childbed in *Fædrelandet*⁷⁶—that was the third experiment.

IV.

And it came to pass that the Brother went on one of his daily walks on Østergade etc. and there met the poet and grammarian I. Levin.⁷⁷ He unlocked the lock on his mouth so that he could speak again, and he said: "Listen, Israel, my Israel, until now you were only my friend, but I wish hereby to appoint you as the sole reader of my upbuilding discourses and also as the privileged reader of them for *The Corsair*'s sweet and lovable housemaids; furthermore, you will receive coffee from my silver coffee pot, sugar from my earthen sugar bowl, and a cigar from Siesbyes, and, in addition, you will be permitted to walk arm-in-arm with me on Vimmelskaftet—if you find out for me whether I have slain *The Corsair*." And Levin wagged his tail, put up one of his paws, and said: "That I shall do, master!" And Israel returned and wagged his tail and said:

"Here I am, master. I have visited *The Corsair*, as you ordered me to do, and felt of the teeth; it is not quite dead yet, but it will not be long. Then the Brother said [*preceding four words crossed out; Levin's lines continue*] Now do I get coffee from your silver coffee pot and a cigar from Siesbyes and sugar from your earthern sugar bowl?"

Then the Brother had a fit of philosophizing and said: "Levin, go to hell!"

That was the fourth experiment.

The Corsair, no. 276, January 2, 1846, col. 2-6:

How the Wandering Philosopher
Found the Wandering
Actual Editor of *The Corsair*[78]

It is a remarkable story, as horse dealer Nathanson[79] is wont to say.

The secret, actual, veritable editor of *The Corsair*, he about whom there has been as much inquiry as for casino stock, he for whose sake the publisher of *The Corsair* was innocently put on bread and water[80] and nevertheless still did not confess, he for whom Gudenrath, Leerbeck, Normann, Paulsen, and Falkenthal[81] have searched as zealously as for the man who hit the policeman on the head with a cane and who, like Coronato, the great Venetian bandit, has been heard from every week, except when he has been placed under arrest—he has now been found. He was found by sheer accident, since the search for him had ceased (as is usually the case in such matters); he was found as one finds a handbag, a pocketbook, and the honest finder[82] has produced him in *Fædrelandet*[83] without claiming any reward for it.

The remarkable incident that brought everything to the light of day is as follows. There lives here in the city a great and famous recluse and philosopher called Frater Taciturnus,[84] or the Silent Brother. That, however, is only his hermit name; he has another, under which he strolls the streets[85] every day, but it would be indiscreet to mention it. Coronato the Terrible took him into his confidence. One evening the two strollers were coming back from a spree; the punch had been strong, the sky was blue, the moon sailed in quiet majesty upon it—it was one of those moments in life when hearts are opened. Coronato took the Silent Brother's arm and said:

"Brother! I want to tell you something in confidence. My well-being, my life, depends on it, but you will see how much I trust you. I am Coronato, the veritable editor of *The Corsair*." "I shall not, God punish me, tell anyone," answered Frater Taciturnus, the Silent Brother. —Let us go in, then, and drink another glass of punch, said Coronato. —Yes, let us do that, answered the Silent Brother.

A few days before Christmas, *Gæa, Æsthetisk Aarbog*, came out, containing a review of Frater Taciturnus's books by Mr. P. L. Møller.[86] The article was shabby and could well be called a *Corsair* article, a scurvy, vile article. When *Frater Taciturnus* saw it, he said: The devil with secrecy any longer!

He went to *Fædrelandet*. Just as he came in the door, he shouted: Now I will identify the secret actual editor of *The Corsair*. —Excellent! said *Fædrelandet*; that is precisely our principle. In our no. 2052 issue,[87] we ourselves explained that under certain circumstances it is not only justifiable but can also have a good effect to identify anonymous authors . . . . . who is he, anyway? —It is the editor of *Gæa*, P. L. Møller. —Great! But are you absolutely sure of it? —Am I sure of it? One evening when our souls opened up in sympathetic harmony, he threw himself on my breast and confided it to me, and I even swore God to punish me if I told it; but now that he has been so mean as to place me in *Gæa*, I am telling it. —You are right, Mr. Frater Taciturnus; silence is a virtue all right, but *Alles mit Maszen* [everything in moderation], as the Germans say. But may I give you a word of advice? —Two, if you wish! I am very infuriated at the moment. —Well, you see, if you identify him now, you will not ruin him completely, for there are still people who consider *The Corsair* a tolerably well-edited paper. —But it is a scurvy, an ungrateful paper that does not spare even me, *Fædrelandet*, and I cannot manage to stamp it out. —If you now declare that "*The Corsair* is a loathsome paper," we shall kill two flies with one blow, for people will, of course, believe what is said by you (*Fædrelandet* bows respectfully), Denmark's greatest mind, the author of Denmark's thickest books.[88]

Oh, you are too good! answered Mr. Frater Taciturnus and looked down modestly. You see with the eyes of friendship! If my words have weight, it must be because they are expressed in Denmark's best newspaper, edited by Denmark's greatest giver of toasts.

Oh, don't mention it!

When the mutual excitement had subsided, *Fædrelandet* brought pen and ink, and Frater Taciturnus sat down to write.

The pen writes so forcefully, he said when he stopped a moment for breath, but then I am terribly infuriated. Now I have declared P. L. Møller to be the editor of *The Corsair*,[89] and I have done it so unequivocally that tomorrow the Chancellery will have to collar him.

FÆDRELANDET. That's all very fine, great genius of a philosopher, but *The Corsair* itself! Do not forget *The Corsair*! For God's sake, don't pull any punches!

THE SILENT BROTHER (*dipping the pen again*). Just take it easy. Now I'm going to kill it. You may as well arrange the funeral ..... See, there it is! Now it is done! Now you will also see a little proof of my astuteness. To think that that damned paper could take it into its head to put me in it and make me immortal,[90] immortal in *The Corsair*, my friend! I won't have it. Do you know what I have said to prevent it?

FAEDRELANDET. No, you indescribably great mind!

THE SILENT BROTHER. You can say that, all right. You would never have thought of this. I have added: "Would that I might get into *The Corsair* now."[91] This is a thought-experiment:[92] either I get into *The Corsair* now or I do not.[93] If I do, well, I asked for it myself, and *The Corsair* consequently is doing me a service. If I do not—well, hurrah! Then I don't get in, and that is just what I want.

FÆDRELANDET (*with eyes full of tears*). Great, great man!

THE SILENT BROTHER. Sensible, discriminating paper!

FÆDRELANDET (*with a start*). But it just occurred to me: you don't need the thought-experiment! You have just now killed *The Corsair*.

THE SILENT BROTHER. That is surely true! In my haste I forgot that.

FÆDRELANDET. I am as happy over this affair as I would be if the whole world would eat horse meat on the thirteenth of January this year.[94]

THE SILENT BROTHER. And I am as happy as I would be if Heiberg[95] had got one of my books stuck in his throat.

FÆDRELANDET. I believe I shall celebrate the occasion by taking a ride on a district judge.

THE SILENT BROTHER. I shall do something for the poor. I

shall imagine the thought-experiment that I have given a rix-dollar to a poor woman with five small children. Imagine her joy! Imagine those innocent children seeing a rix-dollar![96]

FÆDRELANDET. You are a noble man!

THE SILENT BROTHER. I am in good humor, and that makes me kind. I am happy, you are happy, we are happy.

BOTH. Hurrah!

Epilogue

THE CORSAIR. Congratulations, both of you!
               Congratulations, both of you!
               Off to your summer residence.
BOTH. We say many thanks.

The Corsair, no. 277, January 9, 1846, col. 1-4, 6, 7:

The New Planet

Heiberg,[97] Olufsen,[98] Søren Kierkegaard! You great philosophers and astronomers! Cock-a-doodle-doo! A new planet[99] has appeared!

Den Frisindede[100] is absolutely in seventh heaven; the provincial newspapers screech and look up like hens when the hawk is in the sky.

Just as Quartermaster General Saaby enters the royal box at the theater, so this planet without the scantiest reason steps among the other planets and draws all the lorgnettes upon itself.

Heiberg, Olufsen, Søren Kierkegaard! Let us four have a sensible little chat about this planet. Søren Kierkegaard, you speak first.

SØREN KIERKEGAARD. I am a philosopher and houseowner in Copenhagen. I pay taxes on my house on Nytorv[101] and pay a fee for my license as an experimenter.[102] I maintain that this planet is a tramp, an obtrusive fellow,[103] a vagrant. I consider it the duty of the police to see to it that this person's appearance does not bring any criticism or other misfortune upon us citizens of the city of Copenhagen. *Uebrigens* [in addition], I shall write nineteen upbuilding discourses[104] about him—whereby the only one who will not be built up will be my publisher, bookseller Philipsen.

THE CORSAIR. Fine! Mr. Professor Heiberg, you speak next.

HEIBERG. I would like to bid a hearty welcome; it proves my astronomical prophetic power. Two years ago I predicted in my *Urania*[105] that within a month two large, bright stars would appear. But only one appeared. Whatever happened to the other one has been beyond me until now. This year I predicted no stars at all, and one has made its appearance. A mathematical calculation—mathematics is of utmost importance. Astronomy now shows:

> a. Predicted: 2 stars. Appeared: 1.
> b. Predicted: 0   "   Appeared: 1.
>
> Total: Predicted: 2   "   Appeared: 2.

The honor of astronomy is saved; I congratulate myself.

THE CORSAIR. O Heiberg! The Naval Hospital is Denmark's second Hven.[106] Herr Olufsen, what do you say about the planet?

OLUFSEN. I maintain that it is a comet. Now the comets know that I am watching them, and so they deck themselves out as planets just to fool me. If I am not a clumsy clod, it is a comet!

KIERKEGAARD. Yes, but it has no tail, Mr. Professor!

OLUFSEN. It has no tail? Well, who says so? You have no tail either, and yet you are a comet.

KIERKEGAARD. What, am I a comet? Well, then——Oh, I almost——

OLUFSEN. Don't get excited! You fly off the handle so fast! Now I'll probably be in *Fædrelandet* tomorrow. But it is true just the same. What, then, is a comet?

KIERKEGAARD. It is an eccentric brilliant light that appears at irregular times to us mortals . . . . .

OLUFSEN. Well, aren't you a comet then? Are you not a brilliant body, a light?

KIERKEGAARD. Yes, I am a light, that is correct.

OLUFSEN. So be it, and you cannot deny that you are eccentric, too. Who is your tailor?[107]

KIERKEGAARD. Fahrner.

OLUFSEN. The establishment no longer belongs to Fahrner; Ibsen has taken it over. Are you trying to make me believe that Ibsen has sewed your trousers according to his own ideas?[108]

KIERKEGAARD. No, according to my legs.

OLUFSEN. Well, it is easy enough to make puns. Nevertheless, little man, I too have trousers made by Ibsen, but each pant leg is always just as long as the other, if I do not expressly order it otherwise in order to look like a genius. Of course, you are a comet.

HEIBERG. Mr. Olufsen, you are getting personal . . . . .

OLUFSEN. Why should I put up with his rushing at me so spitefully? Shall I not give as good as I get? And it is fine for you to talk about making personal remarks when I speak of Mr. Kierkegaard's trousers—you who attacked Professor Baden's stockings[109] in the *Flyvende Post*! Are trousers more sacred than stockings? Are they, now? Tell me.

THE CORSAIR. Gentlemen, you are forgetting the planet.

OLUFSEN. As far as I'm concerned the planet can go to the devil.

THE CORSAIR. That is an unastronomical wish, to say nothing of being unchristian.

OLUFSEN. What is your wise opinion? You are putting on such a wise face. Let us hear.

THE CORSAIR. Well, first of all, I have to know if the planet is there. The world is evil. You no doubt remember what happened to Nathanson[110] with the beer bottle.

HEIBERG. If it is there! Doubt not, man! Damn it all, if it isn't sitting up there! And it is really a fearful sight. When a princess makes her appearance or the king enters the theater, one writes a poem—then one is no longer daunted. But when a person gets up in the night and looks at his stars and then this strange foreign thing sits there and stares earnestly into his face without saying a word—then he gets a very odd feeling. Every time I see it I feel uneasy, just as when Carstensen[111] challenged me: I am nervous.

SØREN KIERKEGAARD (*stretches out in the chair and crosses his legs*). What is there to worry about? A new star—one star more to which earthly fame reaches.

HEIBERG. Have you seen it?

SØREN KIERKEGAARD. No, but I can very well imagine what a star looks like.

HEIBERG. Yes, yes! In my *Urania*,[112] with 14 drawings, Reitzel's Publishing House, I myself said that it is by no means mystical superstition to assume that stars have an influence on the earth. Watch out! Something preternatural is going to happen. — — (*in a deep, toneless voice*) What if the horse in Kongens Nytorv[113] got ornery and started to ride its rider! ——

OLUFSEN (*anxiously*). What do you think, *Corsair*? Out with it.

THE CORSAIR. Just like Count Schulin,[114] I am of the same opinion as my head clerk; but I have no head clerk. My private opinion is perhaps this: that it is a comet that has been the best comet for so long that it most graciously has been promoted to a planet with the rank of Star no. 1 of the third class. But well-informed people have expressed some doubts. I talked recently with Orla Lehmann,[115] and he thought that it very likely is only a planet on approval. "Let us wait and see if it takes the oath of office," he said. Mr. Hultmann[116] likewise confided to me that he believed that it was only on trial and that if it did not have the backing of Councilor Collin[117] it once again could easily become a drifting comet without pay. Who knows, then, if some evening when there is a gala ball and illumination it will vanish—like the hope of economy in the government administration. Perhaps the whole planet is only a national dream, an illusion. In any case, I do not believe in signs; I let the planet be the planet, just like the Stemann[118] administration.

Warning

Since the undersigned cannot keep his mouth shut,[119] everyone and everybody is hereby warned not to confide any secret whatsoever to me. Those who already have secrets in my possession are warned to withdraw them within twenty-four hours, since I otherwise will spread them, and, as for the rest, I reserve my rights.

> Respectfully,
> "Frater Taciturnus"
> Bombardier in the
> Philosophical Artillery[120]

Inquiry

Saturday, December 27, a poor philosopher was so unfortunate as to be run over on the way from the fountain in Gammeltorv to the office of *Fædrelandet* and on this occasion to lose a bit of philosophical composure wrapped in some sheets of *Gæa* for 1846. The honest finder is offered a reasonable reward for delivering it to Frater Taciturnus; address Socrates' successor.

The Corsair, no. 278, January 16, 1846, col. 2-8:
S. T.
Mr. Horse Dealer Michael Leonard Nathanson[121]

We beg a thousand pardons for not immediately recognizing you under the label *Frater taciturnus*. —We want to confess honestly that up until now we erroneously believed that behind this label either Søren Kierkegaard or Blok Tøxen or another of our book-learned thinkers was hiding. But now we see that we were wrong. —Well, well, so you have become a philosopher! Yes, that was certainly the best thing to do, since Neergaard declared that the thoroughbred stallion Cheer had spavin and Councilor Michelsen took the rest of the stallions away from you so that you were altogether stallionless in the world.[122] It is in circumstances such as these that the man of character shows that he is a philosopher.

Perhaps you wonder how you came to be recognized, but remember that you yourself were injudicious. In your most recent article in *Fædrelandet*[123] you say that *The Corsair* is a mean, acrimonious, loathsome, nauseating, slanderous, insipid, disgraceful, contemptible public prostitute. Earlier, in *Corvetten*,[124] you wrote exactly the same, except for "public prostitute"—that first came to you with the help of philosophy. Yes, you can really say with Petronius:[125] I will not dispense with the philosophy I know, at least, by Mary, not for two marks.

But there are in addition some other clues whereby we identify you:

(1) You declare that praise in *The Corsair*[126] makes you angry and being attacked makes you happy. We once said of you that you were more interesting than Bøotius[127] and more immortal[128] than a master of ceremonies—well, good lord, that was not such high praise. But you said nothing and sat on it for a whole year, and then when we gave you a few raps you berated us frightfully. Only a deranged man could think of showing his happiness in that way. — —Sorry, my good Nathanson, but you know yourself that it does not quite square up.

(2) In one of your books, *Stages on Life's Way*,[129] you did a very artificial experiment with a young girl. But it is the very experiment that the betrothed Malte reported in *Adresseavisen*. You called him over one day so that he could see "how you trained your girl."[130]

(3) In the same book, p. 298,[131] you say: "Today she said to me that she believed I really was insane."

And you add: "In a certain sense, it cut me to the quick." Poor man! Presumably some wicked men had told her about the twenty-six fake witnesses and about the Randers madhouse, to say nothing of Bidstrup.[132]

(4) On p. 169[133] of the above-mentioned work it reads: "But is there no third party here? No, everything is dark, the lights out everywhere. How rewarding it is to be shut in [in-

desluttet]."¹³⁴ From this we conclude that it was while you were "shut in" at Randers that you wrote all those thick books, and, since you had free board and lodging, light and heat, you could well say that you are satisfied with "one reader."¹³⁵

(5) On p. 75¹³⁶ of your book *Repetition*, it says "I cannot go around dressed like other men; I like to walk in stiff boots!"

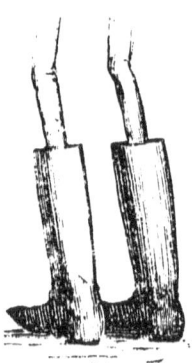

Why not? After all, it goes with your trade. Then, too, you also save garters under your trousers.

(6) In the little book *Prefaces*, p. 7,¹³⁷ you say: "Writing a preface is like straightening out the left leg, pulling the reins to the right, hearing the steed say 'Pst,' and oneself caring not a straw for the whole world."

The horse lover is always detectable through the philosopher, particularly when you get on to ride.

Now we understand at last why you became so incensed at the criticism in *Gæa*.[138] It says there that you are close to speculating yourself crazy. —It was not nice to let you hear that—good lord, after all, we are all men!

Well, Nathanson, this is all the time we have for the present. May all go well! Would that you might be "shut in" again soon; we shall certainly read what you write from in there, so that you really can have it as you ask in *Fædrelandet*: "to be happy yourself over the little world that surrounds you,"[139] and out there "have one reader who is not disturbed by what you write, even if it pleases the whole world to declare it to be nonsense."[140]

Appendix

"How the Frater gets out of the way of a public prostitute."[141]

"How irony calmly and coolly goes in to the Terrible One."[142]

"And how irony calmly and coolly goes out again."[143]

A philosophical member of the editorial staff who has the fixed idea that Michael Leonard Taciturnus[144] is not altogether insane, or, in any case, can be brought back to reason, has written the following:

Most Honorable Mr. Frater Taciturne!

Your latest article[145] in *Fædrelandet* is, of course, like everything you write, a masterpiece of irony and Danish style. As one of your most ardent admirers, the undersigned can have no doubts about that. But the more admiration one has for an author, the more fervently he wishes that the author might be free of any stain that could mar his greatness. I will not deny, most honored Brother, that my admiration for the Brother is sometimes unpleasantly disturbed by a certain feeling, as if something is lacking of that of which, as Holberg[146] declares someplace, a little grain is better than all the frills and flourishes when it is not present—I mean sound understanding and genuine truth. These qualities, indubitably, are doubly important to a literary policeman; they are his policeman's badge, without which he cannot command respect. But here is the rub, Brother; it seems to me that the Brother forgot to take this badge along when the Brother recently posed as

Leerbeck.[147] Obviously, the strong point in the Brother's divine ironic position is that the Brother, *as one praised*[148] by *The Corsair*, has berated *The Corsair* and invited its denunciation[149] instead of its praise. But why did the Brother not do this at the time he was praised? Now it is obvious to all that the Brother did not break his silence until the Brother was criticized in *Gæa*. But—the Brother asks—what does *Gæa*[150] have to do with *The Corsair*? Dear, admirable Mr. Brother, this very question must be asked of you, for it is you, in fact, and no one else who has made these two into one, and thus you must take responsibility for all the consequences. —You see, this is the reason I cannot regard the Brother's present ironic position without fear and misgiving, for, since the strong point is so very weak, the Brother, if I may say so, easily could fall on his ironic backside, and the dialectical result would be just the opposite of what the Brother wished in order to get the laughter on his side.[151] As I said, this is what I wanted to call to the Brother's attention, motivated solely by the zeal of my admiration, and I would be very happy to be enlightened further. I honestly confess that my teeth are not strong enough to crack this nut, but I am sure that is because they are very ordinary teeth such as sit in most men's heads. But I do not doubt that it will be unable to hold its own when the Brother gets his divinely ironic teeth on it; but, dear Brother, do not pull any conjuring tricks and show us another cracked nut instead of the actual one.

I remain
My Honorable Colleague's
Frater Observantissimus

The Corsair, no. 278, January 16, 1846, col. 13-14:

Frater Taciturnus's  Dialectically Authorized

Research Center's Advertisements

Edited by Coronato the Terrible[152]
Printed at Mr. Taciturnus's own expense[153]

Philosophical Announcements

Announcement is herewith made that effective today Mr. F. Taciturnus has received permission from the eminent and profound philosophical magistrate to set up as *irony*[154] here in the city.

Copenhagen, January 10, 1846
Fædrelandet, no. 9

By reason of the above announcement, I herewith respectfully recommend myself as irony to go in and out very coolly and calmly at The Terrible's,[155] as well as to allow public prostitutes to keep the right of way on the sidewalk.[156]

Cheap prices and reliable service guaranteed.

Respectfully
Frater Taciturnus
Irony by Royal Appointment

A philosopher in the habit of suckling ideas desires a philosophical idea or an experiment at his breast, since his own are dead. The most motherly care is guaranteed. Recommended by *Fædrelandet*.

Miscellaneous Announcements

Victor Eremita, former philosopher, of this city, is herewith requested, with eight day's notice, to come forward and explain whether he will again live conjugally with respect to bed and board with his divorced wife, Sound Reason by name, also of this city, since in default of this she will reserve the right to retain undivided possession of the estate or to enter a new and second marriage.

Situation Wanted

A healthy, well-dressed philosopher of prepossessing appearance seeks a place as a literary police club[157] with a family of the philosophical faith. He will furnish his own club, knows all about tailoring and the more subtle dialectics. Salary no object, but good associates and a "little world in whose surroundings he can be happy."[158] Address reply to "Hilarius Bookbinder," care of the office of *Fædrelandet*, where he now works as a volunteer.

Declaration

To avoid collision, I must not fail to announce hereby to the city of Copenhagen's Honorable Association of Public Prostitutes that from now on I shall invariably step aside for the aforementioned corporation.[159]

Nathanson[160]
Horse and Filly Dealer

Since I recently have set up *in republica literaria* as licensed Leerbeck,[161] I recommend myself herewith for the performance of all transactions related to it, such as spying, denouncing, invective, name-calling, and cudgeling etc. etc.

Respectfully
Frater Taciturnus
Self-appointed literary Leerbeck

For rent: the upper floors of the Hilarius Bookbinder house, previously occupied by the undersigned, since I, the undersigned, have departed this life.

Philosophical Composure, retired

Lost and Found Department

Late December, while walking from Nytorv along Vimmelskaftet and Amagertorv to Købmagergade no. 54, second floor, the undersigned lost a padlock marked "Discretion," whereby he, specifically, his mouth, was restrained. Since it is important to my mouth to get its lock back, a reasonable reward is promised to the honest finder.

Frater Taciturnus, Chief[162]

Notice

By this proclamation, dated below, to be read as soon as possible throughout the whole country, each and every person who might believe he has any sound reason to make a claim on Mr. Bombardier[163] Taciturnus's bankrupt estate in charge of the Bidstrup Insane Asylum[164] claim office is given eight days notice to make himself known to the undersigned.

Reason's Claim Office at Bidstrup
January 10, 1846

The Corsair, no. 279, January 23, 1846, col. 1-2:

The gray clouds are silent, the smoke of battle hangs heavily over the terrible battlefield. In an out-of-the-way corner Frater Taciturnus musters his remaining armed forces and balances the accounts.

"Well," he declares, as his eyes survey the powerful remnant, "now I have won my victory. *Das war eine grausame Salbe* [that was a ferocious salvo]! I never would have believed that I was so valiant—but you won't catch Frater Taciturnus napping."

He continues: "When I feel how all my limbs are aching, I can imagine how the ill-fated *Corsair* must feel. He probably has been crippled, so then I have that on my conscience; next time I must control my temper.

"When I go out for a walk[165] these days, people point at me and say: There goes Taciturnus the Terrible! He was the one who crippled *The Corsair*. My strength waxes on that kind of praise so that some day I will take the steeple of St. Peter's and put it on top of the Round Tower,[166] and I will set my friend Heiberg[167] on top of St. Peter's, just for show. Then people will say: Taciturnus the Great did that.

"I will become like Tordenskjold.[168] Mothers will silence their children by saying: Now Taciturnus is coming. I will become a myth, a fable. I will let myself be knighted and called Michael Leonard[169] von Taciturnus-Holofernes.[170] By Jove, what a name!"

He pulls on his collar, takes a majestic step forward, and suddenly stands face to face with—*The Corsair*.

TACITURNUS (*beside himself*). Go to hell!
THE CORSAIR. Good day, great man, how are you feeling?
TACITURNUS. Will you spare me your praise,[171] you villain?
THE CORSAIR. Fine—you wee little man, how are you?
TACITURNUS. Skunk! Libeler!
THE CORSAIR. Good God, you don't want to be either great or not great! Well, you mediocre man, how are you?
TACITURNUS. I am neither great nor not great nor mediocre. I am . . . . . Oh, you are a scoundrel!

The Corsair, no. 280, January 30, 1846, col. 9-11:

Now there's the devil to pay—two crazy Michael Leonard Nathansons[172] have announced themselves.

Saturday there was a knock at the door, and in came a man with two witnesses. Sweat stood in great drops on his brow; he was pale, and in an abusive voice he said:

"May I have the latest number of *The Corsair*?"

The paper was brought, he took it, opened it up, closed it again, looked around, and shouted: "That is scurvy! Such an attack on me now when I have no publication!"

"With whom do I have the honor of speaking?" asked the editor.

The stranger looked up and said: "My name is Nathanson, horse dealer Nathanson; you know me, all right."

"Ah, so it is you!"

He stared into space for a moment and then began again: "I have been to the *Berlingske* Nathanson with an article against you, but he said he could not accept it because then people would think that he himself was the Crazy Nathanson."

"But you do have your *Corvet*,[173] after all."

"It has been discontinued," shouted the man. "I am defenseless; I have no publication."

"So that is why you write in *Fædrelandet*?"

"Then I went to *Fædrelandet*," he went on, staring again, "but they threw me out without reading my article."

"What kind of article is it?"

"I will read it aloud to you! It is in poetry (*reads*):

> 'Is it not patently clear
> That Goldschmidt is a man of fear.
> For as long as I piloted my corvette
> He certainly had a hard time of it.

I now declare *The Corsair* to be a scoundrel. Will the honored public excuse me if I do not put it in poetry. With regard to my complaint against Dr. Christensen, I shall shortly have the honor.

Michael Leonard Nathanson' "

EDITOR. This will be printed in *The Corsair*.
STRANGER *(happily)*. Really? Can I depend on it?
EDITOR. Definitely.
STRANGER. Then wait a minute; let me delete "scoundrel."
EDITOR. No, it must remain as it is.
STRANGER. Well, let it stay. It also was villainous to accuse me of having written *Stages on Life's Way*.
EDITOR. What? Didn't you write *Stages on Life's Way*? Are you not Frater Taciturnus?
STRANGER. Not any more than Gustav Michelsen, who took my mares!
EDITOR. Well, well, so you are not horse dealer Nathanson, either . . . . .
STRANGER. What's that? Am I not the Crazy Nathanson? Do you deny that? Are you mad?
EDITOR. Crazy Nathanson is Frater Taciturnus, who writes against us in *Fædrelandet* because he has lost his *Corvet*. It doesn't help to talk.
STRANGER. By the Almighty God in heaven, I am Crazy Nathanson! Here are two witnesses! Witnesses, speak up!
BOTH WITNESSES. He is Crazy Nathanson.
EDITOR. This is scurvy! So there is someone else going around the city passing himself off as you . . . . .
STRANGER. God have mercy! And my wife! . . . . . And my horses! . . . . . I must catch the man!

And out of the door goes Crazy Nathanson.

At this moment he probably has got hold of the other Crazy Nathanson.

Heaven knows how it will all end.

The Corsair, no. 284, February 27, 1846, col. 5:

Literature

Victor Eremita, the brilliant and active author whom we have previously recommended[174] to our readers, has just recently published a new book to which we venture to bring the attention of the public. It is a "mimical-pathetical-dialectical composition,"[175] distinguished by many good ideas, striking observations, and irreproachable language; for the production of the book, credit goes to the name of book printer Bianco Luno. We again bid the honored author welcome to literature and venture to express the hope that the book may find good sale[176] and many readers.

The Corsair, no. 284, February 27, 1846, col. 13:

—Announcement of vacancy: The post of physician in Greenland. We regret that it is not specified whether it is a position as Chief Physician or a subordinate position, whether the appointment is with the over or under leather britches.
—The author of *Either/Or*, Mr. Victor Eremita, wins a prize in

the Industrial Association for a treatise on clothing manufacture in Denmark. The motto of the treatise reads as follows: Experience shows that the trouser legs[177] of cloth trousers in Denmark are *equal in length or one is longer than the other.* *"Tertium non datur"* [There is no third]!

The Corsair, no. 285, March 6, 1846, col. 8-11:

The Great Philosopher

In his latest published book,[178] Mr. Magister S. Kierkegaard has announced that the following pseudonymous authors are one and the same person and that this one person is he himself, Søren Kierkegaard, namely: Victor Eremita, Johannes de Silentio, Constantin Constantius, Vigilius Hafniensis [*sic*], Nicolaus Notabene, Johannes Climacus, Hilarius Bookbinder, William Afham, the judge, and——Frater Taciturnus.[179] ——So, consequently, we have done Mr. Crazy Nathanson[180] an injustice and herewith ask his pardon.

This is the feeling that most powerfully fills us upon this designation of names, but we wonder how the public feels about such a cloudburst of authors? This is the way the snow melts on the mountain tops in the spring; every single snowdrift is dissolved and all flow together into one single, great, foaming, violent mountain torrent, and this mountain torrent is Søren Kierkegaard, the one and only, and the startled public stares at his mighty dialectical leap.

Let the enormous waterfall thunder in roaring pathos, let it plunge with superhuman force from the dizzy heights of speculation down to the deepest depths of thought, let its dialectically gamboling waves reduce the greatest granite cliffs to the whitest dust and throw it in the eyes of men and animals. As for us, we prefer to remain on earth and look on. With Ussing-like[181] tenacity we return to our earlier concerns.

Mr. Kierkegaard uses this occasion also to comment on praise and censure. He does not wish to be praised,[182] it is an inconvenience to him; for him it is the same as when someone takes off his hat to him on the street and then he has to remove his hat, and he would rather not do that. But then one would think that he would tolerate censure so that he could let his hat sit in peace—but he does not want that, either. He "thanks everyone who has kept silent," but he thanks Bishop Mynster,[183] because he has praised him. Consequently, he does not want censure in any form; Bishop Mynster has a monopoly on praising him, and anyone who interferes with that privilege will be subpoenaed and fined heavily. Consequently, all the rest of us should keep our mouths shut.[184]

It is really strange that a man does not have control of the book he buys and pays for with 3 rix-dollars and 64 shillings.[185] If Magister Kierkegaard invites a man to his home and gives him a cup of coffee and says to him: Here you will taste the best coffee you have ever tasted in your life. But you must be absolutely dumb with ecstacy, you must not praise it; the only one who has permission to praise my coffee is Bishop Mynster. Neither must you find any fault with it, for then I will kick you down the stairs—then Mr. Kierkegaard, M.A., is within his rights. If the man refuses to accept the terms, he does not get the coffee. Likewise, if Mr. Kierkegaard, M.A., has a book printed for private circulation among his friends and gives it away, then he can request first of all: Do you acknowledge this book to be perfect, so pure and sensitive that the mere breath of human judgment defiles it? If the man swears a sacred oath on that, he gets the book, bound in morocco with gilded edges, *sub poena praeclusi et*

perpetui silentii [under the pain of ostracism and perpetual silence]. But, when one has honestly and uprightly paid his 3 rix-dollars and 64 shillings and then is told: Read it as you read the Bible; if you do not understand it, then read it over again; if you do not understand it the second time, you may just as well blow your brains out—then a strange feeling comes over one. There is a moment when his mind is confused[186] and it seems to him that Nicolaus Copernicus was a fool when he insisted that the earth revolves around the sun; on the contrary, the heavens, the sun, the planets, the earth, Europe, and Copenhagen itself revolve around Søren Kierkegaard, who stands silent in the middle and does not once take off his hat in recognition of the honor shown to him.[187]

"Who, what, then, is this Søren Kierkegaard?" thousands are certainly asking who have heard mention of him and his enormous books.

Magister artium Søren Kierkegaard, ladies and gentlemen, is a man with two legs[188] like all the rest of us. As far as his activity—partly as a man, partly as a writer—is concerned, this can best be illustrated by an example. He comes walking[189] along Gothersgade, for example, and a man falls and breaks his leg outside the vegetable store, where a woman recently was injured. The Magister stops momentarily and observes: (1) the man's scream and the surprise clearly portrayed on his face as he falls, (2) his shock when he gets up and notices that his own leg is not functioning because it is broken, (3) the pain in his leg that drives all other expressions from his face. This was the time to step in and help the man, if the second stage of the observation did not intervene: (1) the comic busyness and primness of the people hurrying by, (2) their various questions to the suffering man and their arguing with one another about how he is to be taken away, (3) their cursing at the street commissioners and the property owners for not spreading ashes on the sidewalk. —When the observation is finished, the Magister goes home to record the results. You reconcile yourself to him; you expect that now he either will make himself useful to society by writing an article to *Politivennen* about the slippery sidewalks or entertain society with a beautiful and poetic portrayal of misfortune, suffering, death, resurrection, or the like. By no means, he goes home and writes thusly: "If the speculative thinker explains the paradox in such a way that he canceled it and now consciously knows that it is canceled, that consequently the paradox is not the eternally necessary relation of eternal truth to an existing person in the extremities of existence, but only an accidental relation to limited minds—then there is an essential difference between the speculative thinker and the simple man, whereby all existence is fundamentally confused."[190]

Reader, he really did say this about poor minds in his latest book, p. 168; but you easily perceive that it could just as well be said about poor legs.[191]

The Corsair, no. 285, March 6, 1846, col. 11:

*A page of the Almanac for 1846
Designed for* The Corsair's Observatory

March or Thunder-Month* has 31 days.

Magister Søren Kierkegaard drove a devil out of himself
(*Concluding Postscript*).
S. 1   First Sunday in Lent   Frater Taciturnus

M. 2	Johannes Climacus	
T. 3	Nicholaus Notabene	
W. 4	Ember Day	Søren Kierkegaard
		No twilight
		Full moon
T. 5	Victor Eremita	Sun goes down.
F. 6	Hilarius Bookbinder	Day of prayer
S. 7	Vigilius Hafniensis	
	Søren Kierkegaard consumes one reader.	
S. 8	Second Sunday in Lent	Constantin Constantius
M. 9	40 Knights	Johannes de Silentio is knighted as Sir Braggadocio.

* Thunder-Month, so called because Søren Kierkegaard and all his angelic names[192] so thundered and rumbled in literature that they themselves felt the repercussions.[193]

The Corsair, no. 285, March 6, 1846, col. 14:

Three-Syllable Riddle

The two first are of stone,
The third is just the same;
The whole thing has two legs
Rigged out in scrimpy pants.[194]

The person who solves this riddle will receive as prize the latest of S. Kierkegaard's books, elegantly bound.

The Corsair, no. 289, April 13, 1846, col. 9-10.

Sketches. . . .

3.
Aftenbladet reads *Unscientific Postscript* the first time.

4.
Aftenbladet reads *Unscientific Postscript* the second time.

The Corsair, no. 289, April 3, 1846, col. 13:
Catalogue
of
a profuse and choice selection of the newest
and most beautiful
Ornamental Dahlias
available in the year 1846
scheduled for the next display in *The Corsair*'s
Flower Garden. . . .

1. *Dulcinea de Berlingske*, or *Protée de Nathanson*.[195] Flower of the first rank; all shades of color; tightly and muscularly structured with compact leaves, enormous range, unsteady posture, but is without equal in its profuse blossoms.

2. *Beauty of Kierkegaard*, dirty yellow color;[196] of remarkable form, with two unequal lower stems;[197] brilliant and imposing appearance; unrivaled in every respect; the play of colors on the stems is especially superb.

The Corsair, no. 297, May 29, 1846, col. 7:

Selections from
The Corsair's newest and best
Dream Book
published
for the pleasure and enjoyable information of
everyone who desires reliable interpretation of
his dreams. . . .

Short trousers, to see . . . . . means . . . . .
Frater Taciturnus

The Corsair, no. 381, January 7, 1848, col. 8:

Sketches. . . .

II.
Søren Kierkegaard and *Aftenbladet*[198]
in a theological tarantella with castanets

FROM MEÏR GOLDSCHMIDT'S AUTOBIOGRAPHY

Livs Erindringer og Resultater, I–II
(Copenhagen: 1877)

I first met S. Kierkegaard the summer of 1837[199]—it was during my editing period[200] and therefore should have been discussed earlier. I met my former teacher P. Rørdam,[201] and he invited me to his place, or, more accurately, to the home of his mother,[202] who lived in Frederiksberg. Søren Kierkegaard, among others, was there. I certainly was not a calm, attentive observer, but I did form a mental picture of him. He was about seven years older than I. At that time he had a fresh facial coloring but was slender and with rather prominent shoulders; his eyes were sagacious, lively, and masterful, with a mixture of good humor and malice. I happened to walk home with him along Gamle Kongevej, and he asked me whether I had read a book he had recently published, *From the Papers of One Still Living, Published against His Will.*[203] I had read it and remembered best something about H. C. Andersen, but in the extensive sense he meant, I had not; yet, when he asked and explained, I did not allow myself to get involved but said, "Yes, Yes." It amazed me that he spoke so much about his own book, but he did not become ludicrous thereby, for he constantly remained much superior to me. There was a long pause, and suddenly he made a leap and slapped his leg with his thin cane. There was something jaunty about it, but completely different from the jauntiness usually found in the world. The movement was odd and almost painful. I know that I am in danger of remembering the scene with an admixture of later knowledge, but I am certain that there was something that pained, something like this: the learned, slender man wanted to enter into the joy of life but could not or must not. Later I heard that people in the Lyngby area thought that he was in love with or was very fond of a young lady[204] (who subsequently married one of his cousins). He visited the family frequently and liked to be present when there was dancing, enjoyed it, but did not himself dance. Perhaps it was with a happy thought of the Lyngby area that he made the movement. [*I, pp. 214-16*]

At that time [1841] I was led to the second meeting with S. Kierkegaard.

A review[205] of his master's dissertation, *On the Concept of Irony, with Constant Reference to Socrates,*[206] had been sent to me—or not really a review but an ironic address of thanks using his own striking, mannered language. The article was well written, but I still wanted to see the book itself. I read it and concluded that in all fairness a reservation should be made with respect to its contents, and that I did in a brief postscript, for which I again lacked the capacity for a witty, brilliant appreciation, but nevertheless I did make my reservation (no. 51).[207] At the time I did not know whether this Kierkegaard was the same one whom I had met at Mrs. Rørdam's,[208] but shortly thereafter he met me on the street and said that I had now gotten him into *The Corsair,* but he had no grounds for complaint; he thought, however, that the article lacked composition and that I should apply myself to comic writing, that was my task.[209] I took his words as good advice kindly meant, which they also undoubtedly were. Consequently, he also restricted me solely to the comic and denied me the capacity or the calling to manifest earnestness, respect, veneration. But what was the task assigned to me: comic writing? I could not very well ask him about that, and I did not know what it was. Once again I was at a loss; lacking esthetics as theory, as science, I could not see the article's defect—that is, the crude blending of joking and earnestness—and knew nothing that could help me as a model. The phrase "comic writing" scintillated for me as something that presumably was unrelated to Lessing or justified praise and censure but nevertheless was something significant. What, then, was it? After the bright flash he had tossed out, I stood in the dark. There is something very curious about the fact that it was precisely he who should propose the paper or its presumed spirit as a law and goal for me rather than something in me as the law and goal for the paper. But it is also true that without any presentiment on his part or mine he on that day sharpened the tip that was later to stab him.[210]

I can report here a couple of other brief meetings I had with him during that period. [*I, pp. 275-76*]

[*After buying an expensive tailor-made coat, which the tailor had somewhat ostentatiously trimmed in military style with fur collar and braid instead of buttons, Goldschmidt met Kierkegaard on Amagertorv.*] He turned back with me, speaking now of one thing and then of another, as I recall, and then said quietly, with an unmistakable expression of good will, "Do not wear such a coat. You are not a circus rider. One should go about dressed as other people are." I did not tell him that this was the first time and how I felt about wearing the coat, but I went home, sent the coat back, and had the collar and the braid removed. What hurt was only that Kierkegaard had thought I was really pleased with the coat.

On another occasion there was something from his side that hurt me in a similar or more definite way. Without betraying any curiosity, yet with a certain inquisitiveness, he once asked how things went with the production of each issue of *The Corsair*, and I told him very simply. It seemed to surprise him that there was no secrecy at all, and he asked: But how do you have such good information about what goes on in the city? —I answered, which was the truth, that I knew no more than all the others, that I just read the papers and gave my own observations. —But do you not get many anonymous contributions?[211] he asked. —Yes, but very few are worth anything, and most of them are very bad. —How is that? —Because they are information of a private kind. It is repulsive to get such statements even about intimate family relations; there was even one case of a man and his wife informing on each other to me. —I do not want to hear anything about it, shouted Kierkegaard. —That hurt me, for it seemed as if he imputed to me the intention of divulging something to him and implied that I was of a crasser nature than he. It did not prevent him from later asking me to tell him once more about *The Corsair*, and especially about something between me and Pastor Visby. V. had published a prayerbook[212] for prisoners in penitentiaries, and I had criticized it severely. After some time he came to me and said: But, in God's name, how can you attack me that way? You do not even know me! —I replied that I attacked only his name, which was on the title page of the book, just as I, according to the circumstances, attacked others whose names I found in books or in the papers. —Are you aware, asked Kierkegaard, how amusing that story is? —Of that I was unaware.

During these meetings the question was always on the tip of my tongue: What is the task you have assigned me? What is comic writing? But neither did I have the right talents for raising the question, nor did his personality make such an approach easier. [*I, pp. 278-80*]

Then P. L. Møller[213] loomed up. [*I, p. 297*]

[*In* The Corsair, *no. 125, February 10, 1843, Goldschmidt wrote a piece, "The Europe-Weary"* (De Europa-trætte), *which P. L. Møller called a "Cooper-like story"*[214] *and liked very much.*]

It came over me like a fairy tale, a miracle. What had stood before me as unattainable—although, properly understood, it lay as a germ in the first issue of *The Corsair*—I had suddenly achieved without knowing it; like a sleepwalker I had fulfilled the Kierkegaardian task, had produced a piece of comic writing.[215] [*I, pp. 305-06*]

Under the name Victor Eremita, Kierkegaard published *Either/Or*. How P. L. Møller had read and understood the book, I cannot say, and I have difficulty in remembering my own conception. But I think we more or less agreed that Victor Eremita was the most brilliant Greek to emerge again on the modern scene.[216] There was a wealth of thought, wit, irony, mastery, especially the last. He was masterly in everything and could himself be Either/Or, Both/And, if not personally, then in his thought. I vaguely remember that Møller already had reservations and maintained that there was more fantasy than flesh and blood, but that was something I could not really follow and left to the genuine or proper masters to decide. On my own initiative, I wrote the somewhat nebulous and turgid—but also excited—eulogy on the book in *The Corsair* of March 10, 1843.[217]

At the same time, I had been presented with a flask of rare Italian wine, and I wrote an invitation to Victor Eremita and P. L. Møller to come and drink it with me. Obviously the letter could not be sent to Victor Eremita, because even then he was a character S. Kierkegaard did not officially acknowledge and whom I had not absolutely identified with him, either, but established rather by reconstruction. But I sent it along with the invitation to Møller so that he would know which guest would be present, even though invisibly, and so that he would come "garlanded in the Greek mode and in festive spirits." [*I, pp. 318-19*]

The phrase about the fundamental injustice of society[218] was well suited to a youthful, abstruse idea that one's own distinctive individuality had a special, an absolute right over against all the others, the bourgeois; it was in good favor and was ordained to happiness when it strove for poetry and produced intellectual fireworks. Without knowing or wishing to do so, S. Kierkegaard contributed to this, namely, by breaking his engagement.[219] The event illustrated the artistic right of personality over against every bond. It was just as with Goethe, who had thrown over Friederike in Sesenheim,[220] and her reward for the sacrifice and loss of life was that she came to live eternally in literature or the history of literature. Strange things are also told about Kierkegaard, perhaps untrue, but they are told and have the appearance of probability. One time he is supposed to have taken his fiancée to the theater to hear Mozart's *Don Giovanni*,[221] and after a few bars of the overture he led her out again with the remark that this was sufficient: for a proper comprehension of the opera or for the proper mood, there was enough in the few bars. Mood, to get into the mood, that seemed to be the main business of life![222] Kierkegaard became the chief for the esthetic view of life, most certainly not personally, in and through his personality, but through a recasting of him and of Victor Eremita, "the victorious hermit." [*I, pp. 323-24*]

The book[223] occasioned a renewed acquaintance or a new encounter of special significance with S. Kierkegaard, who once again appeared on the streets.[224] I use this expression because at the time it seemed as if he had disappeared and would come out just to do an intellectual errand and then would disappear again. He asked me which character in the book I myself considered best portrayed, and when I gave the opinion that it was the hero, he said: No, it is the mother. —During the writing I had not given her a second thought. —That is just what I thought! he said, elated. He continued: Of course you have read the review in *Fædrelandet*. What do you think is the point? —Presumably it is simply to praise the book. —No, the point is that there are men who want to see in you the author of *En Jøde* but not the editor of *The Corsair*—*The Corsair* is P. L. Møller.[225]

I almost shouted aloud out of fright on Møller's behalf, since I knew both how wrong it was and how unpleasant and damaging such an opinion would be for him. I objected and reminded Kirkegaard how I had told him about *The Corsair* long before I knew Møller, but he smiled, shook his head, and left me.

Møller became dejected when I told him this and laid it upon me as a point of honor to repeat and repeat again the truth to Kierkegaard, which I did as soon as the occasion arose, but the philosopher did not yield and merely said that there were reports in the world more accurate than any police report. —I asked: How in this case can you have a more reliable report than mine? —He laughed in his curious way, and I was tempted to take the whole thing as a joke, but when I gave Møller an account of my misfired errand, he took the matter more seriously and said that it would definitely become a great obstacle for him if such an opinion spread among the public and that it therefore would be best for us to break off our association for a time, which he did, but not altogether, as will be seen later,[226] and without being able to avoid a collision with Kierkegaard. [*I, pp. 371-73*]

[P. L. Møller] considered the meaning and goal of his life to be an appointment as professor of esthetics here at the university after Oehlenschlæger . . . it may also seem mysterious that Møller, precisely when he was so occupied, should be led or should lead himself into a collision with S. Kierkegaard. Nevertheless, the two main threads can be rendered somewhat visible, and finally light can be thrown upon the matter if it is said—and now I say something under which I myself, like many others, must bow my head deeply—that when Møller went to pieces on account of the blow against Kierkegaard, it was the result, on the deepest level, of the fact that S. Kierkegaard stood in a finer, purer, higher relation to women. This relation of good fortune or of grace or, as I call it, of nemesis,[227] along with whatever organic peculiarity to which it may have been joined, I regard as the basis and not the consequence of his enthusiasm, his religious enthusiasm as well. What we essentially are, we are by virtue of what in that respect has been maintained or redeemed in us.

But what motivated Møller to battle with Kierkegaard, and not merely in an ordinary article or treatise but in a critical presentation that seemed to give the impression of being a manifesto originating at or supported by Sorø Academy?[228] First and foremost, of course, an inner impulse, an antipathy, a disagreement with S. Kierkegaard and a conviction of being able to rebuff him with some Hegelian philosophy and practical intellectual competence. But in addition to that the professorship was involved, not only in the way a prospective university teacher must show himself to be master of something significant but also in an extraordinary way. When Møller came out of his resignation and solitariness, when he, with the vitality and hope one has in one's thirtieth year [*1844*], cast aside the thought of being a dislocated proletarian, he grasped for the world with both hands and wanted to be worldly wise. He wanted to give the appearance of not standing alone but of having surrounded himself, like other intelligent folk, with friends and thereby of fulfilling the craving for esteem. With his plan for *Gæa*—the yearbook that was supposed to create a seat of honor in literature and facilitate a move from there to the professorship—and with some help, notably from Oehlenschlæger, he moved to Sorø and found, it seems, a cordial reception, and in Copenhagen it appeared as if his main strength was in Sorø. It was a kind of cunning that perhaps only poets have; they are so simple-minded that in their craftiness they become both ludicrous and pathetic as a result. Without really committing any indiscretion by naming professors from Sorø, Møller created the impression that such gentlemen seemed to contribute their authority, and in many respects the whole work was splendid, perhaps the most lively and energetic he had written. But he had caught a Tartar.

S. Kierkegaard cracked down on him[229] with such vehemence, used such singular language, created or seemed to create such an effect upon the public that the professorship, instead of being brought closer by *Gæa*, was placed at an incalculable distance, and during the conflict itself Møller was seized with a longing to leave Denmark, which he satisfied a little later.[230] [*I, pp. 409-14*]

Immediately after the publication of *Gæa*, S. Kierkegaard was again "visible on the streets,"[231] and when he met me, according to custom, he took me along. As yet I had not read the entire book, in particular had not read the piece about him, and I asked without guile whether he had seen the new book and what he thought about it. What I really wanted to know, of course, was what he thought of "My Uncle's Lumberyard" [*Min Onkels Tømmerplads*].[232] Well, yes, he replied, and talked about my story with some praise. But otherwise he was more silent than usual, obviously his thoughts were elsewhere; perhaps he also believed that my naiveté was feigned.

Evidence of what had preoccupied his thoughts came quickly, namely, in his extremely violent article[233] in *Fædrelandet*, signed by Frater Taciturnus, against *The Corsair* and P. L. Møller. Møller's article in *Gæa* was called, among other things, a "loathsome *Corsair* attack," and Møller himself was called a vagabond and with the greatest recklessness was represented as the real *Corsair* and the evil in it: "where P. L. Møller is, *The Corsair* is."[234]

At that time it was still not customary to cast aside certain literary rules of honor,[235] and not a few were offended by this outburst, which was either an arbitrary declaration or an excited, arbitrary breach of anonymity. But it was most striking to me, who so clearly and repeatedly had initiated Kierkegaard into the actual situation and so urgently had requested him not to hold an opinion that was unfair to Møller and also could do him harm.

Very soon I met him again, but now he had taken a strange, although presumably under the circumstance necessary, position. He adhered strictly to anonymity. Just as I, of course, did not dare to know or say that he was Frater Taciturnus, so he did not want to know that I had anything at all to do with the editing of *The Corsair*. We could talk about Frater Taciturnus, P. L. Møller, and *The Corsair* as matters entirely unrelated to us, and it was without any personal predilection that he sided with Frater Taciturnus and I with the other side. The way in which he began the conversation established this tone immediately; I understood it and maintained it. It was a little light comedy that we played. But, because of the impersonality of the situation, it followed that I could not manage to say to him: I have told you this and that; why have you nevertheless made the declaration against Møller? On the other hand, I could and did say that Frater Taciturnus, however right he might be otherwise, on that point had done an injustice and inflicted an injury. To this, Kierkegaard replied that Frater Taciturnus's right must be seen from a higher point of view. I said that I could not see his higher point of view, and then we talked for a moment about other things.

Now I, too, of course, had to write on the affair.[236] Such a hard blow could not be struck against *The Corsair* without a turnabout, and presumably in that respect something unpleasant would necessarily arise, even though Kierkegaard in our personal meetings had made everything so impersonal, but I put no stock in that. What I wanted most of all at the moment was to show him that I had fulfilled the task he once had assigned to me:[237] to do comic writing. In my opinion, even now, the task was successfully carried out in that I strictly limited the question and gave a sprightly account of the discovery at last of the secret editor of *The Corsair*.[238] This editor resembled the famous Venetian bandit Coronato the Terrible, and although he carried out his acts with the greatest daring, more or less in broad daylight, the renowned police of Venice still had not been able to track him down or form the slightest notion of who he was. But in the moonlight one evening, while having a glass of punch with "The Silent Brother," Frater Taciturnus, he opened his heart and confided to him his secret, yet with the injunction that he must not divulge it, and the Silent Brother had sworn he would be silent. But now Coronato had written a criticism of him, and Frater Taciturnus felt no longer obliged to be silent but went to *Fædrelandet* and told the whole story: Now I will identify Coronato publicly and at the same time demolish *The Corsair*. *Fædrelandet* was pleased with it, and Frater Taciturnus was pleased, saying: I am so happy that I will imagine that I am giving a poor man a dollar.[239]

When I saw this last remark again in the proofs, it struck me as alien, almost as something that flowed from my pen without my knowing it. But I let it stand, because it seemed both witty and pertinent and seemed to be true. It conformed to an opinion floating around that Kierkegaard did not stand in a genuine personal relation to his writings or to his life but carried on everything as a thought-experiment. Was it really so? The answer is not easy; as a general, approximate notion it was already plausible with the publication of *Either/Or*. In the course of the intervening years there had come to be something about him that gave him the appearance of standing at a distance, observing ironically, like one who with conscious superiority—a superiority that seemed to be based both on his intellect and his reputed wealth—could understand everything, also all cares and sorrows, and give the word but not share it. That could, in fact, be a pretense that would vanish if one followed him into his cubbyhole, but who could do that, and how much trouble do we take in that respect with regard to each other before it is too late? Egotistically preoccupied as we generally are, we accept the rumor floating in the air, which, through our arbitrary, superficial association with others, we ourselves broadcast and which, according to the proverb "Where there is smoke, there is fire," does have some truth in it and seems to give pain to an individual. With some malice, I took it to be true and on my own responsibility became an instrument for that indefinite floating rumor and got my pleasure out of it. Later I have noted that others who have written about or against me have been instruments in a similar way for something unjust—just floating in the air.

At that time the bite in my account diminished behind the joking fantasy about Coronato and Frater Taciturnus, and I was so satisfied with it—so childishly satisfied, it may be said—that the next time I met Kierkegaard I asked him whether the article in *The Corsair* was comic writing.[240] —He replied with a long, drawn-out No. —Why not? —Because the question cannot be put. In the first place, it lacks respect. —Respect for what? —For Frater Taciturnus's higher right. —There again we stuck to our positions, and after a few words about other things we parted.

His real reply came in *Fædrelandet*, a new vehement article[241] in which he called *The Corsair*, among other things, "a public prostitute." When the paper was delivered, Møller himself was with me. I read the article and burst into laughter. Møller took the paper, read it, grew very pale, and said: You can laugh at what will come of this! This dirty mix-up, this confusing of my *Gæa* with *The Corsair*, this never would have happened if I had never come to you.

The whole thing took an unexpected bitter turn. Nevertheless, I could not forget the comic element that seemed to be present in Kierkegaard's exaggeration and in the passion with which he maintained that he was a martyr and had wished to be a martyr at the hands of *The Corsair*. If the affair were judged to be an ordinary literary controversy, according to the humor and fantasy of the articles, I would even dare let the matter go to a jury.

After the replies, which I wrote myself, some accompanied by cartoons, my colleagues carried on, and thus the affair was constantly raked up, with side-cuts at him. To what extent this was distasteful to me, I cannot say. My impression of the whole business first emerged clearly at a crucial moment.

As long as the name Kierkegaard was never mentioned, there was still a tinge of impersonality about the controversy. He himself wrote pseudonymously, and he was attacked under one of the many names he himself had invented; consequently, he could not personally step out of the fiction in which he had surrounded our conversations, and when he met me—which happened rarely now—it was with the same courtesy as before, although neither he nor I showed a desire for conversation.

But then he publicly named himself Victor Eremita, Frater Taciturnus,[242] etc., etc., and immediately thereafter he met me on Myntergade and passed me by with an intense, very bitter glance, without wanting to give a greeting or to be greeted.

In the bitterness of that glance, just as in Kierkegaard's entire personal appearance and manner, there was something that verged on the comic. But this vanished and gave place to the loftiness, the ideality that were also present in his personality. There was something about that intense, wild glance that drew the curtain, as it were, away from the higher right[243] that Kierkegaard had asserted earlier and that I had not been able, rather, was unwilling, to see, although I did indeed suspect it. It accused and depressed me: *The Corsair* had won the battle, but I myself had acquired a false no. 1. Nevertheless, a protest also arose in my mind during that moment packed with meaning: I was not one to be looked down upon, and I could prove it. On my way home I decided that I would give up *The Corsair*, and when I told them at home that I was going to do it, they said, Praise God—so happy but so little surprised, as if they had known about it before I did.

It so happened that the first stranger I told about my decision was the same one I had spoken with on the top of Skamlingsbanken[244] and who had offered a wager, a sensible, practical man some years older than I. He reminded me of the proverb that one should not throw out the dirty water before one has the clean water. But there is a youthfulness that need not die with the years and that shows itself, among other ways, in throwing out the water as soon as one thinks it is dirty. His misgivings on my behalf, however, were well grounded. During the last year, *The Corsair* had brought in 4,000 rix-dollars, but I had not saved any of it and at most had a few hundred rix-dollars in addition to a good library. *The Corsair* itself was actually not salable. As soon as I left it, anyone could take the name and continue it. But Flinch, the wood engraver, thought that if I would turn it over to him he could give me 1,500 rix-dollars for it. Reitzel bought a volume of short stories[245] I had written, and thus I gathered together around 4,000 rix-dollars, which I divided, and with one-half I left the country[246] "in order to be done with witticism and to learn something."

I was going on twenty-seven years of age and had edited *The Corsair* for six years. [I, pp. 421-30]

At this time [*December 1847*] Møller was about to travel.[247] Since that evening during the Kierkegaard battle we had not seen much of each other,[248] but of course I looked him up when I returned home,[249] and inasmuch as it was entirely clear that we had neither personally nor willfully done each other any harm, everything was fine between us, although more distant, cooler than before.

On one of the last days of the year, I visited him [Møller] in order to say goodbye—because his departure, which for a long time had been postponed from day to day, finally seemed necessarily at hand—and on that day he was in an especially bad mood. It was still the time when I knew so little about him and understood so little of his whole frame of mind. Meanwhile, it was he who led the conversation.

He congratulated me on now being able to be quoted by Bishop Mynster,[250] yes, in time I would be canonized, and—who knows—the faithful would make pilgrimages to the shrine that concealed my Christianly tempered bones. It is difficult to defend oneself against such congratulations—that I had had to learn for myself during the *Corsair* period—and when I nevertheless tried, he said that nothing would help, that by giving up *The Corsair* I had betrayed myself; it was not natural for me to pursue some "positive good" in public life here at home; the caustic Jewish nature demanded hate, and in hate I had and have my strength. His words had no trace of vulgar anti-Semitism—on the whole, Møller was far removed from that—but were more like a private, comradely conversation and in their quiet bitterness seemed to be based on an irrefutable world-historical fact. Neither were they totally novel at the time, just as they have not become outmoded; it is a view before which one can stand in embarrassment, justly accused, as it were, because there can be a likelihood in them—indeed, an element of truth, but a truth that on the whole and generally speaking is bound to be turned into an untruth.

To free myself from the impact his statement had on me, I shifted the format and asked him: What have you yourself accomplished by not choosing something positive? What effect, even if only literary, has your esthetics had on writing? Where is that for which we once hoped? —What do you have against my writing? —Then, as I remember, I criticized his writing, from "Arion"[251] to his most recently published poetry.[252] It is far worse to criticize a writer orally than in print; it more readily makes for bad blood. One word led to another, and we were a hair's breadth from becoming outright philistine enemies. Fortunately, at the very last moment, I reminded him of the alliance we two had made: that for the sake of the truth of literature we would, if necessary, oppose each other and keep ourselves young and strong in the process. With this reminder of a singular and yet genuine common youthfulness, the storm vanished, and with a kind of elation he said: "Well, let's fight, then! I can find occasion to say a lot on that score. Come on!"

I went home and wrote down almost verbatim what I had said but added my hopes for a bright and happy future as a result of his journey[253] and sent it to him. He sent it back, and it was printed in *Nord og Syd*,[254] Vol. I, p. 166, with the note that it had been communicated to him prior to his departure. [*I, pp. 434-36*]

SELECTED ENTRIES FROM KIERKEGAARD'S JOURNALS AND PAPERS PERTAINING TO ARTICLES, THE *CORSAIR* AFFAIR, AND "AN OPEN LETTER"

Articles

Summons[255]

That the police adjutant must be on the spot whenever the watchman whistles, that the fire chief must get up whenever the alarm goes off, that the censor has no quiet day or night as soon as it pleases an author to set him in motion by his mental activity—I, too, find it to be quite in order that these men receive therefore an appropriate wage, enjoy glory and honor in society, are loved and respected by the entire community. But that I, an unemployed man, who in my life unite what is rarely seen united, have neither business affairs nor wages, that I, without any compensation whatsoever, must be disturbed in my quiet inactivity every time it pleases a joker to attribute to me the authorship of things of which no one wants to be the author—this I do not find to be in order, no more than if someone for a joke were to hang on my door the sign of the police or of the fire chief or to persuade people to think that I am the censor in order to create for me the inconvenience of opening the door at every moment in the day in order to explain that I am neither the one nor the other.

What the majority of readers probably never knew and the others have long since forgotten, what I myself would have forgotten in a short time if the aftereffects did not still pain me, is at this moment still all too much alive in my memory: that six months ago, driven to extremities by the informing voices that denounced me as the author of various articles, I disclaimed in a solemn declaration all association with these pieces, that in order to secure for myself a carefree and undisturbed future, I "begged every reader never to regard me as an author of anything that does not bear my name,"*[256] that as a result of this step I have for a long time now met with sharp glances, derisive looks, mocking faces, which to me were inexplicable until spoken and written expressions made it clear beyond all doubt that people had seen through me, had seen that it was vanity that had led me to bring myself to attention in an unseemly way, that there was actually only one person who regarded me as capable of being the author of those remarkable articles. The mistake was unpleasant for me; the mortification that followed, I have sought to overcome, and I perhaps would have succeeded if the same story had not started all over again. During the past fortnight I have heard that an article in *Ny Portefeuille*[257] has been fathered upon me, two letters in *Berlingske Tidende*[258] (or just one), a letter in *Fædrelandet*,[259] and the big work *Either/Or*.[260] My situation is just as painful as formerly, is even more painful, since it is a repetition. It is just as difficult as before, is even more difficult, since by experience I have learned the distressing consequences that warn me against every step, although a step nevertheless seems necessary, a step that would be just as dangerous for me as it would be for the man Jean Paul[261] tells about, if he, standing on one leg, read a sign saying, "A fox-trap is set here," put his other foot on the ground. If I declare that I have no part either in those articles or in that work, I run the risk of seeing later that people only wanted to get the best of me, that they will again mock me because I am so vain as to believe that anybody could seriously suppose that I, in one way or another, was capable of writing those articles, a book of around eight hundred pages, or to write half of it, if one assumes that there are two authors. If I remain silent, then the daily scene repeats itself, then in some way I must do the honors of an author, receive courtesies and lying-in visits appropriate to an author, endure an ironic smile that gives me a presentiment of what I can expect if I am so imprudent as to

* See *Fædrelandet*.

disclaim the authorship. In order to avoid, if possible, this difficult situation, I have decided to do what I hereby do: to call upon Victor Eremita to abandon his pseudonymity so that I can live in peace and at ease, to call upon him to do this as soon as possible, so that it will not be said later that I have pretended to be an author, although I myself know that in this respect I am as innocent as a child born yesterday.

As far as the newspaper articles are concerned, I would wish that the writers would do the same, but since the matter seems almost forgotten because of *Either/Or*, I will not call upon them to do what I, if they did it, would always regard as a proof of the noble rectitude that has sympathy for the calamities of others.

Copenhagen, Feb. 22, 1843

S. KIERKEGAARD
Magister Artium

P.S. I have placed my summons in this paper[262] so that Victor Eremita, if he does not live here in the city, will receive it as quickly as possible, and in conclusion I request that he not delay longer than is absolutely necessary.—*Pap.* IV B 19 February 22, 1843

There is something curious about my little secretary, Mr. Christensen.[263] I wager that he is the one who in various ways is scribbling pamphlets and things in the newspapers, for I often hear the echo of my own ideas, not in the way I am accustomed to writing them but in the way I casually toss them out orally. And I who was so kind to him, paid him well, conversed with him for hours, for which I also paid, for the simple reason that he should not feel mortified and humiliated because his poverty made it necessary for him to be a copyist. I made him an initiate in the whole affair, cast a veil of mystery over the whole thing, made the time as pleasant as possible in every way. —The little article in *Portefeuille*[264] a few days before *Either/Or* was published is certainly by him. It really was not very nice of him. After all, he could have confided in me and told me that he hankered to be an author, but his authorship does not have a good conscience. He no doubt notices that I have changed a little toward him, although I was just as polite and considerate as before. On the other hand, I have stopped his inquisitive snooping around my room; he must be kept at arm's length; I hate all plagiarizing pirates.—*JP* V 5688 (*Pap.* IV A 141) *n.d.*, 1843

A Literary Unpleasantness in Berlingske Tidende, *no.*

In *Berlingske T.*, no. ,²⁶⁵ under the rubric "Literature,"* I find my name brought in such close association with the authorship of various pseudonymous works that the article, which also touches upon a little book of mine, is headed by my name. The fictional opening (what a curious effect is produced by a prosaic colon) is continued in a fictional way in that the reviewer of those books and the exhibiter of my person, with an ingenious allusion to oriental tales (with which the article, given the absence of any other similarity, has a certain similarity because of its ahistorical character), assumes that I must be in the possession of a magic wand—if I, as rumor says, have written so many pseudonymous books. Yes—if! But, now, if not! Oh, so I have no magic wand. Lacking it, I can be of service to that reviewer only by way of a cordial and sincere wish: that all clumsy reviewers be kept on Blocksberg.²⁶⁶

It is indeed true that a rumor says, or, more correctly, has said (because after a while one does grow weary of talking about such things), that I am the author. But from this it does not follow that what the rumor says is true. To print a rumor does not make it more true, and if an attempt is made to deceive a little by means of the form, this simply shows the uncertainty—that the report is indeed a rumor. What, then, is the purpose of it all, and what are the consequences for me? I have always regarded pseudonymity as a bill of divorcement between an author and his work and therefore do not regard

---

* Note. The article is not from the honored editorial staff of this paper but is contributed.

myself as justified, any more than I regard the reviewer as justified, in making any attempt to join what is to be separated. Neither could it occur to me to want to make a concession to that reviewer, on the occasion of his writing and his colon, by wanting to disclaim the authorship—that would be making too much of too little—yes, it would also be an impossibility, since he speaks indefinitely of many pseudonymous books, and consequently I cannot know which ones he means. Nor could it occur to me to summon the pseudonymous authors to give their names in order to save me, for I regard such a summons as a literary attack. Nor could it occur to me to disclaim authorship of that article in the *Berlingske Tidende*, even though in a certain sense it might be necessary, for that kind reviewer does not seem to be dialectically aware of the confusion he produces by wanting to betray something about the name of a pseudonym while he himself remains unnamed.—*Pap.* VI B 185 *n.d.*, 1845

The *Corsair* Affair

DRAFTS OF WRITINGS FOR POSSIBLE PUBLICATION

A *Request to* The Corsair[267]

Sing sang resches Tubalcain—which translated means: Cruel and bloodthirsty *Corsair*, high and mighty Sultan, you who hold the lives of men like a plaything in your mighty hand and as a whim in the fury of your invective, Oh, let me move you to compassion, curtail these sufferings—slay me, but do not make me immortal! High and mighty Sultan, in your quick wisdom consider what it would not take long for the paltriest of all those you have slain to see, consider what it means to become immortal, and particularly to become that through the testimonial of *The Corsair.* Oh, what cruel grace and mercy to be forever pointed to as an inhuman monster because *The Corsair* inhumanly had spared him! But, above all, not this—that I shall never die! Uh, such a death penalty is unheard of.* I get weary of life just to read it. What a cruel honor and distinction to have no one be moved by my womanly wailing: This will kill me, this will be the death of me—but everybody laughs and says: He cannot die. Oh, let me move you to compassion; stop your lofty, cruel mercy; slay me like all the others.

VICTOR EREMITA

(Here perhaps could be added the words at the end of the postscript to *Either/Or*,[268] which is in the tall cupboard closest to the window.)

In margin: * Slay me so I may live with all the others you have slain, but do not slay me by making me immortal.—*JP* V 5853 (*Pap.* VI B 192) *n.d.*, 1845

Addition to Pap. VI B 192:

Have no fear—why spare me, I have no wife to sigh for me, perhaps to grieve . . . . . over the husband you slay, no beloved to feel the drubbing more devastatingly, no children whose tenderness makes the blow heavier for them than for the father—I have no legitimately acquired distinction in society that can be temporarily embittering to see wasted, I have no famous family name so that an entire family will suffer by the attack upon one single member—spare instead everyone who has anyone who perhaps cannot help but feel violated even though the one who is wounded disdains the attack . . . . . —*JP* V 5854 (*Pap.* VI B 193) *n.d.*, 1845

Deleted from draft of "The Activity of a Traveling Esthetician and How He Still Happened to Pay for the Dinner," 46:1-18:

Finally, a wish: [*text*: would that I might only get into *The Corsair* soon. It is really hard for a poor author to be so singled out in Danish literature . . . he is the only one who is not abused there]. Yes, Victor Eremita has even had to experience the hitherto unheard-of disgrace—of being attacked?*—no, of being immortalized—by *The Corsair*.[269] No doubt it would be highly desirable that this disgrace to literature did not exist at all, that there be no literary publication making money by prostitution, for what is a woman's loveliness if it is for sale for money,** and what is a bit of talent when it is in the service of vile profit†; but if it does exist, then it is more desirable to be in the company of or in agreement with what one respects, even though one disapproves of some particulars, than to sit in the place of honor among the despicable.

In margin: * it is an honor.
In margin: ** without such an author's talent.
In margin: † without a whore's beauty—*JP* V 5860 (*Pap.* VII^1 B 1) *n.d.*, 1845

Penciled addition to draft of "The Activity of a Traveling Esthetician . . . ," 46:8-10:

ubi spiritus ibi ecclesia
ubi P.L.M. [Møller] ibi The Corsair
—*JP* V 5861 (*Pap.* VII^1 B 5) *n.d.*, 1845

Addition to draft of "The Activity of a Traveling Esthetician . . . ," 46:4-5, 20-22:

Hilarius Bookbinder,[270] my superior, has been flattered in *The Corsair*.

FRATER TACITURNUS
Chief of Part Three in
Stages on Life's Way.
—*JP* V 5862 (*Pap.* VII^1 B 6) *n.d.*, 1845

The Dialectic of Contemptibleness[271]

To have to acquire the principle for one's action in the moment of urgency and action is too late: the end result is neither principle nor action. This is why a youth is dedicated to much beautiful reflecting on life for which he as yet has no use; he is practiced in using, purely ideally, much advice about venturing and in suffering many a mitigating solution* for which he** still has no use. And it is the desire and hope of the

---

* against life's spiritual trials
** in actuality

teacher and well-intentioned adults that he eventually will use this counsel in the right way, as coolly and calmly as in the beautiful contemplative time when youth enthusiastically understands what is noble and sublime.

Thus I, too, will now think about or think through the dialectic of contemptibleness, for, after all, I am a young man and have not even remotely experienced anything like being the object of persecution by what is contemptible, I who live happily in my father's house, enthralled by beautiful recollections, resenting no one, and scarcely the object of anyone's slander. But I have been told by my elders that contemptibleness nevertheless exists in the world and that it is in fact possible (even if I shudder at having to go out into such a world) that sometime, many years hence, I may be subjected to considerable whispered slander, the annoyance of offensive gossip, or even the concentrated cowardly persecution of raucous contemptibleness—for I have heard about this from one of my elders. And it is indeed possible, even if it is almost impossible for me to believe it, which I dare say is why this older person said to me: My young friend, it is only *all too* certain—thereby wanting to tell me that he did not wish to believe it, either. But he told me that there were men who had to live on, year after year, knowing how much evil was being said about them, how their character was being attacked and their capabilities envied; and this, he said, was minor and, however reprehensible, yet sometimes excusable, but sometimes contemptibleness could *ex professo* [intentionally] outright choose a person as its victim. You see, I ought to think all this through so that sometime in the persistent daily gossip over the years, sometime in the urgency of danger, I can consider the dialectic of contemptibleness as coolly and calmly as I do now, I, a young person who, like a young maiden, has no acquaintance with the actual world.

When a man says: It is shameful to have to put up with abuse by a contemptible person, and he says this in anger, he very likely believes he is saying something very reasonable, and many who hear it will perhaps think the same. And yet he actually is stating a tautology, actually nothing. To be abused by a contemptible person is really not shameful; for the person abused there can be no shame, and in his contemptibleness the abuser is without shame—thus it cannot be called shame on his part, since it is only a further manifestation and actualization of his contemptibleness. However, it would be shameful of an estimable person, and this is what the man would say: It is shameful that such a worthy person abuses me this way, since I am innocent. It is shameful for me simply because he generally is a good man, and it is shameful for him because he generally is a good man. — Many grieved at Socrates' death sentence, but Xantippe was strident and said: How can it be that an innocent man should suffer this. Socrates answered: Would you rather have me guilty?[272] So also in this matter of being abused by a contemptible person or by a generally good man.

If contemptibleness is unable to insult by abusing, is it then unable to insult at all? No, it cannot—that is, if there is no opposite to abusing. But if there is such a thing, then, quite consistently, it will be able to insult by it. What is its opposite? It is to commend, to praise,[273] to admire.

So if a man said: It is shameful that I have to put up with being praised by a contemptible person, and said this calmly and coolly, many would find this strange talk. Perhaps it would also seem so if I imagined it happening in the confusion and busy urgency of actuality. But whether or not I will be able to think and talk this way in an actual situation—and I have often heard from my elders that actuality changes a person, that what looks so easy for the young man in contemplation or the young girl in her enthusiasm is not so easy in actuality—as I see it now, this is the only consistent conclusion, and I will once again convince myself by thinking the matter through in a hypothetical situation, and I am positive that I will convince everyone of it, as convinced as I am now when nothing* disturbs the proper movement of the dialectic.

* no actuality

—*Pap.* VII¹ B 9 *n.d.*, 1846

The dialectic of contemptibleness, a household remedy for internal use as a mild discutient.—*Pap.* VII¹ B 10 *n.d.*, 1846

Continuation of Pap. VII¹ B 10:

VII¹ B 11 173

I will suppose that there was a city where the prostitutes made a practice of abusing all the decent girls once a week, but there was one young girl who was never abused; on the contrary, she was acclaimed and praised.²⁷⁴ As young girls do, she would throw herself in tears on her mother's neck and say: Oh, Mother, why can't I be abused, too? All my friends look at me suspiciously because I am praised. But then, as mothers do, her mother would admonish patience and say, "Dear child, one does not always get what one wishes. The good often fails to be appreciated in the world, as you are now finding out here in the city where we live by not being abused by those women." But, finally, as mothers do, the mother would heed the girl's wish and request of the persons involved that her daughter might also be abused.²⁷⁵ For in the ordinary world it* is not good to be censured, and also in that city it was not good to be censured by everybody, either. Oh, no, and there, where the respectable matrons judged the behavior of the young girls, there it was not good, not good at all, to be censured—how should respectable matrons demean themselves that way—no, it was dreadful merely to be the object of the slightest criticism. Where the prostitutes were concerned, however, it was desirable to be abused. But it would be inconsistent of those prostitutes to get angry at the teenage girl, for they certainly must see that it was they themselves who had reversed matters and that the young girl, far from crediting herself with the power to force them to abdicate, was trying to identify herself with the prescribed practice in such matters in that city where, as was said, it was not an honor to be censured or even to merit rebuke, but it most certainly was in this situation involving the prostitutes and the young girl.

VII¹ B 11 174

So also here. But, in actuality, might it not appear different to the serene mind of a young person who does not know the world and has not been upset by any humiliation or insult? No, impossible. But could there not be something plausible in it? Yes, that is certainly possible.

In margin: * generally speaking

If, for example, contemptibleness had talent. Indeed, I have heard an elder say that it is inconceivable* that an appreciable talent could sink so low as to be in the service of what is contemptible, inconceivable also because the contemptibleness would have to live in a grand illusion, one that only spite and impotence and darkened understanding could sustain: that its attack actually was an insult. Contemptibleness would have to want to be abusive and then be the only one sufficiently stupid to believe that it was being insulting. A curious kind of madness, unlike the kind in which an insane man fancies that he is the Emperor Napoleon, for the madness of contemptibleness is twofold: it also believes that everybody else agrees with its illusion. Yet let us assume that the talent is the greatest possible, the greatest possible in terms of being capable of entering the service of what is contemptible. What then? Would this change the dialectic of contemptibleness? By no means. It would simply make the contemptible even more loathsome. To be sure, worthiness cannot invest a man with talent, but contemptibleness can and ought to let one forget that the contemptible one has talent, for contemptibleness is related to the essential, talent to the accidental.[276] Modesty and chastity certainly cannot make a girl beautiful, but beauty cannot make a harlot beautiful, simply because she is essentially unbeautiful, whereas the chaste and modest girl lacks beauty only accidentally. And whereas they who are fond of the chaste girl say: It is almost a shame that she did not become beautiful,** one says of the other woman: Would that she had not become beautiful.

What if contemptibleness had money? This, the elder has said, was often the case—what then? Could wealth and fine clothes and great banquets, could all these alter the dialectic of contemptibleness? By no means. They could only accentuate it all the more forcefully, for in poverty contemptibleness wears a mask, so to speak, and has the protection of an excuse, but wealthy contemptibleness is stark naked.[†]

In margin: * and that one never saw it in actuality
In margin: ** this lovable girl
[†] *In margin*: and just as Plato[277] detected pride expressly in Diogenes' tat-

What if contemptibleness is feared and has power? To be sure, the elder has said that it has never reached that point in the world. But I may, after all, imagine the worst without in the remotest manner worrying about any actual situation that might keep me from thinking the thought through and even though I am glad that such a thing can never happen. Would power in the remotest way alter the dialectic of contemptibleness? By no means, for when suppressed and downtrodden, contemptibleness is in a way almost defended; when it has power, it is completely defenseless.[*]

These are my thoughts on the matter. Of course, I am well aware, as the elder says, that it looks simple to an idealistic, inexperienced young man sitting and thinking about such things but that it is quite different in the confusion of life when the passions mount. Therefore, it is good for me to think about this in time, before having to be tested by experiencing it** year after year, or before insurgent contemptibleness makes it completely necessary, for then I would scarcely have the tranquillity I have at present in my ignorance of the world, the tranquillity to sit this way and think and write down my thoughts. No, then I shall have to consult what I have written. It makes me sad to think that sometime, perhaps many years from now, I shall take out this piece of paper and read what I then would be incapable not only of writing but even of understanding. But, away with negative fears of the distant future. I am still a young man, happy in the peacefulness of my paternal home, happy in never having been insulted by anyone—as far as I know.

But what if it happened? Would I join in the laughter at the cheap witticisms of contemptibleness? No, one shows that honor only to pure, innocent, essential wit, even if it touches

---

tered cloak, so one most readily detects contemptibleness in the environment of wealth.

[*] *In margin:* and just as Tacitus[278] detected the contemptible slave mind in the Jewish King Agrippa, because he exercised tyrannical power, so contemptibleness is always seen most readily when it possesses power.

In margin: ** if not an attack.

oneself. Would I be essentially aware of it, as if I were privy to it? No. I shall ponder the Socratic principle:[279] "What difference does it make if people slander a person in his absence; they are quite welcome to beat me up—in my absence." As for being affected, Holberg[280] teaches me that there is always a way out for an intelligent man, a way of wisdom that the defiant fool who just stands there does not know: to get out of the way. As for someone who is worse than a fool, I know that no one is so sure of having the sidewalk to herself as a prostitute[281]—that recognition she enjoys. But if I were extolled as was that young girl in that city, would I put up with it? No, I would regard it as treason against each and every good person who had been abused that anyone who respects the honor of the good should permit this confusion.

Yes, it is easy for a young man to have a tranquil mind; he does not know the world. But that is why he is initiated into many beautiful reflections and much learned counsel. That is what I have done now—oh, everything is so clear to me. I shall now put the date on this paper—January 7, 1846—so that sometime years hence, when it is my turn to be maligned,* accused by this one and that of this and of that, or even if loud-mouthed contemptibleness wants to finish me off, I may then be able to remember this.

A YOUNG MAN

Yesterday I found this manuscript on the street. Perhaps it may be of interest to someone to read it. If later in his life the young man is obliged to practice the dialectic of contemptibleness in the service of actuality, I only wish that he may be able to do it. Then it will make no difference if he is unable to think it through calmly and coolly and with youth's beautiful detached view of the dialectical—something he had regarded as quite difficult—to sit like Archimedes, lost in dialectical contemplation, but not, like Archimedes,[282] amid peril to his life to sit there lost in dialectical reflection, quietly sitting there absorbed in the dialectical, for the latter the young man can-

In margin: * year after year

not do, he cannot sit in the kettle on which the coppersmith is hammering, sit quietly absorbed in dialectical reflection.

—*Pap.* VII¹ B 11 January 7, 1846

Some Instructive Comments on The Corsair's *Drastic Errors*

No. 1

Since I am in the process just now of reading the proofs of a large work[283] that finally will be annexed to the whole project that began and continued through the pseudonymous works, although the book is more closely related to *Philosophical Fragments*, edited by me, and since I am not in the habit of taking on any new work while reading proof, I think it would betray myself and my position as a Danish author not to use this free time to protest what ought to have been protested long ago.

In everyday life, protest is promptly made and rules and regulations and preventive measures are immediately devised when the drinking water in the city is polluted or the baker uses contaminated flour, or even when the streetlights do not burn. But when polluted and contaminated food is offered for sale in the world of the spirit, when there seems to be an enormous customer demand, when, unfortunately, cheating in a sale does not involve getting too little for the money but much too much—then this goes on year after year unprotested, and unprotested it reaches such a peak that there is no transaction in the world of spirit comparable to its size in any way. In everyday life, when suddenly there is too much fresh fish* on the market, the police ban it;[284] but when tainted wit is offered for sale in such a mass that even the rare good witticism is spoiled by the encompassing mass, when it is offered for sale in such quantity that it is like everyday bread, then nothing happens. In civil life, a poor woman is severely punished for *seeming* to be begging from a passerby by making a gesture that really and truly cannot be intrusive. But when a private citizen is assaulted in print, at times regularly

In margin: * of a kind hard to digest

every week, by a maligner setting the dog, so to speak, of irresponsibility, coarse brutality, and passion on him, nothing happens. No, nothing happens; the only thing that happens is that the business flourishes, that few civil employees, even in the higher positions, and no artists and scholars in Denmark are paid on the same scale.

While even our celebrated authors find only a small market for their books, while even the newspapers, which always need to have a rather large circulation, are declining, with the exception of the *Berlingske Tidende*, an institution flourishes and thrives that has made a business of invective and is proud and lofty over having more subscribers than any other paper, yes, proud and lofty as a cliff for being unquestionably the most widely read paper in the entire country, read by all classes from the highest to the lowest, read by all ages, even by schoolchildren. Without any intimation of or depth enough for the comprehension of the difference between Paris and Copenhagen—that what in Paris, as one phenomenon among countless others, may have its significance as witty, but good-natured, envy of men with Continental influence and who in their distance from the attack remain ignorant or virtually ignorant of it—here personal attacks are made on private individuals. They are abused by turn and thereupon thrown to the attentions of the curious, if they are so inclined. Thus in a little city, in a limited context, in ordinary social contacts, in a limited literary scene that does not even have one single critical journal, there flourishes triumphantly a paper with an almost unheard-of number of subscribers,[285] a paper that lives on daring to say and do anything, a paper devoid of ideas, that caters to the passions and is out for profit—and benefits splendidly from the license of contemptibleness to be completely unconstrained.

Not only that, this paper has an office that receives the most private information by way of anonymous letters.[286] Here the question is raised not about the misuse of this information but of the danger in the existence of such a thing. The working class and the ordinary middle class regard *The Corsair* as a servant of a higher justice, as a spiritual counselor, in whom they may find consolation or seek it. It really is a strangely inverted situation. An employer, for example, treats his domestic servant too harshly. Oh, who does not have sympathy for the working class. I know that I do to the best of my ability. But now the servant turns for help to *The Corsair* office. Here no mitigating words of admonition[*] are heard, here the injured party is not initiated into any uplifting view of life that could teach him to bear a wrong with true human pride in humility before God. No, revenge, revenge. Then comes the attack by innuendo—and the injured party is revenged! Which, then, is worse—the sickness or the remedy! And what is the relation between the alleged protest of a misuse of power and the irreparable harm done by the misuse of impotence.

Yes, to top it all off they go even further and dare to announce in the paper that the invective is revenge. Just as the authorities at regular intervals examine and pass judgment on water and bread, so the paper at regular intervals subjects individuals to scrutiny and abuse. In disquieting transmissions attached to the text, we are informed of the reason why this or that person is being persecuted. Besides this, we hear that the rabble-champion will be lenient with this one and that one. Well, let us bow down, then, to this mighty power, let us hold banquets for him, let us offer him** the government. In Denmark one dares to speak freely about the king and the authorities, but beware of speaking freely about *The Corsair*!

And all this is answered with—silent contempt! Truly a curious answer, utterly unrelated to the charge and to the fact that everyone reads the paper! After all, this is not a matter of scholars and scientists fighting each other in big books that few read; it is not a paper eking out a miserable existence in a hole in the wall; nor is it a paper that in its dedication to the service of honor and responsibility insists on knowing what it writes and does. No, it is a paper that without comparison is absolutely the most widely read paper in the country—and that without comparison writes with unparalleled uncon-

[*] *In margin:* are said, for the injured party is initiated into a conspiracy instead.

In margin: ** a fortune and

straint—yes, without comparison, because using it for comparison would already be an insult to everything else written in Denmark. Civil authorities are scandalously kept at bay by means of street-corner loafers whom the executive agent by the letter of the law has to arrest and the solemn court has to judge. And while the authorities are thus shamelessly compelled to fool around jabbing at straw men,[287] *The Corsair* wheels and deals in people, holds their honor and serene private lives in its hands as if they were trifles. For all the rest of us are tied hand and foot, and the authorities have to put up with being made to look like fools lest they abuse their power, because in that case the voice of accusation would become strident. If anyone manifests opposition to *The Corsair* in writing, he must scrupulously observe the obligation of honor, responsibility, and decorum, or the voice of accusation will cry out against him in an appalling way. Give the most skillful fencer his sword, which he wields deftly, clearly winning every competition—but instead of a competitor set ferocious dogs on him, sic them on, but threaten him if he dares to use anything but legitimate fencing strokes, high strokes—criticize him if he tries to protect his legs[288]—and yet this is what the dogs grab at.[*][289]

As a climax to all this, they go on saying the same thing they said when *The Corsair* was an insignificant, little-read paper:[290] It's a small matter not worth talking about—this after *The Corsair* has become, if not the only paper, at least beyond question the one most talked about. No journalist raises his voice—it is not worth the effort. Let us rather say: The effort does not pay, for its reward is to be abused to death, its reward is to be misunderstood until men come to their senses, for then they will readily perceive what I perceive.

[*] *In margin*: Not one of those writing in *The Corsair* accepts the terms of honor and the commitments that every other Danish author respects, which people demand of him; not one is capable of writing a substantially witty article in which some clear, specific idea is reflected with dialectical clarity and a mature view of life in the beautiful refracted light of steady, more deeply meditating wit.

If I paid no attention, in some odd, chance way I would have to be regarded by some as a detached observer, I would have to be completely devoid of sympathy for my fellow men, for the beautiful aspects of private life, for the quiet intimacy of marriage, for the shielding of children's upbringing, and for many other relations that have been injured specifically by this paper; I would have to be completely forgetful of what I owe and what everyone owes to anyone who has been injured and insulted. Yet many a layman who cannot express himself in writing perhaps has regarded it as disloyalty on the part of writers that no one has spoken up on this matter, where it is not a question of defending the individual, for as Frater Taciturnus[291] has said: No reply is to be made unless the phenomenon itself is made the subject under discussion.

But precisely because this paper has turned all relations upside down, it is difficult to do anything of this kind. It takes a little systematic planning. First of all, I must find a man whose external appearance has an abundance of ludicrous idiosyncrasies, because that is what *The Corsair* looks for in particular; I would have to make sure* that I would dare to talk about these things as freely as *The Corsair* speaks brazenly. For here, too, the relations are upside down. *The Corsair* dares to attack anyone, and if someone protests on behalf of the one attacked, he is told: You are simply prolonging the attack, so just be quiet! A really strange remark after the whole country has read the attack and when the situation is such that whatever paper printed the defense would have hardly a tenth as many readers as the attack and *The Corsair* have. Or someone will say that the defense prolongs the period during which the affair is the subject of discussion. A strange remark after *The Corsair* has persecuted one particular man for a whole year. But that is the way the comedy goes. But they say: Do not defend the person being attacked; keep quiet in order not to create a disturbance with this affair. What a choice expression, "to create a disturbance with this affair," when the affair that

In margin: * of his agreement so

must not be disturbed is that the person under attack has been mistreated before everyone's eyes.[*]

Meanwhile, lest someone weak in the head take the opportunity to be superclever, the person who wants to do something has to obtain the consent of the person under attack. This I have done, and the person is: I myself. If *The Corsair* has the right to discuss my thin legs and my ridiculous appearance[292]—and there is indeed limelight for me from the wonder-stool game[293] of contemptibleness—well, then I have the same right and fortunately can do it with perhaps somewhat more calmness than *The Corsair*. Here again the difference will readily be seen to be crucial, for I am well aware of what I look like, and I am sure that few men have been the object of a good-humored jest or a little pleasantry or a little teasing or a smile in passing as I have been. I frankly am not bothered by such things: they express the immediate impression that the people concerned cannot help having, and therein lies the redeeming factor. Many a person who may have overrated my capabilities has gotten some joy out of my legs in compensation; many a maiden who may have overestimated my intelligence has become reconciled to me on the basis of my legs. All this I find extremely innocent and excusable, in fact, amusing. But it is something else when a maligner takes the liberty to fasten, as it were, the eyes of the crowd on them, when he also takes away the excuse of immediacy and instead makes them the object of attention. No doubt I shall resign myself to it; it does more harm to those who are misled than to me. And precisely because I know I can resign myself to it, I am positive that I can have some effect on *The Corsair* as a** phenomenon. Later I shall give a specific example of how even a person's accidental physical ludicrousness can be construed in such a way that the comic gets its due and a good-natured envy gets a little revenge as well, and the whole thing ends in an innocent, elevating rec-

[*] *In margin*: But we go on playing the game of being in Paris.[294]
In margin: ** literary

onciliation, with which everything ends when the idea is present and sheds its benediction on the action. But, alas, when passion and commercial interest determine the issue, when there is no ear for the harmony of the spheres of category relations but only for the rattle of money in the cash box, and when passion is propelled to the extreme by the consciousness that every subscriber buys along with the paper the right contemptibly to dispatch what is being written—this is another matter. —*Pap.* VII¹ B 37 *n.d.*, 1846

Some Instructive Comments on The Corsair's *Drastic Errors*
by
S. Kierkegaard

No. 1

Since I am in the process just now [*essentially the same as* VII¹ B 37, *para. 1-7*].

Yet it is a difficult matter to do something. First[*] I must ... [*essentially the same as* VII¹ B 37, *170:16–171:10*] and, fortunately, I perhaps can do it somewhat more calmly than *The Corsair.*

Next it must be clear that the one who speaks is not a person who has been directly attacked—for the immediate response to that will be: It is irritability. Everything connected with resentment and indignation is eliminated immediately. This I have made sure of by having a pseudonymous author, with whom I am usually confused, demand to be abused although he has been praised,[295] and it did happen—and now I am involved. Indeed, everyone must have wondered why I had not been in *The Corsair* before.

So everything was arranged, as anyone with an overview of the situation perhaps will see. He will easily see that the contender here is not a hot-tempered youth but someone previously known for his ability to wield a pen and who also can devise a plan. If no one else is willing, then I shall make an

---

[*] *In margin:* there must be no reply—(Frater Tac.)—but only indictment.

extremely corruptive literary phenomenon the object of an indictment. There will be no mention here of persons or of their character—no, only of the phenomenon itself. And the one who, even though he bears a heavy responsibility personally for what he has done, and who for that very reason always has made his appearance as one without authority,[296] but who really, *qua* author, has the purest and lightest conscience, this person who, despite financial loss[297] year after year and increased application day after day, asked only to be left alone and dared to deposit his books in Danish literature—this person does indeed have the special substance to accentuate the ethical in being an author.

So much for my literary credentials. If it were a question only of a purely esthetic controversy, about who is the wittiest and such things, the matter would indeed be easily decided by getting *The Corsair*'s dreaded geniuses, man for man and each signing his name, to write in another paper under the same conditions governing every other author who does not profit from the license and privilege of contemptibleness by daring to do anything, since that privilege has already been lost by being held in contempt. If one only would reflect on this calmly, one would readily see how much this phenomenon is based on false alarm. But that is not the nature of the conflict, and just as I as author proudly decline recognition as being wittier than *The Corsair*, inasmuch as I do not care to be witty at all, so also is the controversy itself not very pleasant. Or, more correctly, it is not a controversy; it is an attempt to put a stop, if possible, to the confusing deterioration going on all around. Here it is not a matter of controversy but only a matter of describing, calmly and with the power of persuasion, this whole odious practice, doing it calmly and coolly while that paper will presumably be showering invective and in every way holding one up to the laughter of all the silly fools. Calmly and coolly and not detached from the world to devote myself to contemplation, to keep on thinking in the middle of the disturbance, to be quietly reflective while sitting, as it were, in a kettle on which the coppersmiths are hammering.

As for myself, I believe that I have specific qualifications for this. I am single, I have no wife to grieve even though her husband proudly raises himself above insults, I have no other "myself" forced to wait apprehensively to see what the next week brings, who has to stand anxiously alongside her husband and see what the anxious see, perhaps on a magnified scale,[*] while the husband proudly disregards it. I have no child who might get hold of *The Corsair* in school if he could not find it in his father's house and either is led into the sad error of laughing at his father or becomes indignant at an early age about the world in which he lives where such a thing happens to his father. I am not a schoolteacher the children can greet with laughter, nor a teacher of adults.[**] I have no position or office, am not a clergyman who, in his official position, reluctantly will perhaps become involved in a declaration such as this, for how many readers of the Bible and the hymnbook are there in comparison with the readers of *The Corsair*, which is reading for all, especially for the weaker brethren who have no view of life, and yet anyone who does certainly knows that nothing is more difficult to deal with in fear and trembling than a sense of the comic.

So I stand alone, and it is my desire to stand alone, accustomed to other dismays than the dismay of being caricatured[298] in a childish way; calmly aware of my appearance, I no doubt will take the blows. Accustomed as I am to calling my mind and my thoughts back from other inner consternations to cheerfulness and jest, I will manage all right. But I do know very well where jesting belongs. I wish to stand alone; not even the editors of the paper[299] have the remotest part in the action I am taking. Therefore, if possible, let the whole *Corsair* deal with me, giving private citizens an interval of immunity. No one has asked me to take this step, no one. I am counting on no human support. Although it is routine to say, "Oh, well, it's only *The Corsair*," I know very well that there is nothing people fear so much as to be made to look

---

[*] *In margin*: or, dejected, come upon her maid inquisitively reading *The Corsair*.

[**] *In margin*: I do not have many servants; I shall not be greeted by my subordinates with embarrassed looks.

ridiculous! So I stand alone, and yet there is one who has asked me—no, he is not in the habit of asking, he commands and one obeys, one has no peace until one does. And there is one who is the solitary's support in his solitariness, who is far away from life and in solitariness is in the midst of the tribulation.

No witty polemic will be carried on here; there will be no shrill laughter, and, praise God, I do not enjoy the privilege of daring to allow myself to use cartoons and crudeness as my instruments. I want my comments to be instructive, if possible, then calming and mitigating and not devoid of a certain interesting quality. Occasionally there will be place for a good-natured jest as well, simply to show how such a thing can be done.

To that end I ask the patience of my readers. I remind anyone quick to laugh to be a little slow, not just for my sake but for his own; indeed, it is even possible that I can bear his laughter better than he himself. And if I happen to have enemies or the like who may have cause to feel negatively toward me, I ask them—again not just for my sake but for theirs—to consider one thing: insofar as they wanted me to be chastised in some way, is it becoming of them to wish it to happen by way of *The Corsair's* crudity, do they not think more highly of themselves than to want *The Corsair* as their knight errant. No, then let it be an ennobled person, an authoritative person, so that all will be built up when he chastises me. Every attack by *The Corsair*, whether it attacks the guilty or the innocent, does irreparable harm, because the cure is far more pernicious than the sickness. —*Pap.* VII¹ B 38 *n.d.*, 1846

VII¹
B 38
218

The Corsair's credentials.
It has never established its identity; it has sprung into existence out of filth.

> Everything centers on the totally egotistical personality of an unknown person.
> —*Pap.* VII¹ B 40 *n.d.*, 1846

Addition to Pap. VII¹ B 40:

The Corsair becomes more and more brazen—no one replies—no one dares to reply. Goldschmidt, editor of a book.[300]—*Pap.* VII¹ B 41 *n.d.*, 1846

Addition to Pap. VII¹ B 40:

School life intimidated (Høedt).[301]
A man has said something about Goldschmidt in a public place (Rosenkrantz).[302]
Actors—clergy—

—*Pap.* VII¹ B 42 *n.d.*, 1846

Addition to Pap. VII¹ B 40:

(a)

The Corsair's position

Leveling[303]

good-natured envy (its elevating quality)
contemptible envy[304]
A desire to tear down the great—with the help of a contemptible person so that there is nothing left.—*Pap.* VII¹ B 43 *n.d.*, 1846

Addition to Pap. VII¹ B 40:

(b)

The Corsair's attack, how it works.
Analogies with presentations in the theater, with being booed or abused in a meeting.
Both these analogies still nothing. A person has neither the recourse of contemporaneity against the abuser nor the suffering of just the moment—it lasts longer, sometimes a year.[305]
And this punishment that the executor presumably thinks no one can endure, and God knows whether they flatter-

ingly think they are able to force me to leave the country—who executes it? The authorities? No, lawlessness.—*Pap.* VII¹ B 44 *n.d.*, 1846

Addition to Pap. VII¹ B 40:

(c)

The wittiness of *The Corsair*—not essential wit.

Read *The Corsair*'s witticisms in a book or in another paper, and you will be disgusted, because you then apply criteria.

Cartoons drawn from life.

    For example, depicting me giving a speech[306] to the housemaids in my house (since I am a householder) or riding a hobbyhorse.[307]

Such things anyone can do.—*Pap.* VII¹ B 45 *n.d.*, 1846

Addition to Pap. VII¹ B 40:

(d)

No recourse against *The Corsair*'s attacks

  (1) not in court
  (2) not with a witty polemic—for there is no honor to win this way
  (3) not by showing that it is a contemptible paper—for then everybody will say: We knew that.

The false alarm of witchcraft[308] consists in this.—*Pap.* VII¹ B 47 *n.d.*, 1846

Addition to Pap. VII¹ B 40:

(e)

The ethical[309] and the immoral.—*Pap.* VII¹ B 48 *n.d.*, 1846

Literary Contemptibleness

It could open with an Athenian street scene in the time of Socrates (but historical and only slightly idealized).

(1) In antiquity, a person (the abuser) had to appear in person[310] in the square, and if he lost, he had to take the consequences. Furthermore, anyone who repeated it was immediately equally responsible for what he said.

Anonymity has changed the situation: the person involved remains concealed, and those who read have the defense that they merely read—"for to write such stuff is contemptible." In that way, a secret wretch makes a whole mass of men accomplices in his crime, and everything is confusion, because all this is set in motion at a secret level.

(2) In antiquity, one got to see who it was; one grew weary of seeing the same old abuser etc. There were no fantasies about a Mr. X, which always foster panic and dread.

Through anonymity, these fantasies are produced. And although we generally are sensible, it cannot be denied that the propensity to fantasize in the presence of anonymity betrays great superstitiousness—as does belief in elves and a stupendously great giant in the mountain cave.

(3) In antiquity, the attack was open, and therefore social life, especially for one who had to associate with many people and in public places, was not made precarious by all these strange mystifications and allusions, which amount to nothing.

(4) In antiquity, when the attack itself was over, it was forgotten. By means of the press, these things drag on a long time, and not until a man travels to the provinces two weeks later is the gossip fully under way.—*Pap.* VII¹ B 54 *n.d.*, 1846

N.B. Not to be printed but completed
in optima forma only as a study.

A Personal Statement in Costume[*]

Until now, I definitely was of the opinion that I knew what the most difficult task[311] is, namely, to deal with the comic in fear and trembling, to maintain the conception of responsibil-

---

[*] *In margin*: An action-response in personal costume.

ity rooted in ethical and religious earnestness together with the delight of jest, to bind oneself forever to the charter of duty and at the same time be able to go on adventures as a young soldier of fortune does in legends, to put on the full gear of actuality and at the same time be able to dance lightly and with abandonment, to honor one's father, admire men of excellence, bow to one's superiors, and at the same time be able to care about nothing, be able to frolic in a way that would make eternity itself empty if one lost the impress of its pathos, in a way that would make one's future inconsolable if one lost even the slightest recollection of the pathos. Until now, I indeed thought that since few are born in any generation who actually have a talent for the comic, even fewer develop the maturity that balances the two (earnestness and jest) in a union that for each is equidistant from a mésalliance, in a union that is even more difficult to enter into than it is for an old man to marry a young girl. It seems, however, that from these times I have to learn, if not to change my views (I dare say I am too plodding for that; perhaps my willingness to learn is also a bit doubtful), then at least that I am rather alone in my thinking and perhaps the only one who herewith renounces any reputation for having a sense of the comic. But if I learn that, I actually do not learn anything I have not already learned, and I thus learn that there is no external hindrance to the rightness of my thinking simply because I am so alone in it. This comes close to the question Socrates[312] asked in a similar situation with respect to horses: Does everybody know how to ride them and only one does not, or is it the opposite, instead, that a few individuals who are called riding masters know this art, while the others know nothing about it.

Now my view (in line with my sense of the comic, of course) is that in a small country like Denmark a disproportionate and immoral phenomenon such as *The Corsair* does great harm and is of no benefit whatsoever, of no benefit because it counterfeits and taints the comic and thereby silences the authentic comic, just as a naughty child's impertinence can cause the more sensible person not to come and visit or express himself in a family where such things go on, even if he otherwise loves the family very much, does great harm because it seduces the unstable, the irresponsible, the sensate, those who are lost in earthly passions, seduces them by means of ambiguity, lack of character, and the concealment of brash contempt under the pursuit of the comic.

I can even prove this to be so, but the proof, of course, is valid only on the basis of my understanding of the comic and thus only for the individuals who Socratically assume that the comic is like riding, that only a few know how but the majority do not. The proof is that there is unanimous agreement that the phenomenon (the nature of the paper and its extraordinary circulation) is a mere nothing; this in itself proves that the harm is far from insignificant. If there actually were unanimous agreement that it is nothing at all, this might mean that people do not read the paper, do not subscribe to it, do not discuss its contents; but to fight to get to read it, to read it as no other paper is read, to talk about it and thereby make oneself practically a messenger boy for the paper with a circulation no other paper can even remotely boast of—all this adequately proves, according to my understanding, of course, the unreality in the view that regards it as nothing at all. The unreality of the view demonstrates that the harm is far from insignificant, for even if the situation were the same with respect to the nature of the paper and its circulation, the harm would already be diminished if everybody nevertheless agreed that it is harmful. Franklin[313] advises young managers to pay particular attention to small expenses, believing that they will indeed keep an eye on the large ones, precisely because the large ones, after all, keep an eye on the individual, for the difference is that what is significant keeps an eye on him, keeps him alert, teaches him caution and economy, makes him wise by experience, but he himself has to keep an eye on what is insignificant. In the same vein, perhaps the most dangerous temptations are those that come under the modest label of "nothing at all." The very fact that everybody says it is nothing at all may make it so harmful that the clergy could be better used here than to prepare a new hymnal,[314] which everyone considers to be the demand of the times. The line of development proceeds from reflection through the comic to the religious; that is why the misuse of the comic spreads so rapidly in our day, while everybody believes it is nothing at all—although they still read it and subscribe to it and talk about it as about no other paper.

Now this is my view, and yet it perhaps is right; if so, this again is new proof that the world has the equilibrium and balanced distribution that make it the best of all worlds that the liberals and optimists assume it to be, which, in fact, everyone in our liberal era assumes it to be. You see, to my mind this paper does not have the true conception of the comic, but, on the other hand, it makes a lot of money with its warped conception of the comic—is this not equilibrium in the best of all worlds! There are others who, according to my view, do not properly understand the comic, either, yet are honored, esteemed, and highly regarded. What a balanced distribution in this best of worlds! Now if I, disregarded and spurned by all as one who has no sense of the comic, if I actually did not have it, then I would in fact be the stepchild and the injured party in this best of worlds. On the other hand, if I actually had the proper understanding of the comic and were the only one who had it, but also were held in high esteem by everyone, then the balance would be upset in this best of worlds. But if it is assumed that I have the proper understanding and then at the same time am scorned by everybody and lose money by it, then balance is established in this best of worlds. Therefore, on the one side: honor, prestige, financial gain—and the unsound view. On the other side: dishonor, exclusion, financial loss—and the correct view. If one were not an optimist already, who would not become an optimist with this outlook! Why should one person have everything, why should one person be excluded from everything? No, praise be to the balanced distribution of the good things of life: everyone gets his own, individual effort is favored according to desire. He who aspires to honor, status, and money acquires these goods with the help of his unsound views; he who aspires to a sound point of view must purchase it with financial loss and the disdain of all. This upbuilding observation has frequently inspired me, for it is indeed beautiful that there is balance if one only knows how to evaluate properly the goods of life, how to evaluate money, honor, and prestige, and how to evaluate the possession of a sound view and outlook. The only unfortunate ones are those who hesitate in between, no doubt fearing up to a point to be in error, but also fearing up to a point to be destitute of money* and status with men.

But enough of this, especially if it is understood, but there is one person in particular I wish could and would understand it. One of the editors of that paper is Mr. Goldschmidt,[315] a student, whom I consider to be intelligent and not without a certain talent.** However contemptible the paper may be, it still may be wrong to shove everything onto him,[316] even if he rakes in the money as his own and also the admiration of all those who look up to this phenomenon. Since I am well aware that the eventual end will be terrible and that, in taking their revenge on this editor, the same crowd of unstable, irresponsible, sensate, and erring people will justify themselves and wash their hands without becoming one whit better, I would like to say a simple word to him as a single individual before I can decide to identify him with the paper. I am well aware that the majority will again consider it fatuous confusion for me, who as the one attacked should be quick to scorn, to be so slow, while it is usually so easy to laugh at his witticisms—and then in another way to dispose of the joker. But it was still possible that Goldschmidt in particular was capable of understanding that I, far from fearing *The Corsair*'s wretched abuse, am in the very opposite situation and that I, with a perhaps rather rare fortitude and also a more than ordinary sympathy for a human being, take the great risk of being abused and insulted by the rabble and misunderstood by the better class—simply to keep a human being from being destroyed. Never in my life until now have I actually despised

In margin: * in the hand

In margin: ** He is not without passion but is also led astray by passion; he is not without the power of esthetic despair but also fortifies himself with ethical delusion.

any man. I do not enjoy philandering with emotions; I have respect for my own feeling, which teaches me in my association with a wide variety of men to use far milder and, on the whole, probably far more pertinent categories. But it must not happen, *The Corsair* must not be a phantom that does great harm and on which revenge is taken by holding in contempt—a street-corner loafer who is legally responsible, or a nonentity, which a paper in fact is if it is made the object of personal judgment. No, Goldschmidt will not escape; he, too, will be held in contempt for all the meanness, for every shilling that gives consolation for lost honor.

Even if the most vivid imagination were to think up the most diverse kinds of literary contemptibleness, whether brash lies, or mean persecution of someone who has been unsuccessful, or barefaced blasphemy of the good, or a besmirching meddling in the intimate lives of private individuals, or mean and cowardly spite—in short, whatever it may be, one thing is positive, there will be examples of it in abundance in *The Corsair*. My unqualified judgment of the paper is the same as that of Frater Taciturnus:[317] I want to be abused, I refuse to endure the disgrace of being recommended, praised, and invited in by literary contemptibleness. If the paper had a small circulation, then my judgment would be that it makes no difference whether it praised or abused—this is a judgment on its nature—but the extensiveness of its circulation requires that the judgment be expressed differently. And the judgment, the paper's credit rating, is this: to be abused by it is an honor, to be commended an assault, to write in it utterly contemptible. Therefore, I fear *The Corsair*'s abuse no more than the physician fears the patient's abusive language during an amputation; I am not fighting *The Corsair* any more than the physician is fighting the patient who is resisting the operation.

But Goldschmidt has also published a novel: *En Jøde*.[318] So he has two alternatives: the perchance poor and narrow path that leads one as a publisher of books to close kinship with what must be held in honor—to be a Danish author—and the contemptible path of earning money by being the editor of *The Corsair*. There is no mediation, and there must not be any. The contemptibleness of *The Corsair* must not make for itself a friendly setting by secretly aligning itself with a sympathetic interest for what can be moving and sad in that novel. Precisely that is the danger, and that in turn makes it necessary to treat *The Corsair* at this time in another way and with a decisively ethical assurance. It may already be difficult for unstable people to distinguish between talent and misuse of talent, to champion ethical judgment against mercenary prostitution of talent, but if sympathy is to be gained, then it almost takes ethical elevation to see which is which, and this cannot be presupposed at all in the average individual.

My demand to Mr. Goldschmidt, then, is that in another paper and, as befits a man of honor, under his own signature he explain the basic idea of *The Corsair*, what the paper wants, what justification it has for existence. To reply in *The Corsair* is *eo ipso* to sign the verdict upon oneself. Then I am through; up to the very last I have done everything in my power, and I have nothing to fear, for the only thing I feared momentarily was whether perchance I had judged too harshly—not *The Corsair*, but its editor, or at least had given him occasion to think so. I do not read *The Corsair*; I would not even direct my servant to read it, for I do not presume that a master has the authority to order his servant to go to a place of disrepute. But even if *The Corsair* continued year after year and even if its contents were ever so good, it has existed for six years and stigmatized its name in such a way that it will never be the name of a respectable paper. If it is sad to see a splendid name gradually degenerate, it is an extremely pernicious duplicity when contemptibleness undergoes a change, gradual perhaps, but retains the same name, so that ethical judgment never becomes decisive.

I realize that everyone will think it strange, even foolish, for me to give this appearance of having some power, I who have been demolished. And the proof of this is indeed difficult for me, for although everyone reads *The Corsair*, part of the game is that no one wants it known, and thus I dare mention no names without offending someone. But there is one man I may mention without offense as a reader of that paper and

whose judgment I dare quote. He is the watchman on my
street, a good man, alert and personally attached to me for
several reasons. As I said, he reads *The Corsair*. He believes
that that paper has completely destroyed me, and precisely
because he is a good and gentle soul and likes me, this belief
troubles him. He considers me to be a quiet, industrious
student-type who comes home every night at a respectable
hour; without really understanding what I am doing, he nevertheless respects this domestic pattern—but that I am supposed to be witty, to say nothing of having a standard of wit
that could even remotely be compared with *The Corsair*'s, this
he certainly realizes is not the case, for this Goldschmidt must
be *ein ungeheuer Witzkopf* [a colossal wit], as my barber also
says. You see, if I were to drop a hint to my watchman about
going and beating up this newspaper writer, I believe that he
would do it free, simply because the whole affair makes him
sorry for me. Strange, the watchman is a big, hefty fellow,
and I am anything but that, and I actually find it necessary to
treat him very delicately with regard to the truth, for if I let
one single word fall about still having one or another advantage of the stronger, he would regard me as mad. So it goes
with the watchman, who still likes me, but not so with an
alehouse keeper here in the city whom I know from earlier
days when he was a servant in a family of my acquaintance.
He reads *The Corsair* and is proud of the fact. It was extraordinary to note the change that took place in him after he
began reading about me in that paper, for when I was immortalized,[319] he did not notice that it was I. In the past, when we
met on the street, he was visibly pleased to greet me, his not
unhandsome face took on the most friendly expression, and it
genuinely pleased him when I responded to his almost too
deferential greeting with friendly attention. Ah, but then
came the change; his greeting did not, so to speak, hasten to
meet me as soon as he caught sight of me. No, the precipi-
tousness of the past was curbed; he acted as if he did not see
me and let me get very close before he greeted me. Nor did he
snatch off his hat—no, his arm movement was slow and
grudging and finally became so deliberate that he almost kept

VII[1]
B 55
233

his hat on, and it ended with his ceasing to greet me at all. As stated, the alehouse keeper reads *The Corsair*. He believes that what appears in the newspapers is public opinion, the voice of the people and of truth. Since he cannot manage to read all the papers, he has limited himself to *The Corsair*, which he takes together with another alehouse keeper. He gets it on Sunday morning and reads it aloud to his whole family. He saves each number in order to have them all bound later, which will be done if the maid, who sneaks in later to read it, does not, deplorably, throw some away. Our alehouse keeper assumes that people can make mistakes, even alehouse keepers, a king, a court, even the supreme court, but anything that appears in print he regards as infallible. He says, "Is it possible that anything can be a lie which is printed in countless copies, is read all over the country, and, from what I hear, no one yet has ventured to refute!" This explains his altered opinion of me, so altered that he who once would have felt highly flattered to converse with me is supposed to have said, "No alehouse keeper can in decency be in the room or in association with a man whom public truth has branded that way." What a curious contrast: the very same thing has been said in higher places about *The Corsair* writer—and yet all agree about reading it. How fortunate for me that I never go to parties, how fortunate that even if I did go to parties I would hardly seek the company of alehouse keepers in particular.

My watchman's judgment of the esthetic attack is consistently the same: "If worse comes to worst, he could more easily put up with having his trousers stolen than with having them cartooned[320]—that he could not survive." Here again I have to treat the strong man delicately, for to me his judgment seems odd. If my trousers were stolen and I had no others to put on, I very likely would not survive it, assuming that I had to go out just the same, for I probably would catch a cold. It is another matter if I am allowed to keep them on, for then I shall derive a benefit and pleasure from my trousers such as no one else in the whole kingdom has: I have them on—this I have in common with all who wear trousers—and at the same time the whole city has the pleasure of seeing me wearing them—pleasure, yes, perhaps even benefit. Now it is true that once upon a time I thought I would be able to do a little bit for a single human being[321] through my literary efforts. Illusion, vanity! Could it be that I merely mistook the medium and may still prove to be beneficial? The medium of being beneficial has been discovered; I carry it around with me all the time: it is my trousers. Not even the biggest book has created such a big sensation. It almost makes one think that what the times demand is my trousers; I wish that every one of its demands would be as innocent, for the demand is that I wear them and, at most, perhaps will bequeath them some day to the city. Petrarch believed that his Latin writings would make him immortal, and his erotic poetry did just that. Fate is even more ironic toward me. Despite all my diligence and efforts, I have not been able to fathom what the times demanded, and yet it was so very close to me; how incredible that it did not occur to me, that someone else had to say that it was my trousers. What rare luck, for my life acquires exceptional significance; to my contemporaries I acquire significance by means of my trousers, but for a later generation perhaps my writings will help a little.

Ironically, the whole affair suits me, because, as I have said elsewhere,[322] my literary work is dialectical in double-reflection; for that reason, it would be completely frustrating, yes, even high treason against the idea, if, for example, I allowed my portrait or picture to be published. On the other hand, it may be asked whether I am not even responsible for creating for my work all the support that in complete consistency with the idea may result from the dissemination of my caricature, my trousers sketched with me in them. Only the idea, the thought, the true consistency of the thought, engages me; I follow it into whatever external situation it leads me—to being admired or to being abused—I follow it confidently. Just as a child holding its mother's hand walks in danger without recognizing it, so I hold the hand of consistency and walk in danger, because I know that in the idea the danger has been surmounted.

In one respect, I shall have an advantage in taking this particular step, one that I value rather highly, although most people would consider it anything but that, would think it much more as a loss, an injury I bring upon myself. To be specific, just about everybody has read that paper (although it dare not be said that anyone except my watchman and that alehouse keeper does it—this is part of the game); innumerable people, ladies and gentlemen, have assured themselves by a personal appraisal that I wear trousers and that they correspond to the description. In deference to the demand of the times, I have candidly replied to everyone who has asked if these "really" were the famous trousers that they could positively say that they actually had seen them with their own eyes. Furthermore, compared with that paper which has brought up the whole affair, the paper in which I write has but few readers.[323] Finally, whatever anyone says, I certainly am the one who has first priority to my trousers—and yet I know that because I write about this everybody will say, "Good lord, how dull of Kierkegaard to be concerned about something like that." But I wonder whether all these people have a clear idea of what the something is that I am concerned about, that it is not the trousers, which I am even willing to give to the city, that it is not people's nosey interest in reading about them and seeing them, but it is the fact that this is the way it is and that they then deny it, that they do not regard this as being a trifling matter and cease to read and to look, but that they do both and say: It is a trifling matter, and it all begins all over again. I am not disturbed, therefore, by the humiliating judgment that what I say is dull, especially dull compared with the witticisms in that paper; the only thing that concerns me here is that the phenomenon be disclosed with all its implications, no matter whether it is my trousers or someone else's trousers that come to be so very popular. As a matter of fact, everybody in Copenhagen but me properly understands the comic.[324] Fine, so be it. But what do they mean when they say my comments are dull? It means that they are playing a game of hide-and-seek, and now my dullness comes along and interferes somewhat with the game. The game is this: they pretend that just a few people read that paper, as if it endured a miserable life in a despised little out-of-the-way corner of existence, as if it had the support of an insignificant number of subscribers—and so it is dull to pay any attention to it, foolish to propagate it more by talking about it. But this mystification is precisely the game, because, see, it is just the opposite, and to make it even more so they play this game that no one reads it and therefore no one should get excited about it. And everybody plays this game, and for that very reason everyone agrees that what I am doing is dull, because I am stupid enough to disclose the nature of this mystification in its self-contradiction.

For anyone to criticize and protest this matter disturbs the game, and therefore any protest is dull, for the whole affair is indeed nothing at all; what everybody is so keen on is called nothing at all simply so that it can continue. Very strange. That most widely read paper writes about it, everybody talks about it, and yet it must not be mentioned—lest it be circulated. According to my understanding of the comic, this whole situation is highly comic, in the same way that it would be comic, for example, if a very crippled person were to confide this fact very secretively to another, since he himself believes that no one can see it by looking at him. In the same vein, it is comic that everybody knows it and that it then must be kept secret, and therefore the person who is trying to do a little merely to impede it must not talk about it—in order not to circulate it. Consequently, the difference is that it is acceptable to talk about it in order to circulate it, but it is unacceptable to talk about it with the intention of halting the circulation, and the reason is that this talking contributes to its being circulated. If the category of the comic is usually contradiction,[325] then this situation is essentially comic. With respect to something that has limited circulation, it is altogether true that protest contributes to its circulation, but this cannot possibly be true of something that has extraordinary circulation, and therefore the protest will scarcely reach half of those who know all about it.

Suppose a child comes home from playing with other children and has learned a bad word—what will happen? Well, if the mother is a silly woman who chatters with other women about bringing up children, she probably will scold and slap and in her zeal perhaps teach the child even more bad words. If, however, she is a woman who has preserved her maidenly purity, ennobled by the beautiful concern of mothering love, she would think that just because the child heard such a word once, it did not necessarily follow that it would stick with him so that he would never forget it; if he never heard it again, it would disappear without a trace as if he had never heard it—and for that very reason she would not admonish or censure him. All honor to the loving mother's quiet solicitude that daily, alertly watched over her child, although externally it looked as if she were doing nothing, because she neither slapped nor scolded, nor did she nag. But if a child came home after several years in a boarding school and his mother learned to her dismay that he was brashly using such bad words again and again and in a way that seemed to betray that he knew that they were bad and was so corrupted by his comrades that he almost took delight in it, would it not be ridiculous of his mother to say to herself: No use to admonish and advise and punish him lest his attention be drawn to them—then he no doubt will forget the bad words. Or if a man came to the mother's house and found occasion to protest, and the mother would shush him and say: Just don't speak about those bad words to the boy lest he learn them—would that not be ludicrous?

The fact that the only contemptible and the most widely circulated paper in Denmark is read by everyone, although it is supposed to be a secret, sheds new light on it and reveals that its apparent courage is nothing but cowardice and that it enjoys vile, cowardly protection against the law by means of street-corner loafers[326] and against protest by hiding under the skirts of the public. This dreadful paper, which with an emblem of a pirate ship[327] to stimulate terror cries for revenge, really ought to have these explanatory words on its title page: Printed for private circulation among friends. One does not discuss in writing something that is privately printed for friends.[328] Thus it is incidental that it is printed; it could just as well be circulated in manuscript form, which would produce the queer inverse situation that the most widely circulated paper would not even have the character of being in print. The slogans that bakeries put into cookies are also printed, to be sure, but this is quite incidental and is done simply because it would be too much work to write so many. Menus, too, are sometimes printed. But this situation reaches a ridiculous climax with *The Corsair*. It has all the appearance of being a newspaper—it has an editorial staff, contributors such as P. L. Møller, who even specifies in the lexicon of authors[329] that he is a contributor, both lyric and satiric—and yet *The Corsair* actually is a facilitating and expediting agent that town gossip and rumor and scandal have invented and publish themselves—privately, in manuscript form, for friends.

But the queerest and most comic aspect of this situation is that it prompts that paper itself to regard itself as terrifying. Incidentally, cowardice and the vilest cravenness often confuse themselves with courage. This paper, the most timid of all, as newspapers go, which finds the path of contemptibleness up the back steps until, finally, modesty so prevails that workhouse inmates are permitted to subscribe lest the domestics become offended by being named as subscribers, this timid paper is itself probably aware of the connection, but from that it does not follow that it should not be able to devote its cowardice to continuing the game, which in fact is suggested by the pirate ship, the game of playing pirate, the game of being feared and of being brave.

A game such as this is very tempting to cowardice; cowardice is always eager to be confused with its opposite, bravery, courage, to say nothing of a terrible pirate. In various countries, Jews are generally regarded as cowards, and yet it is a fact that there is a strong propensity in young Jewish men to go around dressed as officers[330] and wanting to look like officers. Goldschmidt's novel *En Jøde*[331] emphasizes this point with psychological mastery, which always indicates experience and familiarity with life, something for which the author of this novel must always be commended. The hero, as the main character in a novel is called, therefore the hero, Jacob Bendixen, does indeed have this very same military and warlike propensity. He even rises to lieutenant in the Polish army, and when he comes home again, he is continually being taken for an officer,[*] even by people who knew him fairly well. This military quality must be included in an understanding of Jacob Bendixen's development, which in the third part of the book is interesting in a way that the first two parts are not. In one place the author has even sketched for us with a few strokes Jacob Bendixen's interesting face: the oriental face refined by intelligence to the point where the dominant intelligence almost makes his nationality unrecognizable. If one were to complete this picture in his imagination, it would be impossible to picture him in anything but a bold braid-trimmed officer's coat. If it were not against police ordinances, it would even be fitting to imagine him carrying a sword, at least a concealed weapon, on his person. Just to walk around carrying a dagger[332] takes a little courage, even to take to one's heels carrying a dagger takes courage; moreover, there is also the danger that he could fall and be stabbed by the dagger. In fact, the real coward can be spotted by his being so afraid that he does not even dare to stand close to a gun. Bold is he, however, who even dares go around carrying the murderous weapon on his person. But to go around carrying such a weapon does not always mean that one is going to use it. It is common knowledge that Jean Paul[333] proposes that the National Guard in a certain city carry sticks, as well as rifles, swords, and bayonets—in order to have something for their protection.

What I have written may indeed be dull; everyone may think it dull; everyone may be a connoisseur of the comic. Good lord, by way of my trousers my importance is almost on the point of becoming dangerous to my fellow citizens. It almost looks as if I—that is, my trousers—am about to rise to

[*] *In margin:* In part two, that moving account of Jacob Bendixen proposing to the students that they play pirate[334] seems to be prophetic, but not in the sense that he ends by becoming a pirate—no, but that he gets his wish by getting a chance—to play pirate.

the position of tyrant in Copenhagen, despite all the men of distinction. I am sorry about this, but it actually is the case. Young girls, who in all innocence might wish that some equally innocent and proper person would appreciate their finery and loveliness, are defrauded. The king himself, driving through the streets and desiring and enjoying the greetings of his subjects, is defrauded. All I need to do is put on my trousers, and all eyes are on me—that is, on my trousers. But since this is the case, since my trousers are so potent, it is good for me to do something dull to mitigate, if possible, the great influence of my trousers. And strange to say, I conclude with this so that the game may have an element of witchcraft. Just as Aladdin's lamp was altogether unimpressive, likewise my trousers are as unimpressive and inconspicuous as possible— even if they were red with a green stripe or green with a red stripe! But again, how ungracious of me to have regarded these trousers as a trivial matter and merely to have asked the tailor to make them of ordinary mixed gray wool cloth, and then to have these very trousers help to make me almost important, for when it rains on the preacher, it drips on the sexton, and when the trousers gain supremacy, I, too, advance a little—I, a poor solitary wretch with no sense of the comic, one to whom life therefore shows pity and gives that pair of trousers.

VII[1]
B 55
242

You see, the poet does, after all, exaggerate a little so that the pathos and the comic may stand out. For example, to depict the topsy-turvy situation in Athens, Aristophanes[335] had a sausage dealer become the supreme power in the country. So it was in the play; in actuality it was not quite that bad. But in Copenhagen a pair of trousers has actually attained the position of highest standing and importance. I wonder what Aristophanes would think of that? Certainly he would be envious of this comedy I am writing herewith, but that contemptible paper and the curious are so muddled that they do not grasp the comedy of this, which is comic only according to my view of the comic.

Far be it from me, then, to complain over the upsidedownness of things; after all, I derive both use and importance by wearing the trousers, and then, too, it is just possible that I have an inner spiritual resource, an inner life that is superior to all else, a life that I enthusiastically know can belong just as fully to any man as to me, even to the poorest pauper, if he will turn inward, but certainly not if he turns outward and makes a habit of fixing his attention on my trousers or on anything equally insignificant.

Most of those who have read this far perhaps will concede that my style has a composure that obviously does not indicate agitation or irritation, which, however, could almost be excusable, if one considers how loathsome it must be to be reminded continually of human triviality this way. It is an easy matter to fritter oneself away on trifles; it is an easy matter to take a single person by storm in order to tempt him, if possible, to abandon what inspires him, the conception of what infinite significance there still is in being human and that every single individual can attain the highest if he wills it. It might be said that I could, after all, avoid this whole affair by withdrawing. If I were weak, I might do that. But in an age as devoid of character and full of ferment as this one, anyone who has any character ought to remain at his post. And my orders read not to retreat a hairbreadth. My task is to expose the phenomena, not directly but indirectly, and it is my duty in this respect to put up with everything without retreating. For some time now, I have been aware of that paper and its insinuating misuse of the comic.[336] It is not at all true that I got into all this by a rash step;[337] in time, when people have settled down sufficiently to have the tranquillity to read, I would like to report in detail on a plan[338] I have made. I never speak of my plans before I have done what I want to do or must do. If it can be done, it will make interesting reading. I know very well who I am, I know very well that something can be learned from me, that if I were to put into print my total view of life as I existentially express it one level lower, I would be esteemed by many, but that I will not and dare not do it without becoming false to my idea.—*Pap.* VII¹ B 55 *n.d.*, 1846

Addition to Pap. VII¹ B 55:

In conclusion, let us test the correctness of what was said at the very beginning. When this article is read, everybody, the public, the crowd, will say: It is rather dull, peculiar, imprudent, shameless. And that is exactly right, for the day when everyone says of any statement of mine: That is right, then I will say to myself, as that man did when the people applauded him: Did I say something stupid?[339] Or, more accurately, I will say to myself: Obviously you must have said something stupid. That is the way all the people, the public, the crowd, talk. But then there will be a young man who still has the flourishing vigor of childhood or early youth in his cheeks, in whose blush the idea dwells with feminine modesty. His heart will pound mightily when he reads it, and he will understand that this is still worth living for, this: to be consistent to the uttermost, humble before God, proud toward men, which, God be praised, God has granted to every human being if he wills it. See, to me this is enough, enough beyond all measure. And this preference for a young man I learned, yes, it is true, I learned it from a seducer, alas, from him who, praise God, seduced me when I was a young man. But this seducer was no lascivious fellow nor a man grown old in excesses—no, he was an old man, and he had grown old in wisdom. Socrates[340] knew very well why he loved young men. He understood very well how much men lose in the course of the years through association and traffic and comparison, learning little by little, little by little, little by little to take the way of compromise, to bargain, to make a deal, how they, little by little, little by little, little by little (most dreadful of all sophisms) lose the inwardness of the hidden man, the blushing modesty of the young man. Therefore, my reader will be a young person, or he will be an old person who sadly smiles during the reading because he is reminded sadly of youth, an old person who in the evening of life renews his youth. What lies in between is difficult, my reader, but easy for one who despises, mocks, and derides me. But to me the youth is the most cherished, whether he walks alone on the beach and longs for the ideals or whether he walks alone in the swarming crowd, which jeers at him because he refuses it and longs for the ideals. This youth is enough for me, I ask no more. Yes, just as a girl desires only one adornment, to lie in her grave with a myrtle wreath on her brow, so I ask only for this consciousness: he was laughed to scorn by all the people, by the crowd, by the public, but he could make a young man's heart beat.—*Pap.* VII¹ B 56 *n.d.*, 1846

An Action-response in Personal Costume

Goldschmidt is not without passion but is also led astray by passion; he is not without the power of esthetic despair but also fortifies himself with ethical delusion.

I fear *The Corsair*'s abuse no more than the physician fears the patient's abusive language during an operation.—*Pap.* VII¹ B 57 *n.d.*, 1846

Addition to Pap. VII¹ B 57:

Postscript. Perhaps within three days after reading this, Mr. Goldschmidt will reply, agreeing or disagreeing, in another paper;[341] then he can always demand time to prepare. If not, then my judgment is set. It will please me if he does that, but I am equally at ease if he does not. I cannot do more for one who with deference but also with confidence perhaps has seen in me more than was there, but nevertheless something of what was there. Then comes my turn to be abused. Of such things I am ignorant, but when he praises me[342] and I accidentally come to know about it, I must do something. I am at ease, even more so than before, because I was still somewhat hesitant to come to the final conclusion about him.—*Pap.* VII¹ B 58 *n.d.*, 1846

Addition to Pap. VII¹ B 57:

Note. Now I hear that the new book, *Concluding Unscientific Postscript*, is supposed to have been commended in *The Cor-*

sair,³⁴³ but in a moderated way. I am not so dense that I do not see that from its own point of view *The Corsair* has wanted to make it as good as possible. It has not wanted to abuse, because even it has a notion of what is unseemly; it has not wanted to give high praise, because it does have the notion that from my point of view it would in fact be an insult. So it has chosen a third way: an acknowledging trade announcement. But that cannot be done; I will not agree to that.—*Pap.* VII¹ B 59 *n.d.*, 1846

Some Good-natured Gossipy Remarks

It is a matter of common knowledge that a trifle, a nothing, creates the biggest sensation and especially gossip. I have been pleased to corroborate this by having an insignificant pseudonymous little article in *Fædrelandet*³⁴⁴ create much more of a sensation, because it dealt with Mr. P. L. Møller,³⁴⁵ than all my writing put together. I am positive that my whole life will never achieve the importance that my trousers³⁴⁶ have come to have. Yes, one might almost think that my trousers have become what the age demanded, and, if so, I sincerely hope that the demand of every age may be as moderate for the person concerned, for, good lord, it does not demand trousers from me; after all, it merely demands that I wear them, and this demand really does not embarrass me, inasmuch as I have made a practice of wearing trousers since I was four years old, but it never really occurred to me that this would become so extraordinarily important to others. But since my literary efforts have never been so fortunate as to satisfy the demands of the age, I thought to myself: If you can do it in such an easy way by means of your trousers, then everything is fine again. I always make a little self-sacrifice, but what is that compared with the significance. Just yesterday my servant reminded me to put on a new pair, but I thought to myself: That won't do; perhaps the new ones will not satisfy the demand of the age. But the old ones certainly do. Innumerable ladies and gentlemen have personally made sure that I am wearing them, and, according to what I could discern from their facial expressions, those trousers completely satisfied the demand of the age. To accommodate the demand of the age, I have candidly and freely replied to anyone who asked if they *actually* were the trousers—presumably so that he could relate that he personally had *actually* seen them—I have answered him solemnly, as is seemly in this important matter: Yes. —Whether they are my trousers or someone else's makes no difference to me, but for someone ardently trying to hold to a concept of the greatness in or potential for every man, there is something sad about having an abundance of observations that seem to bear witness only to irresponsibility, silliness, crudity, and the like.

But to move on. I now go from my trousers to something just as unimportant: Literatus P. L. Møller. The manuscript of my latest book[347] was ready by the middle of December 1845, and a few days before Christmas I delivered the manuscript in its entirety, as I am in the habit of doing, to the printer. Thus I was finished and at leisure, had the time and opportunity to do what I otherwise could not do, and in my joy and gratitude over being finished, I felt like doing somebody a little service. Then came P. L. Møller's brilliant *Gæa*.[348] Among other things, it contained a little attack (after praising the pseudonyms) on one of the pseudonyms. Usually I pay no attention to such things, but this was different. Mr. P. L. Møller is sufficiently well known in Danish literature, and for that reason I knew very well that I would make some people happy by challenging him; therefore the article in *Fædrelandet* included the lines: "obtrusive as he (P.L.M.) is and known to many, I really believed I would be doing some people a service by challenging him for once."[349] It is so seldom that P.L.M. comes out so openly that I could not let the opportunity pass. Therefore, far from being an article responding in self-defense to an attack, it was a service I wanted to do for others. The main point of the article was to get Mr. P.L.M. out of literature and the respectable company of famous Danish authors and into the dance hall of *The Corsair*, to which, according to an article he himself revised in the lexicon of authors,[350] he had already contributed both poetry and satire. What a real psychological satisfaction it was for me to see how quickly* Mr. P.L.M. took the hint. He came right out and bowed very deferentially in *Fædrelandet*[351]—and then off he went, that is, he disappeared.[352] Where he went, I do not know, but he vanished like a sneeze—and from that time on, according to my barber, things have been very busy in *The Corsair*'s dance hall.

Further, for now I go on to something just as unimportant as Mr. P.L.M.—to *The Corsair*. They are all trivialities—my trousers, Mr. P.L.M., and *The Corsair*—and thus are subjects only for gossip, which goes against my grain, for although I have a Greek enthusiasm and love for conversation, gossip has always been repugnant to me. But in saying this, I do not want to wrong anyone for the sake of a whim by lumping three paltry things together in order to round off a phrase, for I feel that I must make an exception: I owe my trousers the apology that they are altogether innocent in all this gossip.

I shall write more briefly about *The Corsair*. It is my private opinion that such a disproportionate and immoral phenomenon does great harm by inveigling the unstable and tempting the semieducated; to me it is a national disgrace that such a phenomenon flourishes on such a scale. But, you see, *The Corsair* had immortalized and flattered me.[353] Occasionally I do take notice of such things, for, looking at it polemically, I believe that one cannot be done with the incompetent criticaster who wants to assert himself everywhere if one does not go to the bottom of things and set a precedent when one is praised by the incompetent.** I wanted to do something, and just today I find among some old papers a little offhand piece[354] written in my days of immortality, even if I did not have the time and opportunity then, since I was fully occupied as an author with my own ideas. Add to that the fact that it was a difficult thing to do effectually. Since that paper, according to my barber, is supposed to be ironic and extremely witty, I was afraid it would manage to make a

In margin: * and how perfectly.

In margin: ** Note. Therefore I also did this earlier,[355] on the occasion of an article in *Berlingske Tidende*, a generally decent and respectable paper.

joke of the matter, even capitalize on it, as if it were my intention to say something witty at its expense and thereby prompt it to be witty also. As I see it, that would have been the most dreadful responsibility to assume. So time went on, and my leisure commenced, during which the matter presumably would come up again. And what happens—along comes Mr. P.L.M., most opportunely for me. Precisely because I now could start from a kind of attack, I would be able to prevent the dreadful falsification of regarding my little *inserat* [insertion] as a compliment; I could make it so emphatic that that paper would have to abandon every hope of maintaining a kind of relationship to me as a high-ranking ally by continuing to pamper me and my immortality, for I, too, am supposed to be ironic and witty—how close lies the loathsome copula of misunderstanding! And I succeeded, all right, for, according to my barber, no one should be abused as I have been.

That is the whole story. It is not simply a rash step[356] on my part; I knew very well what I was doing and why. I find everything that has happened quite in order, but it would pain me if a first-rate person did not quickly perceive this; it would pain me if he, out of misunderstanding, condemned me for what I deliberately did out of sympathy for others,[357] did what the majority of the better individuals were prevented from doing for professional reasons, because of circumstances, by not being an author, etc. This step has satisfied me so much that I would not wish it undone at any price. I leave it to anyone in a position to do something to consider whether it is defensible to let a paper go on under the guise of being nothing at all when it is circulated all over, is read even by schoolchildren, yes, even has the brass to meddle with teacher-pupil relationships, when it broadcasts lies and slander on the greatest possible scale, persecutes men whose wives perhaps also feel violated by it. Therefore, I repeat my Catonian *praeterea censeo* [furthermore, I am of the opinion],[358] it is necessary that it be done. As everyone knows, after first begging very obsequiously, insolent beggars, when refused, pursue a person up and down the street with their begging for alms. Literary contemptibleness, which in the literary world stands *au niveau* [on the same level] as such a pack of beggars does in civic life, has tried to employ the same tactic: when no one deems it worthy of reply, it follows behind a man incessantly and continuously, bullying him until he quite likely grows tired of hearing it.—*Pap.* VII^1 B 69 *n.d.*, 1846

A Polite Suggestion

From the very beginning, neither the pseudonymous writers nor I have asked for a public but, polemically opposed to any kind of phantasmic nonentity, have always been satisfied with a few individual readers, or, indeed, with that single individual.[359]

In all consistency, therefore, this suggestion is to the few, among whom those individuals or the single individual may be sought, the few who could and would be more interested in a consistent point of view, diligently, competently, and sacrificially worked out, than in my trousers,[360] the binding of my books, or what printed pieces of impertinence the naughty boy of literature happens to think up. It is almost too much that I, who only wished indirectly to become slightly important to a single individual by editing or writing books, suddenly became important to everybody—because of my old gray trousers. Consequently, anyone who is anything of a dialectician and is willing to spend some time in practicing [*indøve*] double-reflection[361] will readily perceive that it was the consistency of my life-view as an author that made me do everything negative, and precisely thereby consistently, to support the books, even though I also hoped to contribute indirectly to exposing a contemptible literary phenomenon in all its baseness. If my books become popular, then I have been misunderstood, and if I prompt it myself, then I have been guilty of high treason against my idea and my life-view, although few are sufficiently dialectical to understand how. But if it gets to be a questionable good to read or to have read them, if a person becomes almost ashamed or almost fears to be laughed at for having read a big book[362] all the way through, then the opportune time has come—for my readers—then a single individual will go away in solitude and read, he will read and be pleased or displeased. But if it pleases him, as a reader he is still not my adherent in a herd sense, in an external and ridiculous sense—he is himself a man. Just as I have been sufficiently dialectical to perceive this in all its consistency, so too I also have had the courage to act[363] accordingly. I am no fool who believes that the world becomes better because it praises me or, worse, because it censures me—no, the issue is simply one of preventing faddish opinions. This is the hint to that single individual, who will understand that I am utterly and completely in the service of my idea precisely at the point where the crowd interested in my trousers believes that I am trapped. In my opinion, to be victorious in the world does not mean that I conquer but that I persevere in everything, do everything the idea commands so that it can be victorious.

I do not believe it actually can be said that I have been a disgrace to the nation to which I have the honor to belong, to the mother tongue[364] that, next to thinking, is my love, to the literature I dare say I have served unselfishly. On the other hand, I am not settling the question of whether the friendly city in which I live and the inhabitants of the same are honored by having rabble-barbarism rise up against me. It is certainly true that I myself challenged it to do so by way of a pseudonym[365]—absolutely right, and for two reasons. In the first place, because it was in pursuance of my idea—only that single individual will understand this—and, in the second place, because I hoped thereby to give the naughty boy of literature occasion really to exercise his brazenness or, if this is putting it too mildly, since, of course, even a naughty child does not insist on making money from his contemptible behavior, consequently to give the contemptible, avaricious prostitute of literature occasion to be exposed properly in his brazenness. More and more people will gradually come to understand this, even though at the moment I am subject to the most varied misinterpretations, and also by some of the better people, which personally pains me, even though in the idea I am more than at ease. Gradually it will be understood that when rabble-barbarism has achieved wide circulation and flourishes prosperously, it does no good to remain silent, but neither does it do any good to get into conflict with it; one must only help it to make itself even more lunatic and ask to be abused—then it will be exposed, and it will burst. When this is understood, it will also be understood that what kept others from doing what I have done was not so much a higher wisdom or an especially calculating wisdom but rather a slight timidity.*

In margin: * for to oppose the government, especially when one is part of a group, now that is really something, but when this involves just a little danger, a little inconvenience, and there is nothing to gain, neither honor nor status—then courage is not readily at hand.—*Pap.* VII¹ B 70 *n.d.*, 1846

A Bit of Factual Information

From much that has been written the last three months, according to my barber, in that organ of literary contemptibleness in this country, together with something that just now came to my attention in a more respectable paper (*Kjøbenhavnsposten*),[366] I must conclude that there are a few people who curiously connect everything I write or edit, big or small books, with a little article in *Fædrelandet*[367] written three months ago by Frater Taciturnus against Mr. P. L. Møller. It created a sensation[368] at the time, for, needless to say, the biggest sensations are created by nothing at all, and this article, after all, dealt with Mr. P.L.M. Anyone who thinks but a moment of this strange connecting-together will quickly perceive that it completely turns everything upside down. As a rule, it would hardly occur to me to say anything, but since I can factually prove in a few words the impossibility of this connection, I will do it. The manuscript of *Concluding Unscientific Postscript*[369] was completely finished in the middle of December and delivered complete to the printer a few days before Christmas, as the records of book printer Luno[370] can prove. That little review of *En Hverdags His-*

torie[371] was begun in the middle of December, which Giødwad[372] must be able to corroborate. Not until then, consequently after that time, did Mr. P.L.M.'s *Gæa* come out containing the piece[373] that prompted that little article. Thus it was *after I was finished* with what I had regarded as my task for four and one-half years, a task that claimed all my time and attention. I wrote that little article with the stated intention of doing a few people a service.[374] Rarely does one see Mr. P.L.M.'s name, and what I stated in the article is true: "obtrusive as he (P. L. Møller) is and known to many, I really believed I would be doing some people a service by challenging him."[375]

Of course, I consider the article in *Fædrelandet*[376] to be insignificant, at most something that one writes to do someone a service. If there can be one person here in the country who considers it anything else, who regards that little article as far more important than all the pseudonymous books,[377] who believes that everything I do focuses on that little article and thereby even less on the one on whom the article focuses— this must be considered an optical illusion. If that same one has a friend who for friendship's sake abandons himself to the same illusion, this must be regarded as a matter of friendship.—*Pap*. VII¹ B 71 *n.d.*, 1846

A Literary Signal Shot

In a limited setting, where the sediment has difficulty in settling, in a limited setting, where neither a great confluence nor the powerful wind of momentous events is the daily pattern, in a limited setting, it is at times necessary in the interests of truth and the good to use precautionary procedures that are utterly superfluous in a larger setting. In small rooms, care must be taken to air out once in a while; care must be taken to keep the water clean in a small reservoir, a precaution not at all necessary if the reservoir is the sea. In the same vein, it is common knowledge that the great urban centers of Europe, Paris and London, conceal a great mass of demoralization, but the contexts are so vast that the sediment can actually become sediment, the wind so strong that the noxious gases still cannot reach the point of polluting the atmospheric air. One thousand prostitutes in Paris are of no great importance. There is literally a great class of inhabitants who literally and veritably can go on unaware of them.

In a small town, however, one prostitute would be intolerable, because it would be impossible to overlook her in a town where a settling of the sediment is out of the question, since the whole life of the town is in a goldfish bowl. If the inhabitants of a small town were to overlook the presence of such a creature, there would be something false about it that in an immoral way would essentially make such a prostituted creature interesting, because everyone could check on everyone else and know it was a lie if someone said he did not know about it.

But so it is also in a limited literary setting. When the context is so small that, for better or for worse, we all simply have to put up with rubbing elbows, then overlooking must be used with great circumspection. In a limited literary setting, it is, regrettably, impossible to express in an ordinary way that sediment is sediment, because we live so close to one another. The individual cannot be reproached for this any more than the small-town resident can be reproached for living in a town where the urban principle "to overlook" must be exchanged for the principle of riddance, or at least that of labeling sediment for what it is. Therefore, in a limited literary setting, literary rabble-barbarism,* irrespective of its having talent or not, simply and solely by having attained a kind of range and scope, makes overlooking a wrong tactic for those of quality, because, for better or for worse, it is no secret that this overlooking is a lie, and, in any case, it is not believed. Therefore, this overlooking, instead of repressing, works as a stimulating ingredient in favor of propagating rabble-barbarism more widely, until, finally, this overlooking, which supposedly expressed distinction and superiority, can take on the appearance of fear when the rabble-barbarism

VII¹
B 72
261

In margin: * literary prostitution

attains greater and greater circulation. And again it is the case, simply because of the limited setting and the scope and range of circulation, that more and more people will become confused about what is what, all the more since rabble-barbarism, encouraged by its extensiveness, will become more and more rash and brazen. When that is the case, other rules of procedure must be adopted. In a limited setting, it is never wise to want to live in the delusion that one is living in a large setting; it is better to know the circumstances and then to act according to them.

It certainly has not escaped my attention, nor am I ignorant of the potential consequences in a small setting, that over the last few years literary prostitution has attained such alarming circulation that, however much it is generally considered to be and remains sediment, it is so far from factually being sediment that instead it is the most conspicuous of all, and by having practically the largest subscription list[378] of forty-three papers and other organs, it is assured of being read as no other paper is. Therefore, it both amazes and alarms me that those who really must be considered to be called—not to engage in conflict with the prostituted (for one should not engage in conflict with them) but to label them[*]—have been silent, have wanted to delude us into thinking that our setting is large and thereby have helped rabble-barbarism to gain more and more headway.

As far as I am concerned—for I, too, am an author in Danish literature and therefore am interested in this situation—since I have thought that just as a singer should watch his diet before a concert and just as a pregnant woman should follow every precautionary measure, so, too, an author who has been concentrating his effort uninterruptedly on one coherent work, regardless of what others think of this work, must consider it to be of such importance that he must maintain the strictest dietetic regimen with respect to everything else and observe every precautionary rule. This I have done and for that reason have remained silent.

[*] *In margin*: very explicitly

But in the middle of 1845 I was finished with *Concluding Unscientific Postscript*, the entire manuscript, which, according to my invariable practice, I delivered to the printer.*[379] Simultaneously, I decided to take action against the literary rabble-barbarism and its tyranny among us. I was prompted both by my grateful joy over having finished my book in so short a time and by a well-intentioned consideration for others, and, since I was finished, I dared to expose myself to any unpleasantness without concern. Perhaps someone will perceive, if he reads this, that what has been construed in so many ways by the hasty and foolish as a rash and hasty step[380] on my part was carefully calculated and thoughtfully considered.

As I said previously, this was the situation in the last days of December 1845. Then even Governance[381] came to my aid with a little hint. Mr. P. L. Møller,[382] who, according to an article he himself revised in the lexicon of authors,[383] had contributed both poetry and satire to *The Corsair*,** helped me by providing the occasion in a signed article in *Gæa*.[384] I could not let such a fortunate opportunity go by unused (for Mr. P. L. Møller rarely signs his name, and although his name does not add much, it is still something compared with an anonym).

The article did in fact have an effect. Mr. P.L.M. himself unquestionably has realized that it was damnably unfortunate that he signed his name. In a polite, almost obsequious—especially in consideration of my indictment—signed little notice,[385] he retracted, and then where he went,[386] I do not know, but, according to what my barber told me, from that time on there was in *The Corsair* a lot of hustle and bustle in

In margin: * Note. Since, for better or for worse, we are accustomed to the brashest lies in print and it does no good to ignore this in a limited setting, I want to make sure in advance that no cheeky fellow will be able to attenuate this fact and therefore refer to Bianco Luno,[387] who, after all, keeps a record and can testify that this is so.

In margin: ** Perhaps some few who remember the hue and cry raised because I committed the enormous crime of denouncing Mr. P.L.M. as an author writing in *The Corsair* now see the brazenness of the lies that were told, for there is hardly a better guarantee than the article revised by the author himself in the lexicon of authors.

the dance hall of literary contemptibleness. But in other papers as well.—*Pap.* VII¹ B 72 *n.d.*, 1846

JOURNAL ENTRIES

March 1846

the ninth

The *Concluding Postscript* is out; the pseudonymity has been acknowledged;[388] one of these days the printing of the "Literary Review"[389] will begin. Everything is in order; all I have to do now is to keep calm, be silent, depending on *The Corsair* to support the whole enterprise negatively, just as I wish. From the standpoint of the idea, I am at present as correctly situated in literature as possible, and also in such a way that to be an author becomes a deed.[390] In itself, it was a most capital idea to make a break with *The Corsair* in order to prevent any direct advances[*] at the very moment I was through with the authorship[391] and, by assuming all the pseudonyms, ran the risk of becoming an authority of sorts. This is why right now, when I am advancing polemically against the age, I owe it to the idea and to irony to prevent any confusion with the ironical bad brandy *The Corsair* serves in the dance halls of contemptibleness. Incidentally, it has happened here, as it frequently does, that despite all my deliberation a something more eventuates that is due not to me but to Governance. It always happens this way: that to which I give the most thought I always understand far better afterwards, both its ideal significance and the fact that it was precisely what I should have done.[392]

But this existence is exhausting; I am convinced that not a single person understands me. The most that anyone, even an

---

[*] *In margin*: Prior to that time nothing could be done; my work for my idea demanded all my time, every minute, and undisturbed as possible. It is really superb that just when someone supposes and is spitefully pleased that I am taking a rash step[393] (and this perhaps evokes some malicious glee) I am just then being most calculating and level-headed. But the best support for all action is—to pray. That is actually the true genius; then one never comes out on the short end.

admirer, would concede is that I bear all this unpleasantness with a certain poise, but that I want it—of course, no one dreams of that. But then, on the other hand, it would again be hasty human thoughtlessness to conclude, if it were understood why I, by virtue of the idea of double reflection,[394] must wish it, that *ergo* he is not suffering at all, is insensitive to all this vulgarity and the brazen lies. Just as if one could not voluntary decide to take upon oneself all tribulations if the idea enjoins it. The article[395] against P. L. Møller was written in great fear and trembling; I did it during the holidays, but for the sake of a regulating resistance I did not neglect going to church or reading my sermon. So also with the article[396] against *The Corsair*. On the other hand, they were properly written, for if I had evinced passion, someone along the way would have found occasion for a direct relation to me. It was amusing and psychologically superb to see the haste with which P. L. Møller[397] got the hint given about withdrawing into *The Corsair*. He came forward, bowed politely, and then withdrew to the place where he is at home.

What pains me most, however, is not the vulgarity of the rabble but the secret participation in it by the better people.[398] I, too, would like to make myself comprehensible to one single person, to my reader. But I dare not, for then I defraud the idea. It is precisely when I am succeeding most, when brutality is at its most shameless peak, that I dare not speak. Finally, it is my responsibility to be consistently unyielding so that I shall not be responsible for several people going completely astray. So be it. I must be silent.

VII¹
A 98
43

The last two months have been very rewarding for my observations. What I said in my dissertation[399] about irony making phenomena stand revealed is so true. First of all, my ironic leap into *The Corsair* goes a long way toward making it perfectly clear that *The Corsair* is devoid of idea. Seen from the point of view of idea, it is dead, even if it finds a few thousand more subscribers. It wants to be ironical and does not even understand irony. Generally speaking, it would have been an epigram over my whole life if it might ever be said: Contemporary with him there existed a bungling ironic journal that sang his praises;⁴⁰⁰ no, hold on—he was abused, and he himself asked for it.⁴⁰¹ —Second, my ironic leap into *The Corsair* shows up the self-contradiction of the environing world. Everyone has been going around saying: It is nothing, who cares about *The Corsair*, etc. What happens when one does it is that one is charged with being rash; they say one has deserved all this (now, you see, it is "all this") because one prompted it; they hardly dare walk in the street⁴⁰² with me, fearing that they too will be in *The Corsair*. The self-contradiction, however, has a deeper basis; in their Christian envy they half wish that the paper may go on, each one hoping that he will not be attacked. They now say that the paper is despicable and nothing; they enjoin the persons under attack not to dare to become angry or make any protest, *ergo*, the paper must flourish. And the public has first the stimulation of envy and then the shameless pleasure of watching the victim of the attack—whether it affects him.* And this phenomenon in such a little country as Denmark, this phenomenon as the one and only prevailing—and this is supposed to be nothing! How well cowardice and contemptibility suit each other in the bond of shabbiness! And when the whole thing bursts some day, Goldschmidt will be the one who suffers; and it is absolutely the same public—and then the world has become such a splendid world!

Furthermore, my observations abundantly strengthen my conviction that when a man consistently expresses one idea, every objection to him contains a self-contradiction of the one who makes it.** They say I am the one who cares about *The Corsair*. What happens? The "Concluding Postscript" was delivered bag and baggage to Luno⁴⁰³ before I wrote against P. L. Møller. Now in the preface⁴⁰⁴ to it (which, incidentally, was written in May of 1845) there was something that seems to suggest the latter (this shows, among other things, how early I was aware of it). Now if I had cared about *The Corsair*,

In margin: * And now has the chance to lie about him: that he is affected, that he is able to hide it but is affected just the same. The latter formula is especially convenient for scandalmongers.

In margin: ** Who thereby is talking not about him but about himself.

I would have made some changes in it simply to avoid the appearance of being so. I know how I fought down the temptation to do it because it pained me to think of Bishop Mynster, for example, saying: And Kierkegaard refers to such a thing even in a book. But I was true to myself in not caring about *The Corsair*—and then what happens? Well, just as expected—allusions to *The Corsair* are found in everything I write. Here is the dead giveaway, for it must be "they" themselves who had *The Corsair in mente* [in mind], since they find it even in something written prior to that time.

Two things in particular occupy me: (1) that whatever the cost I remain intellectually true in the Greek sense[405] to my existence-idea; (2) that in the religious sense it becomes as elevating and ennobling to me as possible. I pray God for the latter. Solitary I have always been; now I really have the opportunity again to practice. My solitary secret is not my grief but is precisely that I have the upper hand, that I transform what is hostile into something that serves my idea without its having any intimation of this itself. Yes, this life is certainly satisfying, but it is also terribly strenuous. From what a tragic side one learns to know men, and how sad that what will look so good at a distance is always misunderstood by contemporaries. But again it is the religious that redeems; here there is sympathy for all, not the garrulous fellow feeling of cliques and henchmen, but infinite sympathy for each and all—in silence.

But without a doubt it is educational to be placed as I am in so small a city as Copenhagen. To work almost to despair with all one's capacities, with deep agony of soul and much inner suffering, to put money into publishing books[406]—and then literally not to have ten men who read them through properly, while on the other hand students and other authors find it almost ridiculously easy to write a big book; and then to have a paper that everyone reads, which has the license of contemptibleness to dare say anything, the most lying distortions (and it is nothing, but everybody reads it); and then the whole pack of envious people who lend a hand by saying just the opposite in order to minimize in that way. Day after day

VII[1]
A 98
45

to be the object of everybody's conversation and attention, and then the business of defending me against an attack in order to attack me more viciously themselves. Every kitchen boy feels justified in almost insulting me in accordance with *The Corsair*'s orders; young students titter and grin and are happy to see a prominent person trampled on; professors are jealous and secretly sympathize with the attacks, and spread them, too, with the appendage, of course, that it is a shame. The slightest thing I do, if it is merely to pay a visit, is twisted and distorted into lies and told everywhere; if *The Corsair* finds out, it is printed and read by everybody, the man I visit is embarrassed, gets almost angry with me, for which he cannot be blamed. Eventually I will have to withdraw and associate only with people I do not like, for it is, after all, almost a wrong against the others. And so it continues, and sometime when I am dead, men's eyes will be opened; then they will admire what I wanted to do and will simultaneously treat in the same way a contemporary who probably is the only one who understands me. God in heaven, who could endure this if there were not an interior place in a man where all this can be forgotten in communion with you.

But my activity as an author is finished[407]—God be praised. It has been granted to me to conclude it myself, to understand myself when it ought to stop, and next to publishing *Either/Or*[408] I thank God for that. I know very well and find it quite in order that people will not see it this way and that it would in fact take but two words from me to prove it so. This has hurt; it seems that I still could have desired that recognition, but let it be.

If I only could make myself become a pastor.[409] Out there in quiet activity, permitting myself a little productivity in my free time, I shall breathe easier, however much my present life has gratified me.—*JP* V 5887 (*Pap.* VII¹ A 98) March 9, 1846

But nothing must be written, not one word; I dare not. Were I to write, I would give the reader a hint and throw the whole thing out of gear. He must not find out anything secretly. I have tossed off a few things during this time that are not bad but that can be used only in a completely different situation.

I have thought of the last version as being like this:

Short and Sweet

In my opinion, an editor is literarily responsible when there is no author. The editor of *The Corsair* is Mr. Goldschmidt,[410] university student, a bright fellow, without an idea, without scholarship, without a point of view, without self-control, but not without a certain talent and a desperate esthetic power. At a critical moment in his life he approached me.[411] I tried indirectly to help him negatively. I praise him for his self-assurance in getting himself established. I believe he has succeeded in what he wanted to do. I had hoped that he would have chosen an honorable way to earn a name for himself; to be honest, it pains me that as the editor of *The Corsair* he *continues* to choose the way of contemptibility to earn money. It was my desire to snatch, if possible, a talented man from being an instrument of rabble-barbarism, but I certainly had no wish to be shamefully rewarded by being immortalized[412] by a paper of contemptibility that ought never to have existed and by which I can only wish to be abused. It is expedient for my life as an author to be abused, and that is why I wished it and asked for it as soon as I was finished, for by the time Frater Taciturnus[413] wrote, Johannes Climacus[414] had already been delivered to the printer a few days before. I had also hoped to benefit others by this step; they do not want it—well, I shall go on asking for abuse because it suits my idea and in order to get some good, after all, out of the existence of a paper like that. It is sad to see the pack of fools and the fatuous who laugh, and yet, at least in this case, they do not know what they are laughing at. God alone knows whether or not I am playing for too high stakes with respect to my contemporaries. My idea requires it; its consistency satisfies me beyond measure—I cannot do otherwise. I beg forgiveness of all the better people who are undialectical or do not have the presuppositions to understand that I must do as I am doing—and then forward: would that I might be abused.[415] However important or unimportant my life as an author, this much is certain: because of my dialectical relation, I am the only Danish author who is so situated that it can serve the idea to have every possible lie and distortion and nonsense and gossip come out, confusing the reader and thus helping him to self-activity and preventing a direct relationship. No other Danish author, when he addresses himself to one hundred, can possibly benefit from the reading of lies and distortions by one thousand readers.* But he benefits me, he benefits me every time he abuses me, and that he will certainly do; he cannot get away from me, and his inability to pursue the good expresses itself in the defiance of an unhappy infatuation and a self-stifling through abusive words, all of which I regret, inasmuch as I meant him well.[416] But his abuse is irrelevant; I could just as well be absent.

If Mr. Goldschmidt will reply in a decent paper and sign his name to it, I will read it; I no longer read *The Corsair*, I would not even direct my servant to read it, for I do not believe it lies within a master's authority to be able to order his servant to go to a place of disrepute.

S.K.

In margin: * No other Dane can benefit from rabble-barbarism's having a widely read organ that has him in its power, when it so pleases a literary tramp.—*JP* V 5888 (*Pap.* VII¹ A 99) *n.d.*, 1846

What really distresses me in the whole affair is to see the mass of the conceited who want to play the loftiest game of intellectuality, and then I am practically the only one who has the Greek mentality[417] and the education of independence for it, and then I am the very one who wanted to work toward something like that, which is directly related to my whole task.—*JP* V 5889 (*Pap.* VII¹ A 101) *n.d.*, 1846

March 16

Given the conditions in the world as it is, to be an author should be the extraordinary employment in life, an employment that escapes the dialectic of the universal (office and whatever pertains to that; a living and whatever pertains to that). Therefore, not only should the author's production be a testimony to the idea, but the author's life should also correspond to the idea. But, alas, of all categories, the category of actuality is the most mediocre. To be an author is to be in a fraternity and is just as cluttered up with finiteness as anything else. Authors are supposed to be of mutual help to one another, criticize one another's writings, talk about what one is going to do, etc. Your intimate friends in particular are supposed to profit from the relationship and have little scraps of news to run around with: "that they personally saw the manuscript, heard part of it, talked with the author, etc."

VII[1]
A 104
50

By taking advantage of my pseudonymity, I have stayed completely clear of this. In the finite sense, I have thereby done irreparable damage to myself, have offended people, have shirked the salutary tradition of small talk, and have given my whole enterprise the appearance of chance and caprice; and even if I were now to show how everything hangs together, what exceedingly rigorous ordering formed the basis, no one would believe it—for it would be inconceivable that anyone should have such a plan and keep quiet about it. Fools, only the person who can keep quiet has such a plan.

When I had finished,[418] I tried to do a little for others. I wrote the two articles against P.L.M. and *The Corsair*.[419] After that, I was happy to review *Hverdags Historien*.[420] The end result will be, I am sure, that people will be led to believe that I am doing it in order to gain favor. Ah, if I wanted to have power and prestige in Danish literature—which I easily could—I would have done just the opposite. I would not have broken so emphatically with *The Corsair*, for its continual nonsense still exerts an influence on mass opinion, and to be commended by it[421] would still be a titillating ingredient. Very quickly I should have put myself at the front as the awaited one, deigned to recognize one or two of the younger ones, taken a negative position toward the older ones—this is how to get ahead in Danish literature, and this is what the younger ones want, and anyone who wants to have power must always line up with the younger ones. But I did exactly the opposite instead—precisely because I do not wish and am too melancholy to want to have status and recognition in the world. I irritate the younger ones, for none of them stands so high that he can slip past me and what I do—I bow to the older writers. The minute I stop, I will be happy to leave everything unchanged in Danish literature, to get Professor Heiberg[422] esteemed as in the past, Bishop Mynster[423] venerated as absolutely as possible—then everything will again be in order. And then I am accused of ambitious vanity. Would that he who accuses might first reflect for a moment. For example, *The Corsair* no doubt fancies that it has enormous power—how then can a person who breaks with it be seeking power?

How fundamentally polemic I am by nature I can best see in the fact that the only path by which the attacks of men can affect me is the sadness I feel on their behalf. As long as I am embattled, I am imperturbable, but when I have supremacy, then I become sad at seeing human folly and contemptibleness. My author-existence is truly as pure as new-fallen snow, removed from all worldly avidity, is in the service of the idea; therefore, the masses, who actually do not understand me, still ought to have a gratifying impression of it. But that is not to be. Well, let them tell lies, let them slander and misrepresent. But certainly every older generation of authors, insofar as they have the innocent and admissible desire to enjoy recognition, must always wish for a successor like me, who, like a woman, desires nothing himself but desires only to elevate the elders.

Meanwhile, everyone has a special license to taunt and attack me in all sorts of ways. They profit in a strange way from my supposed intelligence. They say what they like, and if it is refuted by the facts, then they say: Well, one can't figure it out, for he is so intelligent and cunning and clever. They maintain that I do this and that out of vanity; the facts contradict this, and so they say: Yes, he is so intelligent—that is, he is intelligent enough to do the opposite, but just the same he is vain. A curious argument! If I do the opposite of what vanity bids me do, then either I must be stupid or, if I am intelligent, then I must not be vain. Now if I am conceded to be intelligent—*ergo*, I am not vain. But see, they arrive at the opposite conclusion. Ultimately, it all comes down to this, that men are not able to conceive of an intelligent man not coveting status and power. They assume this (for the good and stupidity are identical) and consequently draw the conclusion: Even if we cannot prove it, he must be vain because he is so intelligent—intelligent enough to do the opposite of what vanity bids him do. But their presupposition contains a veritable confession.

But how many lives are wasted in this confounded garrulousness about others.—*JP* V 5891 (*Pap.* VII^1 A 104)   March 16, 1846

VII^1
A 104
52

And yet my ironic powers of observation and my soul derived such extraordinary satisfaction from gadding about on the streets[424] and being a nobody in this way while thoughts and ideas were working within me, from being a loafer this way while I was clearly the most industrious of the younger set and appearing irresponsible this way and "lacking in earnestness" while the earnestness of the others could easily become a jest alongside my inner concerns. Now this is all upset; the rabble, the apprentices, the butcher boys, the schoolboys, and all such are egged on. But I will not play to such a public. I have nothing to do with it; it lacks the requisite condition for manifesting my irony or its significance for the idea. It was in the encounter with people who, because of their education, I might say, were able to grasp something more profound in me or to have some conception of it—it was in the encounter with such people that my irony was gratified by posing the enigmatic problem, and my wrath found satisfaction in seeing how they disparaged me. But the completely uneducated class, the schoolboys and the butcher boys, of course, have no requisite conditions; this terrain is unsuitable, irony cannot be used here. It is sad to see that there actually are papers written for schoolboys, that already at such an early age they are plunged into the confusion of am-

VII^1
A 107
54

VII^1
A 107
55

biguity. I will give only one situation, yet it is typical. It was with Lieutenant Barth,[425] adjutant of the Hussars. He came walking along with his little son. The father greeted me with his usual, almost excessive attention, stepped aside to allow me the flagstones. If the lad had not known who I was, he might have gotten a notion that I was somewhat extraordinary, but the boy obviously knew me—he was a reader of *The Corsair*. What a combination! Must it not be harmful to children at one moment to read about a man being mistreated in this way, practically inviting the whole bunch of schoolboys to whistle at him on the streets—and then the next moment to see him treated in this manner by his father, or read samples of his writing in Danish school readers.[426]

And now that I have remodeled my external life, am more withdrawn, keep to myself more, have a more momentous look about me, then in certain quarters it will be said that I have changed for the better. Alas, but my idea is not being served as it was then. But then, after all, my writing days are over.[427]—*JP* V 5894 (*Pap.* VII¹ A 107) *n.d.*, 1846

It was a Greek principle[428] that I existentially expressed; now it is disarranged. And what has disarranged it? The fact that the press is used on such a great scale. It is the press that actually destroys all personality. That a cowardly wretch can sit in hiding and write and print for the thousands! All personal conduct and all personal power must run aground on this. It would be most interesting to talk with Socrates about the matter.—*JP* V 5899 (*Pap.* VII¹ A 112) *n.d.*, 1846

January 1847

What I take exception to in all this trouble with literary contemptibleness is, of course, not their attack and insults (I invited them myself)[429] nor their conduct, which, after all, patronizes this contemptibleness; no, it is their meanness, which, because they do not know how to grasp a situation, wants to be ingenious and pass judgment on me, that it was a rash step[430] etc.

But the time will surely come when all these cowards will think it no longer necessary to lie. As soon as the danger is over, they will most likely dare say that I was right. What paltriness we live in! It is so characteristic that right now when Goldschmidt[431] has gone abroad and P. L. Møller[432] has apparently lost his nerve, they are beginning to appreciate my action. And there are those brave, bold journalists who, when it comes to criticizing a poor policeman for losing his temper, use frank, bold, outspoken language: Fie on the hypocrites! It is these loyal supporters of the government, these outspoken journalists, who attack the liberals for every little trifle—where no danger is involved! But where there is a bit of danger (somewhat like firemen being the only ones tried and tested in dangers during times of peace), there has not been one single hint of a word.

But this is why those who should have maintained the pathos with respect to my action are in difficulties with me. Now that the danger is over, they perhaps even want to say what they did not dare say before; but they have a bad conscience about me, they feel that I see right through them, and they are almost afraid that if the opportunity comes, I will, with new recklessness and probably very good reasons, let them pay the penalty for this meanness.—*JP* V 5957 (*Pap.* VII¹ A 214) January 1847

Jan. 24

God be praised that all the assaults of rabble-barbarism have come upon me. Now I have gained time to learn inwardly and to convince myself that it was indeed a gloomy thought to want to live out in a rural parish[433] and do penance in seclusion and oblivion. Now I stand resolved and rooted to the spot in a way I have never been. If I had not been put through the mill of insults, this gloomy idea would have continued to pester me, for a certain kind of prosperity fosters gloomy ideas; if, for example, I had not had private means,[434] I would never, with my disposition to melancholy, have reached the point I have sometimes reached.—*JP* V 5966 (*Pap.* VII¹ A 229) January 24, 1847

220 *Supplement*

To be trampled to death by geese is a lingering death, and to be torn to death by *envy* is also a slow way to die. While rabble-barbarism insults me (for what comes out in a newspaper once would not mean much if it did not give the vulgar the mandate to insult one day after day, abuse one on the public street, schoolboys, brash students, store clerks, and all the scum yellow journalism stirs up), upper-class envy looks on with approval. It does not grudge me that. And does one want to live or does one choose to live under such conditions. No, but I am nevertheless happy that I know I have *acted*.[435] Incidentally, nibbling mistreatment like that is among the most distressing. Everything else has an end, but this does not cease. To sit in church where a couple of louts have the impudence to sit down beside one in order to gawk at one's trousers and insult one so loudly that every word is audible. But this is what I am used to. The fact that brazenness has a mandate in the newspapers makes the smart alecks think they are justified, yes, that they are agents of public opinion. And I realize this, but in a certain sense I have been in error about Denmark, for I did not believe that rabble-barbarism actually was public opinion in Denmark, but I shall gladly testify that this is the case, something that can be factually demonstrated very easily.—*JP* V 5998 (*Pap.* VIII¹ A 99) *n.d.*, 1847

VIII¹
A 133
65

With the press as degenerate as it is, human beings eventually will surely be transformed into clods. A newspaper's first concern has to be circulation; from then on, the rule for what it publishes can be: the wittiness and entertainment of printing something without any relation to communication through the press. How significant! How easy to be witty when misuse of the press has become the newly invented kind of witticism.

VIII¹
A 133
66

For example, they write that a certain well-known person (mentioned by name) wears an embroidered shirt. This is written and then read by the whole market town where the lunatic press thrives. The man is cartooned with an embroidered shirt, and this treatment goes on for half a year—and naturally is the most widely read of everything read in the market town. If this is not either lunacy or idiocy, then I know of no other alternative. People are simply too immediate and momentary, but on this scale it is the *non plus ultra* [unsurpassable]—to use the circulation of the press to discuss for half a year something which, after all, the most addlebrained person ought to be sufficiently human not to talk about for more than five minutes—it can only lead to idiocy.—*JP* V 6007 (*Pap.* VIII[1] A 133) *n.d.*, 1847

After a laborious process of study and development and after painstaking effort continued over a long period, the most gifted intellects of a country eventually become authors—and authors of books. But books are seldom read in this country. The daily newspaper, however, has wide circulation and is read by everybody. Here, then, seen from the point of view of the idea, are all those hollow and bandy-legged, clumsy and flat-footed as well as clumsy-fingered, half-witted but sly, reprehensible fellows called journalists, busily operating, and their cogitations are read by all. *Pro dii immortales* [ye gods]! Suppose there is only one megaphone on a ship and the cook's mate has appropriated it, an act that all regarded as appropriate. Everything the cook's mate has to communicate ("Some butter on the spinach" or "Fine weather today" or "God knows if there's something wrong below in the ship" etc.) is communicated through the megaphone, but the captain has to give his commands solely by means of his voice, for what the captain has to say is not so important. Yes, the captain finally has to ask the cook's mate to help him so that he can be heard, if the cook's mate would be so good as to "report" the order, which, it must be admitted, sometimes gets completely garbled in going through the cook's mate and his megaphone, in which case the captain strains his little voice in vain, for the cook and his megaphone are heard. Finally the cook's mate gets control, because he has the megaphone. *Pro dii immortales!*—*JP* V 6008 (*Pap.* VIII[1] A 135) *n.d.*, 1847

In a way, I am living like a fish in water to which a disagreeable ingredient has been added, making it impossible for fish to breathe in it. My atmosphere has been tainted for me. Because of my melancholy and my enormous work, I needed a situation of solitude in the crowd in order to rest. So I despair. I can no longer find it. Curiosity surrounds me everywhere. I drive thirty-five miles to my beloved forest looking for simple solitude.[436] Alas, curiosity everywhere. These tiresome people are like flies, living off others.

I know very well that Heiberg[437] and his kind Christianly explain my walking the street[438] as so much vanity—that I do it to be seen. I wonder if it is also to be seen that I walk about even more, if possible, in Berlin,[439] where not a soul knows me?—*JP* V 6013 (*Pap.* VIII¹ A 163) *n.d.*, 1847

My life as an author is as shabby and shameful as possible. In a quite different sense, I may be said to have deserved it—and to that extent I suffer for my guilt—that is, in understanding with God. In relation to men, I am as author not only right but also infinitely much more.

But my life is also the most interesting lived by any author in Denmark. For that very reason, I will assuredly be read and studied in the future. All Europe is working toward demoralization—but in Copenhagen things are on such a small scale that my observations and calculations can comprehend them completely. This will come to be extremely interesting. I am like a physician with a detailed anatomical model, but one not so large that it cannot be surveyed.

No one can dream of the slinking meanness that prevails here. Even my tailor was almost afraid[440]—naturally, that he would be dragged into it and written about so that he would lose his customers. This could very well happen, for to whom could one turn to explain such contemptibleness. After all, there is no one, only accomplices—who consequently would find it all even more of a lark.

Even eminent and prominent people are taking part in it. How many people have modesty of idea; most of them must be pressured by considerations, and when this is completely taken away, yes, when it is almost dangerous to reveal decent feelings—well, then coarseness and brutality are just as glaring in prominent people as they are in the rudest man.

The whole thing is a conspiracy, and therefore, ultimately, there is no one to talk to—about how paltry the whole thing is. And the Danish language does not reach much beyond Copenhagen: consequently, anyone chosen as a sacrifice to envy is *eo ipso* trapped.

Just try to tell the petty meanness of Copenhagen in another language—it would be revolting. But this is impossible. For to write about it in Danish is useless, since there is no one to write for except those sworn conspirators, who once again would regale themselves with this new fun.—*Pap.* VIII¹ A 175 *n.d.*, 1847

In order to give a true picture of the bourgeois mentality here in Denmark, it could be amusing to write a little book entitled:

The Story of the Country Called Denmark

Among the "unknown countries" there is also this one—but there are several especially curious things about it that ought to be mentioned.

There is only one city in the country; although it is only a market town, the whole country is as pleased as punch over it. It is called Copenhagen.

Of course, this city has newspapers, several excellent newspapers. But unlike newspapers in other places, they do not discuss political affairs etc. No, here they print news only about what individuals wear, what they eat, where they eat, etc. In no other country is the public mind as strongly developed as in Denmark. If a man does not wear suspenders with his trousers, this is immediately announced in the newspapers and read by the whole nation. Yes, this is done so conscientiously that a debate was carried on in print for more than a year about a particular man's trousers,⁴⁴¹ whether, very strictly considered, they were not an inch too short. The affair dragged on, because it was not clear whether the public mind could allow him to continue walking around with them as they were or whether the public mind needed to take drastic action. —The public mind is prodigiously developed in Denmark. Murder, prostitution, violence, in short, every crime is forgiven except the crime of having different buttons on one's coat than other men have. That is the *crimen læsæ* [criminal offense] against the public mind. As soon as a man stumbles in the street, his full name is immediately announced in the paper, and the public mind judges whether or not it was injudicious. —Denmark is different from other countries in that it does not have one or two ironists. No, here the whole nation is ironical. That is, as soon as it is discovered that someone does not have black buttons on his coat as the others do, then all the other men laugh at him, and in Denmark this laughter is called irony. . . .—*Pap.* VIII¹ A 290 *n.d.*, 1847

. . . it was also one of my remarks,[442] dialectically thrown out and misunderstood,* that had led Goldschmidt in the past to take a new direction, to attack everybody, while in another sense I did everything to save Goldschmidt from the whole stinking mess, but always *dialectically*, in order to give him the chance to become open.—*Pap.* VIII¹ A 420 *n.d.*, 1847

Addition to Pap. VIII¹ A 420:

*The expression was that it was nonsense to be ironical and also a party man who merely attacked the government; irony must make a clean sweep—the very point of which was to indicate to him how cowardly he was toward the public. A total irony such as this may be considered as characteristic of the modern age. But the one who should take on this task must (1) first of all have great personal courage, (2) be very good-natured, (3) have a pure motive and heroic character. I did not dare to assume this enormous task and enormous responsibility.—*Pap.* VIII¹ A 421 *n.d.*, 1847

Contemptible Lack of Character

Mr. Hostrup writes a student comedy,[443] naturally as harebrained and inconsiderate as possible, using no restraints whatsoever—after all, it would be unsporting for someone to have anything against it! Fine. But then should it not keep on being a student comedy—that is, for students. But what happens. The play travels around the whole country, is finally performed in the Royal Theater—and now, as I see today in *Flyve-Posten*,[444] in Norway, and in *Rigstidenden*, the character who supposedly represents me is named outright: Søren Kierkegaard. No doubt the billboards have already carried my name openly in order to attract interest in the play.

And this is supposed to be a student comedy! And consequently the Danish stage has been demeaned to being *The Corsair*!

How cowardly the whole thing is. Either my name should have been on the billboard outside the Student Union from the very first or the whole character should have been removed.

It is loathsome to see how the Danes disgrace themselves and eagerly do their best to exhibit our shame to neighboring countries.—*JP* V 6088 (*Pap.* VIII¹ A 458) *n.d.*, 1847

This is the difference. If persecution comes from the government, one shows up well; a vain person could be tempted for the sake of the cause to go too far because it looks so good to be the object of persecution by such a power. But when one suffers persecution by the mob, the people, the public, in short, the scum that the daily press is able to dredge up, at best by an anonymous dredger—then one has to use nine-tenths of one's energy in minimizing the persecution itself, one cannot very well be celebrated for talking about such things etc. This is the difference: when one is persecuted by the government, by the powers that be, there is a focus on decisions that time and again will make an impact (a fine, a sentence, etc.), but mob persecution or persecution by the public is sheer dailiness, day in and day out, every day the same, every moment a new arrival knowing nothing about a person except that people grin at him in the most impudent way. They know that they are *supposed to do it*, it is their duty, for the press has ordered it. Here there is no question of modesty and bashfulness—they are doing a good deed authorized by the public mind when they ridicule a person, abuse him, shout after him, etc., when they even insult his driver so that he almost becomes afraid because he cannot understand what it all means.

What I do lack is physical strength. My mind is calm. I have always thought of myself as having to be sacrificed; now I have received my orders and I will abide by the command I have been given. Ordinarily I can take it. But when, for example, seeking recreation, I take a drive[445] of 15-20 miles and sit in the carriage in the happy ferment of thought, my body gradually becomes somewhat weak, partly from the riding, partly from the purely mental exertion, and then when I get out and it so happens I am received by a smirking, grinning crowd, and some of those present are even nice enough to call me names, then my physical state is powerfully affected. Or when I have taken a long walk out on some solitary path,[446] lost in my own thoughts, and then suddenly meet three or four louts way out there where I am all alone and they start to call me names, my physical state is powerfully affected. I do not have the physical strength for a fight—and I know nothing that makes me more depressed than such a scene. I have the ability to make any man listen to reason, except the raw boor—to say nothing of three of them who have orders from the press—there can be no discussion with him.

Yet my faith is unshaken that I will remain standing on the spot. There must be an awakening if coarse brutality is not to prevail altogether in Denmark. For me it has had a good side. I really would not have been able to illuminate Christianity the way I have been allowed to do if all this had not happened to me.—*JP* V 6105 (*Pap.* VIII¹ A 544) *n.d.*, 1848

I feel no bitterness at all at the thought of all the indignities I have suffered and all the times I have been betrayed; I never think of escaping all of this all at once, so to speak, by death. If there is time and place for jest in eternity, I am sure that the thought of my thin legs and my ridiculed trousers[447] will be a source of salutary amusement to me. It is a blessed thing to dare say: What I have suffered in that respect I have suffered in God's name for a good cause and because, humanly speaking, I did a good deed in a truly unselfish sacrifice. This I dare to say—directly to God. I am more sure of this than I am sure that I live, more sure than of everything, for I already feel that he will answer: Yes, my dear child, you are right; and he will add: Everything negative, when you sinned, when you were wrong, has been forgiven you in Christ.

I have never been a Diogenes, have never bordered on cynicism; I have dressed properly and decently. I am not responsible for a whole country's being a madhouse. I have been able to crack jokes with an individual over my thin legs. But when it is the rabble, the utterly brutish humanity, the rowdies, silly women, schoolchildren, and apprentices who abuse me—that is the meanness and lack of character of a people directed against one who truly merits something from his people. The most tiresome aspect is that I am the only one who has the right to jest, but on those terms I cannot and will not jest. And yet I need the refreshment of laughter so often. But then, alas, the one who is clearly the wittiest in a little country is the only one who is not witty—but the riffraff and the fools are all witty and ironic.—*JP* VI 6160 (*Pap.* IX A 64) *n.d.*, 1848

IX
A 64
37

I could in the past have joined up with a number of people and then perhaps have demolished that whole literary barbarism. I chose another method; it will surely stand the test. At the moment, it is true, it seems as if I had lost. But until now, this has been the rule for my victories: I always lose in the first lap, but I win in the end. This is rooted deeply in my nature, for I have no immediacy. This shows itself in trifling matters in my life. My personal appearance has no aplomb. Someone looking at me thinks: Look at that one! But he does not notice that I am reflective.

IX
A 92
48

The crowd can always be assisted to victory but, please

IX
A 92
49

note, in such a way that it gains a wrong kind of victory. Goldschmidt's victory was complete: everybody laughed, all the thousands and thousands. And yet that victory will be costly to him; he has me stuck in his throat.

This is how it had to go and must go. Either all this rabble-barbarism will succeed in destroying me—but in that event the reaction will be very serious, for I am too important to Denmark for that, and, basically, I have the respect of many, yes, am really esteemed, especially if this happens to me—or, if this does not succeed and I go unscathed, then its force is spent. As I gradually work deeper and deeper into presenting the enormous pathos of Christianity,[448] that event will acquire ever new modifications. And what then? Then little by little I shall succeed in converting all this gossip and vulgarity from an apparent matter of indifference to an entirely different qualification: a matter of earnestness.

The point is that I understood Goldschmidt and his consorts down to their most tenuous nerve; they understood me not at all. I knew every line of their position; they knew not one of mine.—*Pap.* IX A 92 *n.d.*, 1848

What is destroying Denmark is neither the new nor the old government but the fact that the country, small as it is, even smaller through demoralization, has become a market town where every government is an impossibility, because envy keeps a watch on anything that is something, so that only contemptibility can have a kind of power, or only an approximation of a martyr can rule, not to mention a martyr.

What brought in a new government[449] was not wisdom, patriotism, and the like but an expression of this demoralization. And what will overthrow the new government will again be envy, caprice, pettiness, and the like; it is not the noble, the good, that triumphs—no, it is the same demoralization, which has given itself a new shape.

In this respect, Goldschmidt is not undistinguished. He is like a cholera fly to cholera; it cannot be said that it is he who produces the demoralization (and everybody else is good) but that he makes manifest that there must be demoralization. He is and remains the characterless instrument of envy and demoralization. He has nothing to lose, cannot be attacked, or envied, either; he is safeguarded by means of contemptibility—and then he gnaws and gnaws. And a good many representatives of the old regime think this is fine—because the new government is the victim. How tragic that there is no character at all, no reflection, no consistent point of view anywhere in Denmark, but everything is momentary passion.—*JP* IV 4149 (*Pap.* IX A 303) *n.d.*, 1848

And so I am wasted on Denmark; and everybody pretends that it is nothing, as if they did not know it, because I, if I am not to become an object of sympathy, remain upright. My first name is now a nickname every schoolboy knows.[450] The same name is more frequently used by authors; it appears in comedies[451] all the time now, and everyone knows it is I.

And what was my crime? Was it a bad book I wrote? In that case, persecution such as this would be insanely out of proportion. But that was not the case. Was it because I brazenly attacked something good, decent, beneficial. No, just the opposite. It was demented literary infamy on a scale all out of proportion to the country. Among highly esteemed people, there was and could be but one opinion, but this, of course, was expressed only in private, for each one feared the tyranny of the rabble, but it is definitely true that there is scarcely a reputable man in the country who in indignation has not said repeatedly: It is infamy without comparison. But no one dared to do anything publicly. In various ways they prodded me, at times by imputing to me a kind of secret connection with this ironizing, at times by reminding me that, being independent, I was the only one who could do it.

So I do it—and at once the envy of the exclusive ones uses the opportunity to say that he is mad to do it. Here is the tragedy. The rabble-barbarism would have been powerless against me, but this meanness of being too cowardly to meet me head on polemically, no matter how much it wanted to because it felt my superiority, and then using this situation to give vent to its envy—this is and remains the tragedy.

And yet all this I could have endured easily and cheerfully. But I am much more threatened by another danger that is destroying my urge to write. It is my financial state and the confused financial world of which one can make neither head nor tail. For my kind of writing, time and tranquillity are required. The further I push ahead, the more violent will become the opposition to me from without; already it has gone so far that I am in the hands of the rabble. If, then, I must be occupied with my finances, too, my writing cannot go on. My writing has always been sacrificial, and that is really why I am regarded as mad. But if my private means[452] run out, then my writing automatically ceases.

And if I am toppled, it will be said: He was the extraordinary, he truly did want the truth. Good God! If I were to judge, I would say: He did have a slight understanding of the truth and did do a little to express the true. But what kind of world is it where after I have been demolished I become so extraordinary that no one can match me—what kind of world is it, that is, what does it mean to speak about truth in relation to such a world. If every man were like me and then there were a few extraordinaries, it would mean something, but the present situation is nothing but baseness.—*Pap.* IX A 370 *n.d.*, 1848

How strange, after all, are the outlook of the moment and the outlook of history. In a way, it was just plain cowardice for men to speak about *The Corsair* as nothing at all, but although that is not the case, the majority honestly believe that *The Corsair* will be forgotten quickly; all the other papers look down on it in this respect and console themselves that they belong to history. But if I were to express my opinion to the contrary, this would be interpreted as my supposed instability. And yet *sie irren* [they err]. It is the history of the disintegration of Denmark that we are living—and *The Corsair* is the normal phenomenon of one sort and the March ministry[453] another, but *The Corsair* has a longer life and covers an enormous area. In a certain sense, it was important, that is, in the realm of evil—and to history it is in a certain sense indifferent whether it is good or evil if only it is important, carried through with talent, consistency, and boldness. Up to a point, *The Corsair* has understood this, hence its attempt at being a sort of moral enterprise in which ethical satire would be beneficial to the good (*à la* Aristophanes). I regard it as very important to have gotten this lie exposed, and I was successful in doing it. But, on the other hand, Goldschmidt was in one sense right over against most of his contemporaries, for their supposed disregard was an untruth, insofar as the issue was one about talent, an attempt to ascribe falsely to themselves the ability to overlook his talent because he misused it. I consider it important to my whole historical position that it be scrupulously maintained that I regard the two articles[454] as belonging unconditionally to my total literary activity. Therefore, I must also see about doing what I thought of earlier, publishing in a separate little book[455] the newspaper articles I have written.—*Pap.* IX A 432 *n.d.*, 1848

The thing that has made my situation difficult in the attack of rabble-barbarism upon me is that no one knows how to dance with me. If I had been directly and straightforwardly attacked by them, then I would have done what anyone else under attack does—then the tactic is to get away from it and forget it as quickly as possible. But this is not the case with me. I have an outstanding account against my contemporaries, for the truth is, was, and remains that I did them a good deed,[456] I was altogether magnanimous; in fact, I myself provoked the attack. But of course this means that my tactic cannot be the same. Yet the trouble is that this, like my whole effort, is much too magnificent and elevated for a low tavern like Denmark. The actual reason for my difficulties was that everything is done to submerge such a bold step in the old apathy, making me just another one who is being attacked. All my contemporaries continue to explain everything on the basis of the little multiplication table and therefore misunderstand me. When I took that step, I counted on having the personal strength—and this I do in fact have—to defy all Copenhagen if necessary; I would not shirk from anything but show myself even more than usual—and I knew I was capable of doing it. It was my intention (after seeing what it led to, how one after the other of those attacked got out of the way) to just stand there and calmly make the attack on me a subject of my conversation. I went to Mini's,[457] asked for his copy of *The Corsair*, which they wanted to hide from me (the same thing happened at Pethau's);[458] I read it in the presence of others, talked with them—and I always managed to maintain a light conversational tone. But what happens. Then Gjødvad[459] comes along one day and tells me that people are saying that this is the only thing I talk about etc.—that is, this is supposed to prove that it did affect me. So there it is. I, that is, my tactic, am interpreted in terms of the formerly usable tactic, and Gjødvad, Ploug,[460] and all the rest actually did not know anything but that old device of trying to forget it.—*Pap.* X¹ A 40 *n.d.*, 1849

Goldschmidt[461] wants to win over the public again. Well, in one sense, I do not blame him for that. After all, he is who he is, made to order for exploiting a time of disintegration such as this, to some extent despising himself, desperate, greedy, without character. I have always said that he is not such a rare phenomenon—he goes with moral disintegration just as a cholera fly goes with cholera. In some ways I find it tedious to be obliged to press this point, for I would prefer to concede his talent its due. But I must accentuate the ethical. I shall have small reward for that, for it will no doubt be misinterpreted as irritability.—*Pap.* X¹ A 69 *n.d.*, 1849

Perhaps This Does Merit Being Recorded

Goldschmidt (quite apart from his total lack of character and contemptibleness) certainly had talent but never an idea. During the time he edited it, *The Corsair* never lacked talent; neither will it be forgotten because of that.

Now he says—as I by chance saw somewhere in *Nord og Syd*,⁴⁶² where he defends his actions—that, considering the contemptibleness of the parties, he took an ironic position toward them.

The fact of the matter is this. Whether *The Corsair* had ideas and, if so, the extent to which it had them depended upon and was proved by the extent to which it had sufficient dialectic to maintain and the personal courage to express absolute negativity.

Goldschmidt had no inkling of this. *The Corsair* was liberal, belabored Christian VIII, public officials, etc.; *The Corsair* was an offspring of the opposition. Goldschmidt never had an idea.

Then some time ago I dropped a hint to Goldschmidt that, apart from the immorality of the enterprise, if there ever was to be any question of an idea in it or in any similar undertaking, it must attack everything equally and not be so stupid as to attack the government⁴⁶³ in our day. This hint was imparted *en passant*, with all the dignity I maintained toward him. But I knew my man, and later I had only the little unpleasantness of his telling Professor Nielsen⁴⁶⁴ explicitly (in Aarhus at the Secondary School) that I had said it. It changed him to the extent that a bit of idea did creep into *The Corsair*.[*]

Then he once again took a totally wrong course, stooped to the most contemptible personal remarks, attacked private personalities, etc.—and he immortalized me.⁴⁶⁵

The time had come for me to have a new existential illumination; furthermore, I felt that I owed it to the country of my birth, and it was the result of negativity. For I have considered negativity as the educational means toward the positive I wanted to advance: religiousness. But that I was justified, the only one here at home, was proved by the very step I took

[*] *In margin*: Then in '48 he addressed himself to Christian VIII, and I do not doubt that he wanted to use this to his advantage, that later on he had not attacked him but the opposition. But there I would have put a little obstacle in his way, so that Christian VIII would not have had any dealings with him.

when I changed my course, perfected my idea by directing the negativity against myself, something that would have happened whether P. L. Møller's attack[466] had come or not. Among my papers there is also a little article that is older and was most immediately prompted by the immortalizing, all the more so since Goldschmidt became even dangerous when with *En Jøde*[467] he became the object of a kind of sentimental sympathy—"that as a child he had suffered so much etc."

In taking this step, I had these points in mind with respect to Goldschmidt.

(1) From the standpoint of eternity, he eventually must condemn himself forever, judge that there is no substance at all in him, even come to despise himself. That is what happened.

(2) Or he answers: No, I cannot go around insulting a body of writing I have admired and said I admire, since it has not changed; I shall concentrate only on the little article in *Fædrelandet*.[468]

(3) Or he could have said: No, I will not attack Magister Kierkegaard.

In the last case, it was my intention to deliver a little judgment. To make men aware of the abyss over which they had been hovering, I intended to show (but by attacking fictitious names, thus completely without venom, purely esthetically) how a thing like this ought to be done and also how dangerous it could be if actual persons were involved.

It was my thought to pull Goldschmidt out of all this, locate him as an esthetic journalist in some respectable position on a respectable paper. He was intelligent, the only young man I actually have paid any attention to. He could then have been very serviceable to me in connection with esthetic writings.

This would have been very advantageous to him. He needs such an influence. It is now evident that he can get along very well, once again attract many subscribers, etc., but his life never acquires an idea.

The test to which he was put was administered rigorously. On the day or the day after the article[469] about P. L. Møller came out, he caught me in the street,[470] obviously intending that I should tell him privately what he should do. This I did not do, treated him even somewhat coolly.

A day after the full load of abuse had been poured on me, I met him on the street.[471] He walked past me, I called to him and said: Goldschmidt. He came over. I asked him to walk along with me. I told him that he perhaps had misunderstood all that I previously had pointed out to him, admonished him to give up the *Corsair* enterprise, and said that he even may have imagined that I was putting on a good face with him in order not to be exposed to his attack myself. Now he surely could see that the opposite was the case. I wanted earnestly to repeat what I had said to him. This I did. I urged upon him very earnestly that he must leave *The Corsair*. It was tragicomic when with tears in his eyes (that kind of person is moved to tears easily) he said: You can criticize everything I do in this manner and not say a word about my having any talent.

Having spoken, I bowed, said farewell with the cordiality I had always shown him, but also with the distance I always had observed toward him.

Since that time, I have never spoken with him. That has not been for my sake, because of what he has done to me; I not only forgive him but am not at all angry about it—I am not that inconsistent. No, I wanted to charge it to the situation. I still continued to be regarded as "the ironist"; if I continued putting on a good face after that event, I would have given him support—how appalling—and sanctioned the view that his *Treiben* [activity] was irony. Easygoing as I am, it really has been a burden for me to have to play the angry man.

Meanwhile, he has continued to copy me in a minor way. As mentioned, he now explains that *The Corsair* was the negative above the parties[472]—and now he once again wants to stand above the parties—positively. He reads (and I perhaps do not have many such ardent readers) that the negative is the transition passage. Thus he is putting on the same comedy. For him, then, *The Corsair* becomes the negative, which practically amounts to saying that it was a developmental factor in his life, that he had been in a house of correction. The public cannot understand me, but in this it nevertheless hears ru-

X^1
A 98
78

mored that there is something deep—and so Goldschmidt plays the comedy over again and becomes popular.

As in everything, in this there has been weftlike filling in the fabric of my life, a bonus from Governance: I have learned indescribably much, perhaps have been further rescued from my hypochondria and influenced in a more definitely Christian way.—*Pap.* X¹ A 98 *n.d.*, 1849

X¹
A 120
91

A martyrdom of laughter is what I really have suffered. Anything more than this and more profound than this I dare not say of myself: I am a martyr of laughter. But not everyone who suffers being laughed at, even for an idea, is therefore a martyr of laughter in the strict sense. For example, when a thoroughly earnest man suffers it in a good cause, he does not have the deeper relationship to the martyrdom he suffers. But I am a martyr of laughter, and my life has been designed for that; I understand myself so completely as such that it is as if I now understand myself for the first time—on the other hand, I would find it difficult to understand myself becoming successful in the world. No, in the martyrdom of laughter I recognize myself again. To be able to become just that, I am the wittiest of all, possessing a superlative sense of comedy, could myself have represented laughter on an unsurpassed scale, could also deceptively have lured men out upon thin ice by doing that, thereby becoming what the age required—this superiority, this self-determination is the criterion of the more ideal martyrdom. Quite rightly, I had to direct the laughter upon myself[473] (as Ney[474] directed the soldiers who shot him). And the one who must carry out the order would gladly have been my lieutenant, and it certainly never occurred to him to do otherwise than give me place no. 1.—*JP* VI 6348 (*Pap.* X¹ A 120) *n.d.*, 1849.

X¹
A 120
92

X¹
A 123
93

My Last Word About Goldschmidt[475]

If I were to speak, I would say something like this. I have nothing to reproach him for. I must reproach myself for wronging myself out of perhaps exaggerated good nature and kindness, for having too much faith in him and hoping for some hidden good in him,⁴⁷⁶ for doing him the wrong of putting him to the test so that this had to come out in the open in a decisive way.

Everyone regarded him with contempt; none of those with whom I had any connection associated with him. That was the judgment passed on him, and I thought that it possibly was an injustice to him. He wished to become an author and with that in mind turned to me. I honestly and sympathetically did everything to encourage him and to tear him away if possible from the aberration and perdition of *The Corsair*.

I laid myself open to the possibility (so, in fact, several have told me) that many would take exception to my greeting or accompanying that man on the streets. I laid myself open to the circulation by certain envious circles of the opinion that I secretly humored rabble-irony.

I had entertained the thought of becoming more involved with him. But before that happened there had to be a test. Would he, in connection with the only object of his admiration⁴⁷⁷ and with what he himself had said in print, have the courage and self-respect to say: No, I will not attack him *or* I will attack the little article⁴⁷⁸ he has written but not the earlier books I personally have admired and immortalized and to which I really am deeply indebted.

He did not stand the test. For me it became—if it must be called punishment—a punishment for being the only person here at home who did Goldschmidt the wrong of having too much faith in him and of hoping that there was something good hidden deep down in the man.

An Eastern proverb says: He who first praises and then berates someone lies two times.⁴⁷⁹ That was the snare I stretched for him—an exaggeration. *Ach, ja*, I could have been satisfied with the positive assurance of all the others that he was contemptible.—*JP* VI 6351 (*Pap.* X¹ A 123) *n.d.*, 1849

The way I am being treated is also part and parcel of the infamy. With the aid of the organ of rabble-barbarism, the signal was given to the rabble to call me by my first name[480] only, making it a nickname to be shouted at me. Now a new subtlety is being employed. It is very rare these days to see a new Danish play[481] without a character in it named Søren. Hostrup has one in every one of his plays; Carit Etlar,[482] too, has gotten himself a similar character; so also—Professor Heiberg.[483] There is nothing to say about it; the person concerned would only answer: How unreasonable; after all, it is a common name. But for one thing this is not the case, for otherwise a list of characters from another period would certainly show a similarity; and, finally, it is not quite the case with Heiberg, either, for the name is used in a singular way. The character Søren represents the younger generation, and one of his lines is: You should have followed the advice of the younger generation (or something like that). And later there is a shout of "Hurrah for Søren." The gallery and the rabble find it great to have a subtlety of that sort in the pleasures of the theater—and the authors, after all, are on the outside, without remorse. If I publicized my name, it would become new subject for laughter.—*Pap.* X^1 A 177 *n.d.*, 1849

In the more profound sense of the word, no author or the like actually can have fellow feeling for me. They feel all too well my great superiority and that here any kind of association and the like is unthinkable. In short, I am a phenomenon in the most disastrous situation possible—a phenomenon in a low dive such as Denmark. The law for the persecution I am suffering is quite simple: the rabble are the ones who do it, while the elite are silent out of envy.

And Heiberg,[484] for whom I openly did the greatest service possible by throwing myself at P. L. Møller and *The Corsair*[485]—he not only remains silent, no, secretly he also literally joins in with the rabble.—*Pap.* X^1 A 224 *n.d.*, 1849

Somewhere in one of my journals [*i.e., Pap.* VIII^1 A 139] I have written something that is so true:

My Last Words to my Contemporaries:
Will you who have been my contemporaries please decorate my grave and say: If we had been his contemporaries, he would not have been treated as he was.—*Pap.* X^1 A 240 *n.d.*, 1849

It is true that rabble-barbarism has grown to be a much more serious matter than I anticipated at the time, even though I considered very seriously the step[486] I took and was religiously resolved; that is, I have discovered the baseness and demoralization to be far greater than I had imagined it to be, but of course it has also served to point out that I remain standing.

But for that very reason I must say that it was good that I got involved, for the more earnest the affair grows, the greater is my obligation and my call.—*Pap.* X^1 A 244 *n.d.*, 1849

But it was weak and cowardly and perfidious and in a way contemptible of the elite[487] (for example, Heiberg and his whole gang; on the other side, the more respectable journals) to behave as they did at the time. I was the proudest junior name in literature; it is quite literally true that the literary elite were provoked, but they were careful not to risk a battle; I was an unqualified force, and there was not one who dared to say one single evil or merely critical word about me, and it was sufficiently significant that Goldschmidt knew how to accentuate it.

Then I decide to turn all the rabble-barbarism upon myself[488] in order to put a stop to it if possible. Beyond a doubt, it is the most unselfish act during the period I have been in public life. And what happens? The envious elite think something like this: "Aha, he has trapped himself. We were incapable of weakening him, but now it will happen for sure. The step he took is foolhardy, the battle as unequal as possible: one single man, known by all, against the rabble, who in addition

X^1
A 254
166

X^1
A 254
167

are consolidated by having their organ and a talented man as editor. That he may accomplish something is not impossible, for he is very capable and seems to have a great faith. Well, well, if he does it, so much the better, it will be to our advantage; but in any case—and this will also be to our advantage—he of course will weaken himself." So the envious elite kept quiet, spread the rumor that I was made to expose myself to such a thing. Pfui!

Yet I did accomplish something. Yes, when I think of it, I am amazed. Goldschmidt[489] is obviously paralyzed; the point in *The Corsair* was lost, he goes abroad—returns home and becomes respectable. P. L. Møller[490] is as good as inaudible since then—and goes abroad.

In a certain sense, elite envy has formed an even greater impression of me, but the important thing for it continues to be that I am weakened, and therefore it is important to continue to cling to the notion that it was mad of me to do what I did—and also (strangely enough, for, if this is so, then where is the madness!) that it is nothing, nothing at all to become a sacrificial victim to the rabble.

Incidentally, there was a strain in the novel *En nat ved Bullar-Søe*[491] that actually tempted me to think that it had me in mind (just as the whole novel had a curious relationship to everything I have written, almost a combination of "The Seducer's Diary"[492] and the imaginary psychological construction " 'Guilty?'/'Not Guilty?' "[493] which would be very odd to me if the novel were older); it was a mad crusade that the hero undertook to convert the Finns—it was practically a counterpart to my campaign against the rabble.[494]—*Pap.* X[1] A 254 *n.d.*, 1849

What an accomplishment the *Concluding Postscript* is; there is more than enough for three professors. But of course the author was a someone who did not have a career position and did not seem to want to have one; there was nothing worthy of becoming a paragraph in the system—well, then, it is nothing at all.

The book came out in Denmark. It was not mentioned anywhere at all. Perhaps fifty copies were sold, thus the publishing costs for me, including the proofreader's fee (one hundred rix-dollars), came to about four or five hundred rix-dollars, plus my time and work.[495] And in the meantime, I was caricatured by a scandal sheet that in the same little country had three thousand subscribers, and another paper (also with wide circulation, *Flyveposten*) continued the discussion about my trousers.[496]—*JP* VI 6458 (*Pap.* X^1 A 584) *n.d.*, 1849

"An Open Letter"

[*In margin*: Rudelbach on the Church constitution, para. cxxxi, pp. 243 etc.][497]

X^1 A 669 423

This book has the merit of having shown that the state church gave rise to or contributed to giving rise to the proletariat.

How much there is to this, Rudelbach seems not to have perceived.

In Christendom life is completely unchristian also in terms of what it means to live together with the common man and what this involves.

In this respect my life is like a discovery—alas, in a certain sense I can say that it is a dearly purchased discovery. It is unchristian and wicked to base the state on a substructure of men who are totally ignored and excluded from personal association—even though on Sunday there are touching sermons about loving "one's neighbor."—*JP* IV 4164 (*Pap.* X^1 A 669) *n.d.*, 1849

X^1 A 669 424

Dr. Rudelbach[498] and I

We shall never understand one another.

For him it has long since been definitely settled that he is a Christian. And now he busies himself with history and the external forms of the Church. He has never felt the disquietude of the idea, wondering every single day whether he is now a Christian or not. "Never"—no, because one who has felt this once, one day, one hour, does not let go of it during his entire life, or it never lets go of him.

The idea has involved me in personal self-concern, and therefore I can never find time for projects, for I must begin every day with this concern: Are you a Christian now? Indeed, perhaps this very day there will be an existential collision that will make it clear that you are not a Christian at all.—*JP* VI 6725 (*Pap.* X⁴ A 20) *n.d.*, 1851

On the folder:

The article on Rudelbach
        A part that has not been used, but one that may have some significance.—*Pap.* X⁵ B 120 *n.d.*, 1851

Notations on final copy of "An Open Letter Prompted by a Reference to Me by Dr. Rudelbach":

4. ["the second half is false," p. 51] since I have never sought to use external means or proposed them or had anything to do with something as great as "the Church" but have limited my activity to "the single individual."

6. ["that external conditions and forms will help," p. 54]. As I see it, the so-called old-time Christians* are therefore at this time in the process of plunging full blast—jubilating** in song and dance besides—toward what (Christianly understood) is perhaps the most dangerous of all illusions.

* who have become, to be sure, terribly modern.
** "like a bird rushing into the snare."—*Pap.* X⁵ B 121 *n.d.*, 1851

Addition to Pap. X⁵ B 121:

With just a few strokes on the chart of our situation, let me sketch the movements of my operation.

In my opinion, we ordinary men may be content (and

Christianly this is also permissible), may be humbly content, with being Christians in quiet inwardness. When this is the case, one may also very well be satisfied with the given external forms—yes, it is precisely and truly Christian not to be occupied with external forms. However, I do believe that greater effort ought to be made to develop a competent clergy who would work for the inward deepening of Christianity in individuals* and to guarantee the commonwealth a sound cadre of plain, good Christians (who constitute an indispensable foundation) who are not occupied with reforming either state or Church.

If anyone believes he cannot be satisfied with being such a Christian in hidden inwardness but aspires to something higher, then, in my opinion, there is Christianly only one thing higher—martyrdom, in which one walks alone, forsaken by men and also, humanly speaking, forsaken by God. The frightful, narrow way of this martyrdom, its frightful splendor, must be stated and portrayed because Christians should never forget that it exists [er til], because if it is forgotten, the average Christian would become all too secular, but if it is remembered, being humbled under this lofty ideal will help to develop inwardness in us ordinary Christians.

But there is still one thing more: the way of the lower level—sectarianism, partisanship, politicizing in the realm of the Church, reformation by way of balloting, etc. All this ought to be opposed. It is sad to see that the so-called old-time Christians—perhaps as a result of having once felt a pressure—now have broken loose all the more and join together with what in a Christian sense is their opposite, and now in their old age they represent a most impoverished Christianity (a composite of politics and Christianity); whereas in their earlier days and especially in the earliest times they represented the original, primitive old Christianity.

This is my opinion. The fault of this age is fancying itself to

In margin: * it would be desirable and it is necessary that the pastors strive in a higher degree for the inward deepening of Christianity in themselves and in individuals.

be an age of reformation and, curiously enough, wanting to reform *en masse*. But Providence sends no reformer. If it sends anything, it sends a servant or two—to reform the reformers.

"There is something antiquated about this." To be sure. But watch out. With the help of the year 1848 it will not be long before it will have become the newest of all.—*Pap.* X^5 B 124 *n.d.*, 1851

Addition to Pap. X^5 B 121:

Conclusion

There is something curious about the whole thing; I am almost tempted to believe that Dr. [Rudelbach] has not read any of my writings at all but that it only seems so to him and that he then naturally also must be able to designate the significance of all these writings and to assign them a place in foreign literature and in our own. But I do not find this inexplicable at all. If someone, like me, has read only a few works, he is easily able to keep the lines straight. But if one has read an enormous mass of books, such a mistake can easily take place. It is like many other things. A person who has never traveled further than Roskilde can easily and definitely know where he has been. A much-traveled person, however, one who has traveled around the world many times and been all over, may very readily think and say, when some place is mentioned that he has not actually visited: Yes, I was there the summer of 1835; there is a very high tower with a magnificent view, etc. (but there is no tower at all). So it is also with the notion that the point of my work as an author is supposed to be emancipation of the Church from the state. Inasmuch as I am not occupied with the Church,[*] I am even less occupied with its emancipation from the state—just as there can only be very figurative reference to a view from the tower if there is no tower.

[*] *In margin*: but with influencing the single individual—*Pap.* X^5 B 125 *n.d.*, 1851

Addition to Pap. X⁵ B 121:

Filled with self-concern through having been wounded by the ideals but nevertheless ineffably happy because of this and grateful for it. For, if one is human, as far as the ideals are concerned it is the most fearful presumption that could arise in a human being to want to be more than an unhappy lover, however burning with zeal one's striving may be; but, if one has become the unhappy lover, to be able to forget for one moment that this is the greatest good fortune that can befall a man would be the most dreadful ingratitude, a proof that he no longer sees the ideals that indescribably move and captivate even the most unhappy of all their unhappy lovers—if he sees them.—*Pap.* X⁵ B 126 *n.d.*, 1851

The Old Orthodox   X⁴ A 36 25

who claimed that they were the only true Christians in Denmark.

I have nothing against their separating from us—but it is indefensible that they should achieve this by balloting and without giving up the claim that they are the true Church.

But this is supposed to be the tactic—and then judgment is supposed to fall upon Mynster and his party.   X⁴ A 36 26

In what frame of mind could the honest Spandet[499] make his proposal? Did he look upon it as similar to a motion about gas streetlighting and the like—if so, then of course a vote may be taken, but it was certainly improper to make his proposal in this vein. Or, if he insists that he has regarded it as a matter of conscience, how in the world can he then be satisfied with serving a matter of conscience (which as a "royal service" not only must be promoted quickly and be put through but must also be put through or the one commissioned falls)—by making a motion for balloting and then seeing how many votes it will get.

Even if it did go through, the cause would still be wrongly served, and an *indirect* proof would be given that it is not a matter of conscience for him and that he has bitten off too much.

And if it fails to pass, then perhaps he will step forth in character.—*JP* VI 6728 (*Pap.* X⁴ A 36) *n.d.*, 1851

In margin of Pap. X⁴ A 36:

The Old Orthodox would like to withdraw from the whole Church and yet reserve for themselves the status of being the true Church, and perhaps also (as Rudelbach seems to indicate in his book on the constitution of the Church)⁵⁰⁰ keep all the Church property for themselves, which per capita is not so insignificant, since the Church property is rather considerable and, according to Rudelbach, the true Christians are very few.—*JP* VI 6729 (*Pap.* X⁴ A 37) *n.d.*, 1851

Dr. Rudelbach

is really vapid. Apparently he has not read the portion in *Practice in Christianity*⁵⁰¹ (stating that Christianity does not exist) in such a way that it even remotely occurred to him to compare himself with the ideal and ask himself: But are you yourself a Christian? No, he is definitely and unalterably convinced that he and his party are Christians. And now he has been delighted with the statement and has had Mynster in mind.

And I, on the other hand, quite simply had only myself in mind.—*Pap.* X⁴ A 46 *n.d.*, 1851

That Christianity Always Involves a Double-Danger

is shown even by my life's fragmentary approximation of a Christian existence.

The present step against Rudelbach⁵⁰² involves a double-danger, for those who really gain by it leave me stuck with it—yes, ultimately they may even use it against me.

For the most part men are wary of venturing out except when there is only one danger. So it is with Grundtvig⁵⁰³ at the moment, for if he were to introduce the concept of Christian freedom in a Christian way he would have the secular-minded against him as well as the ecclesiastical establishment. But he unchristianly removes the one danger by a coalition with the friends of the peasants.—*Pap.* X^4 A 79 *n.d.*, 1851

The End of the Affair^{504}
by
S. Kierkegaard

In this paper [*Fædrelandet*, no. 37, February 13, 1851, and 38, February 14, 1851], Dr. Rudelbach, by stating some points of difference, has now explained in somewhat more detail that we two do not agree.

Well, wasn't that just what I said? For how did the affair begin? Toward the end of the little book on civil marriage there is a passage in which Dr. R. succinctly states his whole point of view and his plan of operation: "What is rightly called routine and state Christianity must go. We must fight for the emancipation of the Church from the state by means of free institutions, one of which is civil marriage." This means that the goal is external change through the use of external means. The following note is added to this text: "This is exactly what Søren Kierkegaard seeks to impress upon, to imprint upon, and, as Luther says, to drive home to all those who will listen."

Consequently we two, Dr. R. and I, agree, completely agree! And I, knowing my task and my responsibility, I, who have guarded in the most anxious fear and trembling of conscience lest even a jot or tittle hinting at external change be mixed into these many books but with the most rigorous abstemiousness have fought alone, and solely with the weapons of the spirit, for the inward deepening of Christianity in the single individual, I regard the disagreement between Dr. R. and me to be comparable in kind and scope to that between two physicians (yet it must be kept in mind that in the Christian sense I do not pass myself off as a physician but am rather myself a patient), one of whom thought that external means should be used in a given situation (or at least the addition of external means) and the other thought that only internal remedies should be used, yes, that the use of external remedies amounted to a conspiracy with the disease, a greater danger than if nothing at all were done either with surgery or with drugs! — But enough of this; the works testify to this, and besides, in my earlier article I found and used the occasion to point this out quite adequately. And then we two agree, totally agree!

Thus I find myself prompted and obliged, especially in view of present circumstances,* to make a slight objection: that we two simply do not agree, that I have worked simply and solely for the inward deepening of Christianity in the single individual, and that for the rest (this was added after the article against Dr. R., which was published over my name, had really ended), I humbly acknowledge that there is a far higher task, that a person may collide with the established order in such a way that external change becomes a matter of

---

* The present circumstances are such that every moment these fatal political encroachments are menacing the religious [*changed from*: churchly] domain. And such encroachments become doubly alarming when a mistaken orthodoxy or hyperorthodoxy (which supposedly would be absolutely opposed by its very nature) perhaps inadvertently becomes the amicable ingredient so that political radicalism and this pious radicalism come to stick together through voting by ballot in a *bona caritate* almost like—yes, what I am about to say is *e concessis* [on the basis of the opponent's premises] according to pious radicalism's own rigorous conception of the world and secular-mindedness, for I have a milder conception—almost like Gert Westphaler's unintentional drinking to an oath of friendship with the executioner.[505] Under such circumstances no doubt even the most honest orthodox person—he most likely of all—will admit that I have expressed myself both cautiously and circumspectly when (not as Dr. R. reports, that I have summarily accused him as guilty of this "confounded confusion of Christianity and politics"), sweeping before my own door, I have said: Nothing alarms me as much as anything that even remotely smacks of this confounded confusion of Christianity and politics. And no doubt such a person will also agree with me that Dr. R. does not report quite accurately when he says that I "reject" all free associations as a whole. I have not altogether rejected anything; I have said that I have a suspicion about the kind of associations in which one in formal unity sticks together with one's qualitative opposite, which is being all too free and easy in freely associating.

conscience, so that he must operate not only along the lines of being a witness to the truth but with "the apostle" as the prototype; yet if a person must or desires to venture out in this way, his operation cannot possibly be fashioned with balloting as the model, and he cannot march to the tune of "Let's get together." In fact, I made it [*changed from:* God knows I made this objection] in a way that seems uncalled for, because, among other things, Dr. R. had used a very appreciative statement about me, and then it is always unpleasant to have to make an objection; with such a point of departure it is very easy to infringe on a man. But, after all, I have not had great returns as an author, and therefore I have wanted at least the satisfaction that what I have intended should stand as clearly as possible. And in this respect that little note was extremely misleading.

Therefore I make the objection that we two do not agree. And this is what Dr. R. has followed up in a freer discourse that sticks neither to the text nor to the note nor to the matter itself: the text and the note. Dr. R. presents a few points of difference: we two do not agree.

But what about that note? And how can Dr. R. possibly begin his article by saying that I have seriously misunderstood him? I was the one who stated immediately that we two disagree, that there must be a misunderstanding on Dr. R.'s part. The affair between Dr. R. and me is not a discussion concerning Christianity and politics beginning with my open letter but is that little note in which R. summarily maintained that we two agree. It was not I who began, not I who *invited* discussion; on the contrary, it was that little note by R., and it was I who in a newspaper article *defended* myself against what the note seemed to intend: that without further ado I ought to be regarded as one who is in complete agreement with Dr. R. Therefore my signature stood about midway in the article, indicating that the affair with Dr. R. had really terminated.

But now the disagreement has certainly been substantiated. To me this is the main point. If Dr. R. wants to say that this is a misunderstanding—with pleasure! This is of no importance to me. On the other hand, it is of importance to me that it be

X^5
B 128
327

clearly maintained that we two disagree. "But, honored friend, this is a misunderstanding." Yes, yes, then let it be a misunderstanding.

One can hardly be more compliant, and Dr. R. cannot possibly demand more, especially in a case in which the disagreement, according to my conception, is so manifest that I pledge myself to make it comprehensible to a child, although my reader may well smile at my situation, he who easily sees with half an eye what I could—if not see—at least know without trying. And now, since everything, after all, is supposed to be free in our time, since we are to have civil marriage without wedding ceremony and union, so I too shall be free, and I hope that no one joins me together with Dr. R. by forced union if I have even the slightest misgiving about it.

The disagreement, therefore, has now been substantiated.

I see, however, and with joy, that there is something else that has remained unchanged; I see it with joy, partly because, as mentioned, I know Dr. R. from my father's house, partly because Dr. R. is our learned and expert Dr. R., and finally because it is after I have had to write an article such as my first one—I see with joy that Dr. R. has maintained unchanged his friendly good will toward me. Yes, this time it seems to have found an even stronger expression than the first time, when toward the end of the article it is said of me that I have made the one great sacrifice the world does not know—my time, my diligence, my life.

. . .

I find this last portion very fine, very fine of Dr. R.; I urgently request him to accept my thanks for it.

But it would not be fine of me to keep silent about it, for what is said of me there is much too much. I still am *essentially* only a poet. I have had the task of laying emphasis upon ideality, of applying the ideals, but then the additional task of seeing to it, for the sake of God in heaven, that the horrible thing does not happen that I am confused with the perfection I portray. But with respect to my undertaking, I have not sacrificed either my time or my labor, and least of all my life. The most that can truthfully be said of me is that I, in the service of the idea, have dedicated or consecrated my time, my labor during part of my life, for the fact that I have worked gratis can signify at most that I have sacrificed some money and signifies least of all what I have done least of all—sacrificed my life. On the contrary, to describe my seven years of activity as an author I may use the words of the poet: *Ich habe gelebt und geliebt* [I have lived and loved].[506] I have lived, lived much in a few years, and I have loved—yes . . . . . yes, the ideals, yes, indescribably, and in all honesty I still do. I have not been cheated out of this love, and it has not been pounded out of me, either, but has only been made more intense. Yet I am only a poet. I have been permitted to go on living in almost the childlike situation of a father's son, occupied early and late in portraying the ideals and in testifying that such glorious ones have lived, who, by stepping forth in character, have shown that they had a cause of conscience or that they still were related ethically to the idea and therefore neither sought first of all to become a crowd nor babbled nonsense about being a crowd, hopefully anticipating the results of balloting—such glorious ones, of whom it is literally true that they have sacrificed—for we can all, the clergy as well as the layman, talk, sing, orate, and talk big about sacrificing, but sacrificed!—note this well—sacrificed! Oh, this is so elevated: they have *sacrificed*, sacrificed time and labor (and in return they received nothing but the ingratitude of all!), honor and property (and the reward, the only reward, but all the more abundant, was mockery), a cozy life lived in harmony with men, friendship and love and life, and all for the sake of truth! I, on the other hand, am essentially only a poet who happens also to have been wronged. From the very beginning and continually I have been accused of being a colossal egotist. Perhaps they still do not understand me, that my sickness may be just the opposite. Through much association with the ideals in quiet solitariness I have learned to hate myself, learned to understand what a wretched bungler I am;

X[5]
B 128
329

many a time I have felt that my life could be bought for four shillings—to such a degree have I learned to hate myself. But I love—yes . . . . . yes, the ideals, yes, indescribably!

Added in margin: as one who loves what wounds: the ideals; what infinitely detains: the ideals; as one who loves what, humanly speaking, makes a man unhappy: the ideals; what teaches "to flee to grace": the ideals; what in a higher sense makes a man indescribably happy: the ideals—if in the self-concern of the infinite he can learn properly to hate himself. Indescribably happy, although he nevertheless has had to and has to admit humbly to himself that there is something infinitely higher that he has not reached, and on the other hand so indescribably happy that he simply does not feel it to be something lacking if he perhaps does not happen to find time either to dance[507] or to vote or to clink glasses.—*Pap.* X^5 B 128 *n.d.*, 1851

For "The Accounting."[508] Something, however, which is not to be included.

Concerning Myself

Inasmuch as before God I regard my entire work as an author as my own upbringing or education, I could say: But I have remained silent so long lest, in relation to what I understand before God to be my own education, by speaking prematurely I become guilty of talking out of school. This could then be added to the passage in the final draft of "The Accounting": Before God I call this my upbringing or education etc.

I would have liked very much to use this very expression; lyrically, it would have gratified me to use this expression. But there is something else that holds me back. As is frequently the case, the most humble expression seen from another angle is the very one that is apt to say too much, and so it is here. Precisely this humble expression would accentuate the fact that it is my education, almost in the sense of my being an authority. It is simpler as it stands in "The Accounting," with the addition that I need further education, and the tone is such that it can be said of every man.—*JP* VI 6737 (*Pap.* X⁴ A 85) *n.d.*, 1851

My Tactic

always *disputere* only *e concessis* (to take a man's words when he says something great about himself and then to press the existential consequences upon him), might seem to be "villainous malice and envy." By no means, it is admiration. But it is the admiration of reflection that looks where it is going, and ethically it is irony, which the lack of character in our age needs.—*JP* VI 6739 (*Pap.* X⁴ A 101) *n.d.*, 1851

... Just one word in closing. I dare not say that I had the honor of knowing Bishop M.[509] from my father's house; that would have been an almost unnatural relationship, since there was, in fact, the greatest possible and most distancing difference in the circumstances of life: the honorable conspicuousness of loftiness and the inconspicuousness, yet honorable in its own way, of lowliness.

But from my father's house I do know Bishop M.'s sermons; I inherited many good things from him, among them Bishop M.'s sermons, which for my own upbuilding I have read and do read and will go on reading again and again. I have consulted them—also when I took the step of opposing that literary contemptibleness[510]—and intend to consult them every time I am to act. I have but one thing to say about this man's sermons to everyone who pays any attention to my voice: Listen to him, read him. And again I say: Listen to him, read him. As for myself, I wish that I may feel even more strongly, every time I pick up Bishop M.'s sermons for my upbuilding, the presence of the one who is dead, that departed one who brought me up on Bishop M.'s sermons. Thus I am well provided for religiously, because Bishop M. tells me exceptionally well what to do and the departed one says: Will you do it now, immediately.

But with respect to doing it and doing it immediately, I no doubt am way behind, probably will never do it perfectly. That I have known how to present ideals and accentuate ideality poetically—yet for God in heaven's sake and with honest fear and trembling guarding against being confused with what I have presented[511]—is something quite different, but then I have never pretended to be essentially more than a singular kind of poet. Therefore it is not true, as Dr. Rudelbach says in concluding his reply to me in *Fædrelandet*, no.——,[512] "that I have made the one great sacrifice the world does not recognize, my time, my diligence, my life." This is a misunderstanding, although uncommonly sympathetic, especially after my article in the same newspaper.[513] But it is a misunderstanding; *essentially* I am only a poet. I have not "sacrificed," not "my time," not "my diligence"—the most that can be said is that I have dedicated or devoted my time and my diligence in a part of my life to the service of an idea. And least of all have I sacrificed—"my life." No! *Essentially* I am only a poet who loves what wounds: ideals; what infinitely detains: ideals; what makes a man, humanly speaking, unhappy: ideals; what "teaches to take refuge in grace":* ideals; what in a higher sense makes a man indescribably happy: ideals—if he could learn to hate himself properly in the self-concern of infinity. Indescribably happy, although humbled, deeply, profoundly humbled, before the ideals, he has had to confess and must confess to himself and to others that there is the infinitely higher that he has not reached, yet unspeakably happy to have seen it, although it is precisely this [having seen] and that [ideals] which cast him to the earth, him, consequently the unhappy one. [*Crossed out*:—Well, perhaps for time, but not for eternity: what unspeakable happiness, what bliss! *Underneath here*: S. Kierkegaard.] No, no,

---

* Note. See my thrice-repeated preface to the pseudonymous *Practice in Christianity*,[514] the latest book I published.

the eternally happy one. For eternity! For one can grow weary of all temporal and earthly things, and so it would be tormenting if they were to continue eternally. But the person who receives a vision of ideals instantaneously has but one prayer to God: an eternity! And this prayer is instantaneously heard, for ideals and eternity are eternally inseparable. Thus he, the happy one, has an eternity for contemplation. And should he finish, then he has—what good fortune!—an eternity in which to begin from the beginning. And there is no hurry, there is time enough, plenty of time, still an eternity left . . . . . what ineffable happiness, what bliss!

And in calm weather, when life seems to be tranquilized in illusions, one may think one can do without all this fantasy about ideals, think that all they do is disturb everything, and quite right—they will disturb all the illusions. But when everything is tottering, when everything is splitting up into parties, small societies, sects, etc., when, just because everyone wants to rule, ruling is practically impossible—then there is still one force left that can control men: the ideals, properly applied. For in the first place, the ideals, properly applied, do not come too close to anyone, do not give offense to the ambitions of all, to the ambitions of anyone, which can so easily happen to someone who wants to rule; and in the next place, ideals split up every crowd, seize the individual and keep control of him. I point to my own life. Through my considerable association with the ideals I dare say I have become a good subject—which perhaps is quite a rarity these days when everybody wants to rule.—*JP* VI 6749 (*Pap.* X^6 B 173) *n.d.*, 1851

S. KIERKEGAARD

. . . . . cannot be formed according to the paradigm of balloting (balloting, balloting with discussion, balloting without discussion—O balloting, from, in, with, upon, by balloting) or be done according to the popular song: Let's a few of us get together, hurrah, hurrah, hurrah. Streetlighting and clothes and, with all due respect, the sanitation department can be reformed in this manner; but let us be men: Christianity does not lend itself to reformation in this way.—*JP* IV 4208 (*Pap.* X⁴ A 102) *n.d.*, 1851

..... You have 1,000 pastors—if you had only one who had nevertheless a little to sacrifice for the sake of Christianity, you would be better served. You want to reform the Church—then find first of all one Christian, and let him reform the Church.—*JP* III 3733 (*Pap.* X⁴ A 117) *n.d.*, 1851

X⁴ A 118
67

My Sights

are always directed toward this: Christianity actually does not exist, that is to say, existentially, and this is also why I call myself a poet.

For the sake of this aim it is naturally of importance to me to exclude anything that could be misleading in this respect. At one time it was believed that the need was for a speculative system—this was misleading, for then it was tacitly conceded that we are Christians, that this was certain, and that everything was all right, since the need was only for a system. Nowadays people want to reform the Church—this is equally misleading, as if everything were all right with all of us as Christians. Here, you see, is the difference between me and Rudelbach, who speaks only of a little party, which he calls the Church—they are the true Christians, which, however, I do not think is so.—*Pap.* X⁴ A 118 *n.d.*, 1851

X⁴ A 118
68

Amazing!

Once the objection against Christianity (and this was right at the time when it was most evident what Christianity is) was that it was unpatriotic, a danger to the state, revolutionary—and now Christianity has become patriotism and a state Church.

Once the objection against Christianity (and this was right at the time when it was most evident what Christianity is and the objection was made by the genuinely keen-eyed pagans) was that it was antihuman—and now Christianity has become humanity.

Once Christianity was an offense to the Jews and foolishness to the Greeks, and now it is—culture. For Bishop Mynster[515] the mark of true Christianity is culture.

And now, if Dr. Rudelbach will give up his office and step forth as a solitary man, get rid of misconceived collaboration in the form of political favor, and declare that he is no Christian and that Christianity does not exist at all—that would be something. But this whole muddle of voting by every Tom, Dick, and Harry, which allows for a host of illusions—no, this is nonsense.—*Pap.* X⁴ A 126 *n.d.*, 1851

Vinet

I have now obtained *Der Sozialismus in seinem Princip betrachtet* [Socialism Considered According to Its Principles],[516] by Vinet, translated by Hofmeister.

Reading his foreword to the little book has been enough.

He is not the man [the awaited existential ethicist]. He is a brilliant author who writes something about the single individual but is not in character, does not operate in character, is not existentially higher than all discussion—no, no, he writes something that he then submits to public opinion; he palavers with the public in the usual author fashion.

But nevertheless there is spirit.—*JP* IV 4211 (*Pap.* X⁴ A 185) March 9, 1851

In margin of Pap. X⁴ A 185:

It was Vinet for whom Rudelbach shouted in his book on civil marriage,[517] saying that Vinet and I are in agreement. Curiously enough, I then requested a book by him from the University Library. It was on loan. Some time later it was sent to me. A few days later the librarian told me that the one who had had the book would like to have it again. I returned it at once. It turned out that Martensen[518] was the one who had had it. It was a large book by Vinet in French, and for that reason I did not read any of it. But today I myself have obtained the little book, which I had ordered.—*JP* IV 4212 (*Pap.* X⁴ A 186) March 9, 1851

Independence

How is it that in our time only a wealthy person is regarded as an independent man? I wonder if it is not because we have completely forgotten or transformed into a fable the fact that being able to live on roots, water, and bread is a more secure independence.—*JP* II 1271 (*Pap.* X⁴ A 257) *n.d.*, 1851

Conversation with Bishop Mynster,[519] *May 2*

As I entered, I said that this was just about the time he usually traveled on his visitations and I usually liked to call upon him some time before.

So we talked together about the minister and the department, which I do not note down since it does not concern my cause.

Then the conversation was drawn to more recent events. I mentioned again the tactic with my latest pseudonym[520] and pointed out how without it I could not have taken the position against Rudelbach, which he admitted. I then repeated that even if he had something against this book of mine, which was possible, it was nevertheless a defense of the established order.

Then I turned suddenly to his book[521] and said outright that I had not come to thank him for my copy because there was something in it that I could not approve, and this was why I had been delinquent about visiting him.

We talked about this; yet he was momentarily startled when I turned the conversation this way. So we talked about this. He maintained essentially, as I could well understand, that he had merely said that Goldschmidt[522] was talented, whereupon I pointed out that this could be understood as an understatement. I reminded him that he, too, had enemies and how an enemy might construe his behavior. I repeated again and again that what concerned me was whether his reputation had not suffered too much by directing attention to Goldschmidt in this way.* I pointed out to him that he ought to have demanded a revocation by G.; I told him that, with his permission, I would show how he should have done it—that is, demanded a revocation. The precariousness of it all lay, I told him, in this, that he should keep in mind that he has to represent prestige—and that it was impossible for me to defend his conduct. I pointed out to him how he now had G. in his power, that he could give a turn to the affair—one usually brings out the good in a man by means of the good. The fact that M. had directed attention to G. in this way ought to have made G. aware that a revocation was necessary; since it was lacking, what had been done was also of a different character. But M. was of the opinion that there was still something in the fact that G. had remained silent. I explained again how insidious G. was and that it probably would appear some time.

Then I said to him, "It may seem strange that youth speaks to age in this manner, but for the present will you permit me to do so and allow me to give you some advice: If there is anything about me of which you disapprove, if you would like to give me a whack, do it, do it; I can take it and shall see to it that you do not suffer for it; but, above all, do not do it in such a way that your own prestige comes to suffer thereby. It is your prestige that concerns me."

Again and again I repeated: "I want it said plainly and bluntly," "I want my conscience to be clear," "It must be noted that I have said that I cannot approve of it" (and as I said it, I bent over the table and wrote, as it were, with my hand). To this he replied: "Well, it is very explicit." And I saw to it that every time I said this he replied and indicated that he had heard it.

In other respects my conversation was permeated by all the affection for him I received from my father and still have. I talked much longer than usual. Incidentally, he was more friendly and attentive than usual today. I did something that I otherwise do not do—I spoke a little with him about his family, a subject he brought up himself by saying that his daughter was to be married. And I spoke a little with him about himself, about the joy of his old age, and how grateful he must be. And then again—that he must be sure to watch out for his prestige.

Usually he has to be pressed when I speak of paying him a visit, and generally he is in the habit of saying that I might better come some other time, without saying when. This he did not do today. On the contrary, he said that I would be welcome. And when I said: Is another time perhaps more convenient for you, he replied: Come at the specified time. To which I answered: I would certainly prefer to come at that time; it is very special to me; I am accustomed to it, and "tradition is still a great force." (This was an allusion to something in the conversation.)

And so it went—Thanks, good friend, etc.

I parted from him on the most friendly terms possible.

Incidentally, when we spoke together of Goldschmidt, he made an attempt to point out that he had used "talented" for Goldschmidt and "gifted" for me and that the latter meant much more. To which I answered: That is of no consequence, the question here is your prestige. Thereupon he abandoned this attempt.**

On the whole I was happy to have spoken with him. My affection for him belongs to him, after all, and it does not help much to put in print how devoted to him I am—it would never be understood anyway.—*JP* VI 6757 (*Pap.* X^4 A 270) May 2, 1851

In margin of Pap. X^4 A 270:

* He said that G. was a useful man and that one ought to utilize such people. I replied that there is an impatience that sees only what appears advantageous at the moment but which is dangerous, and that it was a question of whether or not he had not bought too dearly by paying with his prestige.—*JP* VI 6758 (*Pap.* X^4 A 271) *n.d.*, 1851

In margin of Pap. X⁴ A 270:

** The dubious aspect (of the extent to which Mynster did not mean to affront me by grouping me with Goldschmidt in this way) was something that up until now I have not wanted to note down, although I hid it in my memory. When I said that he at least ought to have let G. first disavow his past, M. answered: Then I would have to have read through all of his numerous books. Thus I was supposed to believe that M. was actually ignorant of the fact that there was a paper called *The Corsair*, that G. had edited it for six years, and that M. did not understand that this was what I was aiming at!—*JP* VI 6759 (*Pap.* X⁴ A 272) *n.d.*, 1851

And this [Mynster's and Goldschmidt's use of the numerical] also took place right at the very moment (for Mynster had already nodded toward Goldschmidt but had not yet linked him with me) when I (out of love for my idea and the truth but also genuinely out of love for the old man) had once more lined up against the numerical and had broken sharply with Rudelbach[523] and the Old Orthodox.—*Pap.* X⁴ A 522 *n.d.*, 1852

To Declare Maieutically that One Himself Is Not a Christian[524]

X⁴ A 553 370

Take the Socratic position: error and evil are puffed-up knowledge—therefore Socrates is the ignorant one and remains that until the end. Likewise, to be a Christian has become an illusion, all these millions of Christians—therefore the situation must be reversed and Christianity must be introduced by a person who says that he himself is not a Christian.

This is the way I have understood it. But to what extent ought this tactic be maintained to the end, and to what extent should I stick to it?

For me, the entire operation has been a matter of being honest with myself: whether and to what extent I wanted to become a Christian in the strictest sense. Devoutly (for I felt myself to be ordained to this task, my only one), I intellectually assumed the task of making clear what Christianity is, and the pseudonym[525] also declared himself not to be Christian.

But when the one who enters upon this operation is himself in the situation of having to determine whether he actually wants to become a Christian in the strictest sense, this tactic cannot and ought not to be maintained to the end. Otherwise the most appalling thing could happen—that by jacking up the price of being a Christian he ultimately (let us take the extreme) would get everyone to give up Christianity and he himself would give it up. Furthermore, such a person, himself detached, could take a demonic delight in torturing those who call themselves Christians by attaching to them heavy burdens that he himself has not yet taken up.

So it is with me. But suppose that someone else had undertaken the enterprise of maieutically introducing Christianity, declaring himself not to be a Christian, someone else who from the outset had in deepest inwardness made up his mind about being and wanting to be a Christian in the strictest sense—ought this maieutic position then be maintained to the end, or is there not a difficulty here that is not present in the Socratic position? To be specific, Christianity teaches that a danger is involved, persecution goes along with confessing that one is a true Christian—this is no doubt evaded by the person who in introducing Christianity declares himself not to be a Christian. True enough, the evil in "Christendom" is precisely that all are Christians, and thus there is no danger connected with calling oneself Christian but rather an advantage, and here again, in reverse, the danger might come through not wanting to declare oneself to be a Christian. Yet to this Christianity might reply: "Because there is no danger connected with being a Christian in the sense that these millions are Christian, I do not for that reason take back my word that suffering, mockery, and persecution are still to be expected if one genuinely wants to be a Christian and confesses to being one—and this you evade by introducing Christianity in such a way that you declare yourself not to be a

Christian." And so it is, too. The scruples about claiming to be a Christian, which I have expressed in a little essay, *Armed Neutrality*[526] (because I do not want the point of contention to be my claim that "I am a Christian" but that "I know what Christianity is"), because of the fear that on judgment day God might say to me: You have dared to call yourself a Christian—these scruples are removed by what I have pointed out here, that on judgment day God could very well say to such a person: By declaring yourself not to be a Christian, you have evaded suffering for confessing that you are a Christian (with respect to Socrates,[527] there was no ignominy etc. connected with calling himself wise, something he evaded by calling himself ignorant).

But let us suppose that the person who introduced Christianity maieutically (in order to get rid of the illusion, the notion of being Christian because one is living in Christendom), declaring himself not to be a Christian, let us suppose that he not only from the beginning made up his mind about wanting to be a Christian in the strictest sense but that he completely ordered his life (although continually declaring himself not to be a Christian) according to the requirements of Christianity concerning renunciation, dying to the world,[*] and lived in voluntary poverty and thereby was definitely exposed to the suffering and persecution that are inseparable and are essential Christianity—can he continue to the end with this formula: I am not a Christian? The answer to this must be: Christianity nevertheless always requires the confession of Christ, and yet the suffering he suffers may not necessarily be for Christ's sake; perhaps he could also be secretly proud of having no fellowship with other Christians.

If the formula "I am not a Christian" is to be maintained to the end, then it must be done by an "apostle"[528] but in an entirely new style. He must have an immediate relation to Christ and then only in death explain how it all hangs together. Whether this will ever happen, I cannot say.

[*] *In margin*: and everything involved in "imitation,"[529] dying to the world, being born again, and so on, which I myself was not aware of in 1848.—*JP* II 1962 (*Pap.* X⁴ A 553) n.d., 1852

EDITORIAL APPENDIX

Acknowledgments
267

Collation of Articles in the Danish Editions of
Kierkegaard's Collected Works
269

Notes
271

Bibliographical Note
309

Index
311

ACKNOWLEDGMENTS

The present volume is included in a general grant from the National Endowment for the Humanities. The grant includes a gift from the Danish Ministry of Cultural Affairs. A grant for special research expenses has been received from the A. P. Møller og Hustru Chastine Mc-Kinney Møllers Fund.

The translators-editors are indebted to Gregor Malantschuk and Grethe Kjær for their knowledgeable observations on crucial concepts and terminology.

Former and present members of the International Advisory Board for *Kierkegaard's Writings* (see end page), Brian Macnamara, Todd Nichol, and Jack and Pamela Schwandt have given helpful criticism of the manuscript on the whole and in detail. The index has been prepared by Rune Engebretsen, Steven Knudson, Craig Mason, and Christopher Smith.

Acknowledgment is made to Gyldendals Forlag for permission to absorb notes to *Søren Kierkegaards Samlede Værker*.

Inclusion in the Supplement of entries from *Søren Kierkegaard's Journals and Papers* is by arrangement with Indiana University Press.

The book collection and the microfilm collection of the Kierkegaard Library, St. Olaf College, have been used in preparation of the text and of the Supplement and appendix.

The manuscript, typed by Dorothy Bolton, has been guided through the press by Sanford Thatcher and Gretchen Oberfranc.

Howard V. Hong
Edna H. Hong

COLLATION OF ARTICLES IN THE DANISH EDITIONS OF KIERKEGAARD'S COLLECTED WORKS

| *Vol. XIII* | *Vol. XIII* | *Vol. 18* | *Vol. XIII* | *Vol. XIII* | *Vol. 18* |
| Ed. 1 | Ed. 2 | Ed. 3 | Ed. 1 | Ed. 2 | Ed. 3 |
Pg.	Pg.	Pg.	Pg.	Pg.	Pg.
397	433	9	426	462	34
398	434	9	427	463	35
399	435	10	428	464	35
400	436	11	429	465	36
401	436	12	430	466	37
402	437	13	431	467	38
403	438	13	432	468	39
404	439	15	433	468	39
405	440	15	434	469	40
406	441	16	435	471	41
407	443	18	436	472	43
408	443	18	437	472	43
409	444	19	438	473	44
410	446	20	439	475	45
411	448	22	440	476	46
412	448	22	441	477	47
413	449	23	442	478	48
414	450	24	443	480	50
415	451	25	444	480	50
416	453	26	447	483	51
417	453	26	448	483	51
418	455	28	449	485	52
419	455	28	450	485	53
420	456	29	451	486	54
421	457	30	452	487	55
422	459	31	453	489	55
423	459	32	454	490	56
424	460	32	455	491	57
425	461	33	456	492	58

NOTES

ARTICLES

1. The article appeared in the Copenhagen newspaper *Fædrelandet*, no. 904, June 12, 1842. In a journal entry from 1848, Kierkegaard interprets this article: "As early as the article 'Public Confession' there was a signal shot . . . suggesting that Professor Heiberg was the literary figure I wanted to protect; he and Mynster both were mentioned there and as unmistakably as possible" (*JP* V 6201; *Pap.* IX A 166).

2. The People's Press, a paper published by the Society for the Proper Use of Freedom of the Press (1835-1848) and edited by F. C. Olsen and C. F. Allen.

3. A schoolbook edited by D. Seidelin Birch (10 ed., Copenhagen: 1842).

4. While writing the pseudonymous works, Kierkegaard fostered the impression that he was an idler by being seen often on the streets, by appearing at the intermission of a play or concert, and by frequenting cafés.

5. See "A First and Last Declaration," *Postscript, KW* XII (*SV* VII, unnumbered pages following text).

6. Strangely enough, *The Corsair* did not quote or otherwise use this line later. See Supplement, p. 96.

7. Throughout, "system" refers to Hegelian philosophy and the claims of some Danish Hegelians even to have gone beyond Hegel in systematizing thought and existence. See, for example, *Fragments, KW* VII (*SV* IV 175-77).

8. Rasmus Nielsen (1809-1884), *Den speculative Logik i dens Grundtræk*, fasc. 1-2 (Copenhagen: 1841-42, incomplete). Fascicle 1 begins with ¶11 and ends with ¶21. The overleaf reads: "This outline is to be regarded as a fragment of a philosophical methodology."

9. Volumes I–XXVIII were published between 1751 and 1772. In 1776-1777, five supplementary volumes were published, and in 1780 two index volumes appeared. The *Encyclopedia* is not included in *ASKB*.

10. The Danish *Ark* refers to a full printed sheet, which has eight leaves in octavo (sheet folded three times), four leaves in quarto (sheet folded twice), and two leaves in folio (sheet folded once).

11. Hans Bastholm (1774-1856), ed., *Sophrosyne, et Tidsskrift for den populaire Philosophie*, II, 1831, p. 295, has as a closing statement: "I still have a few words to say to the public after concluding this work, first of all to affirm that God is my witness that I have not written it with any ambitions in mind or for any temporal advantage, but I could very willingly have kept it in my desk along with so many other compositions."

12. Dr. Andreas Frederick Beck (1816-1861), assistant professor of philosophy, University of Copenhagen, had just published *Begrebet Mythus eller den religiøse Aands Form* (Copenhagen: 1842). The preface reads: "The present

work stands in about the same relation to Bruno Bauer's and in part to Feuerbach's works in criticism and philosophy of religion as Professor George's treatise *Mythus und Sage* to Strauss's famous work on the life of Jesus."

13. At its meeting on February 4, 1842, the Royal Society agreed to keep in its custody a work submitted by a Sorø teacher, Johannes Japetus Steenstrup (1813-1897), later a prominent zoologist.

14. See, for example, *Fear and Trembling*, KW VI (SV III 57), on going beyond Descartes; ibid. (59), on going beyond faith; *Fragments*, KW VII (SV IV 181), on going beyond Socrates; *Postscript*, KW XII (SV VII 89, 320), on going beyond Hegel; ibid. (511), on going beyond Christianity.

15. Presumably a reference to Bishop Jacob (Jakob) P. Mynster. During the preceding nine months, Mynster had preached regularly once a month in Slotskirken (Palace Chapel). Mynster (1775-1854) had been a friend of Michael P. Kierkegaard, father of Søren, who himself had great respect and esteem for Mynster until the later years.

16. See note 17 below.

17. Presumably Kierkegaard refers here to the public acclaim given to the festivities in Rosenborg gardens arranged by Georg Carstensen (who also received permission in 1842 to begin Tivoli) and a decline of interest in J. L. Heiberg's operettas. In a later journal entry (*JP* VI 6624; *Pap.* X³ A 99), Kierkegaard writes of a munificent offer (refused) made by Carstensen for an article against Heiberg.

18. Hans Bastholm, *Sophrosyne*, I, 1830, p. 1: "The aphoristic form will frequently be chosen."

19. Peter M. Stilling (1812-1869), prompted by Rasmus Nielsen's volume on speculative logic (see note 8 above), wrote *Philosophiske Betragtninger over den speculative Logiks Betydning for Videnskaben* (Copenhagen: 1842). The Danish for "to establish" is *at stille*, a pun on the name Stilling.

20. Cf. *Postscript*, KW XII (SV VII 154-57).

21. Presumably an ironic allusion to II Corinthians 5:7.

22. Frederik VI (1768-1839), King of Denmark and Norway (1808-1814), King of Denmark (1814-1839).

23. See *JP* IV 4092 (*Pap.* II A 378).

24. See p. 6 and note 12. Kierkegaard's dissertation was reviewed by Dr. Andreas F. Beck in *Fædrelandet*, no. 890 and 897, May 29, 1842, and June 5, 1842.

25. See p. 6 and note 12. Kierkegaard's dissertation on irony is cited a number of times, and similarities to Strauss (see note 26 below) are claimed.

26. David Strauss, *Das Leben Jesu*, I–II (Tübingen: 1834-35); Ludwig Feuerbach, *Das Wesen des Christenthums* (Leipzig: 1841); Johan K. W. Vatke, *Die Religion des Alten Testaments* (Berlin: 1835); Bruno Bauer, *Kritik der evangelischen Geschichte des Johannes* (Bremen: 1840) and *Kritik der evangelischen Synoptiker* (Leipzig: 1841).

27. See Supplement, p. 219, and note 434. The size of the edition of *The Concept of Irony* (1841) is not known. *Either/Or* (1843), *Fear and Trembling* (1843), *Repetition* (1843), and *Fragments* (1844) were printed in editions of 525

copies. *The Concept of Anxiety* (1844) was published in an edition of 250 copies. Dissertations, however, were published in smaller than usual editions. The retail price of *Irony* was 9 marks, or 1½ rix-dollars, or $7.50 (1973 money), for a paperback volume of 350 pages. If the usual 25% bookseller's commission is reckoned, sales of 163 copies of *Irony* would have covered the costs of printing and binding. If the usual small dissertation edition was printed, and if from that one subtracts the free copies supplied to the university, Kierkegaard most likely lost money on the book.

28. *Either/Or*, I–II, under the pseudonym of Victor Eremita as editor, appeared February 20, 1843. The following article appeared in *Fædrelandet*, no. 1162, February 27, 1843.

29. See Horace, *Ars Poetica*, 78. Q. Horatii Flacci, *Opera* (Leipzig: 1828; ASKB 1248), p. 669; *Satires, Epistles and Ars Poetica*, tr. H. Rushton Fairclough (Loeb, New York: Putnam, 1929), pp. 456-57.

30. The identity of author and publisher.

31. The rix-dollar (worth about $5.00 in 1973 money) contained 6 marks or 96 shillings.

32. A rich businessman and landowner in Altona, Slesvig-Holsten, at that time a duchy of Denmark.

33. See Genesis 4:8.

34. A tax on the proceeds of a trade or business.

35. A small, general parish tax for the local church.

36. Lauritz J. Fribert (1808-1855), from 1840 archivist at Sorø Academy and from 1842 editor and publisher of a newspaper.

37. The sentence states Kierkegaard's main reason for using pseudonyms, five of them in *Either/Or*: (1) Victor Eremita, the editor, (2) Mr. A., author of Volume I, except for the portion by (3) Johannes, author of "The Seducer's Diary," although the editor thinks that Mr. A. may have been the author, (4) Judge William, author of most of Volume II, and (5) William's friend in Jutland, the author of "Ultimatum" at the end of Volume II.

38. Published in *Fædrelandet*, no. 1168, March 5, 1843, a few weeks before Kierkegaard left Copenhagen for his second visit to Berlin (May 8-30, 1843). Johan Ludvig Heiberg (1791-1860), Danish poet, dramatist, philosopher, and editor, was the foremost literary critic in Denmark at the time.

39. In "*Litterær Vintersæd*" (Literary Winter Grain), in *Intelligensblade* (ed. J. L. Heiberg), no. 24, March 1, 1843, J. L. Heiberg reviewed *Either/Or*: "One closes the book and says, 'That's enough [*Basta*]! I have enough of *Either*; I do not want any of *Or*.' . . . . The reader whose approach to the book I have described is 'one' . . . . Some individuals may, however, be curious to learn what sort of *Or* the author contrasts to such an *Either*, and they will begin at least to page through the second volume" (p. 291). For Kierkegaard's response, see, for example, in addition to the present article, *JP* VI 6201 (*Pap*. IX A 166) and *Prefaces*, *KW* IX (*SV* V 23, 28).

40. Heiberg, "*Litterær Vintersæd*," p. 288: "like a lightning bolt out of a clear sky, a monster of a book has suddenly plunged down into our reading public; I mean the two big, thick volumes of *Either/Or*, by Victor Eremita,

consisting of fifty-four full, closely printed sheets . . . . The book may be called a monster, for it is impressive by its very mass . . . ."

41. Page reference is to the first edition. See *Either/Or*, I, *KW* III (*SV* I, p. xv).

42. Title page of *Either/Or*, I. The epigraph, in Danish, is from Edward Young, *The Complaint; or, Night-Thoughts on Life, Death, and Immortality*, IV, 629: "Are passions, then, the pagans of the soul? / Reason alone baptized?" Kierkegaard owned *Einige Werke von Dr. Eduard Young*, I–III, tr. J. A. Ebert (Braunschweig, Hildesheim: 1767-72; *ASKB* 1911). There were two Danish translations: *Dr. Edward Youngs Klage eller Nattetanker*, tr. Barthold J. Lodde (Copenhagen: 1783), and *Forsøg til en Oversættelse af Dr. Edward Youngs Klager eller Nattetanker*, tr. Emanuel Balling (Helsingør: 1767). The Danish translation in *Either/Or* does not follow Ebert (p. 95), Lodde (p. 108), or Balling (p. 112).

43. Heiberg, "*Litterær Vintersæd*," p. 289.

44. Cf. James 1:19.

45. Attributed to A. by the editor, Victor Eremita, *Either/Or*, I, *KW* III (*SV* I, p. xvi).

46. Attributed to B. by the editor, Victor Eremita, *Either/Or*, I, *KW* III (*SV* I, p. xvi).

47. See p. 17 and note 39.

48. *Fædrelandet*, no. 1236, May 16, 1843.

49. Delivered January 12, 1841. See *JP* III 3915 (*Pap*. III C 1).

50. *Either/Or*, II, *KW* IV (*SV* II 306-18).

51. See Aristotle, *De Generatione et Corruptione*, I, 2, 315 b; *Aristotelis Latine ex recensione Immanuelis Bekkeri*, I–IV (Berlin: 1831-36; *ASKB* 1076), I, p. 315; *The Works of Aristotle*, I–XII, ed. J. A. Smith and W. D. Ross (Oxford: Oxford University Press, 1908-52), II; *JP* V 5617 (*Pap*. IV A 61).

52. *Two Upbuilding Discourses*, by S. Kierkegaard, appeared May 16, 1843. See *Eighteen Upbuilding Discourses*, *KW* V (*SV* III 7-52).

53. See Horace, *Odes*, III, 3, 1; *Opera*, p. 149; *The Odes and Epodes*, tr. C. E. Bennett (Loeb, New York: Putnam, 1930), 1. 179.

54. See *Fragments*, *KW* VII (*SV* IV 236).

55. Published in *Fædrelandet*, no. 1883, May 9, 1845, just before Kierkegaard left Copenhagen on his third trip to Berlin (May 13-24, 1845). The article is in response to the first published attribution of any of the pseudonymous works to Kierkegaard. The occasion for this divulgence was a review of Kierkegaard's *Three Discourses on Imagined Occasions* (April 29, 1845) and *Stages* (April 30, 1845).

Berlingske Politiske og Avertissements-Tidende, no. 108, May 6, 1845, col. 3-4:

Literature

Mag. Kierkegaard: *Three Discourses; Stages of Life*. It is well known that the hero in the old oriental fairy tales usually has some magic means to make his wishes come true in the real world. One would think that Mag. Kierkegaard possessed a kind of magic wand by which he instantaneously conjures up his books, so incredible has his literary activity been in recent years, if we dare believe the rumor that presumably is correct in claiming him to be the author of *Either/Or* and the series of books that apparently comes from the same hand. Productivity of that kind is not always a clear recommendation, since very often it signifies hasty, superficial work, but this is so far from being the case here that, on the contrary, each of these works is remarkable for a depth of thought that pursues its object to its most minute thread and in addition unfolds a rare beauty and elegance of language, and particularly a fluency that surpasses that of any contemporary Danish writer. When we consider also that an authentic poetic genius is manifest in many places, we cannot refrain from wishing that the author would also venture in directions other than only philosophical hypothesizing that until now has been dominant in his writings. The *Three Discourses on Imagined Occasions*, which he has recently presented to us, are entirely in the same spiritual family as the author's earlier published discourses and are marked by the same beauty of form and richness of content. The discourses are a confessional sermon, a wedding ceremony, and a graveside meditation; in the first one he tells what it means to seek God, in the second he develops the beautiful theme that love in marriage will overcome everything, and, finally, in the third discourse he poignantly portrays death's culmination as the final end of our earthly existence. *Life's Stages*, a collection of three longer sections, which a "Mr. Hilarius Bookbinder has had the kindness to have published," reminds us not a little of *Either/Or*. In the first section, entitled "In Vino Veritas," we meet our earlier acquaintances, Victor Eremita and Constantinus [sic] Constantius, in the company of Johannes the Seducer, a fashion designer, and a young man whom the author as yet has not named. Over brimming glasses, they discuss the old question of the significance of woman but do not arrive at the same conclusion as the poet who declared her to be the creator's most perfect masterpiece; one of them even declares fashion to be a woman because of its nonsensical fickleness that knows no other consistency than to become more and more starkly mad. The next section contains a piece by Judge William (also an acquaintance from *Either/Or*), in which he furnishes new contributions to the proper conception of marriage. The third section contains a tale of woe or, rather, the story of an engagement in the author's well-known style. If we have any negative criticism of these works, it is that the author seems to us to take almost too much time elaborating his reflections, with the result that they sometimes become somewhat prolix; however, we do thank him for the pleasure he has given us through these fine books, and we are happy that he will let us hear from him again soon. —n.

A sequel to the *B.T.* review appeared the same month in *The Corsair*, no. 245, May 23, 1845, col. 13:

Transcript
of
The Corsair's Record of the Testimony

in the case of
Magister S. Kierkegaard
versus
Berlingske.

In the present action that the honorable Magister Kierkegaard has brought against *Berlingske* because the latter has respectfully praised one of the plaintiff's unwritten books and for having represented his language as being just as flourishing as our finances and our butter production, for which reason the plaintiff seeks appropriate satisfaction and to have nullified the expression used—the judgment of the court is:

The alleged praise by the defendant *Berlingske* of the unwritten book by the plaintiff ought to be null and void and in no imaginable and unimaginable way to harm his good name and reputation. —For its manifest part in this case, the defendant is sentenced to a sound thrashing to be divided equally between its own and *Aftenbladet*'s fund for the intellectually indigent.

The conduct of the case has been legal.
Accuracy of transcript certified.
The Corsair.
The Corsair's Witness Chamber. May 16, 1845.

56. Kierkegaard wrote pseudonymous works but never wrote anonymously. By this time, May 9, 1845, he had published pseudonymously: *From the Papers of One Still Living*, ed. S. Kjerkegaard (1838); *Either/Or*, ed. Victor Eremita (1843); *Fear and Trembling*, by Johannes de Silentio (1843); *Repetition*, by Constantin Constantius (1843); *Philosophical Fragments*, by Johannes Climacus (1844); *The Concept of Anxiety*, by Vigilius Haufniensis (1844); *Prefaces*, by Nicolaus Notabene (1844); and *Stages on Life's Way*, ed. Hilarius Bookbinder (1845). During the same period he had published under his own name: *The Concept of Irony* (1841); *Two Upbuilding Discourses* (1843); *Three . . .* (1843); *Four . . .* (1843); *Two . . .* (1844); *Three . . .* (1844); *Four . . .* (1844); and *Three Discourses on Imagined Occasions* (1845).

57. See note 55 above. "Pronoun" is used in the elemental meaning, that is, a word "for a noun," and refers to the expression "same hand."

58. See note 55 above.

59. The reviewer attributes to the author a beauty, elegance, and versatility of language unmatched by any other Danish writer.

60. Ludvig Holberg, *Den ellefte Junii*, III, 6.

61. In Ludvig Holberg's *Mester Gert Westphaler*, II, 4, Gert drinks with his executioner the toast pledging lifelong friendship.

62. A patron of the arts, derived from Caius Maecenas (73?-8 B.C.), Roman statesman, patron of letters, and friend of Horace and Virgil.

63. See note 38 above.

64. Johan N. Madvig (1804-1886), a classical philologist who occasionally wrote reviews for *Maanedsskrift for Litteratur*.

Notes to Pages 26-37   277

65. The pseudonym of Bishop Jacob (Jakob) Peter Mynster, formed from the initial consonant of the second syllable of each name. In *Intelligensblade* (ed. J. L. Heiberg), no. 41-42, January 1, 1844, Mynster had praised *Fear and Trembling*, by Johannes de Silentio, and Kierkegaard's upbuilding discourses.

66. Published in *Fædrelandets Feuilleton*, no. 1890-91, May 19-20, 1845. See *Either/Or*, I, *KW* III (*SV* I 29-113) for an essay on Mozart.

67. After November 1840, Mozart's *Don Giovanni* was not presented at the Royal Theater until February 1845. The fifth and last performance was on May 8, shortly before the publication of the present article. The Danish version used was by Laurids Kruse (Copenhagen: 1807).

68. Diogenes Laertius, II, 22. Socrates said of Heraclitus that what he had understood of his writings was good, and therefore he assumed the same of that which he had not understood. *Diogenes Laërtses filosofiske Historie*, I-II, tr. Børge Riisbrigh (Copenhagen: 1812; *ASKB* 1110-11), I, p. 66; *Lives of Eminent Philosophers*, I-II, tr. R. D. Hicks (Loeb, New York: Putnam, 1925), I, p. 153.

69. Jørgen C. Hansen (1812-1880) played the role of Don Giovanni for many years from 1839.

70. *Mozart's Opera Don Giovanni* (New York: Ditson, n.d.), I, 2; Danish version by L. Kruse (Copenhagen: 1807), I, 2, pp. 4-5.

71. See *Either/Or*, I, *KW* III (*SV* I 81-82).

72. Boline Abrahamsen Kragh (1810-1839) played the role of Zerlina, 1833-1839.

73. I, 13 (I, 9, p. 33).

74. I, 3 (I, 6, p. 18); see *Either/Or*, I, *KW* III (*SV* I 109).

75. Presumably a reference to the concept of nemesis, retributive justice.

76. I, 21 (I, 13, p. 42).

77. I, 28 (I, 20, p. 63).

78. I, 18 (I, 14, pp. 43-45).

79. II, 7 (II, 11, p. 96).

80. II, 4 (II, 4, pp. 78-82).

81. See *Either/Or*, I, *KW* III (*SV* I 110).

82. See *Either/Or*, I, *KW* III (*SV* I 78-83).

83. Cf. Proverbs 25:11.

84. See *Either/Or*, I, *KW* III (*SV* I 79).

85. The serenade, II, 5 (II, 5, p. 83).

86. I, 8 (I, 6, p. 17).

87. *Either/Or*, I, *KW* III (*SV* I 100-02).

88. I, 14 (I, 10, p. 35).

89. See *Either/Or*, I, *KW* III (*SV* I 47-53), on music and language as media.

90. I, 13 (I, 9, p. 34).

91. The piece on *Don Giovanni* was written a half-year before *The Corsair* began its prolonged ridiculing and caricaturing of Kierkegaard's legs and clothes. See Supplement, p. 114, and note 107.

92. Presumably the young Mr. A. who was the pseudonymous author of

Either/Or, I, which contains the long essay on music and on Mozart's *Don Giovanni* in particular.

93. Published in *Fædrelandet*, no. 2078, December 27, 1845. Peder Ludvig Møller (1814-1865) contributed to *Gæa* (Copenhagen: 1846 [actually published in December 1845]), which he edited, a long piece entitled *"Et Besøg i Sorø"* (A Visit in Sorø), in which he includes a lengthy but superficial consideration of Kierkegaard's pseudonymous works, particularly *Stages* (see Supplement, pp. 96-104). The present article by Frater Taciturnus is a reply to P. L. Møller's article and at the end (p. 46) contains Kierkegaard's public initiation of the *Corsair* affair. See Supplement, pp. 108-12, for the first reply by *The Corsair* to Kierkegaard's article.

94. Carsten Hauch (1790-1872), Danish poet and novelist and at the time a teacher at the famous Sorø Academy.

95. A character in J. L. Heiberg's *Recensenten og Dyret*.

96. *Stages on Life's Way*, with emphasis on " 'Guilty?'/'Not Guilty?' " See Supplement, pp. 96-104.

97. *Stages, KW* XI (*SV* VI 371-72). On the Danish *Experiment* etc., see *Repetition, KW* VI, note on subtitle.

98. See Supplement, p. 100.

99. Georg Christoph Lichtenberg, *Ueber Physiognomik wider die Physiognomen, Vermischte Schriften*, I-IX (Göttingen: 1800-06; *ASKB* 1764-72), III, p. 479. The line is used as the motto of "In Vino Veritas," *Stages, KW* XI (*SV* VI 14).

100. Kierkegaard did not know that P. L. Møller had made use of oral and written comments by Hauch. In a letter (November 1, 1845) to Møller, Hauch wrote: "The observations I have expressed regarding Kierkegaard I readily turn over to you for your use, since I am convinced that you will use them with discretion; meanwhile, you will bring upon yourself a hard battle with Denmark's most subtle dialectician" (quoted by Helge Toldberg, "*Goldschmidt og Kierkegaard*," in *Festskrift til Paul Rubow* [Copenhagen: 1956], p. 235, ed. tr.). Later (January 1870), in a letter to H. P. Barfod, Hauch wrote: "Whatever expressions I may have used in private conversation [and letters], these occurred under the spontaneous influence of the moment and very definitely should not have been made public, all the more so because my views of S. K. and his significant work have become very much modified over the years" (*Søren Kierkegaards Efterladte Papirer*, III, *1844-1846*, p. 221).

101. An expression used by a host after the guest has thanked him for the meal. Literally, may it be of good to you, may it "become you well."

102. See Supplement, pp. 99-102.

103. See *Stages, KW* XI (*SV* VI 415-20).

104. See, for example, *Fear and Trembling, KW* VI (*SV* III 57-58); *JP* I 772-80.

105. See, for example, *Fragments, KW* VII (*SV* IV 205, 271); *JP* II 2277 (*Pap.* III A 211).

106. *Stages, KW* XI (*SV* VI 438 fn.).

Notes to Pages 42-47

107. Jean Paul, *Des Feldpredigers Schmelzle Reise nach Flätz, Sämmtliche Werke*, I–LX (Berlin: 1827; *ASKB* 1777-99), L, p. 33. See Supplement, p. 104.

108. *Lærerige Fortællinger af Cervantes*, I–II, tr. Charlotte D. Biehl, (Copenhagen: 1780-81), I, pp. 309 ff. See Supplement, p. 101.

109. The protagonist in "The Seducer's Diary," *Either/Or*, I, and, in *Stages*, one of the speakers at the banquet in "In Vino Veritas."

110. Feminine form of *quidam*. See note 103 above.

111. Cf. *redintegratio in statum pristinum*, *Repetition*, *KW* VI (*SV* III 185).

112. See Supplement, p. 102.

113. Hans Christian Andersen. See Supplement, p. 99.

114. See *Postscript*, *KW* XII (*SV* VII 546); *JP* I 617-81; V 5865 (*Pap.* VII[1] A 83).

115. See *Erasmus Montanus*, IV, 3, in which Per Degn answers in broken Latin Erasmus's learned question and makes a great impression on the others, who are incapable of entering into the conversation.

116. An allusion to Socrates' mode of conversing. See, for example, Plato, *Gorgias*, 490 c; *Platonis quae exstant opera*, I–XI, ed. Fridericus Astius (Leipzig: 1819-32; *ASKB* 1144-54), I, pp. 370-71; *Udvalgte Dialoger af Platon*, I–VII, tr. C. J. Heise (Copenhagen: 1830-55; *ASKB* 1164-66 [I–III]), III, p. 110; *The Collected Dialogues of Plato*, ed. Edith Hamilton and Huntington Cairns (Princeton: Princeton University Press, 1963), p. 272; *Fragments*, *KW* VII (*SV* IV 195).

117. See Supplement, p. 208 (*Pap.* VII[1] A 98), and note 390, also pp. 213, 239 (*Pap.* VII[1] A 99; X[1] A 254).

118. *Stages*, *KW* XI (*SV* VI 371).

119. *Stages*, *KW* XI (*SV* VI 452).

120. *The Corsair*, no. 251, July 4, 1845, col. 3. See Supplement, p. 96.

121. Victor Eremita, editor of *Either/Or*, is praised in *The Corsair*, no. 269, November 14, 1845, col. 14. See Supplement, p. 96.

122. See Supplement, pp. 143, 191 (*Pap.* VII[1] B 55). The relationship between Møller and *The Corsair* referred to in the two Latin phrases was already known in literary circles, not least through Møller's own sketch supplied for Erslew's *Forfatter-Lexicon*, II, K-R (title page dated 1847, but the fascicles had been appearing periodically since 1843), p. 406. Fascicle no. 7 (fascicle no. 2 of vol. II, K-R) had already been advertised in *Adresseavisen*, no. 37, February 13, 1845. See Historical Introduction, p. xxviii.

123. In the latter portion of his article in *Gæa*, P. L. Møller names a number of the teachers at Sorø and makes sarcastic observations about them. Kierkegaard's brother Peter, however, is respectfully recognized.

124. Published in *Fædrelandet*, no. 9, January 10, 1846, in reply to the long article ridiculing Taciturnus-Kierkegaard in *The Corsair*, no. 276, January 2, 1846, col. 2-6. Although Kierkegaard's acknowledgment of the pseudonymous works had not yet appeared (*Postscript*, February 27, 1846), Goldschmidt knew of the relationship. See p. 24 and note 55; Supplement, pp. 97-100, 112-15, 146.

125. Meïr Goldschmidt (1819-1887), writer and editor of *The Corsair* (1840-1846) and of *Nord og Syd* (1847-1859). On Goldschmidt and Kierkegaard, see Historical Introduction, pp. vii-xxix, and Supplement, pp. 138-52.

126. *En Jøde* (A Jew) (Copenhagen: 1845), published pseudonymously with Goldschmidt's name on the title page as editor. The book offended many Danish Jews because it was impolitic to separate the Jews as a special group and a profanation to portray their intimate family and religious life. On the other hand, it was well received by many reviewers and by Kierkegaard, who distinguished between Goldschmidt as an author and as the editor of *The Corsair*.

127. The reference is to the last paragraph of "Diapsalmata," *Either/Or*, I, *KW* III (*SV* I 27).

128. See Supplement, p. 213 (*Pap.* VII^1 A 9).

129. See pp. 46, 172 (*Pap.* VII^1 B 38).

130. For over six months, *The Corsair* ran pieces ridiculing Kierkegaard, particularly his physique and his dress. The attack lasted longer, was of a different kind, and had a public response different from what Kierkegaard had anticipated. See Supplement, p. 209, and note 398. Therefore this article, Kierkegaard's second, was the last one he published on the *Corsair* affair.

131. See Historical Introduction, pp. xxiii-xxiv.

132. The "responsible editor" named on the title pages of *The Corsair* was one or another of a series of fronts for legal purposes. Goldschmidt remained in the background as active editor and publisher. See Supplement, p. 108, and note 80.

133. See p. 46 and notes 120, 121.

134. See *Stages*, *KW* XI (*SV* VI 281).

135. See Supplement, p. 190 (*Pap.* VII^1 B 55), and note 327.

136. See Historical Introduction, pp. xxxvi-xxxviii.

137. On Kierkegaard's two-track authorship, see "A Glance at a Contemporary Effort in Danish Literature" and "A First and Last Declaration," in *Concluding Unscientific Postscript*, *KW* XII (*SV* VII 212-56, [545-49]), and *The Point of View*, *KW* XXII (*SV* XIII 529-43).

138. Throughout his life, Kierkegaard steadfastly stayed clear of party affiliations of all kinds. Here the reference is particularly to the Grundtvigians, with whom Rudelbach was associated. The primary basis of Kierkegaard's aversion to parties and factions was his emphasis upon the authentic single individual in the context of the universally human and upon Christianity as addressed to every man.

139. Georg Frederik Ursin, *Regnebog eller Anviisning hensigtsmæssigen at udføre Huus- og Handelsregning* (Copenhagen: 1824). On the overleaf of the title page, one rix-dollar is promised for the first reporting of an error. The book was published when Kierkegaard was in his fourth year of school.

140. In Greek mythology, Tantalus was a Phrygian king who for his crimes was punished by confinement in water that receded when he tried to drink and near a tree whose fruit always eluded his grasp—hence the word

"tantalize." Here the phrase has a more direct reference to any situation or activity with unfulfilled and unfulfillable promises.
141. Acts 5:29.

ADDENDA

1. For a discussion of the status of the items in the Addenda, see Historical Introduction, p. xxxv fn.
2. The occasion for the three letters in the Addenda was an unsigned article in *Fædrelandet*, no. 1139, February 4, 1843, col. 5-6:

> An old fable relates that here in Denmark there is supposed to be a most excellent legal system; this has been believed for many years by many good-natured, superstitious people in the upper classes. We are convinced that it is extremely important that the superstition be eradicated, and therefore we believe that a small, but very characteristic, contribution to the portrayal of our legal system, an event that recently took place here in Copenhagen, merits publicizing, because it shows how very easily and without any protest people here in Denmark can be brought up for criminal interrogation and subjected to all the resulting suspicions and injury. The story is as follows: some papers, which, as far as we know, related to an embezzlement of an estate, disappeared from the Department of Justice. His Excellency Stemann searched and did not find them either. It was thought that the court bailiffs who had handled the papers must have misplaced them, and a criminal interrogation of the bailiffs was held. The interrogations yielded no information, which was quite natural, for shortly afterward the papers were found on a shelf in the office of His Excellency Stemann or of another Justice Department official. Can something like this happen in any other civilized country where there is any guarantee of personal rights? Is this a desirable legal climate, one in which criminal interrogation is made even though there is not a shred of evidence that any offense, to say nothing of a crime, has taken place? Cannot this legal system be called wholly devoid of guarantees, and cannot men's most sacred rights be said to be improperly safeguarded in any sense, when a high-ranking person's unverified and, as we learn, unverifiable and unjust charge is sufficient to bring down upon a poor simple man a criminal interrogation with all its consequences? And yet we are supposed to listen to big Danish lawyers and their parrots saying that we have a desirable legal system. We are forced to believe that such persons either do not know what a well-ordered legal system is or that they are speaking contrary to their better judgment.

Poul C. Stemann (1764-1855) was a Danish statesman and supporter of the monarchy who served as presiding officer of the Board of Justice and Interior Department, 1827-1848.

3. Published in *Berlingske Tidende*, no. 33, February 5, 1843. See p. 61 and note 1.

4. Henrik Stampe (1713-1789), Danish jurist, professor, statesman, and Attorney General (1753-1782).

5. Christian Colbjørnsen (1749-1814), Norwegian-Danish jurist, statesman, and lawyer of the Exchequer (1780-1785).

6. Anders Sandøe Ørsted (1778-1860), foremost Danish jurist, professor, writer, and Attorney General (1825-1848).

7. See p. 13 and note 31.

8. Published in *Berlingske Tidende*, no. 35, February 7, 1843. See p. 61 and note 1.

9. See p. 63 and notes 4-6.

10. See Holberg, *Erasmus Montanus*, III, 2.

11. Virgil, *Aeneid*, I, 135.

12. A landmark in central Copenhagen, finished in 1642 as an observatory and as the tower of Trinitatis Church.

13. Published in *Fædrelandet*, no. 1143, February 8, 1843. See p. 61 and note 1.

14. See p. 63 and note 2.

15. See pp. 63-65.

16. *Fædrelandet*, no. 1141, February 6, 1843; a reference to and comments upon "A Letter," pp. 63-65. See p. 66, fn.

17. See pp. 66-68.

18. See p. 63 and notes 4-6.

19. Published in *Ny Portefeuille*, I, 7, February 12, 1843, col. 198-216. See p. 78 and note 1.

20. Cf. *The Battle between the Old and the New Soap-Cellar*, in *KW* I (*Pap*. II B 3, 5); *Fragments*, *KW* VII (*SV* IV 211); *Stages*, *KW* XI (*SV* VI 391); *JP* II 1581 (*Pap*. II A 808): *høiere Galskab*, also translated as "higher lunacy."

21. Lucid intervals. In a journal entry from 1839, the expression *lucida intervalla* appears; see *JP* V 5434 (*Pap*. II A 576).

22. Oehlenschläger, *Tragødier*, I-IX (Copenhagen: 1844; *ASKB* 1601-05), IX, p. 36.

23. Cf. Sophocles, *Antigone*, 620-24; *Sophokles's Tragoedier*, I-II, tr. P. G. Fibiger (Copenhagen: 1821-22), II, p. 40; *The Complete Greek Tragedies*, I-IV ed. David Grene and Richard Lattimore (Chicago: University of Chicago Press, 1959-60), II, p. 180; *Stages*, *KW* XI (*SV* VI 251).

24. Attributed to Democritus. Cf. Cicero, *De divinatione*, I, 37; *M. Tulli Ciceronis Opera*, I-VI, ed. J. A. Ernesti (Halle: 1756-57; *ASKB* 1224-29), IV, pp. 636-37; *De senectute, De amicitia, De divinatione*, tr. William A. Falconer (Loeb, Cambridge: Harvard University Press, 1953), p. 313.

25. See Jerome, *Chronicle*, 171, 2.

26. A road from the West Gate (Vesterport) of old Copenhagen.

27. Henrich Steffens, *Malkolm*, I-II (Breslau: 1831).

28. A reference to Hegel's philosophy. See *System der Philosophie*, *Werke*, I-XVIII, ed. Ph. Marheineke et al. (Berlin: 1832-40; *ASKB* 549-65), VII, 1, p. 695; *Jubiläumsausgabe* [*J.A.*], I-XXVI, ed. Herman Glockner (Stuttgart: 1927-40), IX, p. 721; *Hegel's Philosophy of Nature*, tr. A. V. Miller (Oxford: Clarendon Press, 1970), para. 375 *Zusatz*, p. 444: "Nature has become

another to itself in order to recognize itself again as Idea and to reconcile itself with itself."

29. See Jens Baggesen, *Ja og Nej, Danske Værker*, I–XII (Copenhagen: 1845; *ASKB* 1509-20), I, p. 198.
30. See Genesis 37:9.
31. Not a direct quotation. See *Werke*, X¹, p. 4; *J.A.*, XII, p. 20; Hegel, *Aesthetics*, I–II, tr. T. M. Knox (Oxford: Clarendon Press, 1975), I, pp. 1-2.
32. Philine to Wilhelm in Goethe's *Wilhelm Meisters Lehrjahre*, *Werke*, I–LVI (Tübingen: 1828; *ASKB* 1641-68), XIX, p. 57; *Wilhelm Meister*, I–II, tr. R. O. Moon (London: Foulis, 1947), I, p. 202.
33. See Hegel, *Wissenschaft der Logik*, I, *Werke*, IV, pp. 177-83; *J.A.*, IV, pp. 655-61; *Hegel's Science of Logic*, tr. A. V. Miller (London, New York: Allen & Unwin, Humanities Press, 1969), pp. 523-28. See *Either/Or*, I, *KW* III (*SV* I, pp. v-vi); *Stages*, *KW* XI (*SV* VI 350).
34. Barère de Vieuzac, in his *Mémoires*, I–IV (Paris: 1842-44), recounts that in 1807 Talleyrand gave this reply to the Spanish ambassador, who reminded him of promises made in the interest of Charles IV of Spain. See *The Concept of Anxiety*, *KW* VIII (*SV* IV 376); *Stages*, *KW* XI (*SV* VI 317).
35. Cf. Romans 12:15.
36. See Genesis 4:1-9.
37. See Genesis 4:17.
38. Genesis 4:10.
39. Cf. street violinist, *Either/Or*, I, *KW* III (*SV* I 14-15).
40. Henrik Hertz, *Sven Dyrings Hus* (Copenhagen: 1837), I, 8, p. 36.
41. In Norse mythology, Forsete, the son of Balder and Nanna, is the god of justice and peacemaking. Literally, the name has the same root as "providence": to see forward.
42. The old lady who wrestled Thor to the floor at Utgard-Loki's in the tale "Thor, Uller, and Tyr." See N.F.S. Grundtvig, *Nordens Mythologi* (2 ed., Copenhagen: 1832; *ASKB* 1949), p. 435.
43. *Amors Geniestreger* (Copenhagen: 1830), a play by Henrik Hertz.
44. Daniel F. E. Auber, *Den sorte Domino*, III, 4 (Cavatine).
45. Presumably sycophants or talebearers, who at times were paid to be silent.
46. Peter Wessel Tordenskjold (1691-1720), Norwegian-Danish naval hero.
47. *Odyssey*, XII, 166-200.
48. *Den danske Krønike af Saxo Grammaticus* (Copenhagen: 1851; *ASKB* 2008-10), Book IV, p. lxviii (p. 159 in Müller and Velschow's edition).
49. Cicero relates this about Cato the Elder. *De divinatione*, II, 24: *M. Tulli Ciceronis Opera*, IV, p. 678; Loeb, p. 429.
50. See Matthew 27:24.
51. Herodotus, II, 172. *Die Geschichten des Herodotos*, I–II, tr. Friedrich Lange (Berlin: 1811; *ASKB* 1117), I, pp. 212-13; *Herodotus*, I–IV, tr. A. D. Godley (Loeb, New York: Putnam, 1921), I, p. 485.
52. A popular vote whereby leaders could be exiled for a time. The votes were scratched on pieces of earthenware.

284 Notes to Pages 84-93

53. Delicate, refined, classical wit.
54. See Deuteronomy 32:35; Romans 12:19.
55. See John 3:1-2.
56. Cf. *Postscript, KW* XII (*SV* VII 162).
57. See Ludvig Holberg, *Jean de France*, V, 2.
58. Cf. Matthew 12:36.
59. The demagogue Hyperbolos. See Plutarch, *Alcibiades*, 13; *Plutarchs Levnetsbeskrivelser*, I–IV, tr. Stephan Tetens (Copenhagen: 1800-11; *ASKB* 1197-1200), II, pp. 331-33; *Plutarch's Lives*, I–XI, tr. Bernadotte Perrin (Loeb, New York: Macmillan, 1914-26), IV, pp. 30-31.

SUPPLEMENT

1. On September 29, 1841, 10:00 A.M.–2:00 P.M., 4:00–7:00 P.M., Kierkegaard, in accordance with long-established custom in European universities, made public defense of his published dissertation, *The Concept of Irony, with Constant Reference to Socrates* (Copenhagen: September 16, 1841).

The *Magister* degree was the highest postgraduate degree in the Philosophical Faculty and corresponded to the doctor's degree in other faculties of the University of Copenhagen. In 1854, those with M.A. degrees were declared to be Doctors of Philosophy.

For a review of the dissertation, see *The Corsair*, no. 51, Supplement, pp. 92-93.

2. Part of the method of *The Corsair* was to encourage the funneling of gossip and the betrayal of the private lives of employers, statesmen, and others by their servants, barbers, secretaries, etc. See Supplement, p. 178 (*Pap.* VII^1 B 54).

3. See Supplement, p. 91, and note 1. On Goldschmidt's estimate of the review, see Supplement, p. 139.

4. *The Concept of Irony, KW* II (*SV* XIII 326).
5. Ibid. (*SV* XIII 112-13).
6. Ibid. (*SV* XIII 250-51).
7. Ibid. (*SV* XIII 142-43).
8. Ibid. (*SV* XIII 250-51).
9. Danish *Mellemhverandre*, a special term devised by Kierkegaard. See *The Concept of Irony, KW* II (*SV* XIII 262 fn.), and note.
10. Ibid. (*SV* XIII 115).
11. Ibid. (*SV* XIII 118-19).
12. Ibid. (*SV* XIII 212).
13. Ibid. (*SV* XIII 151)
14. Ibid. (*SV* XIII 113).
15. Ibid. (*SV* XIII 117).
16. Ibid. (*SV* XIII 225).
17. Ibid. (*SV* XIII 150-51). "Weigh salt" refers to a game in which two persons stand back to back, lock arms, and then tip back and forth as a kind of human teeter-totter.

18. On the review of *Irony* in *The Corsair* and the added postscript, Elias Bredsdorff writes: "it was not unfriendly toward Kierkegaard but ironized in a friendly way over his mannered language. Goldschmidt, however, who in the meantime had read *The Concept of Irony*, felt that the review had passed lightly over the contents of the book itself, which had made an impression upon him, and therefore he himself added the following postscript . . . ." *Goldschmidts "Corsaren"* (Copenhagen: Sinistra-Klubben, 1962), p. 92 (ed. tr.).

19. *Either/Or*, I–II, ed. Victor Eremita (Copenhagen: Feruary 20, 1843).

20. See p. 17, note 38. In order to help remedy what he regarded as the Danish public's need for esthetic-artistic education, J. L. Heiberg had established *Kjøbenhavns flyvende Post* (1827-30) and its successor, *Den flyvende Posts Interimsblade* (1834-37). In his *Intelligensblade* (1842-44), Heiberg appeared to be even more critical and intellectually aristocratic than formerly. In *En Sjæl efter Døden* (A Soul after Death; 1841), there is a brilliant and devastating satire of Danish society.

In an article, "*Smaa Skjermydsler*" (Little Skirmishes) (*Intelligensblade*, no. 9, July 15, 1842), Heiberg attacked the Copenhagen papers one by one for having carried "dishonest reports" of the public's reception of Hertz's *Perspektivkassen* when it was performed in the Royal Theater. Heiberg maintained that "the public's acclaim of the entire performance was overwhelming" and that "the few booers consisted of such subjects as Lt. Carstensen and similar nullities." Subsequently, Carstensen (remembered now as the founder of the amusement park Tivoli) initiated an exchange of letters with Heiberg and then printed selections from the correspondence in his journal *Figaro*.

21. See Supplement, p. 211, and note 406.

22. See p. 24 and note 55.

23. Mendel Levin Nathanson (1780-1868), businessman and editor of the *Berlingske Tidende*, 1838-1858. The works attributed to him here were fictitious.

24. Danish: *Tankeexperiment*. See note 92 below.

25. Editor of *Stages on Life's Way* (Copenhagen: April 30, 1845).

26. Presumably Adolph E. Boye (1784-1851), editor of *Nyt Aftenblad* and of Ludvig Holberg's and Johan Herman Wessel's works.

27. Peter Orla Lehmann (1810-1870), popular Danish politician, lawyer, orator, and writer. Although he was better known at the time than Kierkegaard, *The Corsair*'s prediction has been substantially fulfilled.

28. Editor of *Stages*. See p. 46.

29. See p. 38 and note 93.

30. Sorø, in southwest Sjælland, about forty miles from Copenhagen, was and still is the home of Denmark's most famous school, Sorø Academy, which at that time was also an academy in the strict sense, an assemblage of learned persons with provision for pursuing their own interests.

31. Eventually the approach to Kierkegaard made by *The Corsair*. See Supplement, p. 114, and note 107.

32. See p. 38 and note 94.

33. *Slottet ved Rhinen* (Copenhagen: 1845).
34. See Supplement, p. 96, and note 25.
35. See p. 24 and note 56.
36. P. L. Møller's highest esteem (see p. 100 below) was for "The Seducer's Diary," *Either/Or*, I, for which Kierkegaard may have used Møller as the model. See Frithiof Brandt, *Den unge Kierkegaard* (Copenhagen: 1929), pp. 160-304. For high praise of *Either/Or*, see Supplement, pp. 93-95 (*The Corsair*, no. 129).
37. On this discussion of Kierkegaard's works, see pp. 39-40.
38. Langelinie, the fashionable promenade along the Copenhagen harbor.
39. Hans Christian Andersen (1805-1875). See p. 44 and note 113.
40. See *Fear and Trembling*, *KW* VI (*SV* III 85, 106, 147-48, 164).
41. A drama, *Nie-boska Komedja* (Paris: 1832), by Zygmunt Krasinski (1812-1859).
42. *Prefaces*, *KW* IX (*SV* V 21-30, 51-53).
43. See Supplement, p. 96, and note 27. The piece about Lehmann may be the one in *The Corsair*, no. 231, February 21, 1845, col. 1, that ends: "Our view is that if one is to be a dog, whose dog one is is a secondary question. As far as designations are concerned, we make only this observation: when one licks spit for Christian VIII, one is servile, but when one licks spit for Drewsen and Lehmann, one is liberal." Lehmann and Johan C. Drewsen (1777-1851) were leaders of the Liberal party.
44. See pp. 24-27.
45. Frederik Christian Sibbern (1785-1872), professor of philosophy, University of Copenhagen.
46. *Either/Or*, I, *KW* III (*SV* I 273-412). See Goldschmidt's observations on this theme, Supplement, p. 144.
47. *Stages*, *KW* XI (*SV* VI 175-459). On the term "experiment," see note 92 below. Møller understood the term in the Baconian sense of the "vexation of nature." Therefore "experiment" is used here.
48. See pp. 39-40 fn.
49. See p. 42 and note 108.
50. See *Stages*, *KW* XI (*SV* VI 193-94).
51. Ibid. (*SV* VI 259-70).
52. Cf. p. 43.
53. *Stages*, *KW* XI (*SV* VI 13-83).
54. Ibid. (*SV* VI 85-174).
55. Ibid. (*SV* VI 437-38).
56. See p. 42 and note 107.
57. See pp. 38-46.
58. In the preface to *Either/Or*, I, *KW* III (*SV* I, p. xvi), the editor, Victor Eremita, commissions the book to seek out "a single reader."
59. See p. 40.
60. See Supplement, p. 97; Møller's statement about Hauch's house and his participation in the conversation is not substantiated. See also p. 40 and note 99. For Goldschmidt's idea of the impression given by Møller's article in *Gæa*, see Supplement, pp. 144-45.

Notes to Pages 105-08

61. See Supplement, p. 199 (*Pap.* VII¹ B 69).
62. The entire piece (*Ny kongelig Samling* 3217, 4°), especially parts I and II, is patterned on Genesis 1. The quoted terms and phrases are from the article by Frater Taciturnus in *Fædrelandet*, no. 2078, December 27, 1845 (see pp. 38-46 above).

Møller's article was not published. The manuscript bears the marks of initial editing in Goldschmidt's hand, according to Helge Toldberg, who gives the following interpretation of Møller's exclusion from the *Corsair*-Kierkegaard controversy: "It is probable that he [Goldschmidt] looked at the article with a view to its use and attempted an accommodating editorial revision, but he had to give this up, because Møller's self-preoccupation showed through so strongly that the article could have substantiated Kierkegaard and others of like mind in their false supposition that Møller was the driving force in *The Corsair*. Goldschmidt had been punished once [see Supplement, p. 108, and note 80] and had continued in the spotlight. Now all that was lacking was that he should be cheated out of the honor of being the sole editor; now, as later, it was to him a matter of honor that *The Corsair* be regarded as his work. Therefore, he wanted to take up the fight without Møller's help . . . ." "*Goldschmidt og Kierkegaard*," in *Festskrift til Paul Rubow*, p. 226 (ed. tr.).

Although Goldschmidt and others launched and continued the attack on Kierkegaard, the line of attack had already been suggested by Møller in *Gæa*. See Supplement, p. 96.

63. See Supplement, p. 104, and note 58.
64. See pp. 39-40, 42-43. On the Danish *Experiment*, see note 92 below.
65. See p. 46.
66. See p. 44.
67. See p. 46.
68. See pp. 41, 45.
69. See pp. 38, 40 and notes 94, 99.
70. See p. 45.
71. See p. 44.
72. Cf. p. 46.
73. A conflation of Frater Taciturnus (author of Part Three of *Stages*) and Hilarius Bookbinder (editor of *Stages*).
74. See p. 47 and note 127.
75. See p. 46.
76. See pp. 38-46.
77. The philologist Israel S. Levin (1810-1883) had been Kierkegaard's amanuensis and proofreader for the early pseudonymous manuscripts—hence, one reader.
78. *The Corsair*'s reply to Frater Taciturnus's article, "The Activity of a Traveling Esthetician . . . ," in *Fædrelandet*, no. 2078, December 27, 1845. See pp. 38-46.
79. Michael Leonard Nathanson (1795-1862), Danish hippologist, businessman, and horse dealer, by some called Crazy Nathanson. On the instigation of relatives, he was placed a number of times in an asylum in Randers

and later in a Copenhagen mental hospital (Bidstrup). Between August 8, 1845, and January 15, 1846, he published twenty-two issues of *Corvetten-Politivennen*, in which there were attacks on *The Corsair*. After trouble with the police in Jutland, he was declared insane and was sent with his family to Brazil in 1847.

Nathanson's name was originally Isaak; it was changed at baptism (Hamburg, 1843). Because the initials are the same as those of Mendel Levin Nathanson, editor of *Berlingske Tidende*, readers have sometimes confused the two men.

80. Goldschmidt spent twenty-four days in jail in June 1843 for violation of press regulations. See p. 49 and note 132.
81. Police and Justice Department officials.
82. Cf. p. 66.
83. See p. 46.
84. Ibid.
85. Kierkegaard was Copenhagen's "greatest peripatetic," as Villads Christensen has called him in *Peripatetikeren Søren Kierkegaard* (Copenhagen: 1965). Andrew Hamilton, in the earliest English account, *Sixteen Months in the Danish Isles*, I–II (London: 1852), II, pp. 268-70, wrote:

> There is a man whom it is impossible to omit in any account of Denmark, but whose place it might be more difficult to fix; I mean Søren Kierkegaard. But as his works have, at all events for the most part, a religious tendency, he may find a place among the theologians. He is a philosophical Christian writer, evermore dwelling, one might almost say harping, on the theme of the human heart. There is no Danish writer more in earnest than he, yet there is no one in whose way stand more things to prevent his becoming popular. He writes at times with an unearthly beauty, but too often with an exaggerated display of logic that disgusts the public. All very well, if he were not a popular author, but it is for this he intends himself.
>
> I have received the highest delight from some of his books. But no one of them could I read *with pleasure* all through. His "Works of Love" has, I suppose, been the most popular, or, perhaps, his "Either—Or," a very singular book. A little thing published during my stay gave me much pleasure, "Sickness unto Death."
>
> Kierkegaard's habits of life are singular enough to lend a (perhaps false) interest to his proceedings. He goes into no company, and sees nobody in his own house, which answers all the ends of an invisible dwelling; I could never learn that anyone had been inside of it. Yet his one great study is human nature; no one knows more people than he. The fact is *he walks about town all day*, and generally in some person's company; only in the evening does he write and read. When walking he is very communicative, and at the same time manages to draw everything out of his companion that is likely to be profitable to himself.
>
> I do not know him. I saw him almost daily in the streets, and when he was alone I often felt much inclined to accost him, but never put it into

execution. I was told his "talk" was very fine. Could I have enjoyed it, without the feeling that I was myself being mercilessly pumped and sifted, I should have liked [it] very much.

86. See Supplement, pp. 96-104.
87. Nov. 25, 1845, col. 16445.
88. A repetition of phrases in a review of *Either/Or* in *The Corsair*, no. 129, March 10, 1843. See Supplement, pp. 93-95.
89. See p. 46.
90. Ibid.
91. Cf. p. 46.
92. See pp. 39-45; *Either/Or*, II, *KW* IV (*SV* II 149, 174); *Fragments*, *KW* VII (*SV* IV 179); *Stages*, *KW* XI (*SV* VI 35, 376). On the Danish *Experiment*, see *Repetition*, *KW* VI, note on subtitle. For P. L. Møller's use of the term, see Supplement, pp. 100-02, 106-08.
93. See p. 46; *Either/Or*, I, *KW* III (*SV* I 22-23).
94. January 13, 1846, was the feast day of St. Hilary. Hilarius Bookbinder was the editor of *Stages*. Horse meat is a reference to Michael Leonard Nathanson. See Supplement, p. 108, and note 79.
95. J. L. Heiberg. See p. 17 and notes 38-40.
96. See Supplement, p. 147.
97. J. L. Heiberg. See p. 17 and note 38. Heiberg was an accomplished mathematician and had considerable interest in astronomy. He had an observatory in his house and from 1843 to 1845 published a number of pieces on astronomy in his yearbooks *Urania*, which name he took in modified form from that of Tycho Brahe's observatory. See Supplement, p. 114, and note 106.
98. Christian F. R. Olufsen (1802-1855), Danish astronomer, professor of astronomy, and director of the Copenhagen observatory.
99. P. L. Møller's *Gæa*. See p. 38 and note 93.
100. *Den Frisindede* (The Liberal-minded), a general newspaper (1835-1846) founded by Caspar Claudius Rosenhoff (1804-1869). J. L. Heiberg, in *En Sjæl efter Døden* (A Soul after Death), had pilloried the paper for its preoccupation with trivia that all could comprehend and its exclusion of reflection and all large issues. Nevertheless, the paper was confiscated and Rosenhoff fined so often that in 1846 he closed the paper.
101. Kierkegaard was born in his father's house, Nytorv 2 (now 27), and together with his brother Peter inherited the house in 1838.
102. See Supplement, p. 111, and note 92.
103. See p. 45.
104. In 1843 and also in 1844, Kierkegaard published *Two . . . , Three . . . ,* and *Four Upbuilding Discourses*. The remainders were purchased in 1845 by Philip G. Philipsen (1812-1877), who bound the first lot under the title *Atten opbyggelige Taler* (Eighteen Upbuilding Discourses; 1845) and the second short lot under the title *Sexten . . .* (Sixteen . . . ; 1852). Philipsen was the seller of most of the discourses but was publisher of none (see Supplement, p. 211,

and note 406), except as purchaser and distributor of the remainders. The reference to "nineteen" may indicate the inclusion of *Three Discourses on Imagined Occasions* (April 29, 1845).

105. See Supplement, p. 112, and note 97.

106. A small island between Sjælland and Sweden that Tycho Brahe used for his important astronomical work, 1576-1597. The main building there was named Uranienborg, hence Heiberg's *Urania*. During the summer of 1845, Heiberg had spent some time on Hven preparing pieces on the island and on Sophie Brahe for *Urania* . . . *1846* (pp. 54-169, 171-240). The Heibergs' home, in which a small observatory had been arranged, was in the garden house of the old naval hospital on Christianshavn.

107. Here and in the following lines is the beginning of *The Corsair*'s repeated ridicule of Kierkegaard's clothes and physique, resulting in his being taunted by children and others when he appeared on the streets of Copenhagen. See Supplement, pp. 208-09, 217-18, 220, 222-23, 225-27, 229, 237-38.

In 1877, thirty-one years after the *Corsair* affair, Georg Brandes wrote: "My earliest memory of Kierkegaard is that when as a child I did not draw down my trousers carefully and evenly over the long boots customary at the time, the nursemaid said warningly to me: 'Søren Kierkegaard.' " *Søren Kierkegaard, Samlede Skrifter*, I-XVIII (Copenhagen: 1899-1910), II, p. 25 (ed. tr.).

108. The Danish reads *efter sit eget Hoved*—literally, "according to his own head." In English, the play on "head" and "trousers" (and "legs" in the next line) is lost.

109. Professor Torkil Baden (1765-1849), philologist and art historian, was the son of Professor Jacob Baden (1735-1804), philologist and translator. The latter's translations, especially of Horace, came under considerable criticism. A parody by one von Schmidten of Jacob Baden's translation of Horace (*Kjøbenhavns flyvende Post*, no. 21, 1828) prompted a defense by Torkil Baden in *Kjøbenhavnsposten* (no. 27, 1828). Then J. L. Heiberg defended the parody in an article (*Kjøbenhavns flyvende Post*, no. 27, 1828). A little later, the same paper (no. 42, 1828) printed a malicious piece on "the natural history of ducks," which included a description of the "*Anas Torkillus* (in Danish: *Torkil-And* [Torkil-duck], also *Bade-Torkil* because it refreshes itself by bathing, but only in dirty water, distinguishable by its rather long legs, which are blue-striped below the knee and black down to the ankle." J. L. Heiberg, *Prosaiske Skrifter*, I-XI (Copenhagen: 1861), X, pp. 435-36 (ed. tr.).

110. See Supplement, p. 108, and note 79. Information on the beer bottle allusion has not been located. One suggestion is that Nathanson, after being struck on the head with a beer bottle, claimed to have seen nonexistent stars.

111. See Supplement, p. 94, and note 20.

112. *Urania Aarbog for 1846*, ed. J. L. Heiberg (Copenhagen: 1845), pp. 144-45. The title page carries the line "with title-page vignette and 14 lithographs."

113. In the center of Kongens Nytorv there was and still is l'Amoureux's equestrian statue of Christian V. Variations on the themes of horses and riders appear in words and cartoons in succeeding issues of *The Corsair*.

114. Johan S. Schulin (1694-1750), Danish statesman, foreign minister, 1735-1750.
115. See Supplement, p. 96, and note 27.
116. Not identified.
117. Jonas Collin (1776-1861), Finance Department deputy, 1841-1848.
118. See p. 63 and note 2.
119. A reference to Frater Taciturnus (Taciturn or Silent Brother), who wrote the piece in *Fædrelandet* about P. L. Møller and *The Corsair*. See p. 46.
120. See Supplement, p. 126.
121. See Supplement, p. 108, and note 79. S.T. is the abbreviation of *salvo titulo* (title omitted), used ironically here, inasmuch as Nathanson had no title.
122. Part of *The Corsair*'s method was to assassinate by association: Kierkegaard with Nathanson, Tøxen, et al. Jorgen Karstens Blok Tøxen (1776-1848), Danish writer, had been charged by *The Corsair* with participation in seditious activities and with acceptance of an annual pension in return for the betrayal of his alleged co-conspirators. Tøxen brought legal charges against *The Corsair*. Throughout 1844, Tøxen was repeatedly ridiculed in *The Corsair* (no. 175, 181, 183-85, 205) as a reckless writer and ludicrous character. Gustav Michelsen (1800-1846), a veterinarian, cooperated with Nathanson in trying to introduce the "Nathanson stallion" as the provincial breed in Jutland. Jens V. Neergaard (1775-1864), a veterinarian, severely criticized both Nathanson and Michelsen for their endeavors.
123. Article by Frater Taciturnus, pp. 47-50, where F.T. does not use the extensive language attributed to him here. See, however, Kierkegaard's journal entries and unpublished drafts of articles, for example, Supplement, pp. 161-66 (*Pap.* VII^1 B 10-11).
124. See Supplement, p. 108, and note 79.
125. Presumably an adaptation of Petronius's bargaining over writing poetry for two marks. Cf. Holberg, *Jacob von Tyboe*, I, 7.
126. See p. 46.
127. See Supplement, p. 96, and note 26.
128. See Supplement, p. 96, and note 28.
129. " 'Guilty?'/'Not Guilty?' " *Stages, KW* XI (*SV* VI 175-459).
130. The specious designation of Crazy Nathanson as the subject of the article does not obscure Kierkegaard as the intended and actual subject. The crudity and rawness of this section must have been particularly painful to Kierkegaard, for whom the Regine relationship was profoundly private and deeply cherished.
131. Pagination from first Danish edition of *Stages on Life's Way*. See *KW* XI (*SV* VI 359).
132. See Supplement, p. 108, and note 79.
133. *Stages, KW* XI (*SV* VI 211).
134. The Danish *indesluttet* and other forms of the word (used by Kierkegaard particularly in *Either/Or, Fear and Trembling, The Concept of Anxiety*, and *Stages*), usually translated as "inclosed" or "inclosing reserve," literally mean, *mutatis mutandis*, "shut in" or "shut up."

135. See Supplement, p. 104, and note 58.
136. Pagination of first Danish edition of *Repetition*. See *KW* VI (*SV* III 212).
137. Pagination of first Danish edition of *Prefaces*. See *KW* IX (*SV* V 7).
138. See Supplement, pp. 96-104.
139. Cf. p. 46.
140. Cf. p. 44.
141. Cf. p. 49.
142. Ibid.
143. Ibid.
144. See Supplement, pp. 108, 117, and notes 79, 122.
145. See pp. 47-50.
146. Ludvig Holberg (1684-1754), Norwegian-born Danish dramatist and scholar. The reference has not been located.
147. John E. Leerbeck (1805-1860), after 1841 police lieutenant and chief clerk of the police magistrate's office. The reference is to the title "The Dialectical Result of a Literary Police Action." See p. 47; Supplement, p. 108.
148. See p. 46; Supplement, p. 96.
149. See p. 46.
150. See Supplement, pp. 96-104.
151. See p. 47.
152. See Supplement, pp. 121-22.
153. See Supplement, p. 211, and note 406.
154. See Supplement, pp. 91-93.
155. See Supplement, pp. 121-22.
156. See Supplement, p. 121, and note 141; p. 125.
157. Reference to title on p. 47.
158. See p. 46.
159. See p. 49; Supplement, pp. 121, 124.
160. See Supplement, p. 108, and note 79.
161. See Supplement, pp. 122-23, and note 147.
162. See p. 46.
163. See Supplement, p. 117.
164. See Supplement, p. 108, and note 79.
165. Ibid., and note 85.
166. See p. 68 and note 12. Sankt Petri Church, near the university, has an exceptionally high steeple.
167. See Supplement, p. 112, and note 97.
168. See p. 82 and note 46.
169. See Supplement, pp. 108, 117, and notes 79, 122.
170. Holofernes was an Assyrian general who was killed by his Israelite captive, Judith, as related in the Apocrypha (Judith 2:4).
171. See p. 46.
172. See Supplement, pp. 108, 117, and notes 79, 122.
173. See Supplement, p. 108, and note 79.

Notes to Pages 130-37   293

174. See Supplement, p. 96.

175. The subtitle of *Concluding Unscientific Postscript*, by Johannes Climacus, ed. S. Kierkegaard, published February 27, 1846. Upon completing the manuscript of *Postscript* late in December 1845, Kierkegaard wrote "The Activity of a Traveling Esthetician . . ." (see pp. 38-46), which initiated the *Corsair* controversy. See Supplement, pp. 208-10 (*Pap.* VII^1 A 98).

176. Actually, the very opposite of this cordial wish was the case; about 100 copies of *Concluding Unscientific Postscript*, the central work in Kierkegaard's writings, were sold during Kierkegaard's lifetime. See *JP* VI 6458 (*Pap.* X^1 A 584).

177. See Supplement, p. 114, and note 107.

178. *Concluding Unscientific Postscript*, *KW* XII (*SV* VII [545-49]); see Supplement, p. 130, and note 175.

179. The pseudonymous authors or editors of the following works: Victor Eremita, *Either/Or* (1843); Johannes de Silentio, *Fear and Trembling* (1843); Constantin Constantius, *Repetition* (1843); Vigilius Haufniensis, *The Concept of Anxiety* (1844); Nicolaus Notabene, *Prefaces* (1844); Johannes Climacus, *Philosophical Fragments* (1844) and *Concluding Unscientific Postscript* (1846); Hilarius Bookbinder, *Stages on Life's Way* (1845); William Afham, *Stages*; Judge William, *Either/Or*, II; and Frater Taciturnus, *Stages*.

180. See Supplement, p. 108, and note 79; pp. 117-21, 127, 128-30.

181. A reference to Henrich Ussing (1743-1820), known for his contentiousness, and his son Tage Algreen-Ussing (1797-1872), characterized as having "sharp critical powers and an energetic will, together with an amazing capacity for work." *Dansk Biografisk Lexicon*, I-XIX, ed. C. F. Bricka (Copenhagen: 1887-1905), XVIII, p. 133 (ed. tr.).

182. See p. 46.

183. See p. 7 and note 15; *Postscript*, *KW* XII (*SV* VII [548]).

184. See Supplement, p. 116, and note 119.

185. With the rix-dollar reckoned at approximately $5.00 (1973 prices), the paperbound *Postscript* (482 pp. quarto) cost about $18.00. See p. 13 and note 31.

186. Cf. *Postscript*, *KW* XII (*SV* VII 191).

187. See p. 46.

188. See Supplement, p. 114, and note 107.

189. See Supplement, p. 108, and note 85.

190. See Supplement, p. 133, and note 186.

191. See Supplement, p. 114, and note 107.

192. Pseudonyms. See Supplement, p. 131, and note 179.

193. *The Corsair's* attacks since January 2.

194. See Supplement, p. 114, and note 107.

195. See Supplement, pp. 95-96, and note 23.

196. Danish: *isabelfarvet* (Isabella-colored), a term based on the color, according to legend, of the Spanish princess Isabella's linen, which she vowed would not be changed during the siege of Ostend (1601-1604).

197. See Supplement, p. 114, and note 107.

198. Ibid. *Nyt Aftenbladet*, December 14, 15, 17, 1847 (no. 291, 292, 294), carried a long review of *Works of Love*. See *JP* V 6098 (*Pap.* VIII¹ A 496).

199. Should be 1838. The book mentioned below was published June 9, 1838.

200. In 1837, when Goldschmidt was 18 years old, he started a newspaper, the *Næstved Ugeblad*, primarily as a vehicle for his stories.

201. Peter Rørdam (1806-1883), pastor in Lyngby. Earlier he had been much admired by Meïr Goldschmidt when he taught at the Westenske Institut in Copenhagen.

202. Cathrine G. Teilmann Rørdam (1777-1842). It was also at the Rørdam residence in Frederiksberg that Kierkegaard had met Regine Olsen for the first time in May 1837.

203. Published June 9, 1838, with Ki[j]erkegaard named as editor. The book (in *Early Polemical Writings*, *KW* I) is mainly a criticism of Hans Christian Andersen's novel *Only a Fiddler*.

204. Peter Rørdam's sister Bolette (1815-1887) was engaged to Peter Købke, who died in 1839; she later married Nicolai L. Feilberg (1806-1899).

205. See Supplement, pp. 92-93.

206. Published 1841. *KW* II (*SV* XIII).

207. See Supplement, p. 93, and note 18.

208. See Supplement, p. 138, and notes 201, 202, 204.

209. See Supplement, pp. 141, 147.

210. See Supplement, pp. 105-37.

211. See Supplement, p. 91, and note 2.

212. Carl Holger Visby (1801-1871). His *Bønnebog til Brug i Arrester og Straffeanstalter* was reviewed in *The Corsair*, no. 113, December 18, 1842, col. 1-2, 8.

213. P. L. Møller (1814-1865), Danish literary critic, writer, and editor. See Historical Introduction, pp. x-xiii, xxiv-xxix; p. 38 and note 93; Supplement, pp. 198-99, and note 352.

214. Many of James Fenimore Cooper's works had been translated into Danish and were widely read.

215. See Supplement, pp. 139, 147.

216. For an estimate of Victor Eremita in *The Corsair*, see Supplement, p. 96.

217. No. 129; see Supplement, pp. 93-95.

218. In a discussion of Goethe's *Werther*, Goldschmidt said Werther should have gone away and in solitude resolved the love affair with Lotte. P. L. Møller exclaimed, "You are a child; you have misunderstood the book completely. It is a protest against society; society is always in the wrong." Goldschmidt, *Livs Erindringer*, I, p. 321 (ed. tr.).

219. On this theme in the *Papirer*, see *JP* VII, pp. 31, 68, "Engagement," "Regine Olsen," and *Kierkegaard: Letters and Documents*, p. 516, under "Regine Olsen." Here Goldschmidt entirely misconstrued Kierkegaard's thought

Notes to Pages 142-49   295

and act by identifying them with a romantic individualism intensified as a special artistic prerogative, modeled on Goethe's love affairs. See Supplement, p. 144, for a later statement by Goldschmidt.

220. The most celebrated, and briefest, of Goethe's affairs was with Friederike Brion, whom he met when he was studying law at Strasbourg in 1770-1771. She is celebrated in Goethe's autobiography, *Aus meinem Leben*.

221. On Mozart and *Don Giovanni*, see pp. 28-37; *Either/Or*, I, *KW* III (*SV* I 29-113); *JP* III 2785-91.

222. *Either/Or*, I-II, is a dialogue without a resolution, which is left to the reader. Goldschmidt has not only omitted volume II but has concentrated on the esthetic view of volume I and has understood that only on a superficial level, for even the young Mr. A., author of volume I, has reflectively seen through the esthetic way of life and become a sardonic ironist.

223. *En Jøde* (A Jew). See p. 47 and note 126.
224. See Supplement, p. 108, and note 85.
225. See p. 46 and note 122.
226. See Supplement, p. 148.
227. Later, Goldschmidt wrote a number of pieces on nemesis; volume II of Goldschmidt's *Livs Erindringer og Resultater* is subtitled "Nemesis." See Paul V. Rubow, *Goldschmidt og Nemesis* (Copenhagen: Munksgaard, 1968).
228. See Møller's article in *Gæa*, Supplement, pp. 96-104, especially pp. 97-98.
229. See pp. 38-46.
230. In late December 1847, P. L. Møller left Denmark on a travel stipend and never returned. In 1851 he settled in France. See Supplement, p. 150.
231. See Supplement, p. 108, and note 85.
232. *Gæa*, ed. P. L. Møller (Copenhagen: 1846), pp. 110-29. Goldschmidt again used the pseudonym Adolph Meyer.
233. See pp. 38-46.
234. See p. 46.
235. In the context of *The Corsair*, this is an unexpected term.
236. See Supplement, pp. 105-36. Goldschmidt wrote the earlier pieces, and others wrote the later pieces in the extended attack on Kierkegaard. See Supplement, pp. 146-49.
237. See Supplement, pp. 139, 141.
238. See Supplement, pp. 108-12.
239. See Supplement, p. 112.
240. See Supplement, pp. 139, 141, 147.
241. See pp. 47-50, particularly pp. 47, 49.
242. "A First and Last Declaration," *Postscript*, *KW* XII (*SV* VII [545-49]), published February 28, 1846. In no. 276 (January 2, 1846), *The Corsair* had already identified Frater Taciturnus with Kierkegaard through the cartoons, and in no. 277 (January 9, 1846) it linked the two names by using a cartoon of Taciturnus as a representation of Kierkegaard. See Historical Introduction, p. xx, and note 73.

243. See Supplement, pp. 146, 148.

244. A wooded, elevated area near Kolding in South Jutland, the site of folk festivals (1843-1859) in support of the movement to aid Danish interests in Slesvig-Holsten. Goldschmidt was one of the main speakers at the 1844 festival.

245. *Fortællinger*, by Adolph Meyer (Copenhagen: 1846).

246. Goldschmidt sold *The Corsair* and withdrew after editing no. 315 (October 2, 1846). On October 7, he departed for Kiel and travels in Germany and Italy. He returned in the autumn of 1847. See *Livs Erindringer*, I, p. 432.

247. See Supplement, p. 145.

248. See Supplement, p. 144.

249. See Supplement, p. 150, and note 246.

250. A reference to the introductory portion of the first issue of Goldschmidt's new journal, in which Goldschmidt says: "Freedom came into men's consciousness with Christianity . . . a revelation that showed men that their home was neither in a particular temple nor in a particular state . . . .." *Nord og Syd*, I, 1848, pp. 12-13 (ed. tr.).

251. P. L. Møller, *Gæa* (Copenhagen: 1846), pp. 323-30.

252. P. L. Møller, *Billeder og Sange* (Copenhagen: 1847), a volume of previously published and recent poems.

253. See Supplement, p. 145, and note 230.

254. See Supplement, p. 232, and note 461.

255. Not published.

256. "Public Confession," by S. Kierkegaard, *Fædrelandet*, no. 904, June 12, 1842. See p. 5.

257. "Literary Quicksilver," *Ny Portefeuille*, I, 7, February 1843, col. 198-216. See pp. 73-86; Supplement, p. 155 (*Pap.* IV A 141), and note 264.

258. "A Letter" and "Another Letter," *Berlingske Tidende*, no. 33, 35, February 5, 7, 1843. See pp. 63-68.

259. ["A Letter"], *Fædrelandet*, no. 1143, February 8, 1843. See pp. 69-72.

260. Published pseudonymously (Victor Eremita), February 15, 1843, first advertised in *Adresseavisen*, no. 43, February 20, 1843.

261. Source not located. Cf. p. 104; see *Stages, KW* XI (*SV* VI 40).

262. The piece was intended for the *Berlingske Tidende*.

263. Peter Vilhelm Christensen (1819-1863).

264. See Supplement, pp. 73-86, and note 257.

265. *Berlingske Tidende*, no. 108, May 6, 1845. See p. 24 and note 55.

266. In legend, the name of the area in the Harz Mountains where the witches would meet on Walpurgisnacht. See Goethe, *Faust*, I, 6.

267. A reply to the immortalizing reference to Victor Eremita, editor of *Either/Or*, in *The Corsair*, no. 269, November 14, 1845, col. 14. See Supplement, p. 96. The piece, marked by the reckless flamboyance of the writing in *The Corsair*, was written before P. L. Møller's article appeared in *Gæa*, December 1845. It was not published.

268. "My moral principle, at your service: my highest ethical maxim is to consider all existence as an old story or chronicle, in which, as the narrative

proceeds, a person reads, with indescribable delight and sheer surprise, only about himself" (*Pap.* IV B 59). The postscript was not used in *Either/Or.*
269. See p. 46 and note 121.
270. See Supplement, p. 96, and note 25.
271. This and the following entries were not published.
272. *Diogenes Laertius,* II, 35; Riisbrigh, I, p. 72; Loeb, I, p. 165.
273. Cf. p. 46.
274. Ibid.
275. Ibid. "Would that I might only get into *The Corsair* soon."
276. The Danish editors' suggestion that *det Forfærdelige* (the terrible) should read *det Tilfældige* (the accidental) has been followed here.
277. *Diogenes Laertius,* VI, 8 and 26. Cf. ibid., II, 36; VI, 41. Riisbrigh, I, pp. 233, 240-41. Cf. ibid., I, pp. 72, 247. Loeb, II, pp. 9, 29. Cf. ibid., I, p. 167; II, p. 43.
278. Cf. *Historiae,* V, 8; *Sämmtliche Werke,* I–III, tr. Johann S. Müllern (Hamburg: 1765; *ASKB* 1283-85), III, p. 568. See also *Cajus Cornelius Tacitus,* I–III, tr. Jacob Baden (Copenhagen: 1773-97; *ASKB* 1286-88), III, p. 474; *The Histories of Tacitus,* I–II, tr. Clifford H. Moore (Loeb, New York: Putnam, 1925-31), II, pp. 188-89.
279. Cf. *Postscript, KW* XII (*SV* VII 481).
280. See note 146 above. One version of the anecdote is as follows: One day on a Copenhagen street, Holberg met an officer and a dandy, who said to him, "We will not get out of the way for a fool." "Then I will indeed get out of the way for two," Holberg replied as he bowed to them and walked around them.
281. See pp. 47, 49.
282. Plutarch recounts (*Marcellus,* 19) that when a soldier commanded Archimedes to come to Marcellus, Archimedes said he wanted to finish working on some geometrical figures, whereupon the soldier killed him. *Plutarchs Levnetsbeskrivelser,* I–IV, tr. Stephan Tetens (Copenhagen: 1800-11: *ASKB* 1197-1200), III, pp. 283-84; Loeb, V, pp. 486-87.
283. *Concluding Unscientific Postscript to the Philosophical Fragments,* published February 27, 1846.
284. See *Either/Or,* I, *KW* III (*SV* I 26).
285. Goldschmidt stated that *The Corsair* had a large circulation, but "never over 3,000" (*Livs Erindringer,* I, p. 264). "In the last year [1845], *The Corsair* had yielded 4,000 rix-dollars [ca. $20,000, adjusted to 1973 prices]" (ibid., p. 430). In *The Corsair,* no. 270, November 21, 1845, col. 14, the publisher stated: "Now only a few hundred subscriptions are needed to round out the number at 5000" (ed. tr.).
286. See Supplement, p. 91.
287. See p. 49 and note 132.
288. See Supplement, p. 114, and note 107.
289. See *Two Ages,* p. 95, *KW* XIV (*SV* VIII 88).
290. See Supplement, p. 167, and note 285.
291. See p. 44.

292. See Supplement, p. 114, and note 107.
293. A game in which the one who is "it" sits blindfolded on a stool within the circle of players. An interrogator quietly collects from them questions about the person on the stool, who then tries to determine who has asked each wondering question about him.
294. See Supplement, p. 167.
295. See p. 46.
296. Kierkegaard frequently used the phrase "without authority" for himself and his writings. See *On My Work as an Author, The Point of View, KW* XXII (*SV* XIII 494).
297. See Supplement, p. 211, and note 406.
298. See Supplement, p. 114, and note 107.
299. The editors of *Fædrelandet*, to which Kierkegaard considered sending the article but did not.
300. Although Meïr Goldschmidt was the author of *En Jøde* (A Jew) (Copenhagen: 1845), the title page reads "by Adolph Meyer, edited and published by M. Goldschmidt."
301. References to F. L. Høedt (1820-1885), a part-time teacher at Borgerdyds School, Christianshavn, 1844-1845, appeared in *The Corsair*, no. 208, 209, 211, September 6, 13, 27, 1844.
302. Baron Iver Holger Rosenkrantz (1813-1873), an official in the admiralty and a diplomat, appears in many issues of *The Corsair*, including no. 247, 258, 260, June 6, August 22, September 12, 1845. Later, upon the publication of Baron Rosenkrantz's papers (1876), Goldschmidt wrote: "In the strict sense he was not a public personage, and insofar as a border was transgressed by drawing him into publicity, I am responsible and must regard it as entirely proper that now after thirty-one years he enters a complaint against me before public judges." *Livs Erindringer*, I, p. 471 (ed. tr.).
303. See *Two Ages*, pp. 84-96, *KW* XIV (*SV* VIII 79-89).
304. Ibid., pp. 81-84 (*SV* VIII 76-79).
305. In Kierkegaard's case, the main attack by *The Corsair* lasted six months. The last cartoon appeared considerably later (January 7, 1848). With some other persons, the attacks were not as intensive but lasted even longer.
306. Cf. Supplement, pp. 113, 126.
307. See Supplement, p. 119.
308. Cf. *Fragments, KW* VII (*SV* IV 241); *Postscript, KW* XII (*SV* VII, p. vi).
309. Cf. Goldschmidt's later critique of P. L. Møller's writing, Historical Introduction, pp. xxvi-xxvii.
310. See *Two Ages*, p. 91, *KW* XIV (*SV* VIII 85).
311. The main point of contrast between Goldschmidt and Kierkegaard was the nature and the art of the comic. See Supplement, pp. 139, 141, 147, 148. On the comic, irony, and humor, see *JP* II 1669-1769 and pp. 585-86.
312. See Plato, *Apology*, 25 a-b; *Platonis opera*, VIII, pp. 116-19; *Collected Dialogues*, p. 11.
313. Kierkegaard owned Franklin's autobiography and writings in a German edition: *Benjamin Franklin's Leben und Schriften*, I-IV, tr. A. Binzer (Kiel:

Notes to Pages 180-93   299

1829; *ASKB* 1871-72). The reference is to *Der arme Richard, oder der Weg zum Wohlstand*, IV, p. 105.

314. In a number of works, Kierkegaard ironizes over the extravagant claims made for the crucial importance of a new hymnal. See, for example, *Stages, KW* XI (*SV* VI 247, 281); *Postscript, KW* XII (*SV* VII 415-18, 486-87); *Two Ages*, p. 102, *KW* XIV (*SV* VIII 95); *From the Papers of One Still Living*, in *KW* I (*SV* XIII 83); *The Moment, KW* XXIII (*SV* XIV 170). Grundtvigians in particular pressed for a new hymnal, which did not come until after Martensen succeeded Mynster as bishop in 1854.

315. See p. 47; Supplement, pp. 139, 141, 143.

316. See Supplement, p. 143.

317. See p. 46.

318. See p. 47 and note 126.

319. See Supplement, p. 46.

320. See Supplement, p. 114, and note 107.

321. See Supplement, p. 104, and note 58.

322. See *Postscript, KW* XII (*SV* VII 546).

323. This piece was written for possible publication in *Fædrelandet*, but it was not submitted. On circulation, see Supplement, p. 167, and note 285.

324. See note 311 above.

325. See *Postscript, KW* XII (*SV* VII 43, 70-71, 260, 306, 402, 434, 447); *JP* II 1737, 1741, 1747, 1750 (*Pap.* III A 205; V A 85; VII[1] A 19; VIII[1] A 478).

326. See p. 49 and note 132.

327. From January 31, 1845 (no. 228), *The Corsair* bore a pirate ship emblem as part of its masthead. The supplement to no. 227 displayed the emblem with the caption: "*The Corsair* assaults Cape Reiersen [Christian Reiersen (1792-1876), official censor of unlicensed papers] (whenever this picture is seen in the future, it is a sign that *The Corsair* has been published)."

328. In his journal *Arena* (Copenhagen: 1843, no. 1-6), no. 1-2, p. 9, P. L. Møller states that he wanted to write "as one does with books that are not to appear in bookstores, 'Manuscript for Friends' " (ed. tr.).

329. See p. 46 and note 122.

330. See Supplement, p. 140.

331. See Adolph Meyer (Meïr Goldschmidt), *En Jøde* (Copenhagen: 1845), pp. 210-11, 214-15, 237, 340, 357-59, 376-78, 405, 439, 459.

332. In *Arena*, no. 3-4 (June 1843), p. 71, in an article on *The Corsair* and Goldschmidt, P. L. Møller writes of his first meeting with Goldschmidt, whom he expected to find "surrounded by daggers and pistols" (ed. tr.).

333. Source in Jean Paul (Richter) not located. Kierkegaard owned *Vorschule der Aesthetik*, I-III (Vienna: 1813; *ASKB* 1381-83), and *Jean Paul's sämmtliche Werke*, I-LX (Berlin: 1826-28; *ASKB* 1777-99).

334. *En Jøde*, p. 208; see Supplement, p. 190, and note 327.

335. Aristophanes, *The Knights; Des Aristophanes Werk*, I-III, tr. J. G. Droysen (Berlin: 1835-38; *ASKB* 1052-54), II, pp. 313-431; *Aristophanes*, I-III, tr. Benjamin B. Rogers (Loeb, New York: Putnam, 1924), I, pp. 124-259. See *Stages, KW* XI (*SV* VI 383).

336. See note 311 above.
337. See Supplement, pp. 200, 207, 210, 218 (*Pap.* VII^1 B 69, 72, A 98, 214).
338. See Historical Introduction, pp. xv-xix.
339. See Plutarch, *Phocion*, 8; Loeb, VIII, p. 143.
340. See *Phaedrus*, 249 a; *Platonis opera*, I, pp. 177-78; *Collected Dialogues*, p. 495. Cf. *The Concept of Irony*, *KW* II (*SV* XIII 119-20, 273-74).
341. Entry VII^1 B 55 (Supplement, pp. 178-94) was not published, and consequently the challenge to Goldschmidt was not given. It may have been that the decisive, silent meeting of Kierkegaard and Goldschmidt on Myntergade took the place of the published challenge. It is not known precisely when entries VII^1 B 57-58 were written, but most likely it was the end of February 1846, inasmuch as entry VII^1 B 59 refers to *Postscript*, which was published February 27, 1846, and "immediately thereafter he met me on Myntergade . . . ." See Supplement, p. 149.
342. See p. 46 and notes 120-21.
343. No. 284, February 27, 1846. See Supplement, p. 130.
344. See pp. 38-46.
345. See Supplement, p. 141, and note 213.
346. See Supplement, p. 114, and note 107.
347. *Concluding Unscientific Postscript*, published February 27, 1846.
348. See Supplement, pp. 96-104.
349. Cf. p. 45. The quotation is composed of two separated phrases, plus the concluding summary paraphrase.
350. See p. 46 and note 122.
351. See Supplement, pp. 104-05.
352. After his reply to Kierkegaard in *Fædrelandet* (see Supplement, pp. 104-05), P. L. Møller wrote a piece (see Supplement, pp. 105-08) for *The Corsair* that Goldschmidt did not use. He had received a state stipendium for foreign travel and study, and after publishing a volume of old and new poems, *Billeder og Sange* (Copenhagen: 1847), his reviews and articles from 1840-1847, *Kritiske Skizzer*, I–II (Copenhagen: 1847), he left Denmark in late December 1847 and never returned. In the meantime, relations between him and Goldschmidt had cooled and finally reached the point of antagonism (see Supplement, pp. 150-52).
353. See p. 46; Supplement, p. 96.
354. See Supplement, pp. 157-58 (*Pap.* VI B 192).
355. See pp. 24-27.
356. See Supplement, p. 194, and note 337.
357. Cf. pp. 105-12, the interpretation in *The Corsair*.
358. The elder Cato (234-149 B.C.) concluded his speeches in the senate with "Ceterum [or Præterea] censeo Carthaginem esse delendam" (Furthermore, I am of the opinion that Carthage must be destroyed).
359. See, for example, *Upbuilding Discourses in Various Spirits*, *KW* XV (*SV* VIII 116).
360. See Supplement, p. 114, and note 107.

361. See p. 44 and note 114.
362. An allusion to J. L. Heiberg's review of *Either/Or*. See p. 17 and notes 39–40.
363. See Supplement, p. 208, and note 390.
364. See *Stages*, *KW* XI (*SV* VI 454-55).
365. See p. 46.
366. In *Kjøbenhavnsposten*, no. 73-74, March 27-28, 1846, there appeared a review of *Concluding Unscientific Postscript* by Prosper naturalis de molinasky (P. L. Møller). Later it was included in Møller's *Kritiske Skizzer fra Aarene 1840-47*, I–II (Copenhagen: 1847), II, pp. 253-69. See Historical Introduction, pp. xxiv-xxv.
367. See pp. 38–46.
368. See Supplement, pp. 105-36.
369. See note 347 above.
370. Christian Peter Bianco Luno (1795-1852), the printer who printed most of Kierkegaard's books. The manuscript of *Postscript* was delivered on December 30, 1845. See *JP* V 5871 (*Pap.* VII[1] A 2).
371. *Two Ages*, a review of *To Tidsaldre*, by Thomasine Gyllembourg (1773-1856), the mother of J. L. Heiberg.
372. Jens Finsteen Giødwad (1811-1891), editor of *Fædrelandet* and Kierkegaard's middleman in the publication of the pseudonymous works.
373. See Supplement, pp. 38-46.
374. See p. 45.
375. Ibid. See Supplement, p. 198, and note 349.
376. See Supplement, pp. 38-46.
377. See p. 24 and note 56.
378. See Supplement, p. 167 (*Pap.* VII[1] B 37), and note 285.
379. See Supplement, p. 203 (*Pap.* VII[1] B 71).
380. See note 337 above.
381. See *JP* III, pp. 896-97.
382. See Supplement, p. 141, and note 213.
383. See p. 46 and note 122.
384. See Supplement, pp. 96-104.
385. See Supplement, pp. 104-05.
386. See Supplement, p. 199, and note 352.
387. See Supplement, p. 203, and note 370.
388. At the end of his *Postscript* (February 27, 1846), in three and one-half unnumbered pages, "A First and Last Declaration" acknowledges Kierkegaard's relation to the pseudonymous works.
389. See Supplement, pp. 203-04, and note 371.
390. See *The Point of View*, *KW* XXII (*SV* XIII 543-44). To Kierkegaard, confronting *The Corsair* was an ethical, social act of general benefit. Loner though he always was, he nevertheless felt abandoned by the commoners on the streets, who, after the incessant ridicule by *The Corsair*, avoided or taunted him, and also by the literary-political elite, who, although now re-

lieved as objects of *The Corsair*'s treatment, in turn gave Kierkegaard the silent treatment or criticized the action as rash or called the whole thing a trifle not worth thinking about.

391. The term *Concluding* in *Concluding Unscientific Postscript* signifies Kierkegaard's intention to terminate his writing, except for occasional writing of reviews (*Two Ages*, Adler's works).
392. See *The Point of View, KW* XXII (*SV* XIII 556-75).
393. See note 337 above.
394. See p. 44 and note 114.
395. See pp. 38-46.
396. See pp. 47-50.
397. See Supplement, pp. 104-05.
398. See note 390 above.
399. See *The Concept of Irony, KW* II (*SV* XIII 324-25).
400. See p. 46 and notes 120-21.
401. Ibid.
402. See Supplement, p. 108, and note 85.
403. See Supplement, p. 203 (*Pap.* VII[1] B 71), and note 370.
404. *Postscript, KW* XII (*SV* VII, pp. vii-viii).
405. See *Postscript, KW* XII (*SV* VII 305-06).
406. At this time (1846) Kierkegaard was still his own publisher, defraying the entire cost of production of the 17 books already published, none of which had been sold out (1838-1846), in editions of 525 copies (*The Concept of Anxiety*, 250 copies). In 1845, the stock of *Discourses* was remaindered (see *Kierkegaard: Letters and Documents, KW* XXV, Letter 119), and when all other remainders were sold to Reitzel in August 1847 (see Letter 152), only *Either/Or* was sold out. Through honoraria in the later years, Kierkegaard eventually came out ahead on the book publishing but received almost nothing for his undiverted time and work as a writer. Fortunately, his inheritance made the phenomenal enterprise possible. See Supplement, p. 219 (*Pap.* VII[1] A 229), and note 434.
407. See Supplement, p. 208 (*Pap.* VII[1] A 98), and note 391.
408. With the exclusion of the dissertation on irony and *From the Papers of One Still Living*, the authorship proper began with *Either/Or*.
409. On this theme, see, for example, *JP* V 5873, 5947, 5961, 5966 (*Pap.* VII[1] A 4, 169, 221, 229). Kierkegaard very seriously and over a long period of time considered halting all writing after the *Postscript* and taking a rural parish or a post at the pastoral seminary.
410. See p. 47 and note 125.
411. See Supplement, pp. 139-41, 143.
412. See p. 46 and notes 120-21.
413. See pp. 38-46.
414. See Supplement, p. 203 (*Pap.* VII[1] B 71), and notes 347, 370.
415. See p. 46.
416. See Supplement, pp. 139,143.

417. See Supplement, p. 211 (*Pap.* VII[1] A 98), and note 405.
418. See Supplement, p. 208 (*Pap.* VII[1] A 98), and note 391.
419. See pp. 38-46, 47-50.
420. See Supplement, pp. 203-04 (*Pap.* VII[1] B 71), and note 371.
421. See p. 46 and notes 120-21.
422. See p. 17 and note 38.
423. See p. 7 and note 15.
424. See Supplement, p. 108, and note 85.
425. Søren Christian Barth (1803-1895).
426. Cf. H. J. Thue, *Læsebog i Modersmaalet for Norske og Danske* (Kristiania: 1846), pp. 486 ff. As a university student, Thue had spoken from the floor at Kierkegaard's defense of his dissertation on September 29, 1841.
427. See Supplement, p. 208 (*Pap.* VII[1] A 98), and note 391.
428. See Supplement, p. 211, and note 405.
429. See p. 46.
430. See note 337 above.
431. See Supplement, p. 150, and note 246.
432. See Supplement, p. 199, and note 352.
433. See Supplement, p. 212, and note 409.
434. Kierkegaard and his brother Peter each inherited a substantial sum (with part of which they bought the family house at the liquidation auction) from their father following his death on August 9, 1838. During the next 10 years, Kierkegaard lived, and fairly well, on this money and paid the full publication costs of his first 17 books (see p. 211 and note 406), only one of which sold out. F. Brandt and E. Rammel, in *Kierkegaard og Pengene* (Copenhagen: 1935), point out that Kierkegaard received a writer's honorarium from Reitzel after August 1847 and reckon that Kierkegaard's total net from sales and honoraria was an average of 300 rix-dollars per year over 17 years (1838-1855). This they calculate as equaling 1,500 D. kr. in 1935, or approximately $300 annually, which in 1973 would be roughly $1,500. In 1846, Kierkegaard entertained the idea of seeking a state grant (*JP* V 5881; *Pap.* VII[1] B 211), which was not uncommon as patronage of the arts and letters. He did not pursue this notion. In December 1847, the brothers sold the house (Nytorv 2), and Kierkegaard kept part of his share of the proceeds in government bonds, which deteriorated badly in the war period, put some into shares, which he held through the bad times of 1848-1849, and kept some in cash, which also deteriorated because of rampant inflation.

In the later years of his life, Kierkegaard became more stringent about his expenses. He divided what funds he had into units, which were placed in the custody of his brother-in-law Henrik Ferdinand Lund of the National Bank. Shortly before his death he drew out the last portion.

435. See Supplement, p. 208 (*Pap.* VII[1] A 98), and note 390.
436. For Kierkegaard, one of the results of the continued ridiculing and caricaturing of his physique and clothes was a change in the attitudes of people on the streets, where Kierkegaard loved to walk and converse (see

Supplement, p. 108, and note 85). Therefore, during 1847 he made numerous carriage excursions, particularly to the wooded countryside north of Copenhagen, especially to Gribs Skov. For details, see *JP* V, note 1606.
  437. See p. 17 and note 38.
  438. See Supplement, p. 108, and note 85.
  439. At the time, Kierkegaard was considering a journey to Stettin and a longer journey in the fall, but he did not go. See *JP* V 6035 (*Pap*. VIII¹ A 227).
  440. The tailor feared that *The Corsair*'s relentless caricaturing of Kierkegaard's clothes might possibly affect his trade. See Supplement, p. 114, and note 107.
  441. Ibid.
  442. See, in addition to the following entry, Supplement, pp. 139, 141, 147, 148, 179-79, on the comic task.
  443. Jens Hostrup's *Gjenboerne* was first presented in the Hofteater by the Studenterforening on February 20 and again on March 9, 1844. Among its characters is a theologian named Søren Kirk. Subsequently, the play was presented in Odense on December 19, 26, 1845, January 1, 11, 18, 28, February 23, and March 9, 1846. On June 27, 30, and July 2, 1846, it was presented in the Royal Theater in Copenhagen. Søren Kirk was then called Søren Torp.
  444. No. 283, December 6, 1847, in which *Rigstidenden* of Norway is quoted: "Mr. Smith was somewhat absent-minded yesterday and got all confused in the Søren Kierkegaardian syllogisms" (ed. tr.).
  445. See Supplement, p. 222 (*Pap*. VIII¹ A 163), and note 436.
  446. One of Kierkegaard's favorite walks was to Otteveiskrogen (Nook of Eight Paths) in Gribs Skov, Denmark's largest forest, north of Copenhagen.
  447. See Supplement, p. 114, and note 107.
  448. By this time, Kierkegaard had abandoned his idea of writing no more and of going to a country parish. *Upbuilding Discourses in Various Spirits* was published March 13, 1847, *Works of Love*, September 29, 1847, and *Christian Discourses*, April 26, 1848. By the middle of 1848 he was working on *The Sickness unto Death* and *Practice in Christianity*.
  449. The allusion is presumably to a crowd demonstration before Christiansborg on March 21, 1848, followed by a change in the form of government. See note 453 below.
  450. Georg Brandes recalls a nursemaid's pejorative use of Kierkegaard's name. See Supplement, pp. 114, 238 (*Pap*. X¹ A 177), and notes 107, 480.
  451. See Supplement, p. 225 (*Pap*. VIII¹ A 458), and notes 443-44. In the 1848-1849 Copenhagen theater season, three of the plays performed used the name Søren for ludicrous characters: Jens Hostrup, *Gjenboerne*, November 15; Hostrup, *En Spurv i Tranedans*, September 10, 15, 25, October 25, November 11; Johanne Luise Heiberg, *En Søndag paa Amager*, September 17, 22, October 29, November 4, 8.
  452. See Supplement, p. 219 (*Pap*. VII¹ A 229), and note 434.
  453. On March 21, 1848, as the result of earlier events, movements, and an enormous demonstration at Christiansborg, King Frederik VII (King Christian VIII had died on January 28, 1848) agreed to the dissolution of the minis-

Notes to Pages 231-38 305

tries. Thereupon the March government, the Moltke-Hvidt government, was formed, and Frederik VII declared that he now regarded himself as a constitutional monarch.

454. The two pieces by Frater Taciturnus in *Fædrelandet*. See pp. 38-50.
455. See *JP* VI 6202, 6217 (*Pap*. IX A 167, 186).
456. See Supplement, p. 208 (*Pap*. VII[1] A 98), and note 390.
457. Jacob Mini's restaurant, Kongens Nytorv 3.
458. Johan Gotfred Conradi-Päthau's restaurant at the corner of Kongens Nytorv and Lille Kongensgade 3, on the second floor above "à Porta."
459. See p. 204 (*Pap*. VII[1] B 71) and note 372.
460. Carl P. Ploug (1813-94), poet, politician, and editor of the newspaper *Fædrelandet* from 1841.
461. In October 1847, Goldschmidt returned from Germany and began a new journal, *Nord og Syd*, quite different from *The Corsair*. See Supplement, p. 151, and note 250; see also p. 233 (*Pap*. X[1] A 98).
462. 1848, I, pp. 223-24.
463. See Supplement, p. 224 (*Pap*. VIII[1] A 420-21).
464. Knud C. Nielsen (1798-1872), rector of the Realskole in Aarhus, 1839-1853.
465. See p. 46 and note 121.
466. The piece in *Gæa*. See Supplement, pp. 96-104.
467. See p. 47 and note 126; Supplement, p. 176 (*Pap*. VII[1] B 41), and note 300.
468. See pp. 38-46.
469. Ibid.
470. See Supplement, pp. 145.
471. See Supplement, p. 146, also p. 143.
472. Cf. Supplement, p. 203.
473. See p. 46.
474. Marshal Michel Ney (1769-1815), Napoleon's most brilliant general and later general of the army against Napoleon after Elba, returned to Napoleon's side, was condemned for treason, and was executed in Paris. He himself gave the order to the firing squad.
475. See p. 47 and note 125.
476. Cf. Supplement, pp. 139, 232-33 (*Pap*. X[1] A 98).
477. See Supplement, pp. 96, 141.
478. See pp. 38-46.
479. *Tausend und eine Nacht*, I-IV, tr. Gustav Weil (Pforzheim: 1841; *ASKB* 1414-17), IV, p. 353.
480. After the first *Corsair* piece (Supplement, pp. 108-12) directed against Frater Taciturnus, Søren Kierkegaard's name appeared frequently during the next two months. The name "Søren" lent itself to the taunting that developed in the streets, partly because it was a euphemistic term for Satan (*for Søren*: what the devil!). See Supplement, p. 229 (*Pap*. IX A 370), and note 107.
481. See Supplement, pp. 225 (*Pap*. VIII[1] A 458), 229 (*Pap*. IX A 370), and notes 443-44, 451.

482. *Tonne gaaer i Krigen*, performed February 16, 17, 20, 21, March 4, 15, 1849.

483. An anonymous play, *En Søndag paa Amager* (1848), was supposedly by J. L. Heiberg but was actually by his wife, Johanne Luise Heiberg, the actress, whom Kierkegaard later celebrated in *The Crisis and a Crisis in the Life of an Actress, KW* XVII (*SV* X 319-38). See Supplement, p. 229 (*Pap*. IX A 370), and note 451.

484. See Supplement, pp. 208-10 (*Pap*. VII^1 A 98), 238 (*Pap*. X^1 A 177), and notes 390, 483.

485. See pp. 28-50.

486. See note 337 above.

487. See Supplement, p. 209 (*Pap* VII^1 A 98), and note 390.

488. See p. 46.

489. See Supplement, pp. 149-50, 232 (*Pap*. X^1 A 69), and notes 246, 461.

490. See Supplement, p. 199 (*Pap*. VII^1 B 69), and note 352.

491. Emilie Carlén, *En Nat ved Bullar-Søen*, a Swedish novel serialized in *Berlingske Tidende*, no. 43-206, February 20–September 4, 1847.

492. The last section of *Either/Or*, I, *KW* III (*SV* I 272-412).

493. The last section of *Stages, KW* XI (*SV* VI 175-459).

494. The *Corsair* affair.

495. See Supplement, p. 219 (*Pap*. VII^1 A 229), and note 434.

496. See Supplement, p. 114, and note 107.

497. Andreas G. Rudelbach, *Den evangeliske Kirkeforfatnings Oprindelse og Princip* . . . (Copenhagen: 1849; *ASKB* 171).

498. See Historical Introduction, pp. xxxvi-xxxviii.

499. Niels Møller Spandet (1788-1858) was a judge and politician who was acquainted with N.F.S. Grundtvig as early as 1811 and remained closely allied with him and his work. In 1850, he proposed in parliament a law regarding Church affairs.

500. See p. 241 and note 497.

501. *KW* XX (*SV* XII 129-34).

502 "An Open Letter," pp. 51-59.

503. Nicolai F. S. Grundtvig (1783-1872), prominent pastor, poet, hymn writer, historian, and politician.

504. See "An Open Letter," pp. 51-59.

505. L. Holberg, *Mester Gert Westphaler*, II, 4.

506. F. Schiller, *Des Mädchens Klage*, st. 2, l. 7, *Schillers sämmtliche Werke*, I–XII (Stuttgart, Tübingen: 1838; *ASKB* 1804-15), I, p. 232. *The Poems of Schiller*, tr. Edgar A. Dowring (2 ed., New York: Hurst, 1871), p. 109.

507. Cf. *Fragments, KW* VII (*SV* IV 178).

508. "The Accounting" is the major portion of a small work (which also includes "My Position as a Religious Writer in 'Christendom' and My Tactic") entitled *On My Work as an Author*, dated March 1849 and published in 1851. In English translation, it is included with *The Point of View for My Work as an Author, KW* XXII.

509. Bishop Jacob (Jakob) Peter Mynster. See p. 7 and note 15.

Notes to Pages 253-63

510. The *Corsair* affair.
511. See *Armed Neutrality*, together with *The Point of View*, *KW* XXII (*Pap.* X⁵ B 107, pp. 288, 290-94, 298-99).
512. *Fædrelandet*, no. 37, 38, February 13, 14, 1851.
513. "An Open Letter," *Fædrelandet*, no. 26, January 31, 1851.
514. *Practice in Christianity*, published September 27, 1850.
515. See note 509 above.
516. Alexander Vinet, *Der Sozialismus in seinem Princip betrachtet*, tr. D. Hofmeister (Berlin: 1849; *ASKB* 874).
517. See p. 51.
518. Hans Lassen Martensen (1808-1884), professor of theology, University of Copenhagen, Bishop Jacob (Jakob) Peter Mynster's successor in 1854.
519. See Supplement, p. 253, and note 509.
520. Anti-Climacus, author of *The Sickness unto Death* (July 30, 1849) and *Practice in Christianity* (September 27, 1850).
521. J. P. Mynster, *Yderligere Bidrag til Forhandlingerne om de kirkelige Forhold i Danmark* (Copenhagen: 1851).
522. See p. 47 and note 125.
523. See "An Open Letter," pp. 51-59.
524. Ibid.
525. Johannes Climacus. See *Postscript, KW* XII (*SV* VII 7, 537, 539).
526. See note 511 above.
527. See, for example, Plato, *Symposium*, 175 e; *Platonis opera*, III, pp. 438-39; *Udvalgte Dialoger af Platon*, I-VII, tr. C. J. Heise (Copenhagen: 1830-55; *ASKB* 1164-66[I-III], II, p. 10; *Collected Dialogues*, p. 530.
528. See "The Difference between a Genius and an Apostle," in *KW* XVIII (*SV* XI 95-109).
529. See, for example, *Practice in Christianity, KW* XX (*SV* XII 217-35); *JP* II 1833-1940.

BIBLIOGRAPHICAL NOTE

For general bibliographies of Kierkegaard studies, see:

Jens Himmelstrup, *Søren Kierkegaard International Bibliografi*. Copenhagen: Nyt Nordisk Forlag Arnold Busck, 1962.

Aage Jørgensen, *Søren Kierkegaard-litteratur 1961-1970*. Aarhus: Akademisk Boghandel, 1971.

Kierkegaard A Collection of Critical Essays, ed. Josiah Thompson. New York: Doubleday (Anchor Book), 1972.

Søren Kierkegaard's Journals and Papers, I, ed. and tr. Howard V. Hong and Edna H. Hong, assisted by Gregor Malantschuk. Bloomington, Indiana: Indiana University Press, 1967.

For topical bibliographies of Kierkegaard studies, see ibid., I–IV (1967-75).

INDEX

about-face, 8-9
actuality, 215
Adler, Adolph Peter, xxxi
Adonis, 78
Adresseavisen, 13, 70, 118
Aftenbladet, 93, 135-37, 276
age, the present, 5-9
Agrippa, King, 164
Aladdin's lamp, 193
Alembert, Jean le Rond d', *Encyclopedia*, 6
Algreen-Ussing, Tage, 131, 293
Allen, Carl Ferdinand, 271
Amasis, King, 93
Amoreaux, Abraham Cesar l', equestrian statue, 115, 290
analogy: child's language, 189-90; cholera fly, xviii, 228-29, 232; contaminated food, 166; geese, xxx, 220; military, 8; prostitute, xx, 47, 49, 117-18, 121, 124, 125, 148, 158, 162, 165; ship and megaphone, 221
Andersen, Hans Christian, xxvii, xxxix, 44, 99, 138, 279, 286; *Only a Fiddler*, 294
anonymity, anonymous, 24-26, 94, 146, 175, 178, 276
ape and apostle, 40
apostle(s), 56-57, 249, 263; and ape, 40; as solitary person, 56-58
Archimedes, 165
Arena, xi
Aristophanes, 80, 193, 231
Aristotle, *De Generatione et Corruptione*, 274
Ark, 271
Athens, 81, 84, 86
attack and defense, 39
Attic salt, 84

Auber, Daniel François Esprit, 283
Auden, Wystan Hugh, vii
author(s), 73-75, 221, 238; work of, 214-15
authority, *see* without authority
autumn, 75-76

Bacon, Francis, 286
Baden, Jacob, 290
Baden, Torkil, 114-15, 290
Baggesen, Jens Immanuel, 283
balloting, 245, 255
Barère de Vieuzac, Bertrand, 283
Barfod, Hans Peter, xxxv, 278
Barth, Søren Christian, 218, 303
Bastholm, Hans, 6, 8, 271, 272
Bauer, Bruno, 10, 271
Beck, Andreas Frederick, 6, 9-12, 271-72
Berlin, xxx, xli, 222, 273, 274
Berlingske Tidende, xx, xlii, 69, 70, 71, 72, 93, 95, 99, 128, 137, 154-56, 167, 274, 275, 276, 281-82, 285, 288, 296; and Kierkegaard's pseudonyms, 95, 156-57; no. 108, 24
Bible, Apocrypha, Judith 2:4, 292
Bible, New Testament:
  Acts 5:29, 56, 281
  II Corinthians 5:7, 8, 272
  James 1:19, 18-19, 274
  John 3:1-2, 85, 284
  Matthew 12:36, 86, 284; 27:24, 83, 283
  Philippians 1:19-25, 22
  Romans 12:15, 79, 283; 12:19, 84, 284
Bible, Old Testament:
  Deuteronomy 32:35, 84, 284
  Genesis 1, 287; 4:1-9, 80, 283;

Bible, Old Testament (*cont.*)
  4:8, 14, 273; 4:10, 80, 283;
  4:17, 80, 283; 37:9, 77, 283
  Proverbs 25:11, 34, 277
Bidstrup Insane Asylum, 119, 126, 288
Birch, David Seidelin, *Naturen, Mennesket og Borgeren*, 4, 271
Blicher, Steen Steensen, xxviii
Blocksberg, 156, 266
bookkeeper, 102
Böotius, Mr., 96, 118, 285
Borchsenius, Otto Frederik Christian William, viii, xxiv
Borgerdydsskole, 298
Boye, Adolph Engelbert, 285. See also Böotius, Mr.
Brahe, Tycho, 289, 290
Brandes, Georg Morris Cohen, ix, xii-xiii, xxi, 290
Brandt, Frithiof, xi, 286, 303
Bredsdorff, Elias, xiv, xxii, 285
Byron, George Gordon, 99

Cain, 80
caricature(s), xx-xxi, xxx-xxxi
Carlén, Emilie Flygare, *En nat ved Bullar-Søe*, 240, 306
Carstensen, Georg Johan Bernhard, 7, 115, 272, 285
Catholic Church, 31
Cato, Marcus Porcius (the Elder), 200, 283, 300
cause and effect, xxix
Cervantes Saavedra, Miguel de, 42, 101
character assassination, xxii, xxx
Chateaubriand, François René, Vicomte de, 99-100
child's language, *see* analogy
cholera fly, *see* analogy
Christendom, 242, 262. See also Christian, Christianity; Rudelbach, A. G.

Christensen, Peter Vilhelm, 155, 296
Christensen, Villads, 288
Christian, Christianity, 243, 272; becoming a, 261-63; and Christian-dumb, 54; and culture, 257; and double-danger, 246-47; established, 52; and externality, 53-55, 57, 243, 247; going beyond, 272; habitual, 51, 52, 59; inward deepening of, 53; as inwardness, 53-55, 243; Mynster's view of, 257; and politics, 243, 246, 248-49, 255; state, 51, 247; then and now, 256-57; within Christendom, 57
Christian V, King, 290
Christian VIII, King, 233, 286, 304
Church, 51; reformation of, 53, 243, 255-56; and externalities, 53-55
Cicero, *De divinatione*, 282, 283
Clausen, Henrik Nicolai, xxxvii
Colbjørnsen, Christian, 63, 67, 72, 282
Collin, Jonas, 116, 291
collision, existential, 242
comedy, the comic, xiv, xvii, 33, 149, 174, 178-82, 188-89, 194; and tragedy, 22; and writing, viii, xxi, xxiv, 139, 141, 147, 148
common man, 241
communication, indirect, 44
Conradi-Päthau, Johan Gotfred, 232, 305
conscience, 57
construction, *see* imaginary construction
contaminated food, *see* analogy
contemptibleness, xviii, 49, 159-66, 173, 177-78, 183-84, 191, 213, 216, 253
contradiction of the infinite, 44, 106
controversy, xxxvii

Index 313

Cooper, James Fenimore, 141, 294
Copenhagen, xxxi, 67, 97, 113, 167, 188, 211, 220, 223
  and London, 204
  and Paris, 167, 204-05
  streets and quarters: Amagertorv, 125, 141; Christen Bernikov Stræde, 401; Christianshavn, 102, 298; Gamle Kongevej, 75, 138, 282; Gammeltorv, 117; Gothersgade, 133; Købmagergade, 125; Kongens Nytorv, 115, 290; Langelinie, 99, 286; Myntergade, xxiii, xliii, 149; Nytorv, 125; Østergade, 107; Peder Madsens Gang, 7; Pistol Stræde, 7; Vimmelskaftet, 107, 125
Copernican system, 86
Copernicus, Nicolaus, 133
Coronato the Terrible, 108, 124, 147-48
corrective, existential-, 56
Corsair, The, viii, xvi, xix, xxviii, xxxiv, xl, xliii, 140, 231, 233, 271, 275-76, 279-80, 284, 285, 288; anonymity, 175; attack on Kierkegaard, xx-xxii, 117, 146-49, 277, 280, 287, 290, 292, 296, 297; caricature of Kierkegaard, xxi, xxx-xxxi, 174, 187; challenge to Kierkegaard, 158-59; circulation of, 167, 174, 180, 183, 188-91, 206, 221, 241; commendation of *Either/Or*, 141-42; commendation of Kierkegaard, 46, 118, 123, 141-42, 215, 279; commendation of *Postscript*, 196-97; devoid of idea, 209, 221; editor of, xl, xliii, 109, 147, 213-14, 240, 280; emblem of, 190, 191; estimate of *Either/Or*, 141-42; and gossip, 199; and irony, xvi-xvii; Kierkegaard's challenge to, 123, 146, 157-59, 172, 183, 210,
231, 239; Kierkegaard's characterization of, 47-50, 107, 110, 117-18, 179-94, 199; and P. L. Møller, xxv, xxviii, xli, 46, 106, 111, 143, 146, 148, 191, 207, 279; motto of, x; and J. P. Mynster, 261; nature of, 140, 151, 167-68, 191; no recourse against, 177; sale of, xxiii, xliii, 150; as Sultan, 157-58; use of satire, xvi-xvii
Corsair affair, the, vii-xxxviii, 127, 159-78, 208, 231-32, 253; an act, xiv, 123, 202, 208, 218, 232, 239, 253, 280, 301-02; benefit to Kierkegaard, 213-14, 226; and contemporaries, 212, 239-40; contemporaries' estimate of, 188, 194, 200, 207, 208-10, 218-19, 222-24, 229-30; harassment of Kierkegaard, 211-12, 216-18, 220, 222, 225-26, 291, 305; irony of, 209-10; Kierkegaard's aims in, xv-xix, 213, 215, 237; nature of, 229-30; results for Goldschmidt, xxiii-xxiv, 149-50; results for Kierkegaard, xxix-xxxiii; results for Møller, xxvi-xxix; results of, 219, 225-30, 236, 238, 240; victor in, 227-28
Corvetten-Politivennen, 118, 128, 134, 288
Crazy Nathanson, xxi-xxii, xxx, 291. See also Nathanson, Michael Leonard
crisis, transitional, 40-41
criticism, 9-12, 28, 140; false, 3, 26
crowd, the, 56, 94, 222, 227, 251. See also number, numerical; public; rabble-barbarism
cynicism, 227

Dagen, 93, 94
Davidsen, Jacob, *Fra det gamle Kongens Kjøbenhavn*, x

314   Index

defamation of character, xx
defense and attack, 39
demand of the times, 181, 188
Democritus, 282
demoralization, xviii
Denmark, xviii, 179, 222-24, 231, 238; disintegration of, 230; as market town, 228; new government of, 228-29, 230, 304-05
Descartes, René, 272
dialectic, dialectical, 24, 40, 44; existential, 44; of the universal, 215; of writing, 44, 187
Diderot, Denis, *Encyclopedia*, 6
Diogenes Laertius, 163, 227, 277
discourses, upbuilding, 51, 277
disintegration, 230, 232
Don Giovanni, characters in: Anna, 29, 30, 36; Commendatore, 30; Don Giovanni, 35; Elvira, 30, 32-33, 34, 35, 36; Leporello, 29, 34; Masetto, 30-31, 36; Ottavio, 32; Zerlina, 28-36. *See also* Mozart, W. A.
Don Quixote, 94
double-danger, 246-47
double-reflection, 44, 187, 201, 209
doubt, 42
Dream Book, 137

earnestness, 58, 179
emancipation, 54; from habitual and state Christianity, 51-52; of the Church from the state, 53-54, 244, 247
enthusiasts, 52
envy, xviii
era, positive, xvii
Erasmus Montanus, 44-45, 279
Erslew, Thomas Hansen, *Forfatter-Lexicon*, xxviii, xli, 191, 207, 279
established order, the, 52, 56-57
esthetic, the, xxxvi, 18, 173; and interpretation, 36; and Kierkegaard, 142

esthetician, traveling, 38, 158-59
eternity, 255
ethical, the, 173; view, xvii
Etlar, Carit, 238
Europe, demoralization of, 222
existence-idea, religious, 211, 215
existential, the, 211; collision, 242; -corrective, 56; dialectic, 44
experiment, experimenting, *see* imaginary construction
externality, the external, 53-55; and change, 53, 57; forms of, 243; indifference to, 56-57

Fædrelandet, xiii, xix, xxi, xxxiv, 9, 66, 68, 69, 99, 106-10, 114, 117, 121, 122, 124, 125, 143, 146, 147, 148, 154, 188, 197, 271, 272, 278, 279, 281, 282, 287, 296; *Fædrelandets Feuilleton*, 277; piece on Frater Taciturnus, 108-12
faith, 272; in forms, 54
fallacy, genetic, 16
felix culpa, xxxiii
Feuerbach, Ludwig Andreas, 10, 271-72
Figaro, 285
Flyveposten, 115, 225, 285, 290
Flinch, Andreas Christian Ferdinand, xxiii, 150
flogging, 13, 57
fly, cholera, *see* analogy
Folkebladet, 4, 92, 271
forms, faith in, 54
Forsete, 81, 283
Franklin, Benjamin, 180
Frater Observantissimus, 123
Frederik VI, King, 8, 272
Frederik VII, King, 304-05
Frederiks Hospital, xxxiii
Fremtoning, x
Fribert, Lauritz J., 15, 273
Frisindede, Den, 112, 289

Gæa, xii, xiv-xv, xix, xxii, xxxiv,

xliii, 38, 40, 104-06, 109, 110, 117, 121, 123, 145-47, 148, 207, 278, 279, 286, 296
gaiety and jest, 42
geese, *see* analogy
genetic fallacy, 16
Gert Westphaler, 248, 276
Gjødwad (Giødwad), Jens Finsteen, xii, 204, 232, 301
Goethe, Johann Wolfgang von, 142, 295; *Aus meinem Leben*, 295; *Faust*, 296; *Die Leiden des jungen Werthers*, 294; *Wilhelm Meisters Lehrjahre*, 283
going beyond, 6, 271, 272
Goldschmidt, Meïr Aaron [pseud. Adolph Meyer], vii-xxix, xxxi-xxxiv, xxxvii-xxxviii, xl, xli, xlii, xliii, 47, 143, 182-84, 228-29, 231, 279, 284, 294, 295, 297, 298, 299; departure from Denmark, xxiv-xxvi, xliii, 150, 219, 240, 296; estimate of Kierkegaard, vii-ix, xxiv, xxix, 139, 149; imprisonment of, xli, 49, 108, 280, 288; and irony, 224; and Kierkegaard, vii-ix, xxiii, xxix, 138-52, 182-83, 184, 196, 212, 213-14, 224, 228, 232-37, 260-61, 294; and P. L. Møller, x-xiii, xxv-xxviii, 143-44, 150-52, 298; and J. P. Mynster, 258-61; *Breve fra og til Meïr Goldschmidt*, viii, xxiv, xxviii; *Breve til hans Familie*, xi; "How the Wandering Philosopher Found the Wandering Actual Editor of *The Corsair*," 108-12; *En Jøde*, vii, xv, xlii, 47, 143, 176, 183, 191-92, 280, 298, 299; *Livs Erindringer og Resultater*, x, xiv, xxii, xxvii, xxix, xxxi, xxxiv, 295, 296, 297. *See also* comedy, the comic, and writing; *Nord og Syd*
gossip, 140; anonymous, 167-68
Gottsched, Hermann, xxxv

Governance, 207, 236
government, and martyr, 228
government, the new (March), xvii-xviii, 228-29, 230-31, 304-05
grace and ideals, 252, 254-55
Greeks, the, 30, 83; mentality, 141-42, 211, 214, 218
Grundtvig, Nicolai Frederik Severin, xxxvi-xxxvii, 246-47, 280, 283
Gyllembourg, Thomasine Christine, *Two Ages*, xxxi, 203-04, 215, 301

half-truth, 51
Hamilton, Andrew, 288
Hamlet, 82
Hansen, Jørgen Christian, 28-29, 34, 36-37, 277
Hauch, Carsten Johannes, xii, xix, xxviii, xxix, xlv, 38, 40-42, 97, 104-05, 106, 278, 286
Hegel, Georg Wilhelm Friedrich, 271, 272, 282; going beyond, 6, 271; *Aesthetics*, 77, 283; *Logic*, 8; *Philosophy of Nature*, 282; *Science of Logic*, 283
Heiberg, Johan Ludvig, xxxv, 8-9, 17-21, 26, 94, 99, 111, 127, 216, 222, 238, 239, 271, 272, 273, 277, 289, 290, 306, 371; in *Corsair*, 112-17; *Recensenten og Dyret*, 278; *En Sjæl efter Døden*, 289; *Urania*, 115, 290
Heiberg, Johanne Luise, 306
Heraclitus, 277
hero(es), xvii, 5, 9
Herodotus, 283
Hertz, Henrik Heyman, *Perspektivkassen*, 285; *Sven Dyrings Huus*, 80, 283
Høedt, Frederik Ludvig, 176, 298
Holberg, Ludvig, 44, 85, 122, 165, 276, 285; *Den ellefte Junii*, 276; *Erasmus Montanus*, 44-45, 279, 282; *Jacob von Tyboe*, 291; *Jean de*

Holberg, Ludvig (*cont.*)
  France, 284; *Mester Gert Westphaler*, 248, 276, 306
Holofernes, 127, 292
Holst, Hans Peter, xxxv
Homer, *Odyssey*, 283
honor, 49
Horace, 276, 290; *Ars Poetica*, 273; *Odes*, 274
horse meat, 111, 289. *See also* Crazy Nathanson
Hostrup, Jens Christian, 225, 304; *Gjenboerne*, 304
human, the universally, 280
Hven, 114, 290
hymnal, new, 180-81
Hyperbolos, 284

idea and music, unity of, 31
ideals, 245, 250, 254-55; and grace, 252, 254-55; and the poet, 250-52; vision of, 55
identity, mistaken, 31
illusion, 255, 263; of being Christian, 52
imaginary construction, 39-40, 42-43, 45, 113, 118, 124, 278, 286, 287, 289; Kierkegaard's use of, 289; P. L. Møller's analysis of, 100-02; P. L. Møller's use of, xiii, 106-08
imagination and voice, 29, 33
imitation, 263
immortalization, 5, 271; of Frater Taciturnus, xx, 111, 127, 213; of Victor Eremita, xiv, 46, 49-50, 96, 118, 130, 157-58, 279
impersonality, 149
impotence, 49
inclosing reserve, 119-20, 121, 291
independence, 258
indesluttet, 119-20, 121, 291
indifference to the external, 56-57
indirect communication, 44
individual, *see* single individual
infinity, the infinite: contradiction of, 44, 106; desire for, 45-46; joy of, 45; self-concern of, 252
institutions, free, 54, 247
Intelligensblade, 17-20, 285
inwardness and Christianity, 53, 243
ironist, xvii, 224, 235
irony, xvi-xvii, 34, 49, 165, 209, 224, 235, 253; and setting, 217
isabelfarvet, 137, 293

Jean Paul [pseud. of Johann Paul Friedrich Richter], 42, 85, 104, 154, 192; and Schmelzle, 42, 104, 279
jest, 179, 227; and gaiety, 42
Jews, ix, 151, 190, 280
Joseph, 77
journalism, xxxi, 220-21, 225, 271
judgment, suspension of, 18-19
Julius Caesar, 83

Kierkegaard, Ane Sørensdatter Lund, xxxix
Kierkegaard, Michael Pedersen, xxxvii, xxxix, 272; and J. P. Mynster, 259; and A. G. Rudelbach, 250
Kierkegaard, Peter Christian, 279, 289, 303
KIERKEGAARD, SØREN AABYE, vii-xlv, 23, 27, 51, 56
  advice to Goldschmidt, 224, 232-35
  aims in *Corsair* affair, xv-xix, 237. *See also Corsair; Corsair* affair
  authorship, 4-5, 24-27, 153-55, 208-12, 214, 215, 216, 218, 231, 271, 291; criticism of, 24-27, 222; as education, 252-53; second phase, xxxi-xxxiii, xxxvi
  and Christianity, 261-63. *See also* Christian, Christianity

Index 317

church attendance, 209
and contemporaries, xxx-xxxi,
  4-5, 209, 212, 229, 239-40
in *The Corsair*, xx-xxii, 105-31
death, xxxiii, xlv
engagement, *see* Olsen, Regine
excursions, 222, 226, 303-04
existence-idea, religious, 211
finances, 219, 230, 303
and M. A. Goldschmidt, vii-ix,
  xxiii, xxix, 138-52, 182-83,
  184, 196, 212, 213-14, 224,
  228, 232-37, 294. *See also*
  Goldschmidt, M. A.
and Greek mentality, 141-42,
  211, 214, 218
harassment of, 212, 216-21, 222,
  225-26, 228. *See also* rabble-
  barbarism
and higher point of view, 146,
  148, 149
home (Nytorv 2), xxxix, 113,
  289, 303
and ideals, 216, 245, 250-52, 254-
  55
as idler, 217, 271
indirect method, 208. *See also*
  maieutic; pseudonymity; Socratic
irony, 217, 233. *See also* ironist;
  irony
language, 93, 99-100
laughter, need of, 227
legs, xxi-xxii, 37, 133-34, 135,
  171, 227, 277. *See also* Kierkegaard, S. A., trousers
Magister degree, 284
and P. L. Møller, 98-104, 144-
  45, 148, 199, 203-04, 207, 209-
  10, 215, 231, 234, 237, 238.
  See also Goldschmidt, M. A.;
  Kierkegaard, S. A., pseudonyms, Frater Taciturnus;
  Møller, P. L.
and J. P. Mynster, xxxviii, xlv,
  7, 26, 132, 151, 211, 216, 245,
246, 258-61, 271-72. *See also*
  Mynster, J. P.
name-calling, xxx, xxxi, 93, 226,
  229, 238, 304, 305
pastorate, *see* Kierkegaard, S. A.,
  rural pastorate
a patient, not a physician, 247
physical condition, 226
a poet, xxix, 250-51, 254, 256
polemic nature, 216
proposed titles and works: "An
  Action-response in Personal
  Costume," 196-97; "A Bit of
  Factual Information," 203-04;
  "*The Corsair*," 175-78; "The
  Dialectic of Contemptibleness," 159-66; "A Literary Signal Shot," 204-08; newspaper
  articles, volume of, 231; "A
  Personal Statement in Costume," 178-96; "A Polite Suggestion," 201-02; "A Request
  to *The Corsair*," 157-58;
  "Some Good-natured Gossipy
  Remarks," 197-201; "Some In-
  structive Comments on *The
  Corsair*'s Drastic Errors," 166-
  75
pseudonyms, xxxii-xxxv, 49-50,
  51, 97-98, 131, 172, 271, 273,
  276
  A., xxxv, xlii, 18, 20, 37, 273,
    274, 277
  A. F. . . . ., 16
  Anti-Climacus, xxxiii, xxxix,
    xliv, 158
  B., 20, 274
  Constantin Constantius, xli,
    131, 135, 275, 276, 293
  Frater Taciturnus, xix-xxi,
    xxiii, xxxiv, xliii, 46, 47,
    50, 108, 109, 110, 125, 126,
    127, 131, 134, 137, 146-49,
    159, 170, 172, 183, 213, 278,
    279, 287, 291, 293, 305; as
    bombadier, 117, 126; im-

KIERKEGAARD, SØREN AABYE (cont.)
mortalization of in *Corsair*, 111, 127, 183, 185, 213; and insanity, 122-23, 126, 129; P. L. Møller's letter to, 104-05; P. L. Møller's article on, 105-08
H. H., xxxiii, xliv
Hilarius Bookbinder, viii, xlii, 46, 96, 97, 125, 131, 135, 159, 276, 287, 289, 293; and horse meat, 111
Inter et Inter, xxxiii, xliv
Johannes Climacus, xxv, xxxiii, xlii, xliii, 131, 135, 213, 262, 276, 293
Johannes de Silentio, xli, 131, 135, 275, 276, 277, 293
Johannes the Seducer, xi, xiii, 42, 273, 275
Judge William, xxvii, 131, 273, 293
Nicolaus Notabene, xlii, 131, 135, 275, 276, 293
Victor Eremita, viii-ix, xii, xiv, xxi, xxiii, xxxv, xli, xliii, 21, 46, 93, 94, 131, 135, 141-43, 149, 155, 273, 274, 275, 276, 279, 285, 286, 293; immortalization of, 46, 49-50, 96, 118, 130, 157-58; and insanity, 124
Vigilius Haufniensis, xlii, 131, 276, 293
William Afham, 131, 293
See also pseudonymity
publishing, 11, 13-14, 95, 211, 241, 272-73
and A. G. Rudelbach, xxxvi-xxxvii, xlv, 51-59, 241-58, 261, 280
rural pastorate, xxxii, xliii-xliv, 212, 219
self-understanding, 251-52
a solitary, 211
student sermon, 22-23

tactic, 231-32, 253
tailor, 114, 222, 304
teaching post, xxxii
trousers, xxi-xxii, 114-15, 120, 131, 135, 137, 186-88, 192-94, 197-99, 201, 222, 223-24, 227, 241. *See also* Kierkegaard, S. A., legs
walking, 37, 108, 127, 217, 222, 226, 288-89, 303-04
and women, 144
works cited:
"The Activity of a Traveling Esthetician and How He Still Happened to Pay for the Dinner" (1845), xiii, xxxiv, 287
Armed Neutrality (1848-49), 263, 307
The Battle between the Old and the New Soap-Cellar (1838), 282
The Concept of Anxiety (1844), 273, 276, 283, 293
The Concept of Irony (1841), viii, 139, 209, 272, 276, 284, 302; review in *Corsair*, 92-93; review in *Fædrelandet*, 9-12
Concluding Unscientific Postscript (1846), xiv, xix, xxiii, xxviii, xxxi-xxxii, 130, 131, 135-36, 166, 196, 198, 203-04, 207, 208, 210, 213, 215, 240-41, 271, 272, 279, 280, 284, 293, 297, 300
The Crisis and a Crisis in the Life of an Actress (1848), xliv
"The Dialectical Result of a Literary Police Action" (1846), xxxiv-xxxv, 279
Eighteen Upbuilding Discourses (1845), 274, 289
Either/Or (1843 and 1849), xxv, xxvii, xxix, xxx, xxxi, xxxv-xxxvi, xlii, 22, 51, 95,

98, 110, 130, 147, 154, 155, 158, 212, 240, 273, 274, 275, 276, 277, 278, 279, 280, 283, 285, 286, 288, 293, 306; authorship of, 13-16; criticism of, 17-20; review in *Corsair*, 93-95, 141-42
"An Explanation and a Little More" (1845), xxxv
Fear and Trembling (1843), 272, 276, 278, 293; Møller's estimate of, 99
For Self-Examination (1851), xxxviii
Four Upbuilding Discourses (1843), 276, 289
Four Upbuilding Discourses (1844), 276, 289
From the Papers of One Still Living, xxvii, 138, 276
"Literary Quicksilver" (1843), xxxv
The Moment (1855), xxxviii
On My Work as an Author (1851), 252
"An Open Letter" (1851), xxxvii-xxxviii
Philosophical Fragments (1844), 166, 271, 272, 276, 278, 289, 293
The Point of View for My Work as an Author (1859), xi, xxxvi, 280
Practice in Christianity (1850), xxxviii, 246, 254, 307
Prefaces (1844), 99, 120, 273, 276, 286, 292, 293
"Public Confession" (1842), xxxv
Repetition (1843), 120, 272, 276, 279, 289, 292, 293
The Sickness unto Death (1849), 288
Stages on Life's Way (1845), viii, xii-xiii, xix, xxxv, 46, 50, 95, 118-20, 129, 159, 240, 274, 275, 276, 278, 279, 280, 282, 283, 285, 287, 289, 291, 293, 306; Møller's criticism of, 98, 190
Three Discourses on Imagined Occasions (1845), 276
Three Upbuilding Discourses (1843), 276, 289
Three Upbuilding Discourses (1844), 276, 289
Two Ages: The Age of Revolution and the Present Age. A Literary Review (1846), xvii, xxii, xxxi, 203-04, 208, 215, 301
Two Upbuilding Discourses (1843), 276, 289
Two Upbuilding Discourses (1844), 22, 274, 276, 289
Works of Love (1847), 288, 294
on writing, 211, 230
Kjøbenhavns flyvende Post, see *Flyveposten*
Kjøbenhavnsposten, xxiv, xliii, 301
Kragh, Boline Abrahamsen, 30, 277
Krasinski, Zygmunt, *die ungöttliche Comedie* (*Nieboska Komedja*), 99
Kts., see Mynster, J. P.

language, 79; Danish, 202, 223; Kierkegaard's, 93, 99-100
Latin school, 102
laughter, 47, 107, 123, 164, 224; martyrdom of, xxx, 236
Leerbeck, John E., 108, 123, 125, 292
legal system, Danish, 63-72, 281
legs, see Kierkegaard, S. A., legs
Lehmann, Peter Orla, ix, 96, 99, 116, 285, 286
Lessing, Gotthold Ephraim, 139
Leucippus, 22
leveling, 176
Levin, Israel Salomon, 107-08, 287

Lichtenberg, Georg Christoph, 40, 278
London and Copenhagen, 204
love, unhappy, 245
lucida intervalla, 73, 282
Lucretius, *De rerum natura*, 74
lunacy, higher, 73
Lundbye, Johan Thomas, xxxi
Luno, Bianco Christian Peter, 130, 203, 207, 210, 301
Luther, Martin, 51, 55, 58
Lyngby, 138, 294

Maanedsskrift for Literatur, 276
madness and poet, 73
Madsen, Peder Erik, 92
Madvig, Johan Nicolai, 26, 276
Maecenas, Caius Cilnius, 26, 276
Magnussen, Rikard Robert, ix, xi, xiii, xviii, xxxiii
maieutic, the, 263
majority, 9, 11
marriage, civil, xxxvii, 51, 250, 257
Martensen, Hans Lassen, xxxvi-xxxviii, 257; *Leilighedstaler*, xxxviii
martyr, 228
martyrdom, 58, 243; of laughter, xxx, 236
mediation, 42-43
Mellemhverandre, 92, 284
metaphor, *see* analogy
Meyer, Adolph, *see* Goldschmidt, M. A.
Michelsen, Gustav, 117, 291
military, the, *see* analogy
Mini, Jacob, restaurant, 232, 305
Mitchell, P. M., xxiv
Møller, Peder Ludvig [pseud. Prosper naturalis de molinasky], vii-viii, x-xvi, xix-xx, xxii, xxiv-xxix, xxxi-xxxii, xxxiv, xxxix, xl, xli, xlii, xliii, xliv, 38-46, 96, 141-52, 197, 238, 278, 279, 286, 287, 289, 294, 300; attack on Kierkegaard, 203, 234; and *Corsair*, 46, 106, 143, 209; departure from Denmark, xxv-xxvi, xliv, 150, 199, 209, 219, 240, 295, 300; draft of article for *Corsair*, xix-xx, 105-08; and Erslew's lexicon, xxviii, xli, 191, 207, 279; esthetics, 151; Kierkegaard's article against, 38-46, 148, 203-04, 209, 210; and professorship in esthetics, xi-xii, xxvi-xxix, 144-45; pseudonym, xxiv, xliii, 301; view of Kierkegaard's pseudonyms, 98; "A Visit in Sorø," xli, xliii; *Kritiske Skizzer*, xliv. *See also* Goldschmidt, M. A., and P. L. Møller; Kierkegaard, S. A., and P. L. Møller
Mother Elle, 81, 283
Mozart, Wolfgang Amadeus, *Don Giovanni*, xxxv-xxxvi, 28-37, 142, 277, 278. *See also Don Giovanni*
music, 29-35, 81-83, 277
Mynster, Jacob (Jakob) Peter [pseud. Kts.], xxxviii, xlv, 7, 26, 132, 211, 216, 245, 246, 258-61, 271, 272, 277, 307; and *Corsair*, 261; estimate of Kierkegaard and Johannes de Silentio, 277; and M. A. Goldschmidt and Kierkegaard, 258-61; and *Nord og Syd*, 151; sermons, 253-54; *Yderligere Bidrag til Forhandlingerne om de Kirkelige Forhold i Danmark*, 307

-n., 24, 25, 274-76
Næstved, vii, xxxix
name-calling, xxx, xxxi, 93, 226, 229, 238, 304, 305
Napoleon, 163
Nathanson, Mendel Levin, 96, 137, 285, 288
Nathanson, Michael Leonard, 108, 115, 117, 121, 125, 127, 131, 287-88, 289, 290, 291; identifica-

Index

tion with Frater Taciturnus, 128-30; identification with Kierkegaard in *Corsair*, 117-23. See also *Corvetten-Politivennen*; Crazy Nathanson
nature, 77
Neergaard, Jens Veibel, 117, 291
nemesis, 30, 144, 277, 295
Ney, Marshal Michel, 236, 474
Nicodemus, 85
Nielsen, Knud Christian, 233, 305
Nielsen, Rasmus, 5-6, 8, 271, 272
Noah's flood, 84
Nord og Syd, xxiv-xxvi, xliv, 152, 233, 280, 296
number, the numerical, 56, 261. See also crowd; public; rabble-barbarism
Ny Portefeuille, 154-55, 282, 296
Nyt Aftenbladet, 285
Nytorv 2, see Kierkegaard, S. A., home

Odysseus, 82
Oehlenschläger, Adam Gottlob, x, xi-xii, xxvi, xxvii-xxviii, 144, 145
Olsen, Frederick Christian, 271
Olsen, Regine, xiii, xl, 291, 294-95
Olufsen, Christian Friis Rottbøll, 112-17, 289
"one," 17-20
orators, 81
organ grinder, 80-81
Ørsted, Anders Sandøe, 63, 67, 72, 282
Orthodox, the Old, 245-46, 261
ostracism, 84, 86, 283

Paris, 171; and Copenhagen, 167, 204-05; and London, 204
party, xvi, 9, 56, 224, 256; affiliations, 280; spirit, 6-7
pastorate, rural, xxxii, xliv, 212, 219
Per Degn, 44-45, 279

Pethau's restaurant, 232, 305
Petrarch (Francesco Petrarca), 187
Petronius, 118, 291
Philipsen, Philip Gerson, 113, 289
Pilate, 83
Plato, 93, 163; *Gorgias*, 279
Ploug, Carl Parmo, 232, 305
Plutarch: *Alcibiades*, 284; *Phocion*, 300
poet(s): and cunning, xiii, 145; and ideals, 250-52, 254; madness of, 73
politics: and Christianity, 53; as externality, 54
power, 164
praise: undeserved, 3-5, 9, 26; undesirable, 161-62
prayer, 255
present age, the, 243-44; need of irony in, 253
pride, spiritual, 52
privacy, invasion of, xviii, xl, 167-68
Prosper naturalis de molinasky, see Møller, P. L.
prostitute, see analogy
Protagoras, 93
Providence, 244
pseudonymity, xix, xx, xxviii, xxxi, xxxii-xxxiii, 24-27, 51, 215, 273, 280; in *Berlingske Tidende*, 99; Kierkegaard's acknowledgment of, 208. See also Kierkegaard, S. A., pseudonyms
psychological familiarity, 45
public, the, 95, 217, 224. See also crowd; number, numerical; rabble-barbarism
publishing, see Kierkegaard, S. A., publishing
punishment, 10
Pushkin, Aleksandr Sergeyevich, 99

quidam, 42, 278, 279

rabble-barbarism, xvi, 202, 205-06, 213-14, 219-20, 225-28, 229, 231, 237-39. *See also* crowd; Kierkegaard, S. A., harassment of; number, numerical; public
Randers Insane Asylum, 119-20, 287
reader(s), 16, 19-20, 44-46; conscientious, 19; one, 104, 107, 120, 201, 209, 273, 287
reading public, 4, 8-9, 25
reasonable man, 41-42, 98, 102
reconciliation, 31
reflection, 43
reformation of Church, 56, 58, 243-44, 255-56
reformers, 244
Reiersen, Christian, 50, 299
Reitzel, Carl Andreas, xxiii, 115, 150, 303
religious, the, double dialectic of, 40
religiousness, 42
resourcefulness, dialectical, 24
restitutio in integrum, 42
reviewers, 156
Richter, Johann Paul Friedrich, *see* Jean Paul
ridicule of Kierkegaard, xx-xxii, xxx-xxxi, xxxiii, 114-15, 131, 133-35, 137, 171, 212, 217, 290, 305. *See also* Kierkegaard, S. A., harassment of; legs; rabble-barbarism; trousers
Rigstidenden, 225
Rørdam, Bolette, 138, 294
Rørdam, Cathrine Georgia Teilmann, 138, 139, 294
Rørdam, Peter, 138, 294
Rosenhoff, Caspar Claudius, 289
Rosenkrantz, Iver Holger, 176, 298
Roskilde, 244
round earth, 85
Round Tower (Rundetaarn), 68, 127, 282
Rousseau, Jean Jacques, 99

Rubow, Paul V., vii, x, xxviii, 295
Rudelbach, Andreas Gottlob, xxxvi-xxxvii, xlv, 51-59, 241-58, 261, 280

St. Peter's (Sankt Petri) Church, 127, 292
Samson, 94
Sanhedrin, 56-57
satire, xvii
Saxo Grammaticus, 82, 283
Schiller, Friedrich, *Des Mädchens Klage*, 251, 306
schismatics, 52
Schlegel, Johan Frederik, xli
Schmelzle, 42, 104, 279
Schulin, Johan Sigismund, 115, 291
sectarianism, sects, 52, 243
seduction, 30-31, 33-35
self-concern, 55, 57, 59, 242, 245
seminary, pastoral, 22
Shakespeare, 77
ship and megaphone, *see* analogy
Sibbern, Frederik Christian, 100, 286
singer, 29, 33-34
single individual, the, xxv, 51, 54-57, 202, 244, 280
sing sang resches Tubalcain, 157
Skamlingsbanken, 150·
Socrates, xvii, 23, 28, 92-93, 117, 161, 177, 179, 195, 218, 263, 272, 277, 279
Socratic, the, 44, 165, 180, 261-63; principle, 165
Sophocles, *Antigone*, 282
"Søren," *see* name-calling
Sorø, 96-97, 285; Academy, xii, xiii, 144, 285
Spandet, Niels Møller, 245, 306
spirit, weapons of, 54
stagecoach, 41, 45, 106
Stampe, Henrik, 63, 67, 72, 282
Steenstrup, Johannes Japetus, 272
Steffens, Henrich, x, 76, 282
Stemann, Poul Christian, 116, 281

Stilling, Peter Michael, 8, 272
Strauss, David Friedrich, 10, 272
Studenstrup, 25
suffering for a cause, 227
superorthodox, the, 52
system, the, 5-6, 8-9, 240, 256

Taciturnus, Michael Leonard, 122, 279
Tacitus, Cajus Cornelius, 164, 297
tailor, 48, 114, 222, 304
Talleyrand-Périgord, Charles Maurice de, 79, 283
Tantalus, 54, 280-81
tarantella, theological, 137
temporal, the, 255
theater criticism, 28
Theologisk Maanedsskrift, xxxvi
Thor, 81, 283
thought-experiment, 96, 106, 111, 112, 147, 285. *See also* imaginary construction
times, demand of the, 181, 188
Tivoli, xxv, 272, 285
Tøxen, Jørgen Karstens Blok, 117, 291
Toldberg, Helge, xii, xvi, 278, 287
Tordenskjold, Peter Wessel, 82, 127, 283
tragedy, the tragic, 33; and comedy, 22
Trinitatis Church, 282
Trop, 38, 278
trousers, *see* Kierkegaard, S. A., trousers

"*Ubi* P. L. Møller, *ibi* The Corsair," xiii, xix, xxviii, 46, 106, 146, 159
ubi spiritus, ibi ecclesia, 46, 106, 159
unity: of idea and music, 31; of voice and mood, 29
universal, the, 215. *See also* human, the universally

upbuilding, the, 175, 182
upbuilding discourses, 51, 105, 107, 113, 277
Urania, 113, 115, 289, 290
Ursin, Georg Frederick, 53, 280
Ussing, Henrich, 131, 293
Utgardi-Loke, 81, 283

Vatke, Johan Karl Wilhelm, 10, 272
velbekomme, 40, 278
vilification, vilifier, 48-49
Vinet, Alexander Rudolf, 257-58, 307
Virgil (Publius Vergilius Maro), 276; *Aeneid*, 68, 282
Visby, Carl Holger, 140, 294
vision of the ideals, 55
voice and imagination, 29, 33

walking, 37, 108, 127, 217, 222, 226, 288-89, 303-04
Weil, Gustav, *Tausend und eine Nacht*, 305
Wessel, Johan Herman, xxviii, 285
Westenske Institut, 294
wish, ironic fulfillment of, 48
wit, 164-65
without authority, 173
wonder stool, 171, 298
Word, the, 56
world, actual, the, 160
writing, 211, 221; comic, 139; dialectic of, 44, 187

Xantippe, 161
Xenophon, 92

Young, Edward, 274
young man and actual world, 160-65
youth, 195

zither player, 34

ADVISORY BOARD

KIERKEGAARD'S WRITINGS

Howard V. Hong, General Editor, *St. Olaf College, 1972-*
Robert L. Perkins, *University of South Alabama, 1972-76.*
Niels Thulstrup, *University of Copenhagen, 1972-76.*
Gregor Malantschuk, *University of Copenhagen, 1977-78.*
John W. Elrod, *Iowa State University, 1977-*
Per Lønning, *University of Oslo, 1977-*
Sophia Scopetéa, *University of Copenhagen, 1978-*

GPSR Authorized Representative: Easy Access System Europe - Mustamäe tee 50, 10621 Tallinn, Estonia, gpsr.requests@easproject.com

www.ingramcontent.com/pod-product-compliance
Lightning Source LLC
Chambersburg PA
CBHW030105010526
44116CB00005B/100